Fourth Workshop on Statistical Parsing of Morphologically Rich Languages

(SPMRL 2013)

Seattle, Washington, USA
18 October 2013

ISBN: 978-1-62993-549-2

Printed from e-media with permission by:

Curran Associates, Inc.
57 Morehouse Lane
Red Hook, NY 12571

CURRAN ASSOCIATES INC. proceedings.com

Some format issues inherent in the e-media version may also appear in this print version.

Printed by Curran Associates, Inc. (2014)

For permission requests, please contact the Association for Computational Linguistics at the address below.

Association for Computational Linguistics
209 N. Eighth Street
Stroudsburg, Pennsylvania 18360

Phone: 1-570-476-8006
Fax: 1-570-476-0860

acl@aclweb.org

Additional copies of this publication are available from:

Curran Associates, Inc.
57 Morehouse Lane
Red Hook, NY 12571 USA
Phone: 845-758-0400
Fax: 845-758-2634
Email: curran@proceedings.com
Web: www.proceedings.com

SPMRL-2013

Fourth Workshop on Statistical Parsing of Morphologically Rich Languages

Proceedings of the Workshop

18 October 2013
Grand Hyatt Seattle
Seattle, Washington, USA

Introduction

The papers in these proceedings were presented at the fourth Workshop on Statistical Parsing of Morphologically Rich Languages (SPMRL 2013), held in Seattle, USA, on October 18th, 2013, in conjunction with the Conference on Empirical Methods in Natural Language Processing (EMNLP 2013). SPMRL is endorsed by the ACL SIGPARSE and SIGLEX interest groups and provides a forum for research in parsing morphologically-rich languages, with the goal of identifying cross-cutting issues in the annotation and parsing methodology for such languages, which typically have more flexible word order and/or higher word-form variation than English.

SPMRL has also been host to discussions on realistic and appropriate evaluation methods that can be applied in the face of morphological and/or segmentation ambiguities; these discussions have culminated in the first shared task for parsing morphologically-rich languages, co-located with SPMRL 2013. The proceedings include nine contributions to the workshop as well as the system descriptions from the shared task. The workshop included keynote talks by Julia Hockenmaier from the University of Illinois at Urbana-Champaign and by Jinho Choi from IPSoft (New York). We would like to thank all submitting authors for their contributions, the program committee for their fine work on reviewing the submissions, the participants of the shared task for their contributions and of course our invited speaker. For their precious help preparing the SPMRL 2013 Shared Task and for allowing their data to be part of it, we warmly thank and the Linguistic Data Consortium, the Knowledge Center for Processing Hebrew (MILA), the Ben Gurion University, Columbia University, Institute of Computer Science (Polish Academy of Sciences), Korea Advanced Institute of Science and Technology, University of the Basque Country, University of Lisbon, Uppsala University, University of Stuttgart, University of Szeged and University Paris Diderot (Paris 7). Finally, we would also like to thank the ACL SIGPARSE and SIGLEX interest groups for their endorsement, for the support of INRIA's Alpage project, and everybody who participated in the workshop and contributed to the discussions.

Yoav Goldberg, Yuval Marton, Ines Rehbein and Yannick Versley (Workshop organisers)

Sandra Kübler, Djamé Seddah and Reut Tsarfaty (Shared Task organisers)

Workshop Organizers:

Yoav Goldberg (Bar Ilan University, Israel)
Yuval Marton (IBM Watson Research Center, US)
Ines Rehbein (Potsdam University, Germany)
Yannick Versley (Heidelberg University, Germany)

Shared Task Organizers:

Sandra Kübler (Indiana University, US)
Djamé Seddah (Université Paris Sorbonne & INRIAs Alpage Project, France)
Reut Tsarfaty (Weizmann Institute of Science, Israel)

Program Committee:

Mohammed Attia (Dublin City University, Ireland)
Bernd Bohnet (University of Birmingham, UK)
Marie Candito (University of Paris 7, France)
Aoife Cahill (Educational Testing Service Inc., US)
Özlem Cetinoglu (University of Stuttgart, Germany)
Jinho D. Choi (IPSoft Inc., US)
Grzegorz Chrupała (Tilburg University, Netherlands)
Benoit Crabbé (University of Paris 7, France)
Gülsen Cebiroglu Eryigit (Istanbul Technical University, Turkey)
Michael Elhadad (Ben Gurion University, Israel)
Richard Farkas (University of Szeged, Hungary)
Jennifer Foster (Dublin City University, Ireland)
Josef van Genabith (Dublin City University, Ireland)
Koldo Gojenola (University of the Basque Country, Spain)
Spence Green (Stanford University, US)
Samar Husain (Potsdam University, Germany)
Sandra Kübler (Indiana University, US)
Jonas Kuhn (University of Stuttgart, Germany)
Alberto Lavelli (FBK-irst, Italy)
Joseph Le Roux (Université Paris-Nord, France)
Wolfgang Maier (University of Düsseldorf, Germany)
Takuya Matsuzaki (University of Tokyo, Japan)
Joakim Nivre (Uppsala University, Sweden)
Kemal Oflazer (Carnegie Mellon University, Qatar)
Adam Przepiorkowski (ICS PAS, Poland)
Owen Rambow (Columbia University, US)
Kenji Sagae (University of Southern California, US)
Benoit Sagot (Inria Rocquencourt, France)
Djamé Seddah (Inria Rocquencourt, France)

Reut Tsarfaty (Weizmann Institute of Science, Israel)
Lamia Tounsi (Dublin City University, Ireland)
Daniel Zeman (Charles University, Czechia)

Invited Speakers:

Julia Hockenmaier, University of Illinois at Urbana-Champaign
Jinho D. Choi, IPsoft Inc., New York

Table of Contents

Workshop Program

Friday, October 18, 2013

7:30-9:00	Breakfast and Registration
	(9:00-10:30) SPMRL I
9:00-9:10	Welcome
9:10-10:05	Invited talk: An HDP Model for Inducing CCGs by Julia Hockenmaier
10:05–10:30	*Working with a small dataset - semi-supervised dependency parsing for Irish* Teresa Lynn, Jennifer Foster and Mark Dras
	(10:30-11:00) Coffee
	(11:00-12:30) SPMRL II
11:00–11:25	*Lithuanian Dependency Parsing with Rich Morphological Features* Jurgita Kapociute-Dzikiene, Joakim Nivre and Algis Krupavicius
11:25–11:50	*Parsing Croatian and Serbian by Using Croatian Dependency Treebanks* Željko Agić, Danijela Merkler and Daša Berović
11:50–12:15	*A Cross-Task Flexible Transition Model for Arabic Tokenization, Affix Detection, Affix Labeling, POS Tagging, and Dependency Parsing* Stephen Tratz
12:15-12:30	Poster teasers

Friday, October 18, 2013 (continued)

(12:30-14:00) Lunch break

(14:00-15:30) Shared task I

14:00-14:10 Shared task intro by Djamé Seddah

14:10–14:20 *The LIGM-Alpage architecture for the SPMRL 2013 Shared Task: Multiword Expression Analysis and Dependency Parsing*
Matthieu Constant, Marie Candito and Djamé Seddah

14:20–14:30 *Exploring beam-based shift-reduce dependency parsing with DyALog: Results from the SPMRL 2013 shared task*
Eric De La Clergerie

14:30–14:55 *Effective Morphological Feature Selection with MaltOptimizer at the SPMRL 2013 Shared Task*
Miguel Ballesteros

14:55–15:10 *Exploiting the Contribution of Morphological Information to Parsing: the BASQUE TEAM system in the SPRML'2013 Shared Task*
Iakes Goenaga, Koldo Gojenola and Nerea Ezeiza

15:10–15:20 *The AI-KU System at the SPMRL 2013 Shared Task : Unsupervised Features for Dependency Parsing*
Volkan Cirik and Hüsnü Şensoy

15:20–15:30 *SPMRL'13 Shared Task System: The CADIM Arabic Dependency Parser*
Yuval Marton, Nizar Habash, Owen Rambow and Sarah Alkhulani

15:30-15:35 Q+A

Friday, October 18, 2013 (continued)

(15:35-16:00) Coffee

(16:00-16:20) Poster session (+ posters from shared task participants)

A Statistical Approach to Prediction of Empty Categories in Hindi Dependency Treebank
Puneeth Kukkadapu and Prashanth Mannem

An Empirical Study on the Effect of Morphological and Lexical Features in Persian Dependency Parsing
Mojtaba Khallash, Ali Hadian and Behrouz Minaei-Bidgoli

Constructing a Practical Constituent Parser from a Japanese Treebank with Function Labels
Takaaki Tanaka and Masaaki NAGATA

Context Based Statistical Morphological Analyzer and its Effect on Hindi Dependency Parsing
Deepak Kumar Malladi and Prashanth Mannem

Representation of Morphosyntactic Units and Coordination Structures in the Turkish Dependency Treebank
Umut Sulubacak and Gülşen Eryiğit

(16:20-18:00) Shared task II + panel

16:20–16:45 *(Re)ranking Meets Morphosyntax: State-of-the-art Results from the SPMRL 2013 Shared Task*
Anders Björkelund, Ozlem Cetinoglu, Richárd Farkas, Thomas Mueller and Wolfgang Seeker

16:45-17:10 Invited talk: Dependency Parsing with Selectional Branching by Jinho D. Choi

17:10-18:00 Panel discussion

18:00-18:15 Closing Remarks

Overview of the SPMRL 2013 Shared Task: A Cross-Framework Evaluation of Parsing Morphologically Rich Languages
Djamé Seddah, Reut Tsarfaty, Sandra Kübler, Marie Candito, Jinho D. Choi, Richárd Farkas, Jennifer Foster, Iakes Goenaga, Koldo Gojenola Galletebeitia, Yoav Goldberg, Spence Green, Nizar Habash, Marco Kuhlmann, Wolfgang Maier, Yuval Marton, Joakim Nivre, Adam Przepiórkowski, Ryan Roth, Wolfgang Seeker, Yannick Versley, Veronika Vincze, Marcin Woliński and Alina Wróblewska

Working with a small dataset - semi-supervised dependency parsing for Irish

Teresa Lynn[1,2], **Jennifer Foster**[1], **Mark Dras**[2] and **Josef van Genabith**[1]
[1]NCLT/CNGL, Dublin City University, Ireland
[2]Department of Computing, Macquarie University, Sydney, Australia
[1]{tlynn,jfoster,josef}@computing.dcu.ie
[2]{teresa.lynn,mark.dras}@mq.edu.au,

Abstract

We present a number of semi-supervised parsing experiments on the Irish language carried out using a small seed set of manually parsed trees and a larger, yet still relatively small, set of unlabelled sentences. We take two popular dependency parsers – one graph-based and one transition-based – and compare results for both. Results show that using semi-supervised learning in the form of self-training and co-training yields only very modest improvements in parsing accuracy. We also try to use morphological information in a targeted way and fail to see any improvements.

1 Introduction

Developing a data-driven statistical parser relies on the availability of a parsed corpus for the language in question. In the case of Irish, the only parsed corpus available to date is a dependency treebank, which is currently under development and still relatively small, with only 803 gold-annotated trees (Lynn et al., 2012a). As treebank development is a labour- and time-intensive process, in this study we evaluate various approaches to bootstrapping a statistical parser with a set of unlabelled sentences to ascertain how accurate parsing output can be at this time. We carry out a number of different semi-supervised bootstrapping experiments using self-training, co-training and sample-selection-based co-training. Our studies differ from previous similar experiments as our data is taken from a work-in-progress treebank. Thus, aside from the current small treebank which is used for training the initial seed model and for testing, there is no additional gold-labelled data available to us to directly compare supervised and semi-supervised approaches using training sets of comparable sizes.

In the last decade, data-driven dependency parsing has come to fore, with two main approaches dominating – transition-based and graph-based. In classic transition-based dependency parsing, the training phase consists of learning the correct parser action to take given the input string and the parse history, and the parsing phase consists of the greedy application of parser actions as dictated by the learned model. In contrast, graph-based dependency parsing involves the non-deterministic construction of a parse tree by predicting the maximum-spanning-tree in the digraph for the input sentence. In our study, we employ Malt (Nivre et al., 2006), a transition-based dependency parsing system, and Mate (Bohnet, 2010), a graph-based parser.

In line with similar experiments carried out on English (Steedman et al., 2003), we find that co-training is more effective than self-training. Co-training Malt on the output of Mate proves to be the most effective method for improving Malt's performance on the limited data available for Irish. Yet, the improvement is relatively small (0.6% over the baseline for LAS, 0.3% for UAS) for the best co-trained model. The best Mate results are achieved through a non-iterative agreement-based co-training approach, in which Mate is trained on trees produced by Malt which exhibit a minimum agreement of 85% with Mate (LAS increase of 1.2% and UAS of 1.4%).

The semi-supervised parsing experiments do not explicitly take into account the morphosyntactic properties of the Irish language. In order to examine the effect of this type of information during parsing, we carry out some orthogonal experiments where we reduce word forms to lemmas and introduce morphological features in certain cases. These changes do not bring about an increase in parsing accuracy.

The paper is organised as follows. Section 2 is an overview of Irish morphology. In Section 3 our previous work carried out on the development of an Irish dependency treebank is discussed followed in Section 4 by a description of some of our prior parsing results. Section 5 describes the self-training, co-training and sample-selection-based co-training experiments, Section 6 presents the preliminary parsing experiments involving morphological features, and, finally, Section 7 discusses our future work.

2 Irish as a morphologically rich language

Irish is a Celtic language of the Indo-European language family. It has a VSO word order and is rich in morphology. The following provides an overview of the type of morphology present in the Irish language. It is not a comprehensive summary as the rules governing morphological changes are too extensive and at times too complex to document here.

Inflection in Irish mainly occurs through suffixation, but initial mutation through lenition and eclipsis is also common (Christian-Brothers, 1988). A prominent feature of Irish (also of Scottish and Manx), which influences inflection, is the existence of two sets of consonants, referred to as 'broad' and 'slender' consonants (Ó Siadhail, 1989). Consonants can be slenderised by accompanying the consonant with a slender vowel, either *e* or *i*. Broadening occurs through the use of broad vowels; *a*, *o* or *u*. For example, *buail* 'to hit' becomes *ag bu**a**l**a**dh* 'hitting' in the verbal noun form. In general, there needs to be vowel harmony (slender or broad) between stem endings and the initial vowel in a suffix.

A process known as syncopation also occurs when words with more than one syllable have a vowel-initial suffix added. For example *imir* 'to play' inflects as ***imr**ím* 'I play'.

Nouns While Old Irish employed several grammatical cases, Modern Irish uses only three: Nominative, Genitive and Vocative. The nominative form is sometimes regarded as the 'common form' as it is now also used to account for accusative and dative forms. Nouns in Irish are divided into five classes, or declensions, depending on the manner in which the genitive case is formed. In addition, there are two grammatical genders in Irish - masculine and feminine. Case, declension and gender are expressed through noun inflection. For example, *páipéar* 'paper' is a masculine noun in the first declension. Both lenition and slenderisation are used to form the genitive singular form: *p**h**áipé**i**r*. In addition, possessive adjectives cause noun inflection through lenition, eclipsis and prefixation. For example, *teach* 'house', *mo t**h**each* 'my house', *ár **d**teach* 'our house'; *ainm* 'name', *a **h**ainm* 'her name'.

Verbs Verbs can incorporate their subject, inflecting for person and number through suffixation. Such forms are referred to as synthetic verb forms. In addition, verb tense is often indicated through various combinations of initial mutation, syncopation and suffixation. For example, *scríobh* 'write' can inflect as *scríobh**aim*** 'I write'. The past tense of the verb *tug* 'give' is *t**h**ug* 'gave'. Lenition occurs after the negative particle *ní*. For example, *tugaim* 'I give'; *ní t**h**ugaim* 'I do not give'; *níor t**h**ug mé* 'I did not give'. Eclipsis occurs following clitics such as interrogative particles (*an, nach*); complementisers (*go, nach*); and relativisers (*a, nach*) (Stenson, 1981). For example, *an **d**tugann sé?* 'does he give?'; *nach **d**tugann sé?* 'does he not give?'.

Adjectives In general, adjectives follow nouns and agree in number, gender and case. Depending on the noun they modify, adjectives can also inflect. Christian-Brothers (1988) note eight declensions of adjectives. They can decline for genitive singular masculine, genitive singular feminine and nominative plural. For example, *bacach* 'lame' inflects as *baca**igh*** (Gen.Sg.Masc), *baca**í*** (Gen.Fem.Sg) and *bacach**a*** (Nom.PL). Comparative adjectives are also formed through inflection. For example, *láidir* 'strong', *níos láid**re*** 'stronger'; *déanach* 'late', *is déana**í*** 'latest'.

Prepositions Irish has simple and compound prepositions. Most of the simple prepositions can inflect for person and number (known as prepositional pronouns or pronominal prepositions), thus including a nominal element. For example, compare *bhí sé ag labhairt **le** fear* 'he was speaking **with** a man' with *bhí sé ag labhairt **leis*** 'he was speaking **with him**'. These forms are used quite frequently, not only with regular prepositional attachment where pronominal prepositions operate as arguments of verbs or modifiers of nouns and verbs, but also in idiomatic use where they express emotions and states, e.g. *tá brón orm* (lit. 'be-worry-on me') 'I am worried' or *tá súil agam* (lit. 'be-expectation-with me') 'I hope'. Noted by Greene (1966) as a noun-centered language, nouns are often used to convey the meaning that verbs often would. Pronominal prepositions are often used in these types of structures. For example, *bhain mé geit* ***aisti*** (lit. extracted-I-shock-**from her**) 'I frightened her'; *bhain mé mo chóta* ***díom*** (lit. extracted-I-coat-**from me**) 'I took off my coat'; *bhain mé úsáid* ***as*** (lit. extracted-I-use-**from it**) 'I used it'; *bhain mé triail* ***astu*** (lit. extracted-I-attempt-**from them**)'I tried them'.

Derivational morphology There are also some instances of derivational morphology in Irish. Uí Dhonnchadha (2009) notes that all verb stems and agentive nouns can inflect to become verbal nouns. Verbal adjectives are also derived from verb stems through suffixation. For example, the verb *dún* 'close' undergoes suffixation to become *dúnadh* 'closing' (verbal noun) and *dúnta* 'closed' (verbal adjective). An emphatic suffix *-sa/-se* (both broad and slender form) can attach to nouns or pronouns. It can also be attached to any verb that has been inflected for person and number and also to pronominal prepositions. For example *mo thuairim* 'my opinion' → *mo thuairim**se*** '**my** opinion; *tú* 'you'(sg) → *tu**sa*** '**you**'; *cloisim* 'I hear' → *cloisim**se*** '**I** hear'; *liom* 'with me' → *liom**sa*** 'with **me**'. In addition, the diminutive suffix *-ín* can attach to all nouns to form a derived diminutive form. The rules of slenderisation apply here also. For example, *buachaill* 'boy' becomes *buachai**llín*** 'little boy', and *tamall* 'while' becomes *tamai**llín*** 'short while'.

3 The Irish Dependency Treebank

Irish is the official language of Ireland, yet English is the primary language for everyday use. Irish is therefore considered an EU minority language and is lacking in linguistic resources that can be used to develop NLP applications (Judge et al., 2012).

Recently, in efforts to address this issue, we have begun work on the development of a dependency treebank for Irish (Lynn et al., 2012a). The treebank has been built upon a gold standard 3,000 sentence POS-tagged corpus[1] developed by Uí Dhonnchadha (2009). Our labelling scheme is based on an 'LFG-inspired' dependency scheme developed for English by Çetinoğlu et al. (2010). This scheme was adopted with the aim of identifying functional roles while at the same time circumventing outstanding, unresolved issues in Irish theoretical syntax.[2] The Irish labelling scheme has 47 dependency labels in the label set. The treebank is in the CoNLL format with the following fields: `ID`, `FORM`, `LEMMA`, `CPOSTAG`, `POSTAG`, `HEAD` and `DEPREL`. The coarse-grained part of speech of a word is marked by the label `CPOSTAG`, and `POSTAG` marks the fine-grained part of speech for that word. For example, prepositions are tagged with the `CPOSTAG Prep` and one of the following `POSTAGs`: `Simple`: *ar* 'on', `Compound`: *i_ndiaidh* 'after', `Possessive`: *ina* 'in its', `Article`: *sa* 'in the'.

At an earlier stage of the treebank's development, we carried out on an inter-annotator agreement (IAA) study. The study involved four stages. (i) The first experiment (IAA-1) involved the assessment of annotator agreement following the introduction of a second annotator. The results reported a Kappa score of 0.79, LAS of 74.4% and UAS of 85.2% (Lynn et al., 2012a). (ii) We then held three workshops that involved thorough analysis of the output of IAA-1, highlighting disagreements between annotators, gaps in the annotation guide, shortcomings of the labelling scheme and linguistic issues not yet addressed. (iii) The annotation guide, labelling scheme and treebank were updated accordingly, addressing the highlighted issues. (iv) Finally, a second inter-annotator agreement experiment (IAA-2) was carried out presenting a Kappa score of 0.85, LAS of 79.2% and UAS of 87.8% (Lynn et al., 2012b).

We found that the IAA study was valuable in the development of the treebank, as it resulted in im-

[1] A tagged, randomised subset of the NCII, (New Corpus for Ireland - Irish http://corpas.focloir.ie/), comprised of text from books, news data, websites, periodicals, official and government documents.

[2] For example there are disagreements over the existence of a VP in Irish and whether the language has a VSO or an underlying SVO structure.

provement of the quality of the labelling scheme, the annotation guide and the linguistic analysis of the Irish language. Our updated labelling scheme is now hierarchical, allowing for a choice between working with fine-grained or coarse-grained labels. The scheme has now been finalised. A full list of the labels can be found in Lynn et al. (2012b). The treebank currently contains 803 gold-standard trees.

4 Preliminary Parsing Experiments

In our previous work (Lynn et al., 2012a), we carried out some preliminary parsing experiments with MaltParser and 10-fold cross-validation using 300 gold-standard trees. We started out with the feature template used by Çetinoğlu et al. (2010) and examined the effect of omitting `LEMMA`, `WORDFORM`, `POSTAG` and `CPOSTAG` features and combinations of these, concluding that it was best to include all four types of information. Our final LAS and UAS scores were 63.3% and 73.1% respectively. Following the changes we made to the labelling scheme as a result of the second IAA study (described above), we re-ran the same parsing experiments on the newly updated seed set of 300 sentences - the LAS increased to 66.5% and the UAS to 76.3% (Lynn et al., 2012b).

In order to speed up the treebank creation, we also applied an active learning approach to bootstrapping the annotation process. This work is also reported in Lynn et al. (2012b). The process involved training a MaltParser model on a small subset of the treebank data, and iteratively, parsing a new set of sentences, selecting a 50-sentence subset to hand-correct, and adding these new gold sentences to the training set. We compared a passive setup, in which the parses that were selected for correction were chosen at random, to an active setup, in which the parses that were selected for correction were chosen based on the level of disagreement between two parsers (Malt and Mate). The active approach to annotation resulted in superior parsing results to the passive approach (67.2% versus 68.1% LAS) but the difference was not statistically significant.

5 Semi-Supervised Parsing Experiments

In order to alleviate data sparsity issues brought about by our lack of training material, we experiment with automatically expanding our training set using well known semi-supervised techniques.

5.1 Self-Training

5.1.1 Related Work

Self-training, the process of training a system on its own output, has a long and chequered history in parsing. Early experiments by Charniak (1997) concluded that self-training is ineffective because mistakes made by the parser are magnified rather than smoothed during the self-training process. The self-training experiments of Steedman et al. (2003) also yielded disappointing results. Reichart and Rappaport (2007) found, on the other hand, that self-training could be effective if the seed training set was very small. McClosky et al. (2006) also report positive results from self-training, but the self-training protocol that they use cannot be considered to be pure self-training as the first-stage Charniak parser (Charniak, 2000) is retrained on the output of the two-stage parser (Charniak and Johnson, 2005) They later show that the extra information brought by the discriminative reranking phase is a factor in the success of their procedure (McClosky et al., 2008). Sagae (2010) reports positive self-training results even without the reranking phase in a domain adaptation scenario, as do Huang and Harper (2009) who employ self-training with a PCFG-LA parser.

5.1.2 Experimental Setup

The labelled data available to us for this experiment comprises the 803 gold standard trees referred to in Section 3. This small treebank includes the 150-tree development set and 150-tree test set used in experiments by Lynn et al. (2012b). We use the same development and test sets for this study. As for the remaining 503 trees, we remove any trees that have more than 200 tokens. The motivation for this is two-fold: (i) we had difficulties training Mate parser with long sentences due to memory resource issues, and (ii) in keeping with the findings of Lynn et al. (2012b), the large trees were sentences from legislative text that were difficult to analyse for automatic parsers and human annotators. This leaves us with 500 gold-standard trees as our seed training data set.

For our unlabelled data, we take the next 1945 sentences from the gold standard 3,000-sentence

A is a parser.
M_A^i is a model of A at step i.
P_A^i is a set of trees produced using M_A^i.
U is a set of sentences.
U^i is a subset of U at step i.
L is the manually labelled seed training set.
L_A^i is labelled training data for A at step i.
Initialise:
$L_A^0 \leftarrow L.$
$M_A^0 \leftarrow \mathit{Train}(A, L_A^0)$
for $i = 1 \rightarrow N$ **do**
  $U^i \leftarrow$ Add set of unlabelled sentences from U.
  $P_A^i \leftarrow \mathit{Parse}(U^i, M_A^i)$
  $L_A^{i+1} \leftarrow L_A^i + P_A^i$
  $M_A^{i+1} \leftarrow \mathit{Train}(A, L_A^{i+1})$
end for

Figure 1: Self-training algorithm

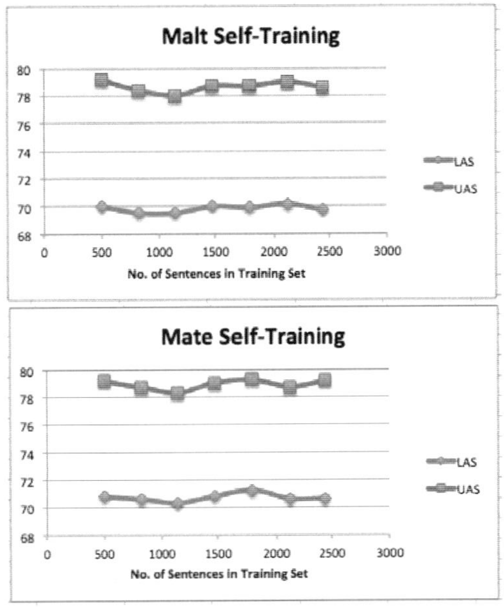

Figure 2: Self-Training Results on the Development Set

POS-tagged corpus referred to in Section 3. When we remove sentences with more than 200 tokens, we are left with 1938 sentences in our unlabelled set.

The main algorithm for self-training is given in Figure 1. We carry out two separate experiments using this algorithm. In the first experiment we use Malt. In the second experiment, we substitute Mate for Malt.[3]

The steps are as follows: Initialisation involves training the parser on a labelled seed set of 500 gold standard trees (L_A^0), resulting in a baseline parsing model: M_A^i. We divide the set of gold POS-tagged sentences (U) into 6 sets, each containing 323 sentences U^i. For each of the six iterations in this experiment $i = [1-6]$, we parse U^i. Each time, the set of newly parsed sentences (P_A) is added to the training set L_A^i to make a larger training set of L_A^{i+1}. A new parsing model (M_A^{i+1}) is then induced by training with the new training set.

5.1.3 Results

The results of our self-training experiments are presented in Figure 2. The best Malt model was trained on 2115 trees, at the 5th iteration (70.2% LAS). UAS scores did not increase over the baseline (79.1%). The improvement in LAS over the baseline is not statistically significant. The best Mate model was trained on 1792 trees, at the 4th iteration (71.2% LAS, 79.2% UAS). The improvement over the baseline is not statistically significant.

5.2 Co-Training

5.2.1 Related Work

Co-training involves training a system on the output of a different system. Co-training has found more success in parsing than self-training, and it is not difficult to see why this might be the case as it can be viewed as a method for combining the benefits of individual parsing systems. Steedman et al. (2003) directly compare co-training and self-training and find that co-training outperforms self-training. Sagae and Tsujii (2007) successfully employ co-training in the domain adaption track of the CoNLL 2007 shared task on dependency parsing.

5.2.2 Experimental Setup

In this and all subsequent experiments, we use both the same training data and unlabelled data that we refer to in Section 5.1.2.

Our co-training algorithm is given in Figure 3 and it is the same as the algorithm provided by Steedman et al. (2003). Again, our experiments are carried out using Malt and Mate. This time, the experiments are run concurrently as each parser is bootstrapped from the other parser's output.

[3]Versions used: Maltparser v1.7 (stacklazy parsing algorithm); Mate tools v3.3 (graph-based parser)

A and B are two different parsers.
M_A^i and M_B^i are models of A and B at step i.
P_A^i and P_B^i are a sets of trees produced using M_A^i and M_B^i.
U is a set of sentences.
U^i is a subset of U at step i.
L is the manually labelled seed training set.
L_A^i and L_B^i are labelled training data for A and B at step i.
Initialise:
$L_A^0 \leftarrow L_B^0 \leftarrow L.$
$M_A^0 \leftarrow Train(A, L_A^0)$
$M_B^0 \leftarrow Train(B, L_B^0)$
for $i = 1 \rightarrow N$ **do**
  $U^i \leftarrow$ Add set of unlabelled sentences from U.
  $P_A^i \leftarrow Parse(U^i, M_A^i)$
  $P_B^i \leftarrow Parse(U^i, M_B^i)$
  $L_A^{i+1} \leftarrow L_A^i + P_B^i$
  $L_B^{i+1} \leftarrow L_B^i + P_A^i$
  $M_A^{i+1} \leftarrow Train(A, L_A^{i+1})$
  $M_B^{i+1} \leftarrow Train(B, L_B^{i+1})$
end for

Figure 3: Co-training algorithm

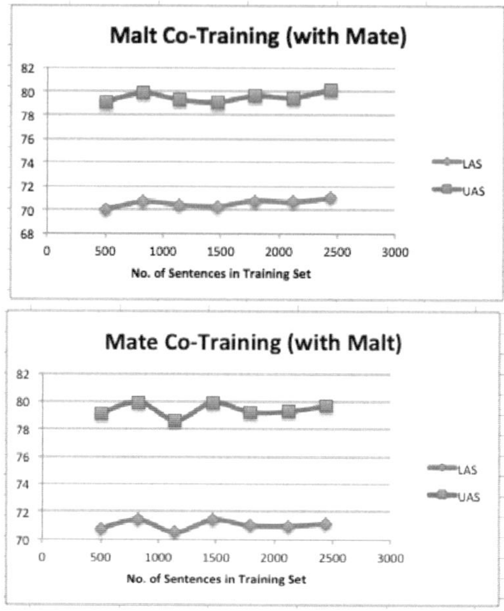

Figure 4: Co-Training Results on the Development Set

The steps are as follows: Initialisation involves training both parsers on a labelled seed set of 500 gold standard trees (L_A^0 and L_B^0), resulting in two separate baseline parsing models: M_A^i (Malt) and M_B^i (Mate). We divide the set of gold POS-tagged sentences (U) into 6 sets, each containing 323 sentences U^i. For each of the six iterations in this experiment $i = [1-6]$, we use Malt and Mate to parse U^i. This time, the set of newly parsed sentences P_B^i (Mate output) is added to the training set L_A^i to make a larger training set of L_A^{i+1} (Malt training set). Conversely, the set of newly parsed sentences P_A^i (Malt output) is added to the training set L_B^i to make a larger training set of L_B^{i+1} (Mate training set). Two new parsing models (M_A^{i+1} and M_B^{i+1}) are then induced by training Malt and Mate respectively with their new training sets.

5.2.3 Results

The results of our co-training experiment are presented in Figure 4. The best Malt model was trained on 2438 trees, at the final iteration (71.0% LAS and 79.8% UAS). The improvement in UAS over the baseline is statistically significant. Mate's best model was trained on 823 trees on the second iteration (71.4% LAS and 79.9% UAS). The improvement over the baseline is not statistically significant.

5.3 Sample-Selection-Based Co-Training

5.3.1 Related Work

Sample selection involves choosing training items for use in a particular task based on some criteria which approximates their accuracy in the absence of a label or reference. In the context of parsing, Rehbein (2011) chooses additional sentences to add to the parser's training set based on their similarity to the existing training set – the idea here is that sentences that are similar to training data are likely to have been parsed properly and so are "safe" to add to the training set. In their parser co-training experiments, Steedman et al. (2003) sample training items based on the confidence of the individual parsers (as approximated by parse probability).

In Active Learning research, the Query By Committee selection method (Seung et al., 1992) is used to choose items for annotation – if a committee of two or more systems disagrees on an item, this is evidence that the item needs to be prioritised for manual correction (see for example Lynn et al. (2012b)). Steedman et al. (2003) discuss a sample selection approach based on differences between parsers – if parser A and parser B disagree on an analysis, parser A can be improved by being retrained on parser B's analysis, and vice versa. In contrast, Ravi et al. (2008) show that parser *agreement* is a strong indicator of parse quality, and in parser domain adaptation, Sagae and Tsujii (2007) and Le Roux et al. (2012) use agreement between parsers to choose which automatically parsed target domain items to add to the training set.

Sample selection can be used with both self-training and co-training. We restrict our attention to co-training since our previous experiments have demonstrated that it has more potential than self-training. In the following set of experiments, we explore the role of both parser agreement and parser disagreement in sample selection in co-training.

5.3.2 Agreement-Based Co-Training

Experimental Setup The main algorithm for agreement-based co-training is given in Figure 5. Again, Malt and Mate are used. However, this algorithm differs from the co-training algorithm in Figure 3 in that rather than adding the full set of 323 newly parsed trees (P_A^i and P_B^i) to the training set at each iteration, selected subsets of these trees ($P_A^i\prime$ and $P_B^i\prime$) are added instead. To define these subsets, we identify the trees that have 85% or higher **agreement** between the two parser output sets. As a result, the number of trees in the subsets differ at each iteration. For iteration 1, 89 trees reach the agreement threshold; iteration 2, 93 trees; iteration 3, 117 trees; iteration 4, 122 trees; iteration 5, 131 trees; iteration 6, 114 trees. The number of trees in the training sets is much smaller compared with those in the experiments of Section 5.2.

Results The results for agreement-based co-training are presented in Figure 6. Malt's best model was trained on 1166 trees at the final iteration (71.0% LAS and 79.8% UAS). Mate's best model was trained on 1052 trees at the 5th iteration (71.5% LAS and 79.7% UAS). Neither result represents a statistically significant improvement over the baseline.

5.3.3 Disagreement-based Co-Training

Experimental Setup This experiment uses the same sample selection algorithm we used for agreement-based co-training (Figure 5). For this experiment, however, the way in which the subsets of trees ($P_A^i\prime$ and $P_B^i\prime$) are selected differs. This time we choose the trees that have 70% or higher **disagreement** between the two parser output sets.

A and B are two different parsers.
M_A^i and M_B^i are models of A and B at step i.
P_A^i and P_B^i are a sets of trees produced using M_A^i and M_B^i.
U is a set of sentences.
U^i is a subset of U at step i.
L is the manually labelled seed training set.
L_A^i and L_B^i are labelled training data for A and B at step i.
Initialise:
$L_A^0 \leftarrow L_B^0 \leftarrow L.$
$M_A^0 \leftarrow Train(A, L_A^0)$
$M_B^0 \leftarrow Train(B, L_B^0)$
for $i = 1 \rightarrow N$ **do**
  $U^i \leftarrow$ Add set of unlabelled sentences from U.
  $P_A^i \leftarrow Parse(U^i, M_A^i)$
  $P_B^i \leftarrow Parse(U^i, M_B^i)$
  $P_A^i\prime \leftarrow$ a subset of X trees from P_A^i
  $P_B^i\prime \leftarrow$ a subset of X trees from P_B^i
  $L_A^{i+1} \leftarrow L_A^i + P_B^i\prime$
  $L_B^{i+1} \leftarrow L_B^i + P_A^i\prime$
  $M_A^{i+1} \leftarrow Train(A, L_A^{i+1})$
  $M_B^{i+1} \leftarrow Train(B, L_B^{i+1})$
end for

Figure 5: Sample selection Co-training algorithm

Again, the number of trees in the subsets differ at each iteration. For iteration 1, 91 trees reach the disagreement threshold; iteration 2, 93 trees; iteration 3, 73 trees; iteration 4, 74 trees; iteration 5, 68 trees; iteration 6, 71 trees.

Results The results for our disagreement-based co-training experiment are shown in Figure 7. The best Malt model was trained with 831 trees at the 4th iteration (70.8% LAS and 79.8% UAS). Mate's best models were trained on (i) 684 trees on the 2nd iteration (71.0% LAS) and (ii) 899 trees on the 5th iteration (79.4% UAS). Neither improvement over the baseline is statistically significant.

5.3.4 Non-Iterative Agreement-based Co-Training

In this section, we explore what happens when we add the additional training data at once rather than over several iterations. Rather than testing this idea with all our previous setups, we choose sample-selection-based co-training where agreement between parsers is the criterion for selecting additional training data.

Experimental Setup Again, we also follow the algorithm for agreement-based co-training as presented in Figure 5. However, two different ap-

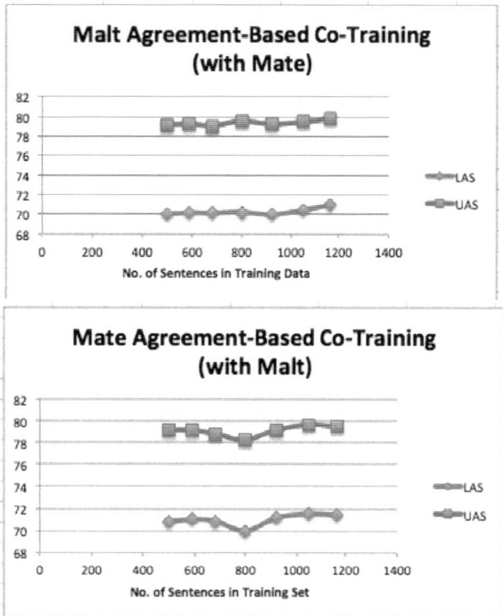

Figure 6: Agreement-based Co-Training Results on the Development Set

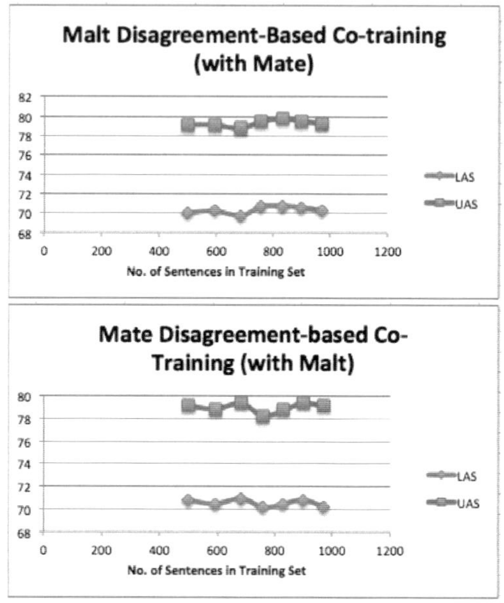

Figure 7: Disagreement-based Co-Training Results on the Development Set

proaches are taken this time, involving only one iteration in each. For the first experiment (ACT1a), the subsets of trees ($P_A^i{\prime}$ and $P_B^i{\prime}$) that are added to the training data are chosen based on an agreement threshold of 85% between parsers, and are taken from the *full* set of unlabelled data (where $U^i = U$), comprising 1938 trees. In this instance, the subset consists of 603 trees, making a final training set of 1103 trees.

For the second experiment (ACT1b), only trees meeting a parser agreement threshold of 100% are added to the training data. 253 trees ($P_A^i{\prime}$ and $P_B^i{\prime}$) out of 1938 trees ($U^i = U$) meet this threshold. The final training set consists of 753 trees.

Results ACT1a proved to be the most accurate parsing model for Mate overall. The addition of 603 trees that met the agreement threshold of 85% increased the LAS and UAS scores over the baseline by 1.0% and 1.3% to 71.8 and 80.4 respectively. This improvement is statistically significant. Malt showed a LAS improvement of 0.93% and a UAS improvement of 0.42% (71.0% LAS and 79.6% UAS). The LAS improvement over the baseline is statistically significant.

The increases for ACT1b, where 100% agreement trees are added, are less pronounced and are not statistically significant. Results showed a 0.5% LAS and 0.2% UAS increase over the baseline with Malt, based on the 100% agreement threshold (adding 235 trees). Mate performs at 0.5% above the LAS baseline and 0.1% above the UAS baseline.

5.4 Analysis

We perform an error analysis for the Malt and Mate baseline, self-trained and co-trained models on the development set. We observe the following trends:

- All Malt and Mate parsing models confuse the `subj` and `obj` labels. A few possible reasons for this stand out: (i) It is difficult for the parser to discriminate between analytic verb forms and synthetic verb forms. For example, in the phrase *phósfainn thusa* 'I would marry you', *phósfainn* is a synthetic form of the verb *pós* 'marry' that has been inflected with the incorporated pronoun 'I'. Not recognising this, the parser decided that it is an intransitive verb, taking 'thusa', the emphatic form of the pronoun *tú* 'you', as its subject instead of object. (ii) Possibly due to a VSO word order, when the parser is dealing with relative phrases, it can be difficult to ascertain whether the following noun is the subject or object. For example, *an chailín a chonaic mé inné* 'the girl whom

I saw yesterday/ the girl who saw me yesterday'.[4] (iii) There is no passive verb form in Irish. The autonomous form is most closely linked with passive use and is used when the agent is not known or mentioned. A 'hidden' or understood subject is incorporated into the verbform. *Casadh eochair i nglas* 'a key was turned in a lock' (lit. somebody turned a key in a lock). In this sentence, *eochair* 'key' is the object.

- For both parsers, there is some confusion between the labelling of `obl` and `padjunct`, both of which mark the attachment between verbs and prepositions. Overall, Malt's confusion decreases over the 6 iterations of self-training, but Mate begins to incorrectly choose `padjunct` over `obl` instead. Mixed results are obtained using the various variants of co-training.

- Mate handles coordination better than Malt.[5] It is not surprising then that co-training Malt using Mate parses improves Malt's coordination handling whereas the opposite is the case when co-training Mate on Malt parses, demonstrating that co-training can both eliminate and introduce errors.

- Other examples of how Mate helps Malt during co-training is in the distinction between `top` and `comp` relations, between `vparticle` and `relparticle`, and in the analysis of `xcomps`.

- Distinguishing between relative and cleft particles is a frequent error for Mate, and therefore Malt also begins to make this kind of error when co-trained using Mate. Mate improves using sample-selection-based co-training with Malt.

- The sample-selection-based co-training variants show broadly similar trends to the basic co-training.

[4]Naturally ambiguous Irish sentences like this require context for disambiguation.

[5]Nivre and McDonald (2007) make a similar observation when they compare the errors made by graph and transition based dependency parsers.

Parsing Models	LAS	UAS
Development Set		
Malt Baseline:	70.0	79.1
Malt Best (co-train) :	71.0	80.2
Mate Baseline:	70.8	79.1
Mate Best (85% threshold ACT1a):	71.8	80.4
Test Set		
Malt Baseline:	70.2	79.5
Malt Best (co-train) :	70.8	79.8
Mate Baseline:	71.9	80.1
Mate Best (85% threshold ACT1a):	73.1	81.5

Table 1: Results for best performing models

5.5 Test Set Results

The best performing parsing model for Malt on the development set is in the final iteration of the basic co-training approach in Section 5.2. The best performing parsing model for Mate on the development set is the non-iterative 85% threshold agreement-based co-training approach described in Section 5.3.4. The test set results for these optimal development set configurations are also shown in Table 1. The baseline model for Malt obtains a LAS of 70.2%, the final co-training iteration a LAS of 70.8%. The baseline model for Mate obtains a LAS of 71.9%, and the non-iterative 85% agreement-based co-trained model obtains a LAS of 73.1%.

6 Parsing Experiments Using Morphological Features

As well as the size of the dataset, data sparsity is also confounded by the number of possible inflected forms for a given root form. With this in mind, and following on from the discussion in Section 5.4, we carry out further parsing experiments in an attempt to make better use of morphological information during parsing. We attack this in two ways: by reducing certain words to their lemmas and by including morphological information in the optional FEATS (features) field. The reasoning behind reducing certain word forms to lemmas is to further reduce the differences between inflected forms of the same word, and the reasoning behind including morphological information is to make more explicit the similarity between two different word forms inflected in the same way. All experiments are car-

Parsing Models (Malt)	LAS	UAS
Baseline:	70.0	79.1
Lemma (Pron_Prep):	69.7	78.9
Lemma + Pron_Prep Morph Features:	69.6	78.9
Form + Pron_Prep Morph Features:	69.8	79.1
Verb Morph Features:	70.0	79.1

Table 2: Results with morphological features on the development set

ried out with MaltParser and our seed training set of 500 gold trees. We focus on two phenomena: prepositional pronouns or pronominal prepositions (see Section 2) and verbs with incorporated subjects (see Section 2 and Section 5.4).

In the first experiment, we include extra morphological information for pronominal prepositions. We ran three parsing experiments: (i) replacing the value of the surface form (FORM) of pronominal prepositions with their lemma form (LEMMA), for example *agam*→*ag*, (ii) including morphological information for pronominal prepositions in the FEATS column. For example, in the case of *agam* 'at me', we include `Per=1P|Num=Sg`, (iii) we combine both approaches of reverting to lemma form and also including the morphological features. The results are given in Table 2.

In the second experiment, we include morphological features for verbs with incorporated subjects: imperative verb forms, synthetic verb forms and autonomous verb forms such as those outlined in Section 5.4. For each instance of these verb types, we included `incorpSubj=true` in the FEATS column. The results are also given in Table 2.

The experiments on the pronominal prepositions show a drop in parsing accuracy while the experiments carried out using verb morphological information showed no change in parsing accuracy.[6] In the case of inflected prepositions, perhaps we have not seen any improvement because we have not focused on a phenomenon which is critical for parsing. More experimentation is necessary.

7 Concluding Remarks

We have presented two sets of experiments which aim to improve dependency parsing performance for a minority language with a very small treebank. In the first set of experiments, the main focus of the paper, we tried to overcome the limited treebank size by increasing the parsers' training sets using automatically parsed sentences. While we do manage to achieve statistically significant improvements in some settings, it is clear from the results that the gains in parser accuracy through semi-supervised bootstrapping methods are fairly modest. Yet, in the absence of more gold labelled data, it is difficult to know now whether we would achieve similar or improved results by adding the same amount of gold training data. This type of analysis will be interesting at a later date when the unlabelled trees used in these experiments are eventually annotated and corrected manually.

The second set of experiments tries to mitigate some of the data sparseness issues by exploiting morphological characteristics of the language. Unfortunately, we do not see any improvements but we may get different results if we repeat these experiments using the larger semi-supervised training sets from the first set of experiments.

There are many directions this parsing research could take us in the future. Our unlabelled data consisted of sentences annotated with gold POS tags. In the future we would like to take advantage of the fully unlabelled, untagged data in the New Corpus for Ireland – Irish, which consists of 30 million words. We would also like to experiment with a fully unsupervised parser using this dataset. Our Malt feature models are manually optimised – it would be interesting to experiment with optimising them using MaltOptimizer (Ballesteros, 2012). An additional avenue of research would be to exploit the hierarchical nature of the dependency scheme to arrive at more flexible way of measuring agreement or disagreement in sample selection.

Acknowledgements

We thank the three anonymous reviewers for their helpful feedback. This work is supported by Science Foundation Ireland (Grant No. 07/CE/I1142) as part of the Centre for Next Generation Localisation (www.cngl.ie) at Dublin City University.

[6] Although the total number of correct attachments are the same, the parser output is different.

References

Miguel Ballesteros. 2012. Maltoptimizer: A system for maltparser optimization. In *Proceedings of the Eighth International Conference on Linguistic Resources and Evaluation (LREC)*, pages 2757–2763, Istanbul, Turkey.

Bernd Bohnet. 2010. Top accuracy and fast dependency parsing is not a contradiction. In *Proceedings of COLING*.

Özlem Çetinoğlu, Jennifer Foster, Joakim Nivre, Deirdre Hogan, Aoife Cahill, and Josef van Genabith. 2010. LFG without c-structures. In *Proceedings of the 9th International Workshop on Treebanks and Linguistic Theories*.

Eugene Charniak and Mark Johnson. 2005. Course-to-fine n-best-parsing and maxent discriminative reranking. In *Proceedings of the 43rd ACL*.

Eugene Charniak. 1997. Statistical parsing with a context-free grammar and word statistics. In *Proceedings of AAAI*.

Eugene Charniak. 2000. A maximum entropy inspired parser. In *Proceedings of the First Annual Meeting of the North American Chapter of the Association for Computational Linguistics (NAACL-00)*.

Christian-Brothers. 1988. *New Irish Grammar*. Dublin: C J Fallon.

David Greene. 1966. *The Irish Language*. Dublin: The Three Candles.

Zhongqiang Huang and Mary Harper. 2009. Self-training PCFG grammars with latent annotations across languages. In *Proceedings of EMNLP*.

John Judge, Ailbhe Ní Chasaide, Rose Ní Dhubhda, Kevin P. Scannell, and Elaine Uí Dhonnchadha. 2012. *The Irish Language in the Digital Age*. Springer Publishing Company, Incorporated.

Joseph Le Roux, Jennifer Foster, Joachim Wagner, Rasoul Samed Zadeh Kaljahi, and Anton Bryl. 2012. DCU-Paris13 systems for the sancl 2012 shared task. In *Working Notes of SANCL*.

Teresa Lynn, Özlem Çetinoğlu, Jennifer Foster, Elaine Uí Dhonnchadha, Mark Dras, and Josef van Genabith. 2012a. Irish treebanking and parsing. In *Proceedings of the Eight International Conference on Language Resources and Evaluation*, pages 1939–1946.

Teresa Lynn, Jennifer Foster, Mark Dras, and Elaine Uí Dhonnchadha. 2012b. Active learning and the Irish treebank. In *Proceeedings of the Australasian Language Technology Workshop (ALTA)*, pages 23–32.

David McClosky, Eugene Charniak, and Mark Johnson. 2006. Effective self-training for parsing. In *Proceedings of the Human Language Technology Conference of the NAACL, Main Conference*, pages 152–159, New York City, USA, June. Association for Computational Linguistics.

David McClosky, Eugene Charniak, and Mark Johnson. 2008. When is self-training effective for parsing? In *Proceedings of COLING*.

Joakim Nivre and Ryan McDonald. 2007. Characterizing the errors of data-driven dependency parsing models. In *Proceedings of EMNLP-CoNLL*, Prague, Czech Republic.

Joakim Nivre, Johan Hall, and Jens Nilsson. 2006. Maltparser: A data-driven parser-generator for dependency parsing. In *Proceedings of the Fifth International Conference on Language Resources and Evaluation (LREC2006)*.

Mícheál Ó Siadhail. 1989. *Modern Irish: Grammatical structure and dialectal variation*. Cambridge: Cambridge University Press.

Sujith Ravi, Kevin Knight, and Radu Soricut. 2008. Automatic prediction of parser accuracy. In *Proceedings of EMNLP*, Hawaii.

Ines Rehbein. 2011. Data point selection for self-training. In *Proceedings of the Second Workshop on Statistical Parsing of Morphologically Rich Languages (SPMRL 2011)*, Dublin, Ireland.

Roi Reichart and Ari Rappaport. 2007. Self-training for enhancement and domain adaptation of statistical parsers trained on small datasets. In *Proceedings of ACL*.

Kenji Sagae and Jun'ichi Tsujii. 2007. Dependency parsing and domain adaptation with LR models and parser ensembles. In *Proceedings of the CoNLL shared task session of EMNLP-CoNLL*.

Kenji Sagae. 2010. Self-training without reranking for parser domain adapation and its impact on semantic role labelling. In *Proceedings of the ACL Workshop on Domain Adaptation for NLP*.

Sebastian Seung, Manfred Opper, and Haim Sompolinsky. 1992. Query by committee. In *Proceedings of the Fifth Annual ACM Workshop on Computational Learning Theory*.

Mark Steedman, Miles Osborne, Anoop Sarkar, Stephen Clark, Rebecca Hwa, Julia Hockenmaier, Paul Ruhlen, Steven Baker, and Jeremiah Crim. 2003. Bootstrapping statistical parsers from small datasets. In *Proceedings of the tenth conference on European chapter of the Association for Computational Linguistics - Volume 1*, EACL '03, pages 331–338, Stroudsburg, PA, USA. Association for Computational Linguistics.

Nancy Stenson. 1981. *Studies in Irish Syntax*. Tübingen: Gunter Narr Verlag.

Elaine Uí Dhonnchadha. 2009. *Part-of-Speech Tagging and Partial Parsing for Irish using Finite-State Transducers and Constraint Grammar*. Ph.D. thesis, Dublin City University.

Lithuanian Dependency Parsing with Rich Morphological Features

Jurgita Kapočiūtė-Dzikienė
Kaunas University of Technology
K. Donelaičio 73
LT-44249 Kaunas, Lithuania
jurgita.k.dz@gmail.com

Joakim Nivre
Uppsala University
Box 635
SE-75126 Uppsala, Sweden
joakim.nivre@lingfil.uu.se

Algis Krupavičius
Kaunas University of Technology
K. Donelaičio 73
LT-44249 Kaunas, Lithuania
pvai@ktu.lt

Abstract

We present the first statistical dependency parsing results for Lithuanian, a morphologically rich language in the Baltic branch of the Indo-European family. Using a greedy transition-based parser, we obtain a labeled attachment score of 74.7 with gold morphology and 68.1 with predicted morphology (77.8 and 72.8 unlabeled). We investigate the usefulness of different features and find that rich morphological features improve parsing accuracy significantly, by 7.5 percentage points with gold features and 5.6 points with predicted features. As expected, CASE is the single most important morphological feature, but virtually all available features bring some improvement, especially under the gold condition.

1 Introduction

During the last decades, we have seen a tremendous increase in the number of syntactic parsers available for different languages, often enabled by the development of syntactically annotated corpora, or treebanks. The added linguistic diversity has highlighted the fact that typological differences between languages lead to new challenges, both in parsing technology and treebank annotation. In particular, it has been observed repeatedly that richly inflected languages, which often also exhibit relatively free word order, usually obtain lower parsing accuracy, especially compared to English (Buchholz and Marsi, 2006; Nivre et al., 2007). This has led to a special interest in parsing methods for such languages (Tsarfaty et al., 2010; Tsarfaty et al., 2013).

In this paper, we contribute to the growing pool of empirical evidence by presenting the first statistical dependency parsing results for Lithuanian, a morphologically rich Baltic language characterized as one of the most archaic living Indo-European languages (Gimbutas, 1963).

Using the newly developed Lithuanian Treebank, we train and evaluate a greedy transition-based parser and in particular investigate the impact of rich morphological features on parsing accuracy. Our experiments show that virtually all morphological features can be beneficial when parsing Lithuanian, which contrasts with many previous studies that have mainly found a positive impact for isolated features such as CASE (Eryigit et al., 2008). Using all available features, we achieve a labeled attachment score of 74.7 with gold morphology (including part-of-speech tags and lemmas) and 68.1 with predicted morphology. The corresponding unlabeled attachment scores are 77.8 and 72.8, respectively.

2 The Lithuanian Treebank

The *Lithuanian Treebank* was developed by the Center of Computational Linguistics, Vytautas Magnus University.[1] The annotated texts are taken from the newspaper domain and thus represent normative Lithuanian language. The treebank contains 1,566 sentences and 24,265 tokens: 19,625 words (9,848 distinct) plus 4,640 punctuation marks (12 distinct). Word tokens in the Lithuanian Treebank are mor-

[1]The treebank creation was one of the tasks of the project *Internet Resources: Annotated Corpus of the Lithuanian Language and Tools of Annotation*, implemented in 2007-2008 and funded by the Lithuanian Science and Studies Foundation.

	SBJ	OBJ	MODIF	PRED	ATTR	DEP	ROOT	TOTAL
Abbreviation	6					457	22	485
Acronym						31	2	33
Adjectival participle	1		28			84	12	125
Adjective	1			63	1,104	157	75	1,400
Adverbial participle			37			28	3	68
Adverb			1,134			193	29	1,356
Conjunction		5				1,171	93	1,269
Infinitive		6		372	9	139	21	547
Interjection						3	6	9
Noun	775	1,097	1,314		1,712	1,415	217	6,530
Numeral		1	22		158	72	6	259
Participle	1			150	430	285	197	1,063
Particle			27	78	1	216	36	358
Preposition		253	168			630	35	1,086
Pronoun	258	170	104		558	424	21	1,535
Proper noun	15	1	22		20	1,307	60	1,425
Roman number						25	3	28
Verb						205	1,844	2,049
TOTAL	1,057	1,533	2,856	663	3,992	6,842	2,682	19,625

Table 1: Cooccurrence statistics on dependencies (columns) and PoS tags (rows) in the Lithuanian Treebank.

phologically and syntactically annotated as follows:

- Syntactic dependencies: 7 different categories listed in Table 1 (columns).
- Part-of-Speech (PoS) tags: 18 different categories listed in Table 1 (rows). These tags simply determine PoS but do not incorporate any additional morphological information.
- Morphological features: 12 different categories listed with possible values in Table 2. The number of morphological features assigned to a word varies from 0 (for particles, conjunctions, etc.) to 9.[2]
- Lemmas: base form of word, lowercase except for proper names.

The syntactic annotation scheme only distinguishes 5 basic grammatical relations (SBJ, OBJ, PRED, ATTR, MODIF) plus an additional underspecified relation (DEP) for other dependencies between words and a special relation (ROOT) for words attached to an (implicit) artificial root node. The dependency structure always forms a tree originating from the root node, but there may be more than one token attached to the root node. This happens when a sentence contains several clauses which do not share any constituents. Table 1 gives statistics on the different dependency relations and their distribution over different PoS tags.

Examples of syntactically annotated sentences are presented in Figure 1 and Figure 2. All dependency relations are represented by arrows pointing from the head to the dependent, the labels above indicate the dependency type.[3] For example, as we can see in Figure 1, *nerizikuoja* (does not risk) is the head of *Kas* (Who) and this dependency relation has the SBJ label. The sentence in Figure 1 contains two clauses (separated by a comma) both containing SBJ dependency relations. The sentence in Figure 2 contains the main clause *Bet štai pro medį praslinko nedidelis šešėlis* and the subordinate clause *kuriame sėdėjau* in which the subject is expressed implicitly (a pronoun *aš* (I) can be inferred from the singular 1st person inflection of the verb *sėdėjau* (sat)). In Lithuanian sentences, the subject is very often omitted, and even the verb can be expressed implicitly. For exam-

[2]For example, the participle *esanti* (existent) is described by 8 feature values: CASE: Nominative, GENDER: Feminine, NUMBER: Singular, TENSE: Present, VOICE: Active, REFLEX: Non-reflexive, PRONOM: Non-pronominal, ASPECT: Positive.

[3]ROOT dependencies are not shown explicitly.

Category	Values	Frequency	Compatible PoS Tags
CASE	Nominative	3,421	Adjective, Noun, Numeral, Participle, Pronoun, Proper noun
	Genitive	4,204	
	Dative	445	
	Accusative	1,995	
	Instrumental	795	
	Locative	849	
	Vocative	10	
GENDER	Masculine	7,074	Adjective, Adverbial participle, Noun, Numeral, Participle, Pronoun, Proper noun
	Feminine	4,482	
	Neuter	283	
	Appellative	1	
NUMBER	Singular	8,822	Adjective, Adverbial participle, Noun, Numeral, Participle, Pronoun, Proper noun, Verb
	Plural	4,624	
	Dual	3	
TENSE	Present	1,307	Adjectival participle, Participle, Verb
	Past occasion	1,352	
	Past	311	
	Past iterative	31	
	Future	123	
MOOD	Indicative	1,950	Verb
	Subjunctive	87	
	Imperative	12	
PERSON	1st	281	Verb
	2nd	41	
	3rd	1,727	
VOICE	Active	456	Participle
	Passive	594	
	Gerundive	13	
REFLEX	Reflexive	526	Adjectival participle, Adverbial participle, Infinitive, Noun, Participle, Verb
	Non-reflexive	3,486	
DEGREE	Positive	1,712	Adjective, Adverb, Numeral, Participle
	Comparative	1,712	
	Superior	1	
	Superlative	94	
TYPE	Cardinal	145	Numeral
	Ordinal	105	
	Multiple	9	
PRONOM	Pronominal	247	Adjective, Participle, Pronoun, Numeral
	Non-pronominal	3,056	
ASPECT	Positive	6,206	Adjectival participle, Adjective, Adverbial participle, Adverb, Infinitive, Noun, Participle, Particle, Preposition, Verb
	Negative	422	

Table 2: Morphological categories in the Lithuanian Treebank: possible values, frequencies and compatible PoS tags.

ple, in the sentence *Jis geras žmogus* (He is a good man), the copula verb *yra* (is) is omitted.

The possible values of different morphological categories are presented with descriptive statistics in Table 2. Given that word order in Lithuanian sentences is relatively free, morphological information is important to determine dependency relations. For example, an adjective modifying a noun has to agree in GENDER, NUMBER and CASE, as in *gražus miestas* (beautiful city), where both the adjective and the noun are in masculine singular nominative. Verbs agree with their subject in NUMBER and PERSON, as in *jūs važiuojate* (you are going) in second person plural. Finally, the CASE of a noun

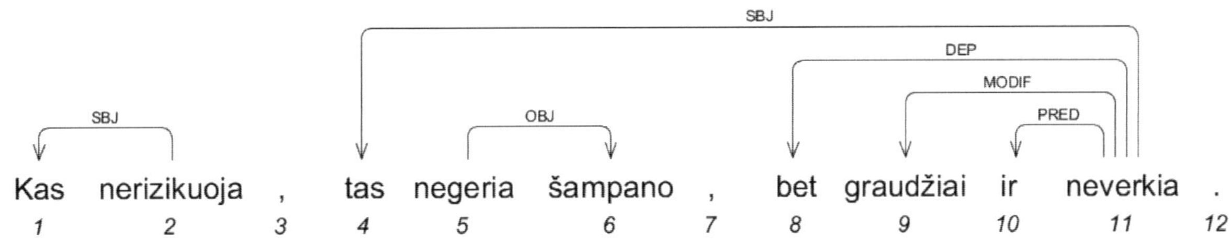

Figure 1: Annotated sentence from the Lithuanian Treebank, consisting of two independent main clauses. Translation: *Who does not risk, that does not drink champagne but does not cry tearfully either.*

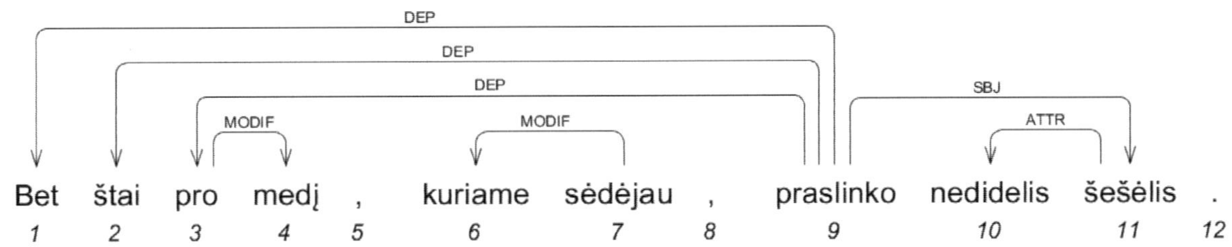

Figure 2: Annotated sentence from the Lithuanian Treebank, consisting of a main clause and a subordinate clause. Translation: *But here through the tree in which I sat passed a small shadow.*

or pronoun is an important indicator of the syntactic relation to the verb, such that nominative CASE almost always implies a SBJ relation. However, the transparency of morphological information is limited by syncretism in CASE, NUMBER and GENDER. Thus, the form *mamos* (mother(s)) can be either plural nominative or singular genitive; the form *mokytojas* (teacher(s)) can be either masculine singular nominative or feminine plural accusative.

3 Parsing Framework

We use the open-source system MaltParser (Nivre et al., 2006a) for our parsing experiments with the Lithuanian Treebank. MaltParser is a transition-based dependency parser that performs parsing as greedy search through a transition system, guided by a history-based classifier for predicting the next transition (Nivre, 2008). Although more accurate dependency parsers exist these days, MaltParser appeared suitable for our experiments for a number of reasons. First of all, greedy transition-based parsers have been shown to perform well with relatively small amounts of training data (Nivre et al., 2006b). Secondly, MaltParser implements a number of different transition systems and classifiers that can be explored and also supports user-defined input formats and feature specifications in a flexible way. Finally, MaltParser has already been applied to a wide range of languages, to which the results can be compared. In particular, MaltParser was used to obtain the only published dependency parsing results for Latvian, the language most closely related to Lithuanian (Pretkalniņa and Rituma, 2013).

In our experiments, we use the latest release of MaltParser (Version 1.7.2).[4] After preliminary experiments, we decided to use the arc-eager transition system (Nivre, 2003) with pseudo-projective parsing to recover non-projective dependencies (Nivre and Nilsson, 2005) and the LIBLINEAR learning package with multiclass SVMs (Fan et al., 2008). Table 3 lists the options that were explored in the preliminary experiments. We first tested all possible combinations of learning method and parsing algorithms and then performed a greedy sequential tuning of the options related to covered roots, pseudo-projective parsing, and all combinations of allow-root and allow-reduce.

In order to use MaltParser on the Lithuanian Treebank, we first converted the data to the CoNLL-X format,[5] treating all morphological feature bundles

[4] Available at http://maltparser.org.

[5] See http://ilk.uvt.nl/conll/#dataformat.

Option	Value
Learning method (-l)	liblinear
Parsing algorithm (-a)	nivreeager
Covered roots (-pcr)	head
Pseudo-projective parsing (-pp)	head+path
Allow root (-nr)	true
Allow reduce (-ne)	true

Table 3: List of MaltParser options explored in preliminary experiments with best values used in all subsequent experiments.

as a single string and putting it into the FEATS column, which means that there will be one boolean feature for each unique set of features. However, in order to study the influence of each individual morphological feature, we also prepared an appropriate format where every morphological feature had its own (atom-valued) column (called CASE, GENDER, NUMBER, etc.), which means that there will be one boolean feature for each unique feature value, as specified in Table 2. In the following, we will refer to these two versions as Set-FEATS and Atom-FEATS, respectively. Another choice we had to make was how to treat punctuation, which is not integrated into the dependency structure in the Lithuanian Treebank. To avoid creating spurious non-projective dependencies by attaching them to the root node, we simply attached all punctuation marks to an adjacent word.[6] Therefore, we also exclude punctuation in all evaluation scores.

We use five-fold cross-validation on the entire treebank in all our experiments. This means that the final accuracy estimates obtained after tuning features and other parameters may be overly optimistic (in the absence of a held-out test set), but given the very limited amount of data available this seemed like the most reasonable approach. We perform experiments under two conditions. In the Gold condition, the input to the parser contains PoS tags, lemmas and morphological features taken from the manually annotated treebank. In the Predicted condition, we instead use input annotations produced by the morphological analyser and lemmatizer *Lemuoklis* (Zinkevičius, 2000; Daudaravičius et al., 2007), which also solves morphological disambiguation problems at the sentence level. Table 4 shows the accuracy of this system for the output categories that are relevant both in the Set-FEATS and Atom-FEATS format.

[6]This is automatically handled by the covered roots option in MaltParser; see Table 3.

Category	Accuracy
POSTAG	88.1
LEMMA	91.1
Set-FEATS	78.6
Atom-FEATS	
CASE	87.2
GENDER	88.3
NUMBER	86.2
TENSE	94.1
MOOD	95.9
PERSON	95.8
VOICE	90.2
REFLEX	93.3
DEGREE	90.3
TYPE	80.7
PRONOM	89.3
ASPECT	93.5

Table 4: Accuracy of the morphological analyzer and lemmatizer used in the Predicted condition.

4 Parsing Experiments and Results

In our first set of experiments, we tuned two feature models in the Gold condition:

- **Baseline:** Starting from the default feature model in MaltParser, we used backward and forward feature selection to tune a feature model using only features over the FORM, LEMMA, POSTAG and DEPREL fields in the CoNLL-X format (that is, no morphological features). Only one feature was explored at a time, starting with FORM and going on to LEMMA, POSTAG, DEPREL, and conjunctions of POSTAG and DEPREL features. The best templates for each feature type were retained when moving on to the next feature.

- **Baseline+FEATS:** Starting from the Baseline model, we used forward feature selection to tune a feature model that additionally contains features over the FEATS field in the Set-FEATS

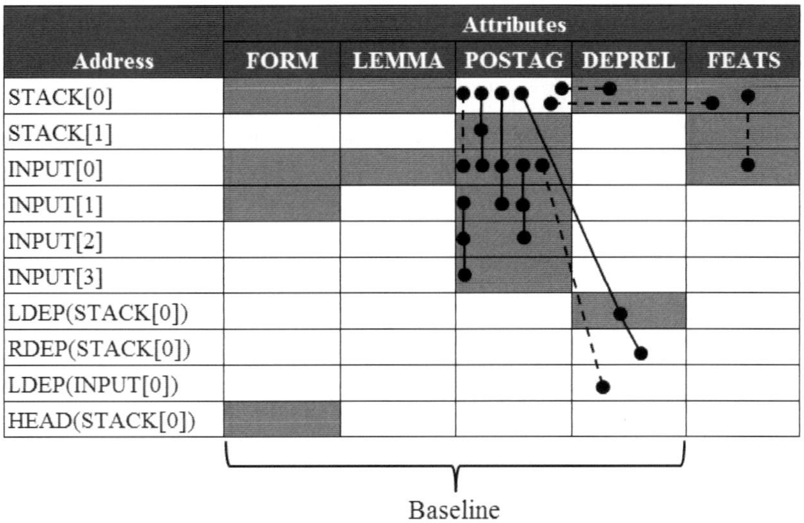

Figure 3: The feature models Baseline and Baseline+FEATS. Rows represent address functions, columns represent attribute functions. Gray cells represent single features, dotted lines connecting cell pairs or lines connecting cell triplets represent conjoined features. The Baseline model contains only features that do not involve the FEATS column.

version, optionally conjoined with POSTAG features.

The features included in these two models are depicted schematically in Figure 3. The Baseline+FEATS model includes all features, while the Baseline model includes all features except those that refer to the FEATS field. In the Gold condition, the Baseline model achieves a labeled attachment score (LAS) of 67.19 and an unlabeled attachment score (UAS) of 73.96, while Baseline+FEATS gets 74.20 LAS and 77.40 UAS. In the Predicted condition, the corresponding results are 62.47/70.30 for Baseline and 68.05/72.78 for Baseline+FEATS. Thus, with the addition of morphological features (all of them together) the Baseline+FEATS model exceeds the Baseline by 7.01 percentage points for LAS and 3.44 for UAS in the Gold condition and by 5.58 percentage points for LAS and 2.48 for UAS in the Predicted condition. To determine whether the differences are statistically significant we performed McNemar's test (McNemar, 1947) with one degree of freedom. The test showed the differences in LAS and UAS between Baseline and Baseline+FEATS for both the Gold and Predicted conditions to be statistically significant with $p << 0.05$.

In our second set of experiments, we started from the Baseline model and incrementally added morphological features in the Atom-FEATS format, one morphological category at a time, using the same five feature templates (three single and two conjoined) as for FEATS in the Baseline+FEATS model (see Figure 3). The order of explored morphological features was random, but only features that increased parsing accuracy when added were retained when adding the next morphological feature. The LAS results of these experiments are summarized in Figure 4 (reporting results in the Gold condition) and Figure 5 (in the Predicted condition). We do not present UAS results because they show the same trend as the LAS metric although shifted upwards. In the Gold condition, the best feature model is Baseline + CASE + GENDER + NUMBER + TENSE + DEGREE + VOICE + PERSON + TYPE, which achieves 74.66 LAS and 77.84 UAS and exceeds the Baseline by 7.47 percentage points for LAS and 3.88 for UAS (MOOD, REFLEX, PRONOM and ASPECT made no improvements or even degraded the performance). In the Predicted condition, the best feature model remains Baseline+FEATS, but using the Atom-FEATS version the best results are achieved with Baseline + CASE + GENDER + TENSE + VOICE + PERSON + REFLEX, which exceeds the Baseline by 5.36 percentage points for LAS and 2.55 for UAS (NUMBER, MOOD, DEGREE, REFLEX, PRONOM and ASPECT made no improvements or even degraded the performance). All these differences are statistically significant. By contrast, the differences between the best models with Atom-FEATS and Set-FEATS are not statistically significant for any metric or condition (with p values in the range 0.35–0.87).

5 Discussion

First of all, we may conclude that the Baseline feature model (without morphological information) does not perform very well for a morphologically rich language like Lithuanian (see Figure 4 and Figure 5), despite giving high accuracy for morphologically impoverished languages like English. However, it is likely that the accuracy of the Baseline model would be a bit higher for the Lithuanian Treebank if PoS tags incorporated some morphological information as they do, for example, in the English Penn Treebank (Marcus et al., 1993).

It thus seems that basic PoS tags as well as lemmas are too general to be beneficial enough for Lithuanian. The simple morphemic word form could be more useful (even despite the fact that Lithuanian is syncretic language), but the treebank is currently too small, making the data too sparse to create a robust model.[7] Thus, the effective way of dealing with unseen words is by incorporating morphological information.

In the Predicted condition, we always see a drop in accuracy compared to the Gold condition, although our case is not exceptional. For example, the Baseline model has a drop in LAS of 4.72 percentage points from Gold to Predicted, but this gap could possibly be narrowed by retuning the feature model for the Predicted condition instead of simply reusing the model tuned for the Gold condition. We also tried training the model on gold annotations for parsing predicted annotations, but these produced even worse results, confirming that it is better to make the training condition resemble the parsing condition. Despite noisy information, morphological features are still very beneficial compared to not using them at all (see Figure 5). Our findings thus agree with what has been found for Arabic by Marton et al. (2013) but seem to contradict the results obtained for Hebrew by Goldberg and Elhadad (2010).

As we can see from both curves in Figure 4 and Figure 5, the top contributors are CASE, VOICE, and TENSE, but the CASE feature gives the biggest contribution to accuracy. It boosts LAS by 6.51 points in the Gold condition and almost 5 points in the Predicted condition, whereas the contribution of all the other morphological features is less than 1 point (and not statistically significant). In a control experiment we reversed the order in which morphological features are added (presented in Figure 4 and Figure 5), adding CASE at the very end. In this case, the addition of all features except case resulted in a statistically significant improvement in the Gold condition ($p = 0.001$) but not in the Predicted condition ($p = 0.24$). However, the contribution of CASE was by far the most important again – increasing LAS by 5.55 points in the Gold condition and by 4.68 points in the Predicted condition. To further investigate the selection of morphological features, we also performed a greedy selection experiment. During this experiment CASE was selected first, again proving it to be the most influential feature. It was followed by VOICE, MOOD, NUMBER and DEGREE in the Gold condition and by GENDER, TENSE, PERSON and TYPE in the Predicted condition. Overall, however, greedy selection gave worse results than random selection, achieving 74.42 LAS and 77.60 UAS in the Gold condition and 67.83 LAS and 72.80 UAS in the Predicted condition.

To find that CASE is the most important feature is not surprising, as CASE has been shown to be the most helpful feature for many languages (at least in the Gold condition). But whereas few other features have been shown to help for other languages, in our case the majority of features (8 out of 12 in the Gold condition) are beneficial for Lithuanian. The so-called agreement features (GENDER, NUMBER and PERSON) are beneficial for Lithuanian (at least in the Gold condition) as well as for Arabic (Marton et al., 2013), but not such languages as Hindi (Ambati et al., 2010) and Hebrew (Goldberg and Elhadad, 2010). In the Predicted condition, their positive impact is marginal at best, possibly because NUMBER is very poorly predicted by the morpho-

[7] We tried to reduce data sparseness a little bit by changing all words into lowercase, but the drop in accuracy revealed that orthographic information is also important for parsing.

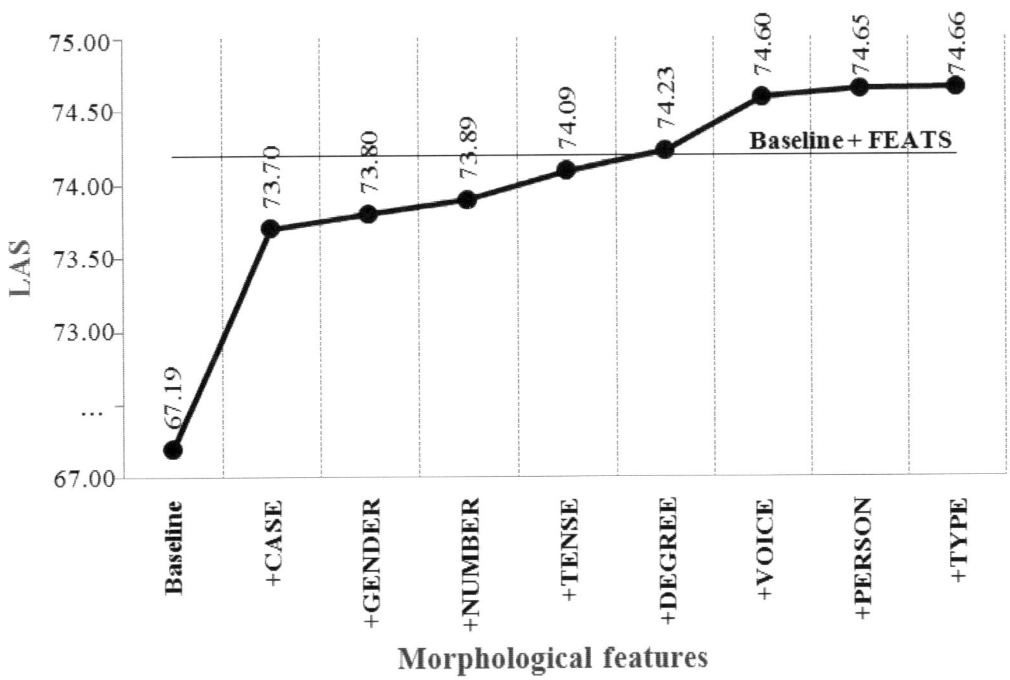

Figure 4: The contribution of individual morphological features in the Gold condition. The x axis represents feature models incorporating different attributes; the y axis represents LAS. The horizontal line at 74.20 represents the LAS of Baseline+FEATS.

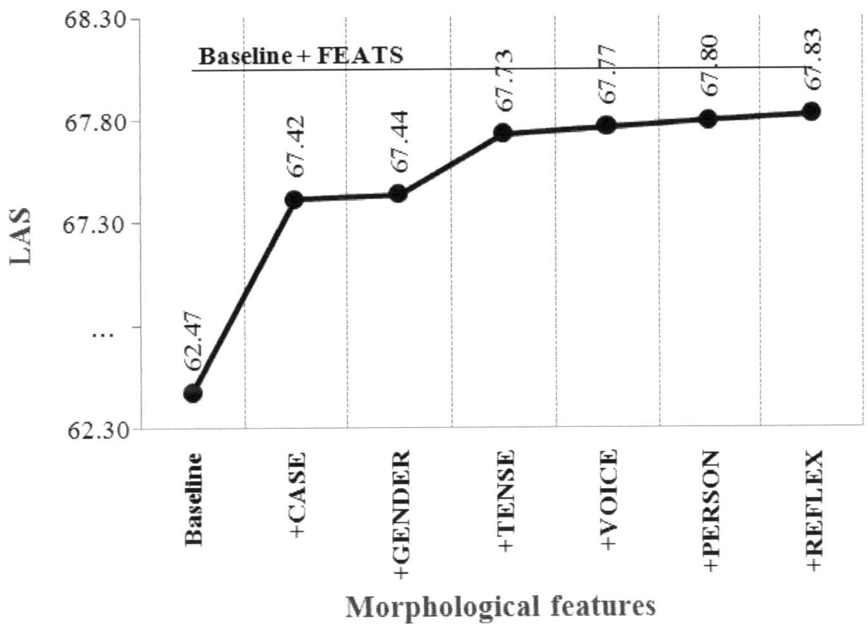

Figure 5: The contribution of individual morphological features in the Predicted condition. The x axis represents feature models incorporating different attributes; the y axis represents LAS. The horizontal line at 68.05 represents the LAS of Baseline+FEATS.

logical analyzer.[8]

It is also worth noting that morphological features have less influence on UAS than LAS, as the gain in UAS over the Baseline is 3-4 percentage points lower compared to LAS. This means that morphology is more important for selecting the type of dependency than for choosing the syntactic head. More precisely, adding morphology improves both recall and precision for the labels SBJ and OBJ, which is probably due primarily to the CASE feature.

Despite the positive effect of morphological information, the best LAS achieved is only 74.66 in the Gold condition and 68.05 in the Predicted condition. An error analysis shows that 38.0% of all LAS errors have an incorrect syntactic head, 12.5% have an incorrect dependency label, and 49.5% have both incorrect. The most commonly occurring problem is the ambiguity between DEP and ROOT dependencies.

For example, in the sentence *atsidūrė Vokietijoje, lankė paskaitas* (he got to Germany, attended lectures) *lankė* (attended) is the dependent of *atsidūrė* (got), because it is the consecutive action performed by the same subject (the subject is expressed implicitly and can be identified according the appropriate verb form). But in the sentence *buvo puiku ir mums, ir jam patiko* (it was great for us and he enjoyed it) *patiko* (enjoyed) is not a dependent of *buvo* (was) but of the root node, because the sentence contains two separate clauses with their subjects and verbs.[9]

Other common ambiguities are among different types of labels that are expressed by the same morphological categories and depends on the context (and the meaning) of the sentence, for example, in the phrase *užželti augalais* (to green with plants), *augalais* (plants) is a dependent of *užželti* (to green) with the OBJ label; in *užsiimti projektais* (to engage in projects) *projektais* (projects) is a dependent of *užsiimti* (to engage) with the MODIF label; and in *pavadinti vardais* (to name with names) *vardais* (names) is a dependent on *pavadinti* (to name) with DEP label. The choice of dependency label in these cases depends on the semantic role of the modifier, corresponding to the question *what* in the first case, the question *how* in the second case, and yet a different relation in the third case. In all these cases morphology does not help to determine the particular label of the dependency relation.

Finally, we note that the results obtained for Lithuanian are in the same range as those reported for Latvian, another Baltic language. Using MaltParser in 10-fold cross-validation on a data set of 2,500 sentences, Pretkalniņa and Rituma (2013) achieve an unlabeled attachment score of 74.6 in the Gold condition and 72.2 in the Predicted conditions, to be compared with 77.8 and 72.8 in our experiments. It should be remembered, however, that the results are not directly comparable due to differences in annotation schemes.

6 Conclusion

In this paper we have presented the first statistical dependency parsing results for Lithuanian. Using the transition-based system MaltParser, we have demonstrated experimentally that the role of morphology is very important for the Lithuanian language. The addition of morphological information resulted in a gain in attachment scores of 7.5 points (labeled) and 3.9 points (unlabeled) with manually validated morphology (the Gold condition) and of 5.6 points (labeled) and 2.5 points (unlabeled) with automatically predicted morphology (the Predicted condition). In the Gold condition, we achieved the best results by adding each morphological feature separately (using the Atom-FEATS representation), but in the Predicted condition adding all features together (using the Set-FEATS representation turned out to be better). The most important morphological feature is CASE, followed by VOICE and TENSE.

Future work includes a more detailed error analysis for the different models, which could throw further light on the impact of different features. It could also be worthwhile to experiment with different feature templates for different morphological categories. For example, for agreement features it seems important to conjoin the values of two words that are candidates for a dependency, while this might not be necessary for features like CASE.

[8]The accuracy is only 86.2%, the lowest of all features.

[9]This type of ambiguity is somewhat artificial, since it arises from the choice to not annotate relations between complete clauses in the Lithuanian Treebank. We expect that parsing accuracy would be improved if all interclausal relations were annotated explicitly.

However, in order to get a major improvement in parsing accuracy, we probably need larger amounts of syntactically annotated data as well as more consistent annotations of interclausal relations.

Acknowledgments

This research is funded by European Union Structural Funds Project "Postdoctoral Fellowship Implementation in Lithuania" (No. VP1-3.1-ŠMM-01) and was initiated when the first author was visiting the Department of Linguistics and Philology at Uppsala University, Sweden.

References

Bharat Ram Ambati, Samar Husain, Joakim Nivre, and Rajeev Sangal. 2010. On the role of morphosyntactic features in hindi dependency parsing. In *Proceedings of the NAACL HLT 2010 First Workshop on Statistical Parsing of Morphologically-Rich Languages*, SPMRL '10, pages 94–102, Stroudsburg, PA, USA. Association for Computational Linguistics.

Sabine Buchholz and Erwin Marsi. 2006. CoNLL-X shared task on multilingual dependency parsing. In *Proceedings of the 10th Conference on Computational Natural Language Learning (CoNLL)*, pages 149–164.

Vidas Daudaravičius, Erika Rimkutė, and Andrius Utka. 2007. Morphological annotation of the Lithuanian corpus. In *Proceedings of the Workshop on Balto-Slavonic Natural Language Processing: Information Extraction and Enabling Technologies (ACL'07)*, pages 94–99.

Gülsen Eryigit, Joakim Nivre, and Kemal Oflazer. 2008. Dependency parsing of Turkish. *Computational Linguistics*, 34.

R.-E. Fan, K.-W. Chang, C.-J. Hsieh, X.-R. Wang, and C.-J. Lin. 2008. LIBLINEAR: A library for large linear classification. *Journal of Machine Learning Research*, 9:1871–1874.

Marija Gimbutas. 1963. *The Balts*. Thames and Hudson.

Yoav Goldberg and Michael Elhadad. 2010. Easy first dependency parsing of modern hebrew. In *Proceedings of the NAACL HLT 2010 First Workshop on Statistical Parsing of Morphologically-Rich Languages*, SPMRL '10, pages 103–107, Stroudsburg, PA, USA. Association for Computational Linguistics.

Mitchell P. Marcus, Beatrice Santorini, and Mary Ann Marcinkiewicz. 1993. Building a large annotated corpus of english: The penn treebank. *Computational Linguistics*, 19(2):313–330.

Yuval Marton, Nizar Habash, and Owen Rambow. 2013. Dependency parsing of modern standard arabic with lexical and inflectional features. *Computational Linguistics*, 39(1):161–194, March.

Quinn Michael McNemar. 1947. Note on the sampling error of the difference between correlated proportions or percentages. *Psychometrika*, 12(2):153–157.

Joakim Nivre and Jens Nilsson. 2005. Pseudo-projective dependency parsing. In *Proceedings of the 43rd Annual Meeting of the Association for Computational Linguistics (ACL)*, pages 99–106.

Joakim Nivre, Johan Hall, and Jens Nilsson. 2006a. Maltparser: A data-driven parser-generator for dependency parsing. In *Proceedings of the 5th International Conference on Language Resources and Evaluation (LREC)*, pages 2216–2219.

Joakim Nivre, Johan Hall, Jens Nilsson, Gülsen Eryiğit, and Svetoslav Marinov. 2006b. Labeled pseudo-projective dependency parsing with support vector machines. In *Proceedings of the 10th Conference on Computational Natural Language Learning (CoNLL)*, pages 221–225.

Joakim Nivre, Johan Hall, Sandra Kübler, Ryan McDonald, Jens Nilsson, Sebastian Riedel, and Deniz Yuret. 2007. The CoNLL 2007 shared task on dependency parsing. In *Proceedings of the CoNLL Shared Task of EMNLP-CoNLL 2007*, pages 915–932.

Joakim Nivre. 2003. An efficient algorithm for projective dependency parsing. In *Proceedings of the 8th International Workshop on Parsing Technologies (IWPT)*, pages 149–160.

Joakim Nivre. 2008. Algorithms for deterministic incremental dependency parsing. *Computational Linguistics*, 34:513–553.

Lauma Pretkalniņa and Laura Rituma. 2013. Statistical syntactic parsing for Latvian. In *Proceedings of the 19th Nordic Conference of Computational Linguistics (NODALIDA 2013)*, pages 279–289.

Reut Tsarfaty, Djamé Seddah, Yoav Goldberg, Sandra Kuebler, Yannick Versley, Marie Candito, Jennifer Foster, Ines Rehbein, and Lamia Tounsi. 2010. Statistical parsing of morphologically rich languages (spmrl) what, how and whither. In *Proceedings of the NAACL HLT 2010 First Workshop on Statistical Parsing of Morphologically-Rich Languages*, pages 1–12.

Reut Tsarfaty, Djamé Seddah, Sandra Kübler, and Joakim Nivre. 2013. Parsing morphologicall rich languages: Introduction to the special issue. *Computational Linguistics*, 39:15–22.

Vytautas Zinkevičius. 2000. Lemuoklis – morfologinei analizei [Morphological analysis with Lemuoklis]. *Gudaitis, L. (ed.) Darbai ir dienos*, 24:246–273. (in Lithuanian).

Parsing Croatian and Serbian by Using Croatian Dependency Treebanks

Željko Agić* **Danijela Merkler†** **Daša Berović†**
*Department of Information and Communication Sciences
†Department of Linguistics
Faculty of Humanities and Social Sciences, University of Zagreb
Ivana Lučića 3, 10000 Zagreb, Croatia
zagic@ffzg.hr dmerkler@ffzg.hr dberovic@ffzg.hr

Abstract

We investigate statistical dependency parsing of two closely related languages, Croatian and Serbian. As these two morphologically complex languages of relaxed word order are generally under-resourced – with the topic of dependency parsing still largely unaddressed, especially for Serbian – we make use of the two available dependency treebanks of Croatian to produce state-of-the-art parsing models for both languages. We observe parsing accuracy on four test sets from two domains. We give insight into overall parser performance for Croatian and Serbian, impact of preprocessing for lemmas and morphosyntactic tags and influence of selected morphosyntactic features on parsing accuracy.

1 Introduction

Croatian and Serbian are very closely related South Slavic languages with complex morphology and relatively free word order. They are mutually intelligible with one another, as well as with Bosnian and Montenegrin, amounting for more than 20 million native speakers.[1] Regarding language technology support, they are considered to be generally under-resourced. More specifically, while a corpus of research on processing Croatian and Serbian on the morphosyntactic and shallow syntactic layer does exist (Tadić et al., 2012; Vitas et al., 2012), approaches to full syntactic analysis of the two languages were up to this point very sparse and very recent (Agić and Merkler, 2013). As linguistic tradition supports dependency-based syntactic formalisms for the two languages (Böhmová et al., 2003; Tadić, 2007), it should be noted that they have not participated in the previous collaborative research efforts in dependency parsing, such as the CoNLL shared tasks (Buchholz and Marsi, 2006; Nivre et al., 2007). Furthermore, regardless of the specific research topic, the communities dealing with natural language processing of Croatian, Serbian and other closely related languages from their group are still to reach the common level of awareness with respect to public availability of their research. Contributions to availability of Croatian and Serbian resources have once again been very few and recent (Tadić and Varadi, 2012), especially for free culture licensing.

Through the line of research we propose here,[2] we seek to provide state-of-the-art in dependency parsing for both Croatian and Serbian. In this first group of experiments, we build on the fact of their close relatedness by using the two Croatian treebanks – Croatian Dependency Treebank (Tadić, 2007) and SETIMES.HR Treebank (Agić and Merkler, 2013) – to build unified parsing models and evaluate them across the languages and domains. As we deal with highly inflectional languages, we also investigate the influence of morphological preprocessing and morphosyntactic feature selection on parsing perfor-

[1] Bekavac et al. (2008) provide a corpus-based comparison of Bosnian, Croatian and Serbian, observing similarities and differences in morphology, syntax and semantics. For further insight regarding Croatian and Serbian morphosyntax, see the respective contemporary grammars (Silić and Pranjković, 2005; Stanojčić and Popović, 2008).

[2] This work was partly financed by the EU FP7 STREP project XLike (FP7-288342).

mance. We aim to use this first inquiry as a decision point regarding further advancements in resource interchangeability in terms of, e.g., annotation projection (Yarowsky et al., 2001) and domain adaptation (Søgaard, 2013). Availability is highly emphasized, as we provide our resources and models to the public under the CC-BY-SA-3.0 license.[3] We stress the essential role of free culture licensing in enabling and maturing NLP for under-resourced languages.

In the following section, we give an overview of related work in computational processing of Croatian and Serbian morphology and syntax. Further, we define the experiment objectives and describe the resources and experiment workflow. We elaborate on the obtained results and conclude by sketching possible future research plans.

2 Related work

Two overviews of current state of language technology development have appeared just recently for the two languages we investigate in this paper.

The Croatian overview (Tadić et al., 2012) states that a few underperforming shallow parsing prototypes for Croatian do exist (Vučković et al., 2008), while deep parsing is left completely unaddressed. In contrast, it indicates that the more basic resources – manually annotated corpora, inflectional lexicons, lemmatizers, morphosyntactic and named entity taggers – are of higher quality and availability. Most of these are available through META-SHARE (Tadić and Varadi, 2012). However, in terms of mandatory preprocessing for dependency parsing, to the best of our knowledge, the only freely available and standard-compliant lemmatization, part-of-speech (POS) or morphosyntactic (MSD) tagging resources are those by (Agić et al., 2013).[4] Their elaboration contains a more substantial overview of preprocessing. Relevant to our research, these models provide the state of the art in preprocessing for both Croatian and Serbian.

Croatian Dependency Treebank (HOBS) project was initiated by (Tadić, 2007). However, its sufficiency in size increase, followed by the first experiments with dependency parsing of Croatian, did not appear soon enough to be included in the CoNLL shared tasks and the overview of (Tadić et al., 2012). Preliminary experiments in transition-based (Berović et al., 2012) and graph-based parsing have been augmented by a hybrid approach which included integrating a graph-based parser (Hall, 2007) and a valency lexicon (Agić, 2012). Due to uncovered partial inadequacies of the HOBS formalism at describing certain syntactic properties of Croatian, a new line of research was initiated, aiming at creating a more simplistic dependency-based formalism for data-driven parsing of Croatian (Agić and Merkler, 2013). It provided a new freely available dependency treebank, the SETIMES.HR Treebank, and derived state-of-the-art dependency parsing models.[5] On the downside, SETIMES.HR is a prototype with currently less than 2 500 sentences and a documented need for addressing certain annotation challenges, such as consistent annotation of complex predicates, an issue that was previously observed and partially resolved in HOBS as well (Berović et al., 2012).

The overview of Serbian language technologies (Vitas et al., 2012) explicitly denotes a satisfactory development level for Serbian preprocessing based on large electronic dictionaries, manually annotated corpora and hand-crafted transducer grammars. These are available through META-SHARE, even if mostly coupled with restrictive licensing. Further, the overview lists some preliminary research in shallow syntactic analysis, while it clearly states that the absence of a formalised syntax of Serbian restricts the development of syntactically annotated corpora and thus hinders the research in full parsing of Serbian, making the creation of a syntactic formalism for Serbian a very urgent task.

Similar to Croatian, research in Serbian shallow parsing deals exclusively with the manual design of rule-based modules (Nenadić, 2000; Nenadić et al., 2003; Vitas et al., 2003) in linguistic development enviroments such as Intex and NooJ (Silberztein, 2004). We also inquired into a case study on the possibilities of resource transfer from English to Serbian (Martinović, 2008), only to conclude that it does not provide any empirical results. Hence, to the best of our knowledge, no experiments in dependency treebank construction and data-driven de-

[3] http://creativecommons.org/licenses/by-sa/3.0/

[4] http://nlp.ffzg.hr/resources/models/tagging/

[5] http://nlp.ffzg.hr/resources/corpora/setimes-hr/

pendency parsing – or, for that matter, any other approaches to deep syntactic modeling and processing – currently exist for Serbian.

3 Experiment setup

In this section, we present the experimental setup by which we aim at subsequently addressing the previously outlined issues with dependency parsing of Croatian and Serbian. We define our goals, describe the utilized resources and lay out the workflow.

3.1 Objectives

We identify the main issues unaddressed by previous research in Croatian and Serbian syntactic processing and use these to define our research objectives. They are listed here as follows.

1. No empirical research was conducted in dependency parsing of Serbian. Even if this fact was justified by the lack of applied research in creating formalisms targeted exclusively at describing syntactic properties of Serbian, we follow the underspecification approach that was successfully implemented in HOBS for Croatian. Namely, as the Prague Dependency Treebank (PDT) formalism for Czech (Böhmová et al., 2003) was altogether ported to Croatian by simply using the PDT annotation manual for annotating Croatian sentences due to minor differences in syntactic structure between Croatian and Czech, we reflect this to the even greater similarity between Croatian and Serbian on all levels of linguistic description. Hence, we use Croatian data to parse Serbian and to serve as a baseline in Serbian parsing.
2. Using Croatian syntactic models for parsing Serbian text serves to establish the need for advanced approaches to porting resources among languages, such as annotation projection.
3. The best dependency parsing models for Croatian are created and tested using a small prototype treebank. SETIMES.HR currently provides state of the art in Croatian dependency parsing. To serve our experiment, we enlarge it by 50% by following the annotation guidelines (Merkler et al., 2013) and provide its new version to the public.
4. Previous experiments were conducted by tenfold cross-validation on treebank data. This is a standard approach to dependency parser evaluation, especially in under-resourced environments. In this setting, observations are positively biased by text domain and phrase transfer due to randomization. We seek to partially account for these effects by designing a set of language- and domain-aware test samples. By these we also target at establishing the need for domain adaptation for parsing.
5. No research was done in investigating the effects of preprocessing and linguistic feature selection to dependency parsing for these languages. As these are highly inflectional, having very large morphosyntactic tagsets, we seek to inspect the impact of preprocessing choices on their dependency parsing. There is ample research on the effect preprocessing has on dependency parsing (Goldberg and Elhadad, 2009; Mohamed, 2011) and on joint morphological and syntactic processing (Bohnet and Nivre, 2012), but none of it included any of the South Slavic languages.

3.2 Workflow

We define three batches of experiments to meet the research objectives:

1. to select the best Croatian dependency formalism with respect to its overall parsing accuracy on Croatian and Serbian – with an emphasis on the most important syntactic categories that match across formalisms – and incidentally to establish the need for annotation projection,
2. to inspect the impact of state-of-the-art automatic preprocessing on dependency parsing of both languages and
3. to establish the importance of specific Croatian and Serbian morphosyntactic features of the most frequent parts of speech in modeling syntactic fenomena for dependency parsing.

In the first batch, we use HOBS in two instances and SETIMES.HR to create parsing models and test them on Croatian and Serbian test samples. Drawing from previous research, we use a standard non-projective graph-based MSTParser generator with second-order features (McDonald et al., 2006), as this setting favors Croatian (Agić, 2012) and related languages such as Czech and Slovene (Buchholz and Marsi, 2006). We are aware of the existence of novel dependency parsers that implement approaches to handling non-local dependencies and outperform MSTParser on a set of languages, such as (Bohnet and Nivre, 2012). They are not included here due to temporal constraints and the fact that we were provided with prebuilt MSTParser models for the HOBS instances and needed to ensure their comparability with SETIMES.HR. As we mainly deal with the concept of resource sharing between closely related languages, we assign a more elaborated parser selection for future research.

For the second batch, we redo the experiments from the first batch in a realistic scenario regarding preprocessing. We use the publicly available state-of-the-art tagging and lemmatization models for Croatian and Serbian (Agić et al., 2013) instead of manual annotation to observe the incurred effects. We do both batches for all three formalisms (two HOBS instances and SETIMES.HR) and provide learning curves.

The third batch of experiments deals with observing the impact of certain morphosyntactic features by removing them from training and test data. We inspect all features involved in subspecification of adjectives, nouns and verbs in compliance with the Multext East specification (Erjavec, 2012), i.e., MTE v5 as its fifth release.[6]

In all batches, we observe labeled (LAS) and unlabeled (UAS) attachment scores. We use approximate randomization for statistical significance testing where applicable and meaningful.

3.3 Treebanks

Two Croatian dependency treebanks are used in this experiment: HOBS (Tadić, 2007) and SETIMES.HR (Agić and Merkler, 2013).

HOBS is available in two instances or implementations. The first one closely follows the PDT annotation guidelines (Böhmová et al., 2003) with several adaptations of predicate annotation (Berović et al., 2012). The second one introduces a set of additional syntactic tags used for the introduction and subclassification of subordinate clauses. It also alters the head attachment rules for subordinating conjunctions. This addition enabled consistency in predicate annotation in clauses and an increase in dependency parsing accuracy (Agić and Merkler, 2013), while taking a turn away from the PDT guidelines and towards specifics of Croatian syntax. In the paper, we refer to this instance of HOBS as HOBS + Sub. Both of them are based on Croatian newspaper text and manually preprocessed. They implement a morphosyntactic tagset based on, but slightly deviated from MTE v4 (Erjavec, 2012). HOBS is available from META-SHARE for research purposes, but its syntactic tags are stripped from this version. HOBS + Sub is not publicly available. Both have been made available to us in whole for conducting this experiment, along with prebuilt MSTParser models compatible with our experimental settings.

SETIMES.HR is based on Croatian newspaper text

Features	HOBS	HOBS + Sub	SETIMES.HR
Sentences	4 626	4 626	3 853
Tokens	117 369	117 369	86 991
Types	25 038	25 038	17 723
Lemmas	12 388	12 388	8 773
MSD tags	914	911	662
Syn. tags	27 (70)	28 (81)	15

Table 1: Basic treebank statistics. Syntactic tag counts are given for the basic and the full tagset (the latter inside brackets) for the two HOBS treebanks.

	set.test		wiki.test	
Features	hr	sr	hr	sr
Sentences	100	100	100	100
Tokens	2 285	2 308	1 878	1 947
Types	1 265	1 246	1 027	1 055
Lemmas	989	979	803	797
MSD tags				
MTE v4 tags	236	237	189	193
MTE v5 tags	233	234	192	195
Syntactic tags				
HOBS	22(37)	23(37)	22(41)	22(44)
HOBS + Sub	22(46)	24(49)	23(49)	22(50)
SETIMES.HR	15	15	15	15

Table 2: Basic statistics for the four test sets. Morphosyntactic and syntactic tag counts are given with respect to the formalism used.

[6]http://nl.ijs.si/ME/V5/msd/html/

from the SETimes parallel corpus.[7] It implements a simplistic new formalism (Merkler et al., 2013) targeting and reaching increased dependency parsing performance while maintaining the information on the main syntactic categories and compliance with the general guidelines for HOBS for these categories (Agić and Merkler, 2013). It is also manually preprocessed, but using the newer MTE v5 morphosyntactic tagset. SETIMES.HR is fully compliant with this tagset. As mentioned, it is freely available for all purposes. With this in mind, following the annotation guidelines, we have expanded its 2 500 sentence prototype by introducing 1 365 new sentences.

Treebank statistics are given in Table 1. HOBS treebanks are larger than SETIMES.HR by approximately 800 sentences, i.e., 30 thousand tokens (30 kw). The morphosyntactic tagsets also differ, favoring SETIMES.HR and MTE v5 by 250 tags if we are to consider the smaller tagset as better in terms of the expressivity vs. preprocessing accuracy balancing. Syntactic tagset of SETIMES.HR has only 15 tags. Tag counts for HOBS treebanks are given by two figures: the first one represents the basic tagset, while the second one includes the subclassification tags. For example, a coordinated predicate is annotated as *Pred* using the basic tagset and as *Pred_Co* in the full tagset. Here, we use only the basic tagset.

As we anticipated given the properties of Croatian syntax, non-projectivity is amply present in both treebanks. Approximately 2% of all dependency relations and more than 20% of all sentences are non-projective, supporting our parser selection.

As the three treebanks – HOBS, HOBS + Sub and SETIMES.HR– formally do implement different approaches to syntactic modeling, issues may be raised regarding the comparability of dependency parsing scores. However, since HOBS and HOBS + Sub are both based on the PDT formalism and SETIMES.HR implements a simplistic formalism that is still based on the PDT and HOBS annotation guidelines and syntactic tagset reduction (Merkler et al., 2013), we consider the comparison to be valid. Moreover, all three formalisms encode the main Croatian syntactic categories by closely following the general guidelines for describing the Croatian syntax (Silić and Pranjković, 2005), thus indicating that comparisons for the main syntactic categories – such as predicates, subjects, objects, prepositional and adverbial phrases – should hold true for the task of dependency parsing irregardless of the formal differences between the models.

3.4 Test sets

The publicly available test sets are obtained from an experiment in lemmatization and tagging of Croatian and Serbian (Agić et al., 2013). They were available in MTE v4 and v5. As HOBS uses the former and SETIMES.HR the latter tagset, they were well-suited for our experiment. We syntactically annotated the test sets threefold, i.e., by using the HOBS, HOBS + Sub and SETIMES.HR formalisms. There are four test samples: Croatian and Serbian parallel sentences from newspaper sources (set.test) and Wikipedia (wiki.test). Their suitability for testing models on closely related languages was thoroughly elaborated by (Agić et al., 2013), where their differences were measured by using inflectional lexicons of Croatian and Serbian and were found to be significant in supporting the difference between the languages. Namely, lexical coverage differed by approximately 10 percentage points in favor of Croatian across the two domains.

Statistics for the test set are given in Table 2. Each sample has 100 sentences or approximately 2 000 tokens. Slight variations in token, type and lemma counts are present and reflect the domain differences. MSD tag and syntactic tag counts reflect the respective formalisms, as not all HOBS and HOBS + Sub syntactic tags are utilized, while all 15 SETIMES.HR tags are present in all the samples. HOBS tag counts are once again given separately for the basic and the full tagset, while only the basic subset was used in the experiment.

Inter-annotator agreement for HOBS, HOBS + Sub and SETIMES.HR is investigated in (Agić and Merkler, 2013). It favors SETIMES.HR over HOBS + Sub and HOBS + Sub over HOBS with a statistically significant difference. The CoNLL shared tasks in dependency parsing (Buchholz and Marsi, 2006; Nivre et al., 2007) used test sets of approximately 5 000 tokens. This may raise an issue regarding the relatively small size of our domain test samples. However, in the experiment, we combine the test sets by domain and by language and also

[7] http://opus.lingfil.uu.se/SETIMES2.php

LAS	set.test hr	set.test sr	wiki.test hr	wiki.test sr	overall
HOBS	59.9	58.7	55.5	55.4	57.6
HOBS + Sub	68.3	66.9	62.4	62.7	65.3
SETIMES.HR	**76.7**	**75.4**	**71.9**	**72.4**	**74.3**
UAS					
HOBS	73.7	75.9	72.3	72.6	73.8
HOBS + Sub	78.1	79.0	76.5	76.5	77.6
SETIMES.HR	**81.6**	**80.6**	**80.0**	**80.6**	**80.8**

Table 3: Parsing accuracy (LAS, UAS) with manual preprocessing. Results are given for each test set and overall, i.e., with all four test sets merged into one.

merge them into a single test set, thus accounting for the size of the individual samples.

3.5 Parser setup

Here we use MSTParser with the non-projective maximum spanning tree parsing algorithm and second order features (`decode-type:non-proj order:2 training-k:5 iters:10`), as it was previously established as the optimal setting for parsing Croatian using MSTParser (Agić, 2012) with a statistically significant margin over the transition-based approach. In training and testing, we separate the MTE v5 MSD tags into POS (CPOSTAG) and full MSD (POSTAG). We do not separate the MSD tags into atomic features, i.e., we do not utilize the FEATS column of the CoNLL-X format. Thus the MSD tags themselves are considered as atomic features in the experiment, both for the full MTE v5 tagset and its reductions.

4 Results and discussion

Here we report and discuss the obtained results. We discuss the results in batches, as in the experiment workflow description. In addition, we give a brief linguistic analysis of the parsing errors considering the difference between the two languages and the fact that Croatian models were used for parsing both Croatian and Serbian text.

4.1 Formalism selection

In the first experiment batch, we trained the parsing models using three treebanks, HOBS, HOBS + Sub and SETIMES.HR, and tested them on our Croatian and Serbian test sets from Wikipedia and newspaper text. We present the overall scores in Table 3, the learning curves are plotted in the first diagram of Figure 1 and the accuracy for selected syntactic categories are given in Table 4.

Regarding the formalism selection process, inspecting the overall observed LAS and UAS, it is evident that models based on SETIMES.HR outperform HOBS-based models by a large margin. They outperform HOBS + Sub by approximately 9 LAS and 3 UAS points, while their overall advantage is even more substantial in comparison with the scores of basic HOBS models – approximately 17 LAS and 7 UAS points. Benefits of explicit annotation of predicates by introducing tags for subordinating syntactic conjunctions are also evident as HOBS + Sub parsers outperform HOBS by 8 LAS and 4 UAS points. These observations maintain the conclusions about the three formalisms given in previous research (Agić and Merkler, 2013).[8] Moreover, the introduction of a held-out test set further steepens these differences, as the previous tests were performed by tenfold cross-validation using treebank data only. The observed differences in overall LAS and UAS scores are shown to be significant by the approximate randomization test ($p < 0.01$).[9]

As stated in the presentation of treebanks in the previous section, since the three formalisms are closely related to one another and to the general guidelines for describing the properties of Croatian dependency syntax, we find this comparison to hold true regardless of the formal differences between the models. Moreover, since the accuracy for the PDT-based formalisms in this and previous experiments with Croatian dependency parsing (Agić and Merkler, 2013) is below the margins set by similar languages such as Czech and Slovene (Buchholz and

[8]Importance of standard compliance should be noted regarding the morphosyntactic tagset impact on the observed results. Namely, HOBS "slightly deviates" from MTE v4 by design, while still claiming *de facto* compliance. As the test sets fully comply with MTE v4 and v5, this has an effect on parsing.

[9]We test by randomly ($prob = 0.5$) inserting alternate syntactic annotations for entire test set sentences and evaluating with respect to annotation style, i.e., selecting to match the sentence annotations against HOBS, HOBS + Sub or SETIMES.HR layer in the gold standard annotation.

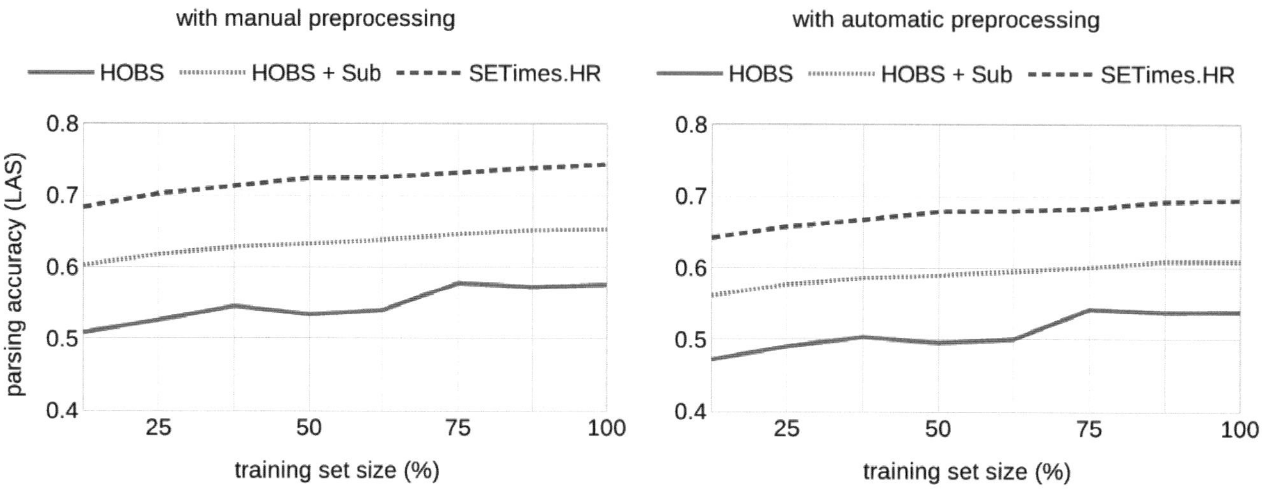

Figure 1: Labeled attachment learning curves for the three treebanks using gold standard and automatic lemmatization and morphosyntactic tagging

Marsi, 2006)[10], we argue that HOBS requires thorough further revision if it is to be the Croatian counterpart of PDT in terms of expressivity and usability in research and practical applications. This is further supported by the data in Table 4, where the assignment of specific syntactic tags is explored. However, extrinsic evaluation would also be beneficial.

The differences in LAS and UAS scores between the two languages are virtually non-existent across formalisms and domains. The parsing models favor Croatian newspaper text by less than 2 LAS points for all three formalisms, while UAS is approximately 1 UAS point higher in Serbian newspaper text for HOBS and HOBS + Sub, in contrast with SETIMES.HR, which scores 1 UAS point higher for the Croatian sample. In the Wikipedia samples, LAS and UAS may be approximated as identical. In total, as a top-performer, the SETIMES.HR model scored 74.5 LAS and 80.9 UAS on Croatian samples and 74.1 LAS and 80.6 UAS on Serbian samples. We believe this indicates that the parsing models trained on Croatian treebank data can be used reliably for both Croatian and Serbian text. We also use these figures to imply no need for syntactic annotation projection between Croatian and Serbian in this test scenario.

The cross-domain differences in LAS and UAS are, in contrast with the cross-language differences, much more substantial. As all treebanks were built on top of Croatian newspaper text, scores are expectedly higher for these test samples in comparison with the Wikipedia samples' scores. This difference amounts to approximately 5 LAS points and 2 UAS points in favor of the newspaper text samples across the two languages and three formalisms.

We plotted the LAS learning curves by merging the test samples into a single mixed-language test set, incrementally creating 8 parsing models per formalism (12.5% to 100% of full size) and testing them on this merged test set. The left plot of Figure 1 represents the learning curves for the three treebanks peaking at previously discussed scores from Table 3. The curves clearly reflect the overall differences in scores. Their rate of increase is consistently comparable, with the overall difference in favor of SETIMES.HR due to its smaller yet still informative syntactic tagset and its formalism better suited for Croatian syntax. With this fact now once again empirically supported, we select the top-performing SETIMES.HR parsing model for further inspection. Thus, our further discussion deals exclusively with parsing using SETIMES.HR.

First we observe parsing accuracy regarding syntactic categories, where we still do compare SETIMES.HR with HOBS + Sub as a final reference point. We merged our test sets by language to provide Croatian and Serbian cross-domain test samples and calculate the LAS per syntactic category for

[10]This holds even with the Slovene treebank of the CoNLL 2006 shared task having more than 2 000 sentences less than HOBS, with both using the PDT formalism

Syntactic tag	HOBS + Sub hr	HOBS + Sub sr	SETIMES.HR hr	SETIMES.HR sr
Adverb	**50.4**	46.6	**50.4**	**47.2**
Attribute	81.4	82.3	**87.9**	**88.4**
Object	56.4	51.3	**68.9**	**70.2**
Predicate	75.1	71.9	**80.7**	**81.2**
Preposition	65.5	**66.4**	**66.4**	64.0
Subject	70.3	71.3	**74.8**	**77.6**

Table 4: LAS for main syntactic tags separated for Croatian and Serbian test set. Manual preprocessing was used. Best scores are boldfaced and split by language.

	set.test		wiki.test		
MTE v4	hr	sr	hr	sr	overall
Lemma	**96.1**	**94.6**	93.9	95.8	**95.1**
POS	95.2	92.3	91.5	90.8	92.5
MSD	86.2	83.4	80.2	81.8	83.1
MTE v5					
Lemma	95.6	94.2	**94.3**	**96.1**	**95.1**
POS	**96.4**	**93.0**	**92.2**	**91.8**	**93.5**
MSD	**86.7**	**84.4**	**80.5**	**82.4**	**83.7**

Table 5: Lemmatization, POS and MSD tagging accuracy on the test sets and overall. Scores are given separately for the two morphosyntactic tagsets used.

the two languages. This data is presented in Table 4. Once again, the language variety is seen to be of no significance to the parsing models. The scores actually alternate in favoring the two languages. SETIMES.HR substantially outperforms HOBS + Sub on the most frequent and arguably the most informative categories, such as predicate and subject (at least 5 LAS points), object (almost 20 LAS points) and attribute (6 points LAS).

4.2 Preprocessing and features

Here we discuss the impact of automatic preprocessing, i.e., lemmatization and MSD tagging on dependency parsing in our test framework. As announced, this discussion deals exclusively with SETIMES.HR. We lemmatize and tag the test samples by using freely available state-of-the-art models for Croatian and Serbian (Agić et al., 2013), parse them using our best SETIMES.HR model and observe LAS and UAS. Preprocessing performance is given in Table 5

	set.test		wiki.test		
LAS	hr	sr	hr	sr	overall
HOBS	57.2	55.9	49.9	51.0	53.8
HOBS + Sub	65.2	62.5	56.7	58.0	60.9
SETIMES.HR	**73.4**	**70.4**	**65.3**	**67.4**	**69.4**
UAS					
HOBS	71.6	71.8	67.4	69.0	70.1
HOBS + Sub	76.2	74.4	71.8	72.5	73.9
SETIMES.HR	**79.4**	**76.9**	**75.2**	**77.8**	**77.4**

Table 6: Parsing accuracy (LAS, UAS) with automatic preprocessing

as a reference point while, more importantly, the dependency parsing scores are given in Table 6. The second plot of Figure 1 provides the learning curves for the automatically preprocessed test sets.

Table 6 scores are easily elaborated using the previously discussed scores with manual, i.e., gold or perfect preprocessing. Namely, the impact of differences between manual and automatic preprocessing on parsing quality basically amounts to a very simple formula: LAS is reduced by 3-4 points and UAS by 2 points when introducing preprocessing noise by automatic lemmatization and tagging. This observation is valid across the languages and domains of our test set and thus applies generally. Keeping in mind the more complex prospective NLP systems for Croatian and Serbian, we consider this fact to be very favorable as the observed 16% error rate in full MSD tagging, 5-6% for POS and lemmatization, amounts for a significantly smaller decrease in parsing quality as quantified by LAS and UAS.

To further support this observation, we conducted an experiment with purposely corrupting lemmatization and tagging. In this, as previously for learning curves, we use the single merged test sample. For lemmatization, we randomly drop lemmas from the manually annotated test sample, replacing them with empty features.[11] For MSD tagging, we implement two procedures. The first is identical with the one for lemmatization, while in the second we replace the valid tag with a randomly selected Croatian tag from the full MTE v5 morphosyntactic tagset. For each

[11]In terms of the CoNLL-X format, we simply replace the valid entry from the LEMMA field by an underscore.

Features	Croatian LAS	Croatian UAS	Serbian LAS	Serbian UAS
Adjective				
Type	74.3	80.7	**74.6**	**81.2**
Degree	74.3	80.7	73.7	80.2
Gender	74.1	80.7	**74.5**	**81.0**
Number	74.5	**81.0**	**74.3**	**80.8**
Case	**75.0**	**81.5**	**74.4**	**81.1**
Noun				
Type	74.3	80.8	72.9	80.0
Gender	74.4	80.8	74.1	**80.7**
Number	74.1	80.7	74.0	**80.7**
Case	73.3	81.0	72.3	80.0
Verb				
Type	**74.6**	**81.3**	**74.3**	**80.8**
Form	74.3	80.9	**74.3**	**81.0**
Person	74.3	**81.0**	73.5	80.0
Number	74.4	80.8	74.1	80.6
Gender	74.4	80.8	**74.4**	**81.0**
Full feature set	74.5	80.9	74.1	80.6

Table 7: Impact of morphosyntactic feature exclusion on parsing. Improvements boldfaced and split by language.

of these scenarios, we provide 11 test sets: stepping by 10% of removals or random insertions, from 0% to 100% preprocessing accuracy. The results are plotted in Figure 2. Evidently, lemmatization is of no influence to dependency parsing using our model. This is an important observation to consider in, e.g., the future tasks of parsing large web corpora of Croatian and Serbian. The large impact of morphosyntactic tagging, i.e., morphosyntactic features on parsing is also evident from the figure. It is also supported by previous research in parsing using SETIMES.HR (Agić and Merkler, 2013), where a significant bias towards MSD-based parsing models was found over the POS-only-based models. Tag removal and tag randomization appear to induce a very similar effect of near-linear functional dependency between tagging and parsing. We note that this is not entirely supported by our realistic preprocessing test scenario. It is purely due to the fact that our noise introduction procedure does not relate to the modus in which the stochastic tagger errs in processing unseen text. Namely, MSD tagging errors

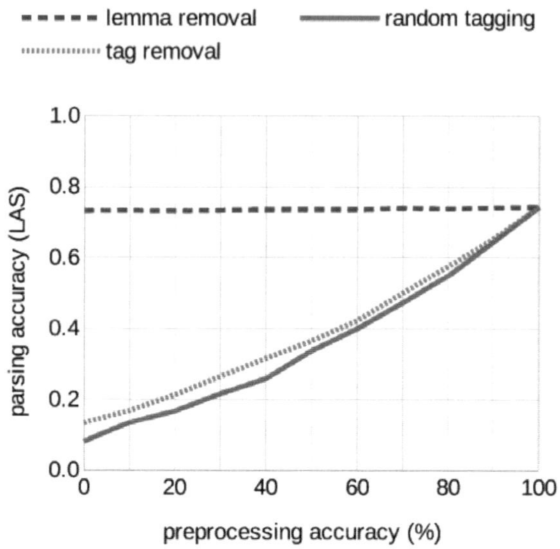

Figure 2: Overall SETIMES.HR parsing accuracy in relation with lemmatization and morphosyntactic tagging

tend to occur on certain morphosyntactic features, corrupting these much more often than entire tags. Thus, even when it yields a feature error, the tagger still provides the parser with other valid features to work with. This consideration of MSD features, in pair with the following set of results, sketches our plans for further research.

Following the previous note on MSD tagset and features, we also implemented a simple experiment in feature weight assessment. In it, we used the SETIMES.HR treebank with full MTE v5 tagset and created from it several instances, each with its own reduced MTE v5 tagset. Each reduction was defined by dropping one MSD feature from one part of speech. More precisely, we dropped all MSD features of adjectives (5 features), nouns (4) and verbs (5). This amounted at 14 different MTE v5 reductions. We trained 14 parsing models using SETIMES.HR with the reduced tagsets and tested them on the test samples merged by language and implementing the respective tagset reductions.

The results are given in Table 7. Most notably, we observed an increase in parsing accuracy when dropping adjective case and verb type. The most substantial decrease occurred with the removal of noun case, indicating the importance of this feature in parsing the two languages. We consider the adjective case removal gain an important observation for future work, as adjectives are the most difficultly

	Adv	Ap	Atr	Atv	Aux	Co	Elp	Obj	Oth	Pnom	Pred	Prep	Punc	Sb	Sub
Adv		0	15	1	0	2	2	5	13	2	1	3	0	2	2
Ap	1		10	0	0	0	2	3	0	1	0	0	0	5	0
Atr	23	9		6	1	0	14	23	3	3	3	0	0	25	2
Atv	0	1	6		0	0	0	0	0	1	26	0	0	1	0
Aux	0	0	0	0		1	0	0	0	0	28	0	0	0	1
Co	0	0	1	0	0		0	0	5	0	0	2	11	0	0
Elp	1	2	12	0	0	0		0	4	3	2	0	0	4	0
Obj	6	3	16	3	0	0	1		0	1	1	0	0	2	0
Oth	14	4	3	0	0	12	1	1		0	0	1	0	1	24
Pnom	3	0	8	0	0	0	3	0	0		24	1	0	3	0
Pred	1	0	2	5	26	0	0	1	1	23		0	0	0	0
Prep	1	0	0	0	1	1	0	0	2	0	0		0	0	0
Punc	0	0	0	0	0	17	0	0	0	0	0	0		1	1
Sb	2	11	26	1	0	0	5	1	4	4	1	0	0		1
Sub	1	0	0	0	0	0	0	0	2	0	0	0	0	0	

Table 8: Confusion matrices for LAS (Croatian: bottom left, Serbian: top right)

tagged category for Croatian and Serbian.

4.3 Error analysis

Here we provide a brief insight to the error instances. We discuss LAS errors for both languages, i.e., instances of invalid head attachments paired with tag misassignments. These are given in Table 8 in the form of two confusion matrices for LAS.

We isolate several clusters of errors with shared linguistic properties. Firstly, the subject-attribute-apposition group (*Sb-Atr-Ap*), in which we find the error instances to be closely related to the order of attachment and assignment in multi-word units representing foreign personal names, titles or functions and occupations of persons. Next, the attribute-adverb-object group (*Atr-Adv-Obj*) expectedly appears as these are inherently ambiguous categories.[12] The predicate-nominal-auxiliary group of errors (*Pred-Pnom-Aux*) reflects the interaction of MSD annotation choices and syntactic annotation principles, as participes are MSD-tagged as adjectives, thus confusing the parser in predicate annotation. Moreover, SETIMES.HR has documented issues with consistency in complex predicate annotation that seek resolution and negatively influence the parsing scores. Lastly, the only error group substantially reflecting the language difference is the one involving predicates and predicate complements (*Pred-Atv*), as it appears only in the Serbian confusions. Namely, the infinitive predicate complement is frequent in Croatian and non-existent in Serbian. Infinitives in Serbian only appear for the future tense paired with auxiliary verbs, confusing the parser to annotate these infinitives as predicate complements as observed in the Croatian training data.

[12]PDT, e.g., has an *AtrAdv*, *AdvAtr*, *AtrObj* and *ObjAtr* ambiguity classes to address this. However, the sum of their frequencies in HOBS is negligibly small ($< 0.03\%$).

5 Conclusions and future work

We have described an experiment with dependency parsing of two closely related and under-resourced languages, Croatian and Serbian, by using parsing models trained on Croatian treebanks. We investigated three different parsing formalisms, the effects of lemmatization, morphosyntactic tagging and feature selection on parsing quality for both languages. We observed state-of-the-art parsing scores. All resources used in the experiment are made publicly available under a permissive license.[13]

The results of this experiment sketch the path for our future research. Experiments with syntactic projection between Croatian and Serbian are not feasible given the negligible differences in the observed scores. In contrast, domain adaptation for parsing the two languages should be investigated given the observed accuracy decrease when moving from newspaper text to Wikipedia. We have already initiated further enlargements of the SETIMES.HR treebank and the test sets with Croatian data from other domains. Experiments with newer and more advanced dependency parsers (Koo and Collins, 2010; Bohnet and Nivre, 2012; Zhang and McDonald, 2012; Martins et al., 2013) should be conducted to provide up-to-date scores.

We are currently experimenting with morphosyntactic tagset design for improved dependency parsing of Croatian and Serbian. We aim at finding the optimal tagset by closely investigating morphosyntactic feature influences and dependencies.

[13]http://nlp.ffzg.hr/

References

Ž. Agić. 2012. K-Best Spanning Tree Dependency Parsing With Verb Valency Lexicon Reranking. In: *Proceedings of COLING 2012: Posters*, pp. 1–12. COLING 2012 Organizing Committee.

Ž. Agić, D. Merkler. 2013. Three Syntactic Formalisms for Data-Driven Dependency Parsing of Croatian. In: *Text, Speech and Dialogue. Lecture Notes in Computer Science*, 8082:560–567. Springer.

Ž. Agić, N. Ljubešić, D. Merkler. 2013. Lemmatization and Morphosyntactic Tagging of Croatian and Serbian. In: *Proceedings of BSNLP 2013*. ACL.

B. Bekavac, S. Seljan, I. Simeon. 2008. Corpus-Based Comparison of Contemporary Croatian, Serbian and Bosnian. In: *Proceedings of FASSBL 2008*, pp. 33–39. Croatian Language Technologies Society.

D. Berović, Ž. Agić, M. Tadić. 2012. Croatian Dependency Treebank: Recent Development and Initial Experiments. In: *Proceedings of LREC 2012*, pp. 1902–1906. ELRA.

A. Böhmová, J. Hajič, E. Hajičova, B. Hladká. 2003. The Prague Dependency Treebank: A Three-Level Annotation Scenario. In: *Treebanks: Building and Using Parsed Corpora*. Springer.

B. Bohnet, J. Nivre. 2012. A Transition-Based System for Joint Part-of-Speech Tagging and Labeled Non-Projective Dependency Parsing. In: *Proceedings of EMNLP-CoNLL 2012*, pp. 1455–1465. ACL.

S. Buchholz, E. Marsi. 2006. CoNLL-X Shared Task on Multilingual Dependency Parsing. In: *Proceedings of CoNLL-X*, pp. 149–164. ACL.

T. Erjavec. 2012. MULTEXT-East: Morphosyntactic Resources for Central and Eastern European Languages. *Language Resources and Evaluation*, 46 (1), 131–142. Springer.

Y. Goldberg, M. Elhadad. 2009. Hebrew Dependency Parsing: Initial Results. In: *Proceedings of IWPT 2009*, pp. 129–133. ACL.

K. Hall. 2007. K-Best Spanning Tree Parsing. In: *Proceedings of ACL 2007*, pp. 392–399. ACL.

T. Koo, M. Collins. 2010. Efficient Third-Order Dependency Parsers. In: *Proceedings of ACL 2010*, pp. 1–11. ACL.

M. Martinović. 2008. Transfer Of Natural Language Processing Technology: Experiments, Possibilities and Limitations – Case Study: English to Serbian. *Infotheca – Journal of Informatics and Librarianship*, 9 (1-2):11–20.

A. Martins, M. Almeida, N. Smith. 2013. Turning on the Turbo: Fast Third-Order Non-Projective Turbo Parsers. In: *Proceedings of ACL 2013*. ACL.

R. McDonald, K. Lerman, F. Pereira. 2006. Multilingual Dependency Parsing With a Two-Stage Discriminative Parser. In: *Proceedings of CoNLL-X*, pp. 216–220. ACL.

D. Merkler, Ž. Agić, A. Agić. 2013. Babel Treebank of Public Messages in Croatian. In: *Proceedings of CILC 2013. Proceedia – Social and Behavioral Sciences*, in press. Elsevier.

E. Mohamed. 2011. The Effect of Automatic Tokenization, Vocalization, Stemming, and POS Tagging on Arabic Dependency Parsing. In: *Proceedings of CoNLL 2011*, pp. 10–18. ACL.

G. Nenadić. 2000. Local Grammars and Parsing Coordination of Nouns in Serbo-Croatian. In: *Text, Speech and Dialogue. Lecture Notes in Computer Science*, 1902:57–62. Springer.

G. Nenadić, I. Spasić, S. Ananiadou. 2003. Morphosyntactic Clues for Terminological Processing in Serbian. In: *Proceedings of the EACL Workshop on Morphological Processing of Slavic Languages*, pp. 79–86. ACL.

J. Nivre, J. Hall, S. Kübler, R. McDonald, J. Nilsson, S. Riedel, D. Yuret. The CoNLL 2007 Shared Task on Dependency Parsing. In: *Proceedings of the CoNLL Shared Task Session of EMNLP-CoNLL 2007*, pp. 915–932. ACL.

M. Silberztein. 2004. NooJ : An Object-Oriented Approach. In: *INTEX pour la Linguistique et le Traitement Automatique des Langue*, pp. 359–369. Presses Universitaires de Franche-Comté.

J. Silić, I. Pranjković. 2005. Gramatika hrvatskoga jezika za gimnazije i visoka učilišta. Školska knjiga, Zagreb.

A. Søgaard. 2013. Semi-Supervised Learning and Domain Adaptation for NLP. Morgan & Claypool Publishers.

Ž. Stanojčić, Lj. Popović. 2008. Gramatika srpskog jezika: za gimnazije i srednje škole. Zavod za udžbenike i nastavna sredstva, Beograd.

M. Tadić. 2007. Building the Croatian Dependency Treebank: The Initial Stages. *Suvremena lingvistika*, 63 (1), 85–92. Hrvatsko filološko društvo.

M. Tadić, D. Brozović-Rončević, A. Kapetanović. 2012. The Croatian Language in the Digital Age. *META-NET White Paper Series*. Springer.

M. Tadić, T. Váradi. 2012. Central and South-East European Resources in META-SHARE. In: *Proceedings of COLING 2012: Demonstration Papers*, pp. 431–438. COLING 2012 Organizing Committee.

D. Vitas, C. Krstev, I. Obradović, Lj. Popović, G. Pavlović-Lažetić. 2003. An Overview of Resources and Basic Tools for Processing of Serbian Written Texts. In: *Proceedings of the Workshop on Balkan Language Resources, First Balkan Conference in Informatics*.

D. Vitas, Lj. Popović, C. Krstev, I. Obradović, G. Pavlović-Lažetić, M. Stanojević. 2012. The Serbian Language in the Digital Age. *META-NET White Paper Series*. Springer.

K. Vučković, M. Tadić, Z. Dovedan. 2008. Rule-Based Chunker for Croatian. In: *Proceedings of LREC 2008*, pp. 2544–2549. ELRA.

D. Yarowsky, G. Ngai, Richard Wicentowski. 2001. Inducing Multilingual Text Analysis Tools via Robust Projection Across Aligned Corpora. In: *Proceedings of HLT 2001*, pp. 1–8. ACL.

H. Zhang, R. McDonald. 2012. Generalized Higher-Order Dependency Parsing With Cube Pruning. In: *Proceedings of EMNLP 2012*. ACL.

A Cross-Task Flexible Transition Model for Arabic Tokenization, Affix Detection, Affix Labeling, POS Tagging, and Dependency Parsing

Stephen Tratz
Army Research Laboratory
Adelphi Laboratory Center
2800 Powder Mill Road
Adelphi, MD 20783
stephen.c.tratz.civ@mail.mil

Abstract

This paper describes cross-task flexible transition models (CTF-TMs) and demonstrates their effectiveness for Arabic natural language processing (NLP). NLP pipelines often suffer from error propagation, as errors committed in lower-level tasks cascade through the remainder of the processing pipeline. By allowing a flexible order of operations across and within multiple NLP tasks, a CTF-TM can mitigate both cross-task and within-task error propagation. Our Arabic CTF-TM models tokenization, affix detection, affix labeling, part-of-speech tagging, and dependency parsing, achieving state-of-the-art results. We present the details of our general framework, our Arabic CTF-TM, and the setup and results of our experiments.

1 Introduction

Natural Language Processing (NLP) systems often consist of a series of NLP components, each trained to perform a specific task such as parsing. These pipelines tend to suffer from error propagation—errors introduced by early components cascade through the remainder of the pipeline causing subsequent components to commit additional errors. Partial solutions from higher-level tasks (e.g., parsing) can aid in resolving the difficult decisions that must be made in solving lower-level tasks, as with part-of-speech tagging the classic "garden path" sentence example "The horse raced past the barn fell." To this end, this paper presents *cross-task flexible transition models* (CTF-TMs), which model multiple tasks and solve these tasks in a more flexible order than pipeline approaches. We implement and experiment with a CTF-TM for Arabic[1] language processing and report experimental results for it on Arabic tokenization (i.e., clitic separation), affix detection, affix labeling, part-of-speech tagging, and dependency parsing.

In addition to error propagation between modules within a parsing pipeline, errors may propagate within the parsing process itself due to the fixed order of operations of the parser. This is common for standard *transition-based* dependency parsing models (McDonald and Nivre, 2007), such as shift-reduce parsers, which incrementally construct a parse by processing the input in a fixed left-to-right or right-to-left fashion. However, using a transition model that allows a more flexible order of operations, such as Goldberg and Elhadad's (2010) parser, allows difficult decisions to be postponed until later, when more of the solution has been constructed. CTF-TMs extend this approach by modeling multiple tasks and providing this flexibility across tasks so that no one task needs to be complete before another can be partially solved.

As a morphologically rich language, Arabic requires a significant number of processing steps. Arabic uses a variety of affixes to inflect for case, gender, number (including dual), and mood, has clitics that attach to other words, permits both VSO and SVO constructions, and rarely includes short vowels in written form. The presence of clitics and the absence of written short vowels are particularly significant sources of ambiguity. As Tsarfaty (2006) argues for Modern Hebrew, a Semitic language that shares these characteristics, we contend that mor-

[1] This paper focuses on Modern Standard Arabic rather than any of the dialects.

phological analysis and parsing should be done in a unified framework, such as a CTF-TM, rather than by separate components.

In this paper, we describe CTF-TMs, which can be used for a wide variety of NLP tasks, and present our Arabic CTF-TM for Arabic tokenization, affix detection, affix labeling, part-of-speech tagging, and dependency parsing as well as the results obtained in applying it to our dependency conversion of the Penn Arabic Treebank (ATB) (Maamouri et al., 2004; Maamouri and Bies, 2004). We find that our Arabic CTF-TM for tokenization, affix detection, affix labeling, POS tagging, and parsing achieves slightly better results than a similar CTF-TM that performs all the tasks except parsing. The CTF-TM that supports parsing appears to be more accurate at distinguishing between passive and active verbs as well as between nouns and adjectives—cases where the context is crucial for proper interpretation due to Arabic's ambiguities. Our system achieves tokenization accuracy similar to Kulick's (2011) state-of-the-art system for a standard split of the ATB part 3, and, in our experiments using ATB parts 1–3, our system achieves the highest labeled attachment, unlabeled attachment, and clitic separation figures (including pronomial clitics) for Arabic yet reported (although no other work can be compared directly).

2 Relevant Arabic Linguistics

Arabic has rich morphology, with a wide array of affixes and clitics and inflecting for case, number, gender, and, occasionally, mood. Coordinating conjunctions, pronouns, and most true prepositions, along with some other particles and the definite article, usually occur as clitics in Arabic. Thus, a space-delimited[2] sequence of Arabic characters may consist of multiple words, and identifying the boundaries between these must be done in order to produce syntactic parses. These boundaries can't be detected perfectly using simple deterministic rules. Significantly, short vowels, which are expressed using diacritics, are not typically written in Arabic, resulting in pervasive ambiguity. For example, active and passive forms of verbs vary only in their diacritics, and nouns and adjectives are both derived from Arabic roots using the same templates and, thus, look similar. A single Arabic token may permit a variety of different analyses, as the example in Table 1 illustrates.

<table>
<tr><td>والى</td><td>wAlY</td><td>'ruler'</td></tr>
<tr><td>و+الى+ي</td><td>w+AlY+y</td><td>'and to me'</td></tr>
<tr><td>و+ألي</td><td>w+<ly</td><td>'and I follow'</td></tr>
<tr><td>و+آل+ي</td><td>w+|l+y</td><td>'and my clan'</td></tr>
<tr><td>و+آلي</td><td>w+|ly</td><td>'and automatic'</td></tr>
</table>

Table 1: Possible interpretations for the text *wAlY* (Habash and Rambow, 2005).

3 CTF-TM Framework

Error propagation is not simply a problem that occurs between components in a pipeline but one that often occurs within a single component's processing. Since transition systems can use the partially built solution for feature generation, incorrect actions taken early on result not only in an invalid final solution, but the invalid partial solution may dissuade the system from making correct decisions with respect to other parts of the solution. If a transition system can postpone decisions it is not confident of until later, the partial solution created by performing other actions may provide more or better information that enables the system to properly resolve more difficult decisions. This "easy-first" strategy is adopted by Goldberg and Elhadad's (2010) parsing system, which starts with an ordered list of unattached words and, in each iteration, creates a new arc between any of the adjacent pairs of words in the list and removes the daughter node (word) from the list.

This strategy is much more *flexible* than shift-reduce style parsing because the system has more options available to it at any one step for building up the solution. However, simply having flexibility within a single component does not reduce error propagation to or from other components in a pipeline and, to mitigate the potential for this, one may use a *cross-task flexible transition model* (CTF-TM) that does not have to wait for lower level tasks to be 100% complete before starting work on higher level tasks.

[2]Technically, space-and-punctuation-deliminated.

McDonald and Nivre (2007) define a *transition system* as follows:

1. a set C of *parse configurations*, each of which defines a (partially built) dependency graph G
2. a set T of transitions, each a function $t : C \rightarrow C$
3. for every sentence $x = w_0, w_1, ..., w_n$
   (a) a unique *initial* configuration c_x
   (b) a set C_x of *terminal* configurations

These systems start at the initial configuration and use a scoring function $s : C \times T \rightarrow \mathbb{R}$ to repeatedly select and follow the locally optimal transition, stopping when a terminal configuration is reached.

We make a few changes to McDonald and Nivre's transition system definition in order to explain our framework. First, to support modeling of multiple tasks, instead of referring to parse configurations, we simply use the term *configuration*, defining it to represent a partially built *solution* rather than a dependency graph. Second, we specify that there exists a routine for enumerating a set of *anchors* for any given configuration. Anchors are an organizational concept for dealing with arbitrary data structures; each anchor acts as a hook into some portion of the configuration that may be changed. Finally, there exist routines for enumerating legal *actions* that can be performed in relation to any anchor and, for training, a routine for verifying that performing a given action will lead to a configuration consistent with the final solution. The performance of an action constitutes a transition between configurations.[3] It is quite straightfoward to adapt Goldberg and Elhadad's (2010) parsing approach to any configuration that is indexable by anchors, and in so doing we are able to create cross-task flexible transition models.

[3] For example, in a fixed order, one-word-at-a-time POS tagging system, there would be only one anchor—the word currently being labeled—but, for a one-at-a-time POS tagger capable of tagging words in any order, the anchor set would contain the entire list of still-unlabeled words. The POS labeling actions for the anchors in each of these cases constitute transitions to new configurations.

4 Our Arabic CTF-TM

4.1 Tasks

Our Arabic CTF-TM system performs the following tasks: split a series of space-delimited Arabic tokens into words (tokenization), identify the bounds of affixes within the words (affix detection), label the affixes (affix labeling), label the words with their parts of speech (POS tagging), and construct a labeled dependency tree (dependency parsing). Tokenization, part-of-speech tagging, and dependency parsing are frequent topics in NLP literature. Affix identification and labeling are parts of morphological analysis that are sometimes completely ignored or are performed using an external morphological analyzer. Identifying affixes and labeling them can help the overall system contend with lexical sparsity issues as well as utilize the information encoded by the affixes (e.g., person).

4.2 Anchors and Actions

The configurations that the system deals with have anchors of two types, token anchors and affix anchors. The initial configuration consists of an ordered list of neighboring token anchors (neighborhood), each of which corresponds to one of the original space-delimited tokens. As processing continues, new token anchors may be created by splitting off clitics, new affix anchors may be created by identifying substrings of tokens as affixes, and token anchors will be removed from the ordered list to become daughter nodes of their neighbors, attached via labeled dependency arcs. The complete list of actions that can be performed on the anchors, which, as described earlier, constitute the transitions between configurations, are as follows:

Tokenization

1. Separate a proclitic of length l from a token anchor, creating a new token anchor for the clitic and reducing the width of the original token
2. Separate an enclitic of length l from a token anchor, creating a new token anchor for the clitic and reducing the width of the original token

Affix Detection

3. Create an affix (prefix) anchor from the first l characters of a token anchor that are not labeled as part of an affix (If the affix is the definite determiner *Al*, which we treat as an affix for consistency with the ATB's tokenization scheme, it is automatically labeled as DET and removed from further processing for the sake of efficiency.)

4. Create an affix (suffix) anchor from the last *l* characters of a token anchor that are not labeled as part of an affix

POS and affix labeling

5. Assign a label *l* to the anchor (Affixes are automatically removed from further processing after labeling)

Dependency parsing

6. Create a dependency arc with label *d* between a token anchor and the preceding unattached neighbor token anchor and remove the attached anchor from the neighborhood
7. Create a dependency arc with label *d* between a token anchor and the following unattached neighbor token anchor with label *l* and remove the attached anchor from the neighborhood
8. Swap the position of two neighboring token anchors (this adds Nivre-style (2009) non-projectivity support as described by Tratz and Hovy (2011))

General

9. Mark an anchor as fully processed and remove it from further processing

The dependency labels, POS labels, clitic lengths, and affix lengths used to define the actions are all collected automatically from the training data. [4]

The actions are subject to the following constraints/preconditions:

1. Labeling is only valid if the anchor has not been labeled
2. Tokens may only be labeled with token labels, prefixes with prefix labels, and suffixes with suffix labels (as determined by the training data)
3. Affix strings observed in the training data may not be labeled with any label not used with them in the training data
4. Token anchors may not be assigned labels that do not cooccur with the labels of any already-labeled affixes and vice versa
5. A prefix creation action may only be applied to a token anchor that doesn't yet have a prefix
6. Proclitics may not be created and detached if the token already has a prefix, and enclitics are similarly restricted by the presence of a suffix
7. Clitics may not be detached from a token that has already been attached to another token via a dependency arc
8. A dependency arc with label *x* may not be created between token anchors T_1 and T_2 if 1) one or both are labeled and 2) no arc between similarly POS tagged anchors exists in the training data
9. Swap actions may not undo previous swaps
10. Marking a token anchor as fully processed may only occur if it has already been labeled, and it must either be 1) the last unattached token or 2) already attached

[4]Training examples with clitics that are invalid (i.e., too long) are discarded at the beginning of training.

4.3 Scoring Function

For our scoring function, like Goldberg and Elhadad, we use the structured perceptron algorithm (Collins, 2002) with parameter averaging. This has previously been shown to produce strong results when modeling multiple NLP tasks (Zhang and Clark, 2008).

4.4 Features

For a given anchor[5], the system extracts features from the partially built solution (e.g., the text, affixes, POS tags, and syntactic dependencies of the anchor and nearby anchors). The same feature templates are used for all action types except the affix labeling actions—affix labeling is applied to affix anchors instead of word-level anchors, and, since all templates are defined relative to an anchor, the templates must be different. The system uses no external resources (e.g., lexicons, morphological analyzers). We leave out a more exhaustive listing and description of the features due to space limitations[6], the fact that the focus of this paper is not on the value of any particular feature template but rather on our overall approach and experimental results, and because we plan to release our code, which will be more helpful for reproducibility efforts.

4.5 Data Preparation

For our experiments, we use the original written form of the data from the latest versions of the first three parts of the Penn Arabic Treebank (ATB) (Maamouri et al., 2004; Maamouri and Bies, 2004) as well as the new broadcast news collection (Maamouri et al., 2012).[7] We convert the constituent trees into dependency trees and adjust the part-of-speech tags.

[5]'A given action' may be more correct technically, but our implementation is set up to share the same set of string-based features across all actions associated with a given anchor.

[6]Simply listing the feature templates in a normal font size with minimal (insufficient) explanation would require well over a page. The set of feature templates is based upon the templates used by Tratz and Hovy's (2011) English parser, which are given in Tratz's (2011) thesis.

[7]We use version 4.1 of ATB part 1, 3.1 of part 2, 3.2 of part 3, and 1.0 of the broadcast news transcriptions.

4.5.1 Dependency Conversion

The two main Modern Standard Arabic dependency treebanks currently available are the Columbia Arabic Treebank (CATiB) (Habash and Roth, 2009) and the Prague Arabic Dependency Treebank (PADT) (Hajič et al., 2004). CATiB has over 228,000 manually annotated words as well as an automatic ATB conversion. It uses only 8 dependency relations (subject, object, predicate, topic, idafa, tamyiz, modifier, and flat) and 6 part-of-speech tags, and it has not yet been publicly released by the LDC. The PADT, which was used in the CoNLL 2006 and 2007 shared tasks (Buchholz and Marsi, 2006; Nivre et al., 2007), is much smaller, with only about 148,000 annotated tokens. Since we want a large annotated corpus with fine-grained labels, we create our own ATB conversion.

4.5.2 Transformations

In addition to converting the ATB's constituent parses to dependency trees, we make a handful of other changes. Following Green and Manning (2010) and others, sentences headed by *X* nodes are deleted because the treebank annotators considered them unbracketable or somehow erroneous. Following Rambow et al. (2005), Treebank sentences headed by *TOP* elements containing multiple *S* daughters are split into separate sentences.[8] Additionally, if the dependency converter concludes that an *S* node without treebank functional tags is dependent upon another *S* node and is separated from it via sentence-final punctuation (e.g., an exclamation point), these *S* nodes are separated into distinct sentences as well. For the broadcast news data, we remove all subtrees headed by *EDITED* tags to make it more closely resemble newswire text.[9]

Since we adhere to the tokenization scheme used by the ATB, and we do not split off the determiner *Al* as its own tree token. Instead, we treat it as a prefix.

The words referred to as *inna and her sisters* are annotated using two different part-of-speech categories and syntactic structures in the ATB. In our conversion, both ATB structures are converted to the same dependency structure headed by the INNA word, similar to CATiB (Habash and Roth, 2009).

We treat the focus particle *AmmA* like a preposition in our dependency structure, following CATiB.

4.5.3 Dependency Label Scheme

Our dependency scheme consists of a total of 35 labels. Many of these are similar to those of Stanford's basic dependency scheme for English (de Marneffe and Manning, 2008), although they are somewhat closer to a similar scheme used by (Tratz and Hovy, 2011). The list of relations is presented in Table 2.

Most of the relations are self-explanatory or correspond to similar labels in either Tratz and Hovy's (2011) scheme for English or CATiB's (Habash and Roth, 2009) scheme for Arabic. A few are new or significantly different from their similarly named counterparts in other schemes and are described in greater detail below.

- *adjnom* — connects the head of an NP to that of a sister NP (occurs with apposition and preposition-like nouns)
- *advcl* — connects verbal nouns to their syntactic governor in what resemble English's adverbial participle clauses
- *advnp* — connects NPs with treebank adverbial function tags (e.g., -LOC, -TMP, -DIR), which are often headed by preposition-like nouns, to what they modify
- *fidafa* — for false idafa (idafa-like structures that are headed by adjectives instead of nouns)
- *kccmp* — connects a clausal complement that is part of a past progressive or habitual construction to the head verb *kana*
- *lakinna* — similar to *cc* but used with the sister of inna *lakinna* instead of coordinating conjunctions
- *part* — particle modifier; connects particles (other than FOCUS_PART) to their governors
- *rcmod* — connects a bare relative clause to its head
- *reladv* — connects an adverbial WH- clause to its governor
- *relmod* — connects the head of a WH- node to the relativized word
- *ripcmp* — connects a clause to the relative or interrogative pronoun that heads it

4.5.4 Part-of-Speech Tag Scheme

The Penn Arabic Treebank uses complex part of speech tags for the entire tree token such as DET+NOUN+NSUFF_FEM_SG+CASE_DEF_GEN. Across the treebank data used in our experiments, there are a total of 579 such tags, which are composed of 179 different parts separated by plus signs. Each part corresponds to a substring of the

[8] The ATB often has multiple sentences, or even entire paragraphs, annotated under a single *TOP* element.

[9] The *EDITED* tag "is used to show the repetition and restarting of constituents that are repaired by subsequent speech" (Maamouri et al., 2012).

adjnom	adjunct nominal	intj	interjection	prep	preposition modifier
advcl	adverbial clause	iobj	indirect object	punct	punctuation modifier
advmod	adverbial modifier	idafa	idafa	*rcmod*	(bare) relative clause modifier
advnp	adverbial noun phrase	**fidafa**	false idafa	**reladv**	relative pronoun adverbial
cc	coordinating conjunction	flat	flat structure	**relmod**	relative pronoun modifier
ccinit	initial coordinating conjunction	**kccmp**	kana clausal complement	**ripcmp**	relative/interrogative pronoun complement
ccomp	clausal complement	**lakinna**	*see text*	sc	subordinating conjunction modifier
combo	combination term	neg	negation	subj	subject
conj	conjunction	obj	object	tmz	tamyiz
cop	copula complement	objcomp	object complement	tpc	topicalized element
dep	unspecified dependency	**part**	particle modifier	voc	vocative
det	determiner	pcomp	preposition complement		

Table 2: Syntactic dependency scheme used in this work. Labels that aren't self-explanatory or similar to the labels used by Tratz and Hovy (2011) for English or CATiB for Arabic (Habash and Roth, 2009) are in bold (for completely new relations) or italics (for similarly named but semantically different relations)

vowelized version of the word.[10] Due at least in part to the enormity of this label set, simpler schemes are often preferred, such as the "Bies" labels (Bikel, 2004; Kulick et al., 2006), Diab's (2007) labels, Kulick's (2011) labels, and CATiB's labels (Habash and Roth, 2009). Marton et al. (2010) find that using simpler schemes allow them to get better parsing results when using predicted POS tags due to the relatively poor performance of taggers trained using the full ATB scheme.

The part-of-speech tag scheme we use is quite similar to that of the original ATB but has several simplifications. These changes are listed below.

1. Possessive and direct object pronoun clitics are all given the same label (PRON_OPP) (50 fewer tags; mapping back to the originals is trival in almost all cases)
2. .VN forms of NOUN and ADJ are merged with their respective more generic categories
3. Interrogative and relative adverbial and pronoun labels are merged together into RI_ADV and RI_PRON
4. Noun suffix labels (e.g., NSUFF_MASC_PL_GEN, NSUFF_MASC_PL_ACC) with genitive or accusative case distinctions are merged because there is no distinction in unvowelized form
5. Labels for dual masculine noun suffixes are merged with their plural counterparts (no distinction in the unvowelized forms)
6. Demonstrative pronoun labels are collapsed to DEM_PRON (person and number information is easily recovered)
7. The words called *inna and her sisters* are labeled INNA instead of PSEUDO_VERB or SUB_CONJ

[10]Since we use the original written form of the data and the internal segmentation of the words are only provided for the vowelized versions, we project the segmentation into the original written forms, discarding any parts that weren't actually written (e.g., case labels associated with unwritten diacritics).

Since our system splits off clitics and identifies the affixes, the tagging is performed at the individual morpheme level instead of producing a single all-encompassing tag for the entire token.

Some of the part-of-speech tags (mostly instances of DIALECT, TYPO, TRANSERR, and NOT_IN_LEXICON tags) are automatically corrected/improved during the dependency conversion based upon the original constituent parse.

4.6 Filtering

Sentences containing invalid clitics are not used in training both because they are erroneous and because including them would require allowing the system to perform actions that should not occur (i.e., splitting off a clitic of length 8); similarly, training examples with more than 20% of their tokens tagged as DIALECT, TRANSERR, LATIN, PARTIAL, GRAMMAR_PROBLEM, and/or TYPO are ignored on the assumption that including them would harm the model. This filtering process is not applied in testing.

4.7 Data Split

We train and test models using three different splits of the data. The first split is based upon the split used by Zitouni et al. (2006) in their diacritization work and is the same as that used by Marton et al. (2013) in their parsing work and by Kulick (2011) in his tokenization and part-of-speech tagging work, in order to facilitate better comparison. However, Marton et al. use the CATiB conversion of a slightly earlier version of the data (3.1, not 3.2), and, thus, the results are not directly comparable. This split places

Part	Use	Files	Sent	Toks	Tree Toks	Affixes
1	train	514	4090	101629	116892	49057
	dev	110	909	22932	26261	11074
	test	110	823	20825	24127	10032
2	train	351	3011	102795	120605	56273
	dev	75	559	20869	24619	11245
	test	75	630	20518	24078	11078
3	train	509	11350	287945	341033	145621
	dev	45	1029	26347	31200	13828
	test	45	992	25299	29938	12220
BN	train	68	5504	82388	98040	48190
	dev	26	1801	29873	35676	17890
	test	26	2082	34361	41192	20366

Table 3: Counts of the number of files, sentences (Sent), original space-delimited tokens (Tok), ATB tree tokens (Tree Toks), and affixes in the experimental data.

the first (in name and chronological order) 85% of the documents in ATB part 3 in training, the next 7.5% in development, and the final 7.5% in test.

In the second split, we use data from the first three parts of the ATB, each of which consists of documents coming from a different newswire source. Parts 1 and 2 are split 70%/15%/15% training/dev/test, and we reuse the split of part 3 just mentioned. Under this setup, we train two different CTF-TMs, one that performs all of the tasks and one that performs all of the tasks except parsing. This enables us to test whether modeling parsing task improves performance on the lower level tasks.

In the final split, we use the splits for parts 1–3 plus the data in LDC's annotated broadcast news transcripts (Maamouri et al., 2012). Unlike parts 1–3, the broadcast news data are drawn from a variety of sources. Files from sources with three or more files are split across training, development, and test, with the latest documents being placed in test. [11] This experiment illustrates how the system performs when additional, out-of-domain data are included.

Statistics for the data are given in Table 3.

4.8 Evaluation Measures

Dependency parsing quality is measured in terms of labeled and unlabeled attachment scores (LAS and UAS), which indicate the percentage of words attached to their correct parent and, in the case of LAS, whose attachment is labeled with the correct dependency. Since a given space-delimited token may not be tokenized into words correctly, the dependency arcs are only counted as correct if they occur between the correct words (spans of character indices). We measure part-of-speech tagging in terms of F-score (F1) and require that the tree token have the correct bounds (was tokenized correctly) and have the correct label.

Normally, we would choose LAS on the development set as the measure for determining the version of the model to keep for testing because it measures performance on the highest-level task (labeled dependency parsing). However, since one of the CTF-TMs does not perform parsing, we instead use POS tagging F1. In general, we observe that the scores are highly correlated, making the point moot. For the ATB part 3 experiment, POS tagging F1 peaks on iteration 437.[12] For the second experiment, POS tagging F1 peaks at iteration 301 for the CTF-TM with parsing and iteration 278 for the one without. For the third experiment, the highest score occurs on iteration 431.

4.9 Results and Discussion

The results for the various experimental setups are presented in Table 4.

ATB 3 Experiment When using the same split of ATB part 3 as Kulick (2011) and Marton et al. (2013), the system correctly tokenizes 99.3% of the space-delimited tokens, similar to Kulick's (2011) accuracy (99.3%) and slightly higher than the 99.0% figure Kulick calculates for MADA. Though these results are obtained using our dependency conversion of the ATB rather than the original, we use the same tokenization scheme. The POS labeling F1 score of 95.8 can't be compared well with any other work due to differences in tag schemes, which vary greatly, as well as use of gold tokenization and other differences. Our system obtains 84.9 UAS and 82.0 LAS, which are higher than Marton et al.'s best results of 84.0 UAS and 81.0 LAS, but they were using a different conversion (CATiB) of a different version of the data (3.1, not 3.2) as well as gold tokenization, so the results are not directly comparable.

Framework Internal Experiment The CTF-TM

[11] We will make the exact list of files used in the training, development, and test sets available.

[12] We run 500 iterations for each experiment, which can take as long as a week using a quad-core machine. However, little improvement is seen after the first 100 iterations.

Train	Eval Data	Tok Acc	POS F1	Affix Bounds F1	Affix Label F1	UAS	LAS
3	3 Dev	99.5	96.6	98.7	98.4	86.3	83.8
3	3 Test	99.3	95.8	98.4	97.9	84.9	82.0
1,2,3	1,2,3 Dev	99.6	97.1	99.1	98.9	88.3	86.0
1,2,3	1,2,3 Test	99.6	96.8	99.0	98.7	87.4	84.8
1,2,3,BN	1,2,3 Dev	99.6	97.1	99.1	98.9	88.5	86.2
1,2,3,BN	1,2,3 Test	99.6	96.8	99.0	98.8	87.5	85.0
1,2,3,BN	1,2,3,BN Dev	99.5	96.0	98.8	98.5	87.4	84.6
1,2,3,BN	1,2,3,BN Test	99.3	95.7	98.7	98.4	86.6	83.8
Without Parsing							
1,2,3	1,2,3 Dev	99.6	96.9	99.1	98.9	NA	NA
1,2,3	1,2,3 Test	99.5	96.5	98.9	98.6	NA	NA

Table 4: Results for the various experiments (Exp) for both the development and test portions of the data, including per-token clitic separation (tokenization) accuracy, part-of-speech tagging F1, affix boundary detection F1, affix labeling F1, and both unlabeled and labeled attachment scores.

that does parsing and the CTF-TM that doesn't achieve similar overall results for the different tasks (other than parsing, of course). However, when looking deeper at the individual POS tagging mistakes that one system made more often by one system than the other, (see Tables 5 and 6), we observe that the parsing CTF-TM does a better job with labeling some parts-of-speech. For instance, the non-parsing system mismarks passive verbs as active more than 29% more often than the other. In Arabic, passive and active forms of verbs are only distinguished by their short vowels, which are typically unwritten, and, thus, the context is of particular importance in distinguishing between the two. The non-parsing system also has more trouble with the distinction between nouns and adjectives, which is likely because adjectives are derived using the same templatic structures as nouns (Attia et al., 2010) and, thus, context is, once again, of great importance.

Gold	Prediction	Errors -parse	Errors +parse	Diff
NOUN	ADJ	297	238	-59
ADJ	NOUN	328	298	-30
VB_IV_PASS	VB_IV	109	80	-29
VB_PV_PASS	VB_PV	86	68	-18
VB_PV	NOUN	104	88	-16
VB_IV	VB_PV	12	22	+10
INNA	SUB_CONJ	9	2	-7
VB_PV	VB_IV	19	13	-6
NOUN	NOUN_PROP	140	134	-6
ADJ	NOUN_PROP	32	27	-5

Table 5: Top 10 POS mistakes made more often by either the CTF-TM with parsing or the CTF-TM without on the ATB part 1, 2, and 3 development set.

Tag	#Gold	Tag	#Gold
NOUN	26195	INNA	1456
ADJ	7491	SUB_CONJ	641
NOUN_PROP	5913	VB_PV_PASS	231
VB_PV	3478	VB_IV_PASS	207
VB_IV	2682		

Table 6: Counts for the POS tags mentioned in Table 5.

Broadcast News Experiment The scores obtained in the experiment with the broadcast news data are slightly lower than in the second experiment. However, this appears to be because the broadcast news portions of the development and test sections are more difficult to parse than the remainder. If we apply the model to the development and test sections of parts 1, 2, and 3, we observe that the results, which are given in Table 4, are higher than those of the model trained without the broadcast news data.

5 Related Work

5.1 Semitic Language Parsing

Much of the Arabic parsing research to date uses the pipeline approach, either running a tokenizer prior to parsing or simply assuming the existence of gold tokenization (Bikel, 2004; Buchholz and Marsi, 2006; Kulick et al., 2006; Nivre et al., 2007; Marton et al., 2010; Marton et al., 2011; Marton et al., 2013). Of course, using gold tokenization results in optimistic evaluation figures.[13]

Other methods exist however. For example, to parse Modern Hebrew, Cohen and Smith (2007) combine a morphological model with a syntactic model using a product of experts. Another alternative is lattice parsing, which can be used to jointly model both tokenization and parsing (Chappelier et al., 1999). Curiously, while researchers of Modern Hebrew parsing find lattice parsers outperforming their pipeline systems (Goldberg and Tsarfaty, 2008; Goldberg and Elhadad, 2011; Goldberg and Elhadad, 2013), Green and Manning (2010) obtain the opposite result in their Arabic parsing experiments, with the lattice parser underperforming the pipeline system by over 3 points (76.01 F1 vs 79.17 F1). Why lattice parsing may help in some cases but not others is not clear.

Some Arabic parsing work focuses on the usefulness of various features and part-of-speech tagsets. Marton et al. (2013) examine various morphological features and part-of-speech tagsets, employing MADA (Habash and Rambow, 2005; Habash et al., 2009) to predict form-based morphological features and an in-house system (Alkuhlani and Habash, 2012) to predict functional morphological features. Dehdari et al. (2011) investigate the best set of features for Arabic constituent parsing and try several approaches for selecting an optimal feature set, finding that the best-first with backtracking algorithm is the most effective in their experiments.

5.2 Other Languages

There has been a flurry of recent research involving the joint modeling of dependency parsing and lower-level tasks[14] for a variety of languages, with most of the attention focused on Chinese. While lacking Arabic's morphological richness, Chinese has its own challenges, such as word segmentation and part-of-speech ambiguities, which have led researchers to develop new unified approaches for processing it. Qian and Liu (2012) train independent models for word segmentation, POS tagging, and parsing but then incorporate them together during decoding. Li et al. (2011), Li and Zhou (2012), Hatori et al. (2011), and Ma et al. (2012) present systems that jointly model Chinese POS tagging and dependency parsing. Li et al. (2011) use a dynamic programming approach similar to Koo and Collins (2010), Li and Zhou (2012) present a shift-reduce style system that uses structured perceptron and beam search, Hatori et al. (2011) implement a shift-reduce style algorithm that utilizes dynamic programming and beam search in the manner of Huang and Sagae (2010), and Ma et al. (2012) extend Goldberg and Elhadad's (2010) easy-first approach to support both dependency parsing and POS tagging and is thus similar to our work. Hatori et al. (2012) extend their previous system to tackle word segmentation, and Ma et al. (2013) build upon earlier work by implementing beam search to get better results. Li and Zhou (2012) side step some of the issues of Chinese word segmentation by parsing structures of words, phrases, and sentences in a unified framework using a structured perceptron and beam search.

Some researchers focus their work on other languages. Lee et al. (2011) present a graphical model for morphological disambiguation and dependency parsing that they apply to Latin, Ancient Greek, Hungarian, and Czech. Bohnet and Nivre (2012) present a shift-reduce style system similar to Li and Zhou's (2012) system that jointly models POS tagging and labeled dependency parsing, achieving state-of-the-art accuracy on Czech, German, Chinese, and English.

6 Conclusion

In this paper, we described cross-task flexible transition models (CTF-TMs) and demonstrated their viability for Arabic tokenization, affix detection, affix labeling, part-of-speech labeling, and dependency parsing, obtaining very strong results in each tasks. We plan to release our software in the near future, including the software for converting the ATB to dependency parses, and would like to release our dependency conversion of the Penn Arabic Treebank via the LDC.

[13] Green and Manning (2010) find that using automatic tokenization provided by MADA (Habash et al., 2009) instead of gold tokenization results in a 1.92% F score drop in their constituent parsing work.

[14] Systems that jointly model POS tagging and *constituent* parsing have existed for some time.

7 Future Work

In the future, we plan to integrate beam search into the training and decoding. We want to add support for the recovery of diacritics, roots, and derivation templates, and we would like to apply modified versions of our system to other languages.

Our choice of anchors, operations, and constraints represent one possible design for an Arabic CTF-TM. Other options, such as creating unlabeled dependencies and adding labels in subsequent operations, restricting clitic separation to a hand-crafted list of clitics, utilizing information from a dictionary or morphological analyzer, or following some sort of coarse-to-fine labeling scheme, are also possible, and we hope to investigate more of these options.

References

Sarah Alkuhlani and Nizar Habash. 2012. Identifying broken plurals, irregular gender, and rationality in arabic text. In *Proceedings of EACL 2012*, pages 675–685.

Mohammed Attia, Jennifer Foster, Deirdre Hogan, Joseph Le Roux, Lamia Tounsi, and Josef Van Genabith. 2010. Handling Unknown Words in Statistical Latent-Variable Parsing Models for Arabic, English and French. In *Proceedings of the NAACL HLT 2010 First Workshop on Statistical Parsing of Morphologically-Rich Languages*, pages 67–75.

Dan M Bikel. 2004. *On the parameter space of generative lexicalized statistical parsing models*. Ph.D. thesis, University of Pennsylvania.

Bernd Bohnet and Joakim Nivre. 2012. A transition-based system for joint part-of-speech tagging and labeled non-projective dependency parsing. In *Proceedings of the 2012 Joint Conference on Empirical Methods in Natural Language Processing and Computational Natural Language Learning*, pages 1455–1465.

Sabine Buchholz and Erwin Marsi. 2006. CoNLL-X shared task on Multilingual Dependency Parsing. In *Proceedings of the 10th Conference on Computational Natural Language Learning*, pages 149–164.

Jean-Cédric Chappelier, Martin Rajman, Ramón Aragüés, and Antoine Rozenknop. 1999. Lattice Parsing for Speech Recognition. In *Proc. of 6ème conférence sur le Traitement Automatique du Langage Naturel (TALN 99)*, pages 95–104.

Shay B Cohen and Noah A Smith. 2007. Joint Morphological and Syntactic Disambiguation. In *Proceedings of the EMNLP-CoNLL 2007*.

Michael J. Collins. 2002. Discriminative Training Methods for Hidden Markov Models: Theory and experiments with Perceptron Algorithms. In *Proceedings of the 2002 Conference on Empirical Methods in Natural Language Processing*.

Marie-Catherine de Marneffe and Christopher D. Manning. 2008. The Stanford typed dependencies representation. In *COLING 2008: Proceedings of the workshop on Cross-Framework and Cross-Domain Parser Evaluation*.

Jon Dehdari, Lamia Tounsi, and Josef van Genabith. 2011. Morphological Features for Parsing Morphologically-Rich Languages: A Case of Arabic. In *Proceedings of the Second Workshop on Statistical Parsing of Morphologically Rich Languages*.

Mona Diab. 2007. Toward an Optimal POS Tag Set for Modern Standard Arabic Processing. In *Proceedings of Recent Advances in Natural Language Processing*.

Yoav Goldberg and Michael Elhadad. 2010. An Efficient Algorithm for Easy-First Non-Directional Dependency Parsing. In *Human Language Technologies: The 2010 Annual Conference of the North American Chapter of the Association for Computational Linguistics*, pages 742–750.

Yoav Goldberg and Michael Elhadad. 2011. Joint Hebrew Segmentation and Parsing Using a PCFG-LA Lattice Parser. In *Proceedings of ACL 2011*.

Yoav Goldberg and Michael Elhadad. 2013. Word Segmentation, Unknown-word Resolution, and Morphological Agreement in a Hebrew Parsing System. *Computational Linguistics*, 39(1):121–160.

Yoav Goldberg and Reut Tsarfaty. 2008. A Single Generative Model for Joint Morphological Segmentation and Syntactic Parsing. *Proceedings of ACL-08: HLT*.

Spence Green and Christopher Manning. 2010. Better Arabic Parsing: Baselines, Evaluations, and Analysis. In *Proceedings of the 23rd International Conference on Computational Linguistics*, pages 394–402.

Nizar Habash and Owen Rambow. 2005. Arabic Tokenization, Part-of-Speech Tagging and Morphological Disambiguation in One Fell Swoop. In *Proceedings of the 43rd Annual Meeting of Association for Computational Linguistics*, pages 573–580.

Nizar Habash and Ryan Roth. 2009. CATiB: The Columbia Arabic Treebank. In *Proceedings of the ACL-IJCNLP 2009 Conference Short Papers*.

Nizar Habash, Owen Rambow, and Ryan Roth. 2009. MADA+TOKAN: A Toolkit for Arabic Tokenization, Diacritization, Morphological Disambiguation, POS Tagging, Stemming and Lemmatization. In *Proceedings of the 2nd International Conference on Arabic Language Resources and Tools (MEDAR)*.

Jan Hajič, Otakar Smrz, Petr Zemánek, Jan Šnaidauf, and Emanuel Beška. 2004. Prague Arabic Dependency

Treebank: Development in Data and Tools. In *Proceedings of the NEMLAR International Conference on Arabic Language Resources and Tools*.

Jun Hatori, Takuya Matsuzaki, Yusuke Miyao, and Jun'ichi Tsujii. 2011. Incremental joint pos tagging and dependency parsing in chinese. In *IJCNLP*, pages 1216–1224.

Jun Hatori, Takuya Matsuzaki, Yusuke Miyao, and Jun'ichi Tsujii. 2012. Incremental joint approach to word segmentation, pos tagging, and dependency parsing in chinese. In *Proceedings of the 50th Annual Meeting of the Association for Computational Linguistics: Long Papers-Volume 1*, pages 1045–1053.

Liang Huang and Kenji Sagae. 2010. Dynamic Programming for Linear-Time Shift-Reduce Parsing. In *Proceedings of the 48th Annual Meeting of the Association for Computational Linguistics*, pages 1077–1086.

Terry Koo and Michael Collins. 2010. Efficient Third-order Dependency Parsers. In *Proceedings of ACL 2010*, pages 1–11.

Seth Kulick, Ryan Gabbard, and Mitchell Marcus. 2006. Parsing the Arabic Treebank: Analysis and Improvements. In *Proceedings of the Treebanks and Linguistic Theories Conference*, pages 31–42.

Seth Kulick. 2011. Exploiting Separation of Closed-Class Categories for Arabic Tokenization and Part-of-Speech Tagging. *ACM Transactions on Asian Language Information Processing (TALIP)*, 10(1):4.

John Lee, Jason Naradowsky, and David A Smith. 2011. A discriminative model for joint morphological disambiguation and dependency parsing. In *Proceedings of the 49th Annual Meeting of the Association for Computational Linguistics: Human Language Technologies-Volume 1*, pages 885–894.

Zhongguo Li and Guodong Zhou. 2012. Unified dependency parsing of chinese morphological and syntactic structures. In *Proceedings of the 2012 Joint Conference on Empirical Methods in Natural Language Processing and Computational Natural Language Learning*, EMNLP-CoNLL '12, pages 1445–1454.

Zhenghua Li, Min Zhang, Wanxiang Che, Ting Liu, Wenliang Chen, and Haizhou Li. 2011. Joint models for chinese pos tagging and dependency parsing. In *Proceedings of the Conference on Empirical Methods in Natural Language Processing*, pages 1180–1191.

Ji Ma, Tong Xiao, Jingbo Zhu, and Feiliang Ren. 2012. Easy-First Chinese POS Tagging and Dependency Parsing. In *Proceedings of COLING 2012*, pages 1731–1746, Mumbai, India.

Ji Ma, Jingbo Zhu, Tong Xiao, and Nan Yang. 2013. Easy-first pos tagging and dependency parsing with beam search. In *Proceedings of the 51st Annual Meeting of the Association for Computational Linguistics (Volume 2: Short Papers)*, pages 110–114, Sofia, Bulgaria. Association for Computational Linguistics.

Mohamed Maamouri and Ann Bies. 2004. Developing an Arabic Treebank: Methods, Guidelines, Procedures, and Tools. In *Proceedings of the Workshop on Computational Approaches to Arabic Script-based languages*, pages 2–9.

Mohamed Maamouri, Ann Bies, Tim Buckwalter, and Wigdan Mekki. 2004. The Penn Arabic Treebank: Building a Large-Scale Annotated Arabic Corpus. In *NEMLAR Conference on Arabic Language Resources and Tools*, pages 102–109.

Mohamed Maamouri, Ann Bies, and Seth Kulick. 2012. Expanding Arabic Treebank to Speech: Results from Broadcast News. In *Proceedings of LREC 2012*.

Yuval Marton, Nizar Habash, and Owen Rambow. 2010. Improving Arabic Dependency Parsing with Lexical and Inflectional Morphological Features. In *Proceedings of the NAACL HLT 2010 First Workshop on Statistical Parsing of Morphologically-Rich Languages*.

Yuval Marton, Nizar Habash, and Owen Rambow. 2011. Improving Arabic Dependency Parsing with Form-based and Functional Morphological Features. In *Proceedings of the 49th Annual Meeting of the Association for Computational Linguistics: Human Language Technologies*, pages 1586–1596.

Yuval Marton, Nizar Habash, and Owen Rambow. 2013. Dependency Parsing of Modern Standard Arabic with Lexical and Inflectional Features. *Computational Linguistics*, 39(1):161–194.

Ryan McDonald and Joakim Nivre. 2007. Characterizing the Errors of Data-Driven Dependency Parsing Models. In *Proceedings of the EMNLP-CoNLL 2007*, pages 122–131.

Joakim Nivre, Johan Hall, Sandra Kübler, Ryan McDonald, Jens Nilsson, Sebastian Riedel, and Deniz Yuret. 2007. The CoNLL 2007 Shared Task on Dependency Parsing. In *Proceedings of the CoNLL Shared Task Session of EMNLP-CoNLL 2007*.

Joakim Nivre. 2009. Non-Projective Dependency Parsing in Expected Linear Time. In *Proceedings of the Joint Conference of the 47th Annual Meeting of the ACL and the 4th International Joint Conference on Natural Language Processing of the AFNLP*.

Xian Qian and Yang Liu. 2012. Joint Chinese Word Segmentation, POS tagging and Parsing. In *Proceedings of the 2012 Joint Conference on Empirical Methods in Natural Language Processing and Computational Natural Language Learning*, pages 501–511.

Owen Rambow, David Chiang, Mona Diab, Nizar Habash, Rebecca Hwa, Khalil Simaan, Vincent Lacey, Roger Levy, Carol Nichols, and Safiullah Shareef. 2005. Parsing arabic dialects. In *Final Report, JHU Summer Workshop*.

Stephen Tratz and Eduard Hovy. 2011. A Fast, Accurate, Non-Projective, Semantically-Enriched Parser. In *Proceedings of EMNLP 2011*.

Stephen Tratz. 2011. *Semantically-Enriched Parsing for Natural Language Understanding*. Ph.D. thesis, University of Southern California.

Reut Tsarfaty. 2006. Integrated Morphological and Syntactic Disambiguation for Modern Hebrew. In *Proceedings of the 21st International Conference on Computational Linguistics and 44th Annual Meeting of the Association for Computational Linguistics: Student Research Workshop*, pages 49–54.

Yue Zhang and Stephen Clark. 2008. Joint Word Segmentation and POS Tagging Using a Single Perceptron. In *Proceedings of ACL 2008*, pages 888–896.

Imed Zitouni, Jeffrey S Sorensen, and Ruhi Sarikaya. 2006. Maximum entropy based restoration of Arabic diacritics. In *Proceedings of the 21st International Conference on Computational Linguistics and the 44th annual meeting of the Association for Computational Linguistics*, pages 577–584.

The LIGM-Alpage Architecture for the SPMRL 2013 Shared Task: Multiword Expression Analysis and Dependency Parsing

Matthieu Constant
Université Paris-Est
LIGM
CNRS

Marie Candito
Alpage
Paris Diderot Univ
INRIA

Djamé Seddah
Alpage
Paris Sorbonne Univ
INRIA

Abstract

This paper describes the LIGM-Alpage system for the SPMRL 2013 Shared Task. We only participated to the French part of the dependency parsing track, focusing on the realistic setting where the system is informed neither with gold tagging and morphology nor (more importantly) with gold grouping of tokens into multi-word expressions (MWEs). While the realistic scenario of predicting both MWEs and syntax has already been investigated for constituency parsing, the SPMRL 2013 shared task datasets offer the possibility to investigate it in the dependency framework. We obtain the best results for French, both for overall parsing and for MWE recognition, using a reparsing architecture that combines several parsers, with both pipeline architecture (MWE recognition followed by parsing), and joint architecture (MWE recognition performed by the parser).

1 Introduction

As shown by the remarkable permanence over the years of specialized workshops, multiword expressions (MWEs) identification is still receiving considerable attention. For some languages, such as Arabic, French, English, or German, a large quantity of MWE resources have been generated (Baldwin and Nam, 2010). Yet, while special treatment of complex lexical units, such as MWEs, has been shown to boost performance in tasks such as machine translation (Pal et al., 2011), there has been relatively little work exploiting MWE recognition to improve parsing performance.

Indeed, a classical parsing scenario is to pre-group MWEs using gold MWE annotation (Arun and Keller, 2005). This non-realistic scenario has been shown to help parsing (Nivre and Nilsson, 2004; Eryigit et al., 2011), but the situation is quite different when switching to automatic MWE prediction. In that case, errors in MWE recognition alleviate their positive effect on parsing performance (Constant et al., 2012). While the realistic scenario of syntactic parsing with automatic MWE recognition (either done jointly or in a pipeline) has already been investigated in constituency parsing (Cafferkey et al., 2007; Green et al., 2011; Constant et al., 2012; Green et al., 2013), the French dataset of the SPMRL 2013 Shared Task (Seddah et al., 2013) offers one of the first opportunities to evaluate this scenario within the framework of dependency syntax.

In this paper, we discuss the systems we submitted to the SPMRL 2013 shared task. We focused our participation on the French dependency parsing track using the predicted morphology scenario, because it is the only data set that massively contains MWEs. Our best system ranked first on that track (for all training set sizes). It is a reparsing system that makes use of predicted parses obtained both with pipeline and joint architectures. We applied it to the French data set only, as we focused on MWE analysis for dependency parsing. Section 2 gives its general description, section 3 describes the handling of MWEs. We detail the underlying parsers in section 4 and their combination in section 5. Experiments are described and discussed in sections 6 and 7.

2 System Overview

Our whole system is made of several single statistical dependency parsing systems whose outputs are combined into a *reparser*. We use two types of single parsing architecture: (a) pipeline systems; (b) "joint" systems.

The pipeline systems first perform MWE analysis before parsing. The MWE analyzer (section 3) merges recognized MWEs into single tokens and the parser is then applied on the sentences with this new tokenization. The parsing model is learned on a gold training set where all marked MWEs have been merged into single tokens. For evaluation, the merged MWEs appearing in the resulting parses are expanded, so that the tokens are exactly the same in gold and predicted parses.

The "joint" systems directly output dependency trees whose structure comply with the French dataset annotation scheme. As shown in Figure 1, such trees contain not only syntactic dependencies, but also the grouping of tokens into MWEs, since the first component of an MWE bears dependencies to the subsequent components of the MWE with a specific label `dep_cpd`. At that stage, the only missing information is the POS of the MWEs, which we predict by applying a MWE tagger in a post-processing step.

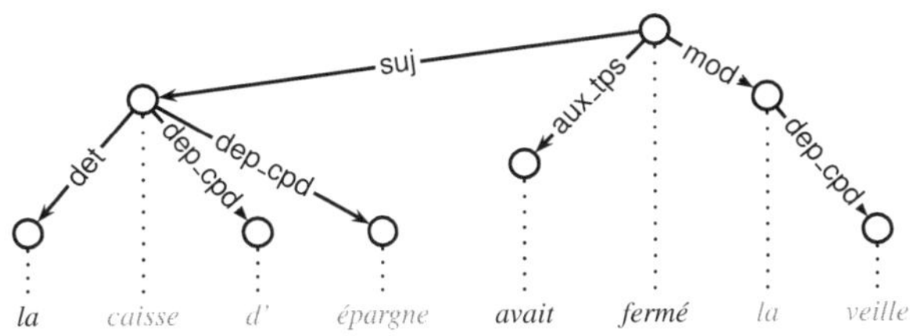

Figure 1: French dependency tree for *La caisse d'épargne avait fermé la veille* (*The savings bank had closed the day before*), containing two MWEs (in red).

3 MWE Analyzer and MWE Tagger

The MWE analyzer we used in the pipeline systems is based on Conditional Random Fields (CRF) (Lafferty et al., 2001) and on external lexicons following (Constant and Tellier, 2012). Given a tokenized text, it jointly performs MWE segmentation and POS tagging (of simple tokens and of MWEs), both tasks mutually helping each other[1]. CRF is a prominent statistical model for sequence segmentation and labelling. External lexicons used as sources of features greatly improve POS tagging (Denis and Sagot, 2009) and MWE segmentation (Constant and Tellier, 2012). Our lexical resources are composed of two large-coverage general-language lexicons: the Lefff[2] lexicon (Sagot, 2010), which contains approx. half a million inflected word forms, among which approx. $25,000$ are MWEs; and the DELA[3] (Courtois, 2009; Courtois et al., 1997) lexicon, which contains approx. one million inflected forms, among which about $110,000$ are MWEs. These resources are completed with specific lexicons freely available in the platform Unitex[4]: the toponym dictionary Prolex (Piton et al., 1999) and a dictionary of first names.

The MWE tagger we used in the joint systems takes as input a MWE within a dependency tree, and outputs its POS. It is a pointwise classifier, based on a MaxEnt model that integrates different features capturing the MWE local syntactic context, and in particular the POS at the token level (and not at the MWE level). The features comprise: the MWE form, its lemma, the sequence of POS of its components, the POS of its first component, its governor's POS in the syntactic parse, the POS following the MWE, the POS preceding the MWE, the bigram of the POS following and preceding the MWE.

4 Dependency Parsers

For our development, we trained 3 types of parsers, both for the pipeline and the joint architecture:

- **MALT**, a pure linear-complexity transition-based parser (Nivre et al., 2006)
- **Mate-tools 1**, the graph-based parser available in *Mate-tools*[5] (Bohnet, 2010)
- **Mate-tools 2**, the joint POS tagger and transition-based parser with graph-based completion available in *Mate-tools* (Bohnet and Nivre, 2012).

[1]Note though that we keep only the MWE segmentation, and use rather the Morfette tagger-lemmatizer, cf. section 4.

[2]We use the version available in the POS tagger MElt (Denis and Sagot, 2009).

[3]We use the version in the platform Unitex (http://igm.univ-mlv.fr/~unitex). We had to convert the DELA POS tagset to the FTB one.

[4]http://igm.univ-mlv.fr/~unitex

[5]Available at http://code.google.com/p/mate-tools/. We used the *Anna3.3* version.

Such parsers require some preprocessing of the input text: lemmatization, POS tagging, morphology analyzer (except the joint POS tagger and transition-based parser that does not require preprocessed POS tagging). We competed for the scenario in which this information is not gold but predicted. Instead of using the predicted POS, lemma and morphological features provided by the shared task organizers, we decided to retrain the tagger-lemmatizer Morfette (Chrupała et al., 2008; Seddah et al., 2010), in order to apply a jackknifing on the training set, so that parsers are made less sensitive to tagging errors. Note that no feature pertaining to MWEs are used at this stage.

5 Reparser

The reparser is an adaptation to labeled dependency parsing of the simplest[6] system proposed in (Sagae and Lavie, 2006). The principle is to build an arc-factored merge of the parses produced by n input parsers, and then to find the maximum spanning tree among the resulting merged graph[7]. We implemented the maximum spanning tree algorithm[8] of (Eisner, 1996) devoted to projective dependency parsing. During the parse merging, each arc is unlabeled, and is given a weight, which is the frequency it appears in the n input parses. Once the maximum spanning tree is found, each arc is labeled by its most voted label among the m input parses containing such an arc (with arbitrary choice in case of ties).

6 Experiments

6.1 Settings

MWE Analysis and Tagging

For the MWE analyzer, we used the tool *lgtagger*[9] (version 1.1) with its default set of feature templates. The MWE tagger model was trained using the Wapiti software(Lavergne et al., 2010). We used the default parameters and we forced the MaxEnt mode.

Parsers

For MALT (version 1.7.2), we used the *arceager* algorithm, and the *liblinear* library for training. As far as the features are concerned, we started with the feature templates given in Bonsai[10] (Candito et al., 2010), and we added some templates (essentially lemma bigrams) during the development tests, that slightly improved performance. For the two *Mate-tools* parsers, we used the default feature sets and parameters proposed in the documentation.

Morphological prediction

Predicted lemmas, POS and morphology features are computed with Morfette version 0.3.5 (Chrupała et al., 2008; Seddah et al., 2010)[11], using 10 iterations for the tagging perceptron, 3 iterations for the lemmatization perceptron, default beam size for the decoding of the joint prediction, and the Lefff (Sagot, 2010) as external lexicon used for out-of-vocabulary words. We performed a jackknifing on the training corpus, with 10 folds for the full corpus, and 20 folds for the 5k track[12].

6.2 Results

We first provide the results on the development corpus. Table 1 shows the general parsing accuracy of our different systems. Results are displayed in three different groups corresponding to each kind of systems: the two single parser architectures ones (joint and pipeline) and the reparsing one. Each system was tested both when learned on the full training data set and on the 5k one. The joint and pipeline systems were evaluated with the three parsers described in section 4. For the reparser, we tested different combinations of parsers in the full training data set mode. We found that the best combination includes all parsers but MALT in joint mode. We did not tune our reparsing system in the 5k training data set mode. We assumed that the best combination in this mode was the same as with full training.

[6] The other more complex systems were producing equivalent scores.

[7] In order to account for labeled MWE recognition, we integrated in the "dep_cpd" arcs the POS of the corresponding MWE. For instance, if the label "dep_cpd" corresponds to an arc in a multiword preposition (P), the arc is relabeled "dep_cpd_P". At evaluation time, the output parse labels are remapped to the official annotation scheme.

[8] More precisely, we based our implementation on the pseudo-code given in (McDonald, 2006).

[9] http://igm.univ-mlv.fr/~mconstan

[10] http://alpage.inria.fr/statgram/frdep/fr_stat_dep_parsing.html

[11] Available at https://sites.google.com/site/morfetteweb/

[12] Note that for the 5k track, we retrained Morfette using the 5k training corpus only, whereas the official 5k training set contains predicted morphology trained on the full training set.

		full			5k		
type	parser	LAS	UAS	LaS	LAS	UAS	LaS
Joint	MALT	80.91	84.74	89.18	78.61	83.16	87.51
	Mate-tools 1	84.60	88.21	91.43	82.02	86.23	90.02
	Mate-tools 2	84.40	88.08	91.02	81.66	85.97	89.38
Pipeline	MALT	82.56	86.22	90.22	80.79	84.71	89.19
	Mate-tools 1	85.28	88.73	91.85	83.23	86.97	90.67
	Mate-tools 2	84.82	88.31	91.45	82.79	86.56	90.26
Reparser	joint only	85.28	88.77	91.70	-	-	-
	pipeline only	85.79	89.17	91.94	-	-	-
	all	86.12	89.36	92.22	-	-	-
	best ensemble	86.23	89.55	92.21	84.25	87.88	91.17

Table 1: Parsing results on development corpus (38820 tokens)

	COMP			MWE			MWE+POS		
	R	P	F	R	P	F	R	P	F
joint Mate-tools 1	76.3	82.4	79.2	74.3	80.6	77.3	70.7	76.7	73.6
pipeline Mate-tools 1	80.8	82.7	81.7	79.0	83.6	81.2	75.6	80.1	77.8
best reparser	81.1	82.5	81.8	79.2	83.0	81.0	76.1	79.8	77.9

Table 2: MWE Results on the development corpus (2119 MWEs) with full training.

Table 2 contains the MWE results on the development data set with full training, for three systems: the best single-parser joint and pipeline systems (i.e. with Mate-tools 1) and the best reparser. We do not provide results for the 5k training because they show similar trends. We provide the 9 MWE-related measures defined in the shared task. The symbols *R*, *P* and *F* respectively correspond to *recall*, *precision* and *F-measure*. *COMP* corresponds to evaluation of the non-head MWE components (i.e. the non-first MWE components, cf. Figure 1). *MWE* corresponds to the recognition of a complete MWE. *MWE+POS* stands for the recognition of a complete MWE associated with its correct POS.

We submitted to the shared task our best (reparser) system according to the tuning described above. We also sent the two best pipeline systems (Mate-tools 1 and Mate-tools 2) and the best joint system (Mate-tools 1), in order to compare our single systems to the other competitors. The official results of our systems are provided in table 3 for general parsing and in table 4 for MWE recognition. We also show the ranking of each of these systems in the competition.

7 Discussion

In table 3, we can note that for the $5k$ training set scenario, there is a general drop of parsing performance (approximately 2 points), but the trends are exactly the same as for the full training set scenario. Concerning the performance on MWE analysis (table 4), the pipeline Mate-tools-1 system very slightly outperforms the best reparser system in the 5k scenario, contrary to the full training set scenario, but the difference is not significant. In the following, we focus on the full training set scenario.

Let us first discuss the overall parsing performance, by looking at the results on the development corpus (table 1). As far as the single-parser systems are concerned, we can note that for both the joint and pipeline systems, MALT achieves lower performance than the graph-based (Mate-tools-1) and the joint tagger-parser (Mate-tools-2), which have comparable performance. Moreover, the pipeline systems achieve overall better than their joint counterpart, though the increase between joint and pipeline architecture is much bigger for MALT than for the Mate parsers (for MALT, compare

training	type	parser	LAS	UAS	LaS	Rank
Full	Reparser	best	85.86	89.19	92.20	1
	Pipeline	Mate-tools 1	84.91	88.35	91.73	3
	Pipeline	Mate-tools 2	84.87	88.40	91.51	4
	Joint	Mate-tools 1	84.14	87.67	91.24	7
5k	Reparser	best	83.60	87.40	90.76	1
	Pipeline	Mate-tools 1	82.53	86.51	90.14	4
	Pipeline	Mate-tools 2	82.15	86.18	89.79	6
	Joint	Mate-tools 1	81.63	85.76	89.56	7

Table 3: Official parsing results on the evaluation corpus (75216 tokens)

training	type	parser	COMP	MWE	MWE+POS	Rank
Full	Reparser	best ensemble	81.3	80.7	77.5	1
	Pipeline	Mate-tools 1	81.2	80.8	77.4	2
	Pipeline	Mate-tools 2	81.2	80.8	76.6	3
	Joint	Mate-tools 1	79.6	77.4	74.1	6
5k	Pipeline	Mate-tools 1	78.7	77.7	74.0	1
	Reparser	best ensemble	78.9	77.2	73.8	2
	Pipeline	Mate-tools 2	78.7	77.7	73.3	5
	Joint	Mate-tools 1	75.9	72.2	75.9	10

Table 4: Official MWE results on the evaluation corpus (4043 MWEs). The scores correspond to the F-measure.

LAS=80.91 for the joint system, and LAS=82.56 for the pipeline architecture, while for Mate-tools-1, compare LAS=84.60 with LAS=85.28). The best reparser system provides a performance increase of approximately one point over the best single-parser system (Mate-tools-1), both for LAS and UAS, which suggests that the parsers have complementary strengths.

When looking at performance on MWE recognition and tagging (2), we can note greater variation between the F-measures obtained by the single-parser systems, but this is due to the much lower number of MWEs with respect to the number of tokens (there are 38820 tokens and 2119 MWEs in the dev set). The MWE analyzer used in the pipeline systems leads to better MWE recognition ($F - measure = 81.2$ on dev set) than when the analysis is left to the bare "joint" parsers (joint Mate-tools 1 achieves F-measure= 77.3).

Contrary to the situation for overall parsing performance, the reparser system does not lead to better MWE recognition with respect to the MWE analyzer of the pipeline systems. Indeed the performance on MWEs are quite similar between the reparser system and the MWE analyzer (for the MWE metric, on the dev set we get F=81.0 versus 81.2 for best reparser and pipeline systems respectively, whereas we get 80.7 and 80.8 on the test set. These differences are not significant). This is because the MWEs predicted by the MWE analyzer are present in three of the single-parser systems taken into account in the reparsing process, and are thus much favored in the voting.

In order to understand better our parsing systems' performance on MWE recognition, we provide in table 5 the MWE+POS results broken down by MWE part-of-speech, for the dev set. Not surprisingly, we can note that performance varies greatly depending on the POS, with better performance on closed classes (conjunctions, determiners, prepositions, pronouns) than on open classes. The lowest performance is on adjectives and verbs, but given the raw numbers of gold MWEs, the major impact on overall performance is given by the results on nominal MWEs (either common or proper nouns). A little less than one third of the nominal gold MWEs

	R	P	F	Nb gold	Nb predicted	Nb correct
adjectives	46.9	75.0	57.7	32	20	15
adverbs	74.7	83.0	78.7	360	324	269
conjunctions	90.1	83.7	86.8	91	98	82
clitics	-	0.00	-	0	1	0
determiners	96.0	96.8	96.4	252	250	242
nouns	72.7	76.2	74.4	973	928	707
prepositions	84.6	84.9	84.8	345	344	292
pronouns	75.0	87.5	80.8	28	24	21
verbs	66.7	66.7	66.67	33	33	22
unknown	0	0	0	5	0	0
ALL	77.9	81.6	79.7	2119	2022	1650

Table 5: MWE+POS results on the development corpus, broken down by POS (recall, precision, F-measure, number of gold MWEs, predicted MWEs, correct MWEs with such POS.

is not recognized (R = 72.7), and about one quarter of the predicted nominal MWEs are wrong (P = 76.2). Though these results can be partly explained by some inconsistencies in MWE annotation in the French Treebank (Constant et al., 2012), there remains room for improvement for open class MWE recognition.

8 Conclusion

We have described the LIGM-Alpage system for the SPMRL 2013 shared task, restricted to the French track. We provide the best results for the realistic scenario of predicting both MWEs and dependency syntax, using a reparsing architecture that combines several parsers, both pipeline (MWE recognition followed by parsing) and joint (MWE recognition performed by the parser). In the future, we plan to integrate features specific to MWEs into the joint system, so that the reparser outperforms both the joint and pipeline systems, not only on parsing (as it is currently the case) but also on MWE recognition.

References

A. Arun and F. Keller. 2005. Lexicalization in crosslinguistic probabilistic parsing: The case of french. In *Proceedings of the Annual Meeting of the Association For Computational Linguistics (ACL'05)*, pages 306–313.

T. Baldwin and K.S. Nam. 2010. Multiword expressions. In *Handbook of Natural Language Processing, Second Edition*. CRC Press, Taylor and Francis Group.

Bernd Bohnet and Joakim Nivre. 2012. A transition-based system for joint part-of-speech tagging and labeled non-projective dependency parsing. In *Proceedings of the 2012 Joint Conference on Empirical Methods in Natural Language Processing and Computational Natural Language Learning*, pages 1455–1465, Jeju Island, Korea, July. Association for Computational Linguistics.

Bernd Bohnet. 2010. Top accuracy and fast dependency parsing is not a contradiction. In *Proceedings of the 23rd International Conference on Computational Linguistics (COLING'10)*, Beijing, China.

C. Cafferkey, D. Hogan, and J. van Genabith. 2007. Multi-word units in treebank-based probabilistic parsing and generation. In *Proceedings of the 10th International Conference on Recent Advances in Natural Language Processing (RANLP'07)*.

M.-H. Candito, J. Nivre, P. Denis, and E. Henestroza Anguiano. 2010. Benchmarking of statistical dependency parsers for french. In *Proceedings of the 23rd International Conference on Computational Linguistics (COLING'10)*, Beijing, China.

Grzegorz Chrupała, Georgiana Dinu, and Josef van Genabith. 2008. Learning morphology with morfette. In *In Proc. of LREC 2008*, Marrakech, Morocco. ELDA/ELRA.

Matthieu Constant and Isabelle Tellier. 2012. Evaluating the impact of external lexical resources into a crf-based multiword segmenter and part-of-speech tagger. In *Proceedings of the 8th conference on Language Resources and Evaluation (LREC'12)*.

Matthieu Constant, Anthony Sigogne, and Patrick Watrin. 2012. Discriminative strategies to integrate multiword expression recognition and parsing. In *Proceedings of the 50th Annual Meeting of the Association for Computational Linguistics: Long Papers - Volume 1*, ACL '12, pages 204–212, Stroudsburg, PA, USA. Association for Computational Linguistics.

B. Courtois, M. Garrigues, G. Gross, M. Gross, R. Jung, M. Mathieu-Colas, A. Monceaux, A. Poncet-Montange, M. Silberztein, and R. Vivés. 1997. Dictionnaire électronique DELAC : les mots composés binaires. Technical Report 56, University Paris 7, LADL.

B. Courtois. 2009. Un système de dictionnaires électroniques pour les mots simples du français. *Langue Française*, 87:11–22.

P. Denis and B. Sagot. 2009. Coupling an annotated corpus and a morphosyntactic lexicon for state-of-the-art POS tagging with less human effort. In *Proceedings of the 23rd Pacific Asia Conference on Language, Information and Computation (PACLIC'09)*, pages 110–119.

Jason M. Eisner. 1996. Three new probabilistic models for dependency parsing: an exploration. In *Proceedings of the 16th conference on Computational linguistics - Volume 1*, COLING '96, pages 340–345, Stroudsburg, PA, USA. Association for Computational Linguistics.

G. Eryigit, T. Ilbay, and O. Arkan Can. 2011. Multiword expressions in statistical dependency parsing. In *Proceedings of the IWPT Workshop on Statistical Parsing of Morphologically-Rich Languages (SPRML'11)*, pages 45–55.

S. Green, M.-C. de Marneffe, J. Bauer, and C. D. Manning. 2011. Multiword expression identification with tree substitution grammars: A parsing tour de force with french. In *Proceedings of the conference on Empirical Method for Natural Language Processing (EMNLP'11)*, pages 725–735.

Spence Green, Marie-Catherine de Marneffe, and Christopher D Manning. 2013. Parsing models for identifying multiword expressions. *Computational Linguistics*, 39(1):195–227.

J. Lafferty, A. McCallum, and F. Pereira. 2001. Conditional random fields: Probabilistic models for segmenting and labeling sequence data. In *Proceedings of the Eighteenth International Conference on Machine Learning (ICML'01)*, pages 282–289.

Thomas Lavergne, Olivier Cappé, and François Yvon. 2010. Practical very large scale CRFs. In *Proceedings the 48th Annual Meeting of the Association for Computational Linguistics (ACL'10)*, pages 504–513.

Ryan McDonald. 2006. *Discriminative Training and Spanning Tree Algorithms for Dependency Parsing*. Ph.D. thesis, University of Pennsylvania.

J. Nivre and J. Nilsson. 2004. Multiword units in syntactic parsing. In *Proceedings of Methodologies and Evaluation of Multiword Units in Real-World Applications (MEMURA)*.

J. Nivre, J. Hall, and J. Nilsson. 2006. Maltparser: A data-driven parser-generator for dependency parsing. In *Proceedings of the fifth international conference on Language Resources and Evaluation (LREC'06)*, pages 2216–2219, Genoa, Italy.

Santanu Pal, Tanmoy Chkraborty, and Sivaji Bandyopadhyay. 2011. Handling multiword expressions in phrase-based statistical machine translation. In *Proceedings of the Machine Translation Summit XIII*, pages 215–224.

O. Piton, D. Maurel, and C. Belleil. 1999. The prolex data base : Toponyms and gentiles for nlp. In *Proceedings of the Third International Workshop on Applications of Natural Language to Data Bases (NLDB'99)*, pages 233–237.

Kenji Sagae and Alon Lavie. 2006. Parser combination by reparsing. In *Proceedings of the Human Language Technology Conference of the NAACL, Companion Volume: Short Papers*, NAACL-Short '06, pages 129–132, Stroudsburg, PA, USA. Association for Computational Linguistics.

B. Sagot. 2010. The lefff, a freely available, accurate and large-coverage lexicon for french. In *Proceedings of the 7th International Conference on Language Resources and Evaluation (LREC'10)*.

Djamé Seddah, Grzegorz Chrupała, Ozlem Cetinoglu, Josef van Genabith, and Marie Candito. 2010. Lemmatization and statistical lexicalized parsing of morphologically-rich languages. In *Proc. of the NAACL/HLT Workshop on Statistical Parsing of Morphologically Rich Languages (SPMRL 2010)*, Los Angeles, CA.

Djamé Seddah, Reut Tsarfaty, Sandra K'ubler, Marie Candito, Jinho Choi, Richárd Farkas, Jennifer Foster, Iakes Goenaga, Koldo Gojenola, Yoav Goldberg, Spence Green, Nizar Habash, Marco Kuhlmann, Wolfgang Maier, Joakim Nivre, Adam Przepiorkowski, Ryan Roth, Wolfgang Seeker, Yannick Versley, Veronika Vincze, Marcin Woliński, Alina Wróblewska, and Eric Villemonte de la Clérgerie. 2013. Overview of the spmrl 2013 shared task: A cross-framework evaluation of parsing morphologically rich languages. In *Proceedings of the 4th Workshop on Statistical Parsing of Morphologically Rich Languages: Shared Task*, Seattle, WA.

Exploring beam-based shift-reduce dependency parsing with DyALog: Results from the SPMRL 2013 shared task

Éric Villemonte de la Clergerie
INRIA - Rocquencourt - B.P. 105
78153 Le Chesnay Cedex, FRANCE
Eric.De_La_Clergerie@inria.fr

Abstract

The SPMRL 2013 shared task was the opportunity to develop and test, with promising results, a simple beam-based shift-reduce dependency parser on top of the tabular logic programming system DYALOG. The parser was also extended to handle ambiguous word lattices, with almost no loss w.r.t. disambiguated input, thanks to specific training, use of oracle segmentation, and large beams. We believe that this result is an interesting new one for shift-reduce parsing.

1 Introduction

DYALOG is a tabular-based logic programming environment, including a language (variant of Prolog), a bootstrapped compiler, and C-based abstract machine. It is mostly used for chart-like parsing (de La Clergerie, 2005b), in particular for a wide coverage French Tree Adjoining Grammar (de La Clergerie, 2005a). However, DYALOG offers all the power of a programming language a la Prolog, with some specific advantages, and it was tempting to try it on statistical parsing paradigms. The SPMRL 2013 shared task (Seddah et al., 2013) was an interesting opportunity to develop a simple (non-deterministic) beam-based shift-reduce dependency parser, called DYALOG-SR, inspired by (Huang and Sagae, 2010).

The main advantage of logic programming is the (almost) transparent handling of non-determinism, useful for instance to handle ambiguous word lattices. DYALOG allows an easy tabulation of items, and their fast retrieval (thanks to full term indexing), needed for the dynamic programming part of the algorithm. Thanks to structure sharing and term hashing, it also reduces the costs related to the tabulation of multiple items (sharing subparts) and to term unification. Logic programs tend to be very concise, with, in our case, around 1500 lines of DYALOG code. However, one of the disadvantages of (pure) logic programming, and of DYALOG in particular, is the handling of mutable structures, which motivated the development of a companion C module (around 850 lines) to handle statistical models (loading, querying, updating, and saving).

We briefly present the implemented algorithm (Section 2) and list the preliminary adaptations done for the 9 languages of the shared task (Section 3). We analyze in Section 4 the official results for DYALOG-SR. Recent developments corrected some weaknesses of DYALOG-SR. In particular, we explain in Section 5 how we seriously improved the parsing of ambiguous lattices, an important new result for shift-reduce parsing. Finally, Section 6 provides some empirical data about the efficiency and complexity of the algorithm.

2 A Dynamic Programming Shift-Reduce parser

We used (Huang and Sagae, 2010) as the starting point for this work, in particular using the same simple *arc-standard* strategy for building projective dependency trees, defined by the deductive system of Figure 1. In a configuration $m{:}\langle j, S\rangle{:}c$, m denotes the number of transitions applied since the axiom configuration, j the current position in the input string, S the stack of partial dependency trees built so far, and c the cost. A *shift* transition pushes the next input symbol on top of the stack while the two *reduce* transitions combine the 2 topmost stack trees, add a new (labeled) leftmost or rightmost dependency edge between their roots, and remove the newly governed subtree from the stack. The delta cost ξ, λ, and ρ denote the cost of each operation w.r.t. the input configuration.

$$\text{input:} \quad w_0 \dots w_{n-1}$$
$$\text{axiom} \quad 0{:}\langle 0, \epsilon \rangle{:}0$$
$$\text{shift}\frac{m{:}\langle j, S \rangle{:}c}{m+1{:}\langle j+1, S|w_j \rangle{:}c+\xi}$$
$$re_{\iota\curvearrowleft}\frac{m{:}\langle j, S|s_1|s_0 \rangle{:}c}{m+1{:}\langle j, S|s_1\, {}_{\iota}\!\curvearrowleft\! s_0 \rangle{:}c+\lambda}$$
$$re_{\curvearrowright\iota}\frac{m{:}\langle j, S|s_1|s_0 \rangle{:}c}{m+1{:}\langle j, S|s_1 \curvearrowright_\iota s_0 \rangle{:}c+\rho}$$
$$\text{goal} \quad 2n-1{:}\langle n, s_0 \rangle{:}c$$

Figure 1: Arc-standard deductive system

From the configurations, the deductive system, and the configuration elements used to determine the transition costs, it is relatively straightforward to design *items* denoting partial configurations standing for equivalence classes of configurations and allowing computation sharing, following the principle of *Dynamic Programming*. The deduction rules are adapted to work on items and beam search (with size b) is then achieved by keeping only the b best items for each step m[1]. By following *backpointers* from items to parents, it is possible to retrieve the best transition sequence and the best dependency tree.

```
item{ step => M,
      right => J,
      stack => S0,  % topmost trees
      stack1 => S1, %
      prefix => Cost,  % max cost
      inside => ICost  % inside cost
    }.
back(Item,Action,Parent1,Parent2,C).
tail(Item,Ancestor).
```

Listing 1: Item structure

Instead of the items proposed in (Huang and Sagae, 2010), we switched to items closer to those proposed in (Goldberg et al., 2013), corresponding to *Tree Structured Stacks* (TSS), where stack tails are shared among items, as defined by Listing 1. The prefix cost corresponds to the maximal cost attached to the item, starting from the initial item. The inside cost is the maximal cost for a derivation from some ancestor item where s_0 was shifted on the stack, and is used to adjust the total cost for different ancestor items. The items are completed by backpointers (using asserted facts `back/5`) and links to the potential stack tails (using asserted facts `tail/2`) needed to retrieve the lower part of a stack when applying a reduce action. Figure 2 shows the adaptation for items of some of the deductive rules.

$$\text{shift}\frac{I = m{:}\langle j, s_0, s_1 \rangle{:}(c, \iota)}{\begin{array}{c} J = m+1{:}\langle j+1, w_j, s_0 \rangle{:}(c+\xi, \xi) \\ \text{tail}(J) \mathrel{+}= I \\ \text{back}(J) \mathrel{+}= (\text{shift}, I, \text{nil}, c+\xi) \end{array}}$$

$$re_{\iota\curvearrowleft}\frac{\begin{array}{c} I = m{:}\langle j, s_0, s_1 \rangle{:}(c, \iota) \\ J = \_{:}\langle \_, s_1, s_2 \rangle{:}(c', \iota') \in \text{tail}(I) \end{array}}{\begin{array}{c} K = m+1{:}\langle j, s_1\, {}_{\iota}\!\curvearrowleft\! s_0, s_2 \rangle{:}(c'+\delta, \iota'+\delta) \\ \delta = \iota + \lambda \\ \text{tail}(K) \mathrel{\cup}= \text{tail}(J) \\ \text{back}(K) \mathrel{+}= ({}_{\iota}\!\curvearrowleft, I, J, c'+\delta) \end{array}}$$

Figure 2: Deductive system on items (fragment)

The stack elements for configuration are dependency trees, but approximations can be used for the item fields `stack` and `stack1`, under the condition that sufficient information remains to apply the transitions and to compute the costs. In practice, we keep information about the root node, and, when present, the leftmost and rightmost dependency edges, the numbers of left and right dependencies (*valency*), and the label sets (*domain*) for the left and right dependencies.

The training phase relies on sequences of actions provided by an oracle and uses a simple *averaged structured perceptron* algorithm (Daume, 2006). The underlying statistical model is updated positively for the actions of the oracle and negatively for the actions of the parser, whenever a point of divergence is found. Several updating strategies may be considered (Huang et al., 2012), and, in our case, we update as early (*early update*) and as often as possible: after completion of Step $m+1$, we update the model locally (i.e. for the last action) whenever

[1]Because we use Dynamic Programming techniques, keeping the b-best items at step m actually corresponds to keep more than the b-best configurations at step m.

- the best item B^O_{m+1} derived from the oracle item O_m at Step m differs from the expected oracle item O_{m+1};
- the oracle item O_{m+1} is not in the beam, for intermediary steps $m < 2n - 2$;
- the oracle item O_{m+1} is not the best item, for the last step $m = 2n - 2$.

We use a relatively standard set of *word features* related to the CONLL fields such as `lex` (FORM), `lemma`, `cat` (CPOSTAG), `fullcat` (POSTAG), `mstag` (morphosyntactic features FEATS). They apply to the next unread word (`*I`, say `lemmaI`), the two next lookahead words (`*I2` and `*I3`), and (when present) to the 2 stack root nodes (`*0` and `*1`), their leftmost and rightmost child (*before* `b*[01]` and *after* `a*[01]`). We have *dependency features* such as the labels of the leftmost and rightmost edges (`[ab]label[01]`), the left and right valency and domains (`[ab][vd][01]`). Finally, we have 3 (discretized) *distance features* between the next word and the stack roots (`delta[01]`) and between the two stack roots (`delta01`). Most feature values are atomic (either numerical or symbolic), but they can also be (recursively) a list of values, for instance for the `mstag` and *domain* features.

A tagset (for a given language and/or treebank) contains a set of *feature templates*, each template being a sequence of features (for instance `fullcat0:fullcat1:blabel0`).

Model management is a key factor for the efficiency of the algorithm, both for querying or updating the costs attached to a configuration. Therefore, we developed a specialized C companion module. A model is represented by a hash trie to factor the prefixes of the templates. Costs are stored in the leaves (for selecting the labels) and their immediate parent (for selecting between the `shift` and `reduce` base actions), ensuring join learning with smoothing of an action and a label. Querying is done by providing a tree-structured argument representing the feature values for all templates[2], with the possibility to leave underspecified the action and the label. By traversing in a synchronous way the model trie and the argument tree, and accumulating costs for all possible actions and labels, a single query returns in order the cost for the b best actions. Furthermore, when a feature value is a list, the traversal is run for all its components (with summation of all found costs).

3 Preparing the shared task

We trained the parser on the training and dev dependency treebanks kindly provided by the organizers for the 9 languages of the task, namely Arabic[3], Basque (Aduriz et al., 2003), French (Abeillé et al., 2003), German (Brants et al., 2002; Seeker and Kuhn, 2012), Hebrew (Sima'an et al., 2001; Tsarfaty, 2013; Goldberg, 2011), Hungarian (Vincze et al., 2010; Csendes et al., 2005), Korean (Choi et al., 1994; Choi, 2013) , Polish (Świdziński and Woliński, 2010), Swedish (Nivre et al., 2006).

Being very short in time, we essentially used the same set of around 110 templates for all languages. Nevertheless, minimal tuning was performed for some languages and for the pred data mode (when using predicted data), as summarized below.

For French, the main problem was to retrieve MWEs (*Multi Word Expression*) in `pred` data mode. Predicted features `mwehead` and `pred` were added, thanks to a list of MWEs collected in the gold treebank and in the French lexicon LEFFF (Sagot et al., 2006). We also added the predicted feature `is_number` to help detecting numerical MWEs such as *120 000*, and also a `is_capitalized` feature. For all data modes, we added a subcategorization feature for verbs (with a list value), again extracted from LEFFF.

For Arabic, Hebrew, and Swedish, the `lemma` feature is removed because of the absence of lemma in the treebanks. Similarly, for Polish and German, with identical CPOS and POS tagsets, we remove the `cat` feature.

For Hungarian, the `SubPOS` morphosyntactic feature is appended to the fullcat feature, to get a

[2]The tree structure of the argument mirrors the tree structure of the templates and getting the argument tree for a configuration is actually a fast and very low memory operation, thanks to unification and structure sharing.

[3]We used the shared task Arabic data set, originally provided by the LDC (Maamouri et al., 2004), specifically its SPMRL 2013 dependency instance, derived from the Columbia Catib Treebank (Habash and Roth, 2009; Habash et al., 2009)

richer set of POS. The set of dependency labels being large (450 labels), we split the labels into lists of more elementary ones for the `label` features.

Similarly, the Korean POS tags are also split into lists, because of their large number (2743 tags) and of their compound structure.

For French, Hebrew, and Korean, in order to compensate initially large differences in performance between the gold and pred modes, we added, for the pred mode, `dict` features filled by predicted information about the possible tags for a given form, thanks to the `dict` lexicons provided by the IMS_SZEGED team.

Finally, we discovered very late that the dependency trees were not necessarily projective for a few languages. A last-second solution was to use the MALT projectivization / deprojectivization wrappers (Nivre and Nilsson, 2005) to be able to train on projectivized versions of the treebanks for German, Hungarian, and Swedish, while returning non projective trees.

4 First results

Under the team label `ALPAGE-DYALOG`, we have returned parsed data for the 9 languages of the shared task, for the **full** and **5k** training size modes, and for the **gold** and **pred** data modes. For each configuration, we provided 3 runs, for beam sizes 8, 6, and 4. The results are synthesized in Tables 2, with LAS[4] on the `test` and `dev` files, contrasted with the LAS for the best system, the baseline, and the mean LAS of all systems. The tables show that DYALOG-SR cannot compete with the best system (like most other participants !), but performs reasonably well w.r.t. the baseline and the mean LAS of the participants, at least in the **gold/full** case.

The system is proportionally less accurate on smaller training treebanks (**5k** case), lacking good smoothing mechanisms to deal with data sparseness. The **pred** case is also more difficult, possibly again because of data sparseness (less reliable information not compensated by bigger treebanks) but also because we exploited no extra information for some languages (such as Basque or Swedish).

The big drop for German in `pred/5k` case comes from the fact we were unable to deprojectivize the parsed test file with Malt[5] and returned data built using an old model not relying on Malt proj/deproj wrappers.

For Hungarian, a possible reason is the high level of multiple roots in sentences, not compatible with our initial assumption of a single root per sentence. New experiments, after modifying slightly the algorithm to accept multiple roots[6], confirm this hypothesis for Hungarian, and for other languages with multiple roots, as shown in Table 1.

language	#roots/sent	single	multiple
Hungarian	2.00	79.22	82.90
Arabic	1.21	87.17	87.71
Basque	1.21	81.09	82.28
German	1.09	90.95	91.29

Table 1: Taking into account multiple roots (on gold/full)

Finally, the Korean case, where we are below the baseline, remains to be explained. For the **pred** case, it could come from the use of the **KAIST** tagset instead of the alternative **Seijong** tagset. For the **gold** case, the results for all participants are actually relatively close.

5 Handling ambiguous lattices

One of the important and innovative sub-tasks of the SPMRL campaign was to parse ambiguous lattices using statistical methods. A *word lattice* is just a Directed Acyclic Graph (DAG) whose edges are decorated by words with their features and whose nodes denote positions in the sentence, as represented in Figure 3 for an Hebrew sentence. A valid analysis for a sentence should follow a path in the DAG from its root node at position 0 till its final node at position n. Each edge may be associated with an unique identifier to be able to refer it.

Lattice parsing is rather standard in chart-parsing[7] and since the beginning, thanks to DYALOG's support, DYALOG-SR was designed to parse ambiguous word lattices as input, but originally using

[4]Labeled Attachment Score, with punctuation being taking into account.

[5]because of non-termination on at least one sentence.

[6]Essentially, the initial configuration becomes $0{:}\langle 0, \mathbf{0}\rangle{:}0$ and the final one $2n{:}\langle n, \mathbf{0} \curvearrowright \star\rangle{:}c$ using **0** as a virtual root node.

[7]being formalized as computing the intersection of a grammar with a regular language.

language	DYALOG-SR test	dev	b	other systems best	baseline	mean
Arabic	85.87	86.99	4	89.83	82.28	**86.11**
Basque	**80.39**	81.09	6	86.68	69.19	79.58
French	**87.69**	87.94	8	90.29	79.86	85.99
German	**88.25**	90.89	6	91.83	79.98	86.80
Hebrew	**80.70**	81.31	8	83.87	76.61	80.13
Hungarian	79.60	79.09	4	88.06	72.34	**81.36**
Korean	88.23	89.24	6	89.59	**88.43**	88.91
Polish	**86.00**	86.94	8	89.58	77.70	83.79
Swedish	**79.80**	75.94	6	83.97	75.73	79.21

(a) gold/full

language	DYALOG-SR test	dev	b	other systems best	baseline	mean
Arabic	83.25	84.24	8	87.35	80.36	**83.79**
Basque	**79.11**	79.03	8	85.69	67.13	78.33
French	**85.66**	0.00	8	88.73	78.16	84.49
German	**83.88**	87.21	6	87.70	76.64	83.06
Hebrew	**80.70**	81.31	8	83.87	76.61	80.13
Hungarian	78.42	79.09	4	87.21	71.27	**80.42**
Korean	81.91	84.50	6	83.74	**81.93**	82.74
Polish	**85.67**	0.00	8	89.16	76.64	83.13
Swedish	**79.80**	0.00	6	83.97	75.73	79.21

(b) gold/5k

language	DYALOG-SR test	dev	b	other systems best	baseline	mean
Arabic	81.20	82.18	8	86.21	80.36	**82.57**
Basque	77.55	78.47	4	85.14	70.11	**79.13**
French	**82.06**	82.88	8	85.86	77.98	81.03
German	**84.80**	88.38	8	89.65	77.81	84.33
Hebrew	**73.63**	74.74	6	80.89	69.97	73.30
Hungarian	75.58	75.74	6	86.13	70.15	**79.23**
Korean	81.02	82.45	6	86.62	**82.06**	83.09
Polish	**82.56**	83.87	8	87.07	75.63	81.40
Swedish	77.54	73.37	8	82.13	73.21	**77.65**

(c) pred/full

language	DYALOG-SR test	dev	b	other systems best	baseline	mean
Arabic	78.65	79.25	8	83.66	78.48	**80.19**
Basque	76.06	76.11	6	83.84	68.12	**77.76**
French	**80.11**	0.00	4	83.60	76.54	79.31
German	73.07	84.69	8	85.08	**74.81**	79.34
Hebrew	**73.63**	74.74	6	80.89	69.97	73.30
Hungarian	74.48	75.55	6	85.24	69.08	**78.31**
Korean	73.79	76.66	6	80.80	**74.87**	76.34
Polish	**82.04**	0.00	8	86.69	75.29	80.96
Swedish	77.54	72.44	8	82.13	73.21	**77.65**

(d) pred/5k

Table 2: Official results

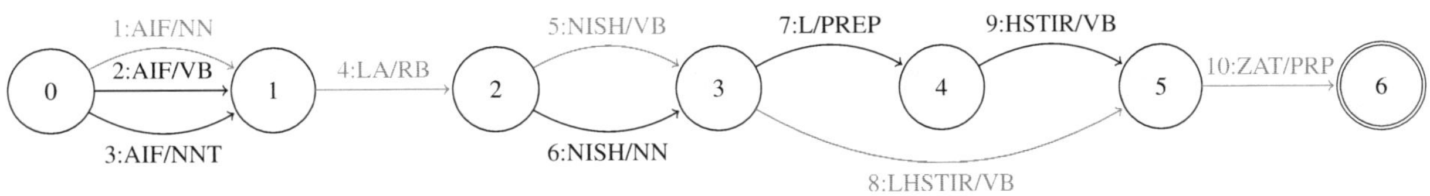

Figure 3: An ambiguous Hebrew word lattice (with gold segmentation path *AIF LA NISH LHSTIR ZAT*)

models trained on standard CONLL non ambiguous sentences. However, the initial experiments with Hebrew lattices (Table 3, using TED metric) have shown an important drop of 11 points between non ambiguous lattices (similar to standard CONLL files) and ambiguous ones.

	Hebrew disamb	nodisamb	Arabic disamb
no training	87.34	76.35	87.32
spec. training		86.75	

Table 3: Results on dev lattices (TED accuracy $*$ 100)

The main reason for that situation is that multiple paths of various lengths are now possible when traversing a lattice. Final items are no longer associated with the same number of steps ($2n-1$) and final items with a large number of steps (corresponding to longest paths in the lattice) tend to be favored over those with a small number of steps (corresponding to shortest paths), because the transition costs tend to be positive in our models.

A first attempt to compensate this bias was to "*normalize*" path lengths by adding (incrementally) some extra cost to the shortest paths, proportional to the number of missing steps. Again using models trained on non-ambiguous segmentations, we gained around 3 points (TED accuracy around 79) using this approach, still largely below the non-ambiguous case.

Finally, we opted for specific training on lattice, with the idea of introducing the new `length` word feature, whose value is defined, for a word, as the difference between its right and left position in the lattice. To exploit this feature, we added the following 9 templates: `length[I,I2,0]`, fullcat[I,I2,0]:length[I,I2,0], lengthI:lengthI2, length0:lengthI, and length0:lengthI:lengthI2.

Then, to ensure that we follow valid lattice paths, the configurations and items were completed with three extra *lookahead* fields la[123] to remember the edge identifiers of the lookahead words that were consulted. Obviously, adding this extra information increases the number of items, only differing on their lookahead sequences, but it is an important element for the coherence of the algorithm.

The reduce actions are kept unchanged, modulo the propagation without change of the lookahead identifiers, as shown below:

$$re_{l\curvearrowleft}\frac{m :< j, S|s_1|s_0, \mathrm{la}_1, \mathrm{la}_2, \mathrm{la}_3 >: c}{m+1 :< j, S|s_1 \,{}_l\!\curvearrowleft s_0, \mathrm{la}_1, \mathrm{la}_2, \mathrm{la}_3 >: c+\lambda}$$

$$re_{\curvearrowright l}\frac{m :< j, S|s_1|s_0, \mathrm{la}_1, \mathrm{la}_2, \mathrm{la}_3 >: c}{m+1 :< j, S|s_1 \curvearrowright_l s_0, \mathrm{la}_1, \mathrm{la}_2, \mathrm{la}_3 >: c+\rho}$$

On the other hand, the shift action consumes its first lookahead identifier la_1 (for a word between position j and k) and selects a new lookahead identifier la_4 (which must be a valid choice for continuing the path $\mathrm{la}_1, \mathrm{la}_2, \mathrm{la}_3$):

$$\text{shift}\frac{m :< j, S, \mathrm{la}_1, \mathrm{la}_2, \mathrm{la}_3 >: c}{m+1 :< k, S|\mathrm{la}_1, \mathrm{la}_2, \mathrm{la}_3, \mathrm{la}_4 >: c+\xi}$$

It should be noted that for a given position j in the lattice, we may have several items only differing by their lookahead sequences $\mathrm{la}_1, \mathrm{la}_2, \mathrm{la}_3$, and each of them will produce at least one new item by shifting la_1, and possibly more than one because of multiple la_4. However, several of these new shifted items are discarded because of the beam. Learning good estimations for the shift actions becomes a key point, more important than for usual shift-reduce algorithms.

In order to do that, we modified the oracle to provide information about the *oracle segmentation path* in the lattice, essentially by mentioning which edge identifier should be used for each oracle shift action. It should be noted that this information is also sufficient to determine the lookahead sequence for each oracle item, and in particular, the new edge identifier la_4 to be retrieved for the shift actions.

An issue was however to align the predicted lattices with the gold sentences (implementing a standard dynamic programming algorithm) in order to find the oracle segmentation paths. Unfortunately, we found that the segmentation path was missing for 1,055 sentences in the provided Hebrew lattices (around 20% of all sentences). Rather than discarding these sentences from an already small training set, we decided to keep them with incomplete prefix segmentation paths and oracles.

Figure 4 shows the strong impact of a specific training and of using large beams, with a TED accuracy climbing up to 86.75 (for beam size 16), close to the 87.34 reached on non-ambiguous lattices (for beam 6). Increasing beam size (around 3 times) seems necessary, probably for compensating the lattice ambiguities (2.76 transitions per token on average). However, even at beam=6, we get much better results (TED=83.47) than without specific training for the same beam size (TED=76.35).

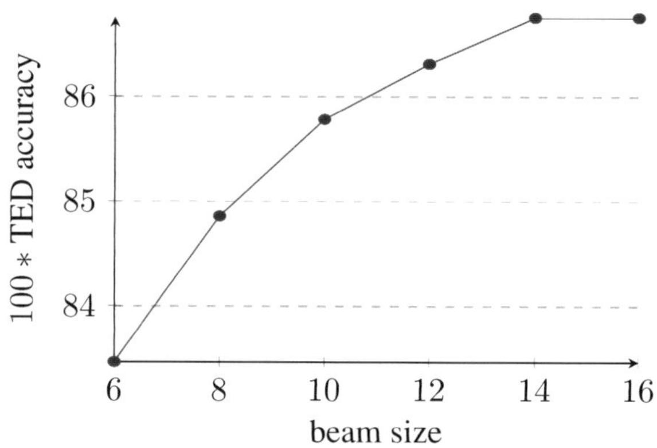

Figure 4: Score on Hebrew lattices w.r.t. beam size

To test the pertinence of the length features, we did some training experiments without these features. Against our expectations, we observed only a very low drop in performance (TED 86.50, loss = 0.25). It is possible that the lex features are sufficient, because only a relatively restricted set of (frequent) words have segmentations with length > 1. In practice, for the Hebrew 5k training lattices, we have 4,141 words with length > 1 for 44,722 occurrences (22.21% of all forms, and 12.65% of all occurrences), with around 80% of these occurrences covered by only 1,000 words. It is also possible that we under-employ the length features in too few templates, and that larger gains could be obtained.

6 Empirical analysis

The diversity and amount of data provided for the shared task was the opportunity to investigate more closely the properties of DYALOG-SR, to identify its weaknesses, and to try to improve it.

The usefulness of beams has been already proved in the case of Hebrew ambiguous lattices, and Figure 5 confirms that, in general, we get serious improvements using a beam, but in practice, beam sizes above 8 are not worth it. However, we observe almost no gain for Korean, a situation to be investigated.

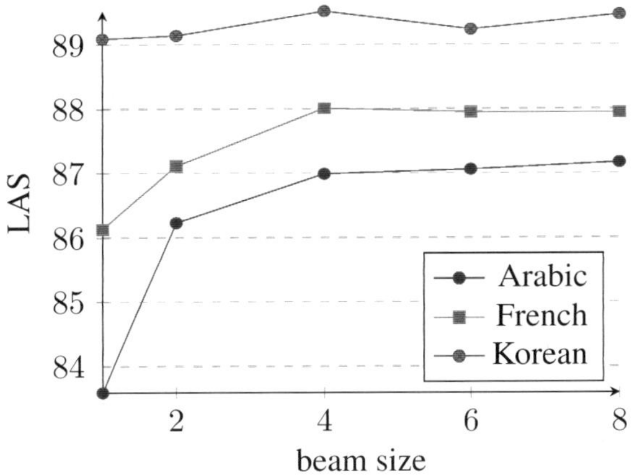

Figure 5: Accuracy evolution w.r.t. beam size

Efficiency was not the main motivation for this work and for the shared task. However, it is worthwhile to examine the empirical complexity of the algorithm w.r.t. beam size and w.r.t. sentence length. As shown in Figure 6, the average speed at beam=1 is around 740 tokens by second. At best, we expect a linear decreasing of the speed w.r.t. to beam size, motivating the use of a normalized speed by multiplying by the size. Surprisingly, we observe a faster normalized speed than expected for small beam sizes, maybe arising from computation sharing. However, for larger beam sizes, we observe a strong decrease, maybe related to beam management through (longer) sorted DYALOG lists, but also to some limits of term indexing[8]. The same experience carried for large beam sizes on the Hebrew lattices does not exhibit the same degradation, a point to be investigated but which suggests some kind of equivalence between beam=4 on non ambiguous input string and beam=12 on ambiguous lattices (also reflected in accuracy evolution).

[8]Even with efficient term indexing, checking the presence of an item in DYALOG table is not a constant time operation.

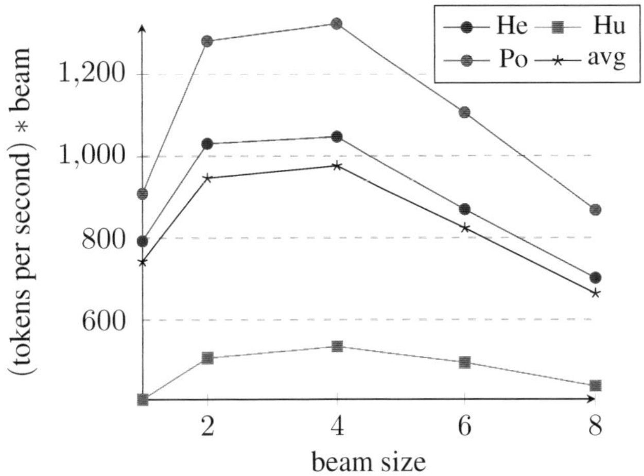

Figure 6: Normalized speed w.r.t. beam size (dev)

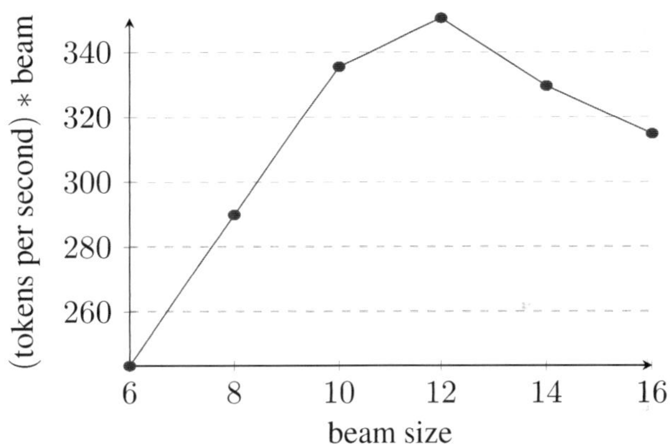

Figure 7: Normalized speed w.r.t. beam size (lattices)

Collecting parsing times for the sentences under length 80 from all training files and for all training iterations, Figure 8 confirms that parsing time (divided by beam size) is linear w.r.t. sentence length both for beam=1 and beam=8. On the other hand, we observe, Figure 9, that the number of updates increases with beam size (confirming that larger beams offer more possibilities of updates), but also non linearly with sentence length.

7 Conclusion

We have presented DYALOG-SR, a new implementation on top of DYALOG system of a beam-based

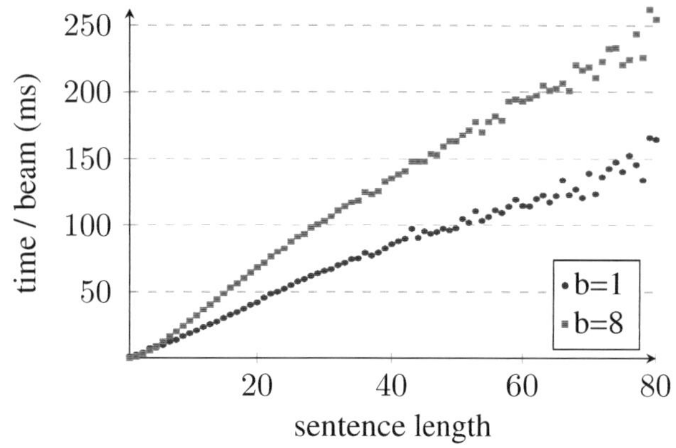

Figure 8: Parsing time w.r.t. sentence length (train)

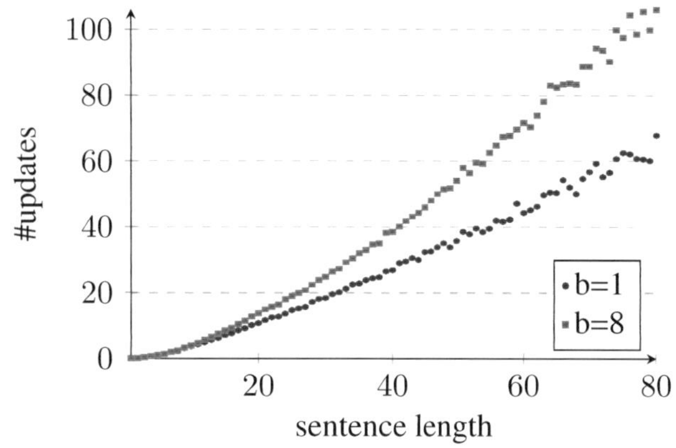

Figure 9: Number of updates w.r.t. sentence length (train)

shift-reduce parser with some preliminary support for training on ambiguous lattices. Although developed and tuned in less than a month, the participation of this very young system to the SPMRL 2013 shared task has shown its potential, even if far from the results of the best participants. As far as we know, DYALOG-SR is also the first system to show that shift-parsing techniques can be applied on ambiguous lattices, with almost no accuracy loss and with only minimal modifications (but large beams).

Several options are currently under consideration for improving the performances of DYALOG-SR. The first one is the (relatively straightforward) evolution of the parsing strategy for handling directly non-projective dependency trees, through the addition of some kind of `SWAP` transition (Nivre, 2009). Our preliminary experiments have shown the importance of larger beam sizes to cover the increased level of ambiguity due to lattices. However, it seems possible to adjust locally the beam size in function of the topology of the lattice, for improved accuracy and faster parsing. It also seems necessary to explore feature filtering, possibly using a tool like MALTOPTIMIZER (Ballesteros and Nivre, 2012), to determine the most discriminating ones.

The current implementation scales correctly w.r.t. sentence length and, to a lesser extent, beam size. Nevertheless, for efficiency reasons, we plan to implement a simple C module for beam management to avoid the manipulation in DYALOG of sorted lists. Interestingly, such a module, plus the already implemented model manager, should also be usable to speed up the disambiguation process of DYALOG-based TAG parser FRMG (de La Clergerie, 2005a). Actually, these components could be integrated in a slow but on-going effort to add first-class probabilities (or weights) in DYALOG, following the ideas of (Eisner and Filardo, 2011) or (Sato, 2008).

Clearly, DYALOG-SR is still at beta stage. However, for interested people, the sources are freely available[9], to be packaged in a near future.

Acknowledgements

We would like to thank the organizers of the SPMRL 2013 shared task and the providers of the datasets for the 9 languages of the task.

References

Anne Abeillé, Lionel Clément, and François Toussenel. 2003. Building a treebank for French. In Anne Abeillé, editor, *Treebanks*. Kluwer, Dordrecht.

Itziar Aduriz, M. J. Aranzabe, J. M. Arriola, A. Atutxa, A. Díaz de Ilarraza, A. Garmendia, and M. Oronoz. 2003. Construction of a Basque dependency treebank. In *TLT-03*, pages 201–204.

Miguel Ballesteros and Joakim Nivre. 2012. MaltOptimizer: an optimization tool for MaltParser. In *Proceedings of the Demonstrations at the 13th Conference of the European Chapter of the Association for Computational Linguistics*, pages 58–62.

Sabine Brants, Stefanie Dipper, Silvia Hansen, Wolfgang Lezius, and George Smith. 2002. The TIGER treebank. In Erhard Hinrichs and Kiril Simov, editors, *Proceedings of the First Workshop on Treebanks*

[9] via Subversion on INRIA GForge at `https://gforge.inria.fr/scm/viewvc.php/dyalog-sr/trunk/?root=dyalog`

and Linguistic Theories (TLT 2002), pages 24–41, Sozopol, Bulgaria.

Key-Sun Choi, Young S Han, Young G Han, and Oh W Kwon. 1994. KAIST tree bank project for Korean: Present and future development. In *Proceedings of the International Workshop on Sharable Natural Language Resources*, pages 7–14. Citeseer.

Jinho D. Choi. 2013. Preparing Korean Data for the Shared Task on Parsing Morphologically Rich Languages. *ArXiv e-prints*, September.

Dóra Csendes, Janós Csirik, Tibor Gyimóthy, and András Kocsor. 2005. The Szeged treebank. In Václav Matoušek, Pavel Mautner, and Tomáš Pavelka, editors, *Text, Speech and Dialogue: Proceedings of TSD 2005*. Springer.

Harold Charles Daume. 2006. *Practical structured learning techniques for natural language processing*. Ph.D. thesis, University of Southern California.

Éric de La Clergerie. 2005a. From metagrammars to factorized TAG/TIG parsers. In *Proceedings of IWPT'05 (poster)*, pages 190–191, Vancouver, Canada.

Éric de La Clergerie. 2005b. DyALog: a tabular logic programming based environment for NLP. In *Proceedings of 2nd International Workshop on Constraint Solving and Language Processing (CSLP'05)*, Barcelone, Espagne, October.

Jason Eisner and Nathaniel W. Filardo. 2011. Dyna: Extending Datalog for modern AI. In Tim Furche, Georg Gottlob, Giovanni Grasso, Oege de Moor, and Andrew Sellers, editors, *Datalog 2.0*, Lecture Notes in Computer Science. Springer. 40 pages.

Yoav Goldberg, Kai Zhao, and Liang Huang. 2013. Efficient implementation of beam-search incremental parsers. In *Proc. of the 51st Annual Meeting of the Association for Computational Linguistics (ACL)*, Sophia, Bulgaria, August.

Yoav Goldberg. 2011. *Automatic syntactic processing of Modern Hebrew*. Ph.D. thesis, Ben Gurion University of the Negev.

Nizar Habash and Ryan Roth. 2009. Catib: The Columbia Arabic Treebank. In *Proceedings of the ACL-IJCNLP 2009 Conference Short Papers*, pages 221–224, Suntec, Singapore, August. Association for Computational Linguistics.

Nizar Habash, Reem Faraj, and Ryan Roth. 2009. Syntactic Annotation in the Columbia Arabic Treebank. In *Proceedings of MEDAR International Conference on Arabic Language Resources and Tools*, Cairo, Egypt.

Liang Huang and Kenji Sagae. 2010. Dynamic programming for linear-time incremental parsing. In *Proceedings of the 48th Annual Meeting of the Association for Computational Linguistics*, pages 1077–1086. Association for Computational Linguistics.

Liang Huang, Suphan Fayong, and Yang Guo. 2012. Structured perceptron with inexact search. In *Proceedings of HLT-NAACL 2012*, pages 142–151.

Mohamed Maamouri, Ann Bies, Tim Buckwalter, and Wigdan Mekki. 2004. The Penn Arabic Treebank: Building a Large-Scale Annotated Arabic Corpus. In *NEMLAR Conference on Arabic Language Resources and Tools*.

Joakim Nivre and Jens Nilsson. 2005. Pseudo-projective dependency parsing. In *Proceedings of the 43rd Annual Meeting on Association for Computational Linguistics*, pages 99–106.

Joakim Nivre, Jens Nilsson, and Johan Hall. 2006. Talbanken05: A Swedish treebank with phrase structure and dependency annotation. In *Proceedings of LREC*, pages 1392–1395, Genoa, Italy.

Joakim Nivre. 2009. Non-projective dependency parsing in expected linear time. In *Proceedings of the Joint Conference of the 47th Annual Meeting of the ACL and the 4th International Joint Conference on Natural Language Processing of the AFNLP: Volume 1-Volume 1*, pages 351–359.

Benoît Sagot, Lionel Clément, Éric de La Clergerie, and Pierre Boullier. 2006. The Le*fff* 2 syntactic lexicon for French: architecture, acquisition, use. In *Proceedings of the 5th Language Resources and Evaluation Conference (LREC'06)*, Genova, Italie.

Taisuke Sato. 2008. A glimpse of symbolic-statistical modeling by PRISM. *J. Intell. Inf. Syst.*, 31(2):161–176.

Djamé Seddah, Reut Tsarfaty, Sandra Kübler, Marie Candito, Jinho Choi, Richárd Farkas, Jennifer Foster, Iakes Goenaga, Koldo Gojenola, Yoav Goldberg, Spence Green, Nizar Habash, Marco Kuhlmann, Wolfgang Maier, Joakim Nivre, Adam Przepiorkowski, Ryan Roth, Wolfgang Seeker, Yannick Versley, Veronika Vincze, Marcin Woliński, Alina Wróblewska, and Éric Villemonte de la Clergerie. 2013. Overview of the SPMRL 2013 shared task: A cross-framework evaluation of parsing morphologically rich languages. In *Proceedings of the 4th Workshop on Statistical Parsing of Morphologically Rich Languages: Shared Task*, Seattle, WA.

Wolfgang Seeker and Jonas Kuhn. 2012. Making Ellipses Explicit in Dependency Conversion for a German Treebank. In *Proceedings of the 8th International Conference on Language Resources and Evaluation*, pages 3132–3139, Istanbul, Turkey. European Language Resources Association (ELRA).

Khalil Sima'an, Alon Itai, Yoad Winter, Alon Altman, and Noa Nativ. 2001. Building a Tree-Bank for Modern Hebrew Text. In *Traitement Automatique des Langues*.

Marek Świdziński and Marcin Woliński. 2010. Towards a bank of constituent parse trees for Polish. In *Text, Speech and Dialogue: 13th International Conference (TSD)*, Lecture Notes in Artificial Intelligence, pages 197—204, Brno, Czech Republic. Springer.

Reut Tsarfaty. 2013. *A Unified Morpho-Syntactic Scheme of Stanford Dependencies*. Proceedings of ACL.

Veronika Vincze, Dóra Szauter, Attila Almási, György Móra, Zoltán Alexin, and János Csirik. 2010. Hungarian dependency treebank. In *LREC*.

Effective Morphological Feature Selection with MaltOptimizer at the SPMRL 2013 Shared Task

Miguel Ballesteros
Natural Language Processing Group
Pompeu Fabra University.
Barcelona, Spain
miguel.ballesteros@upf.edu

Abstract

The inclusion of morphological features provides very useful information that helps to enhance the results when parsing morphologically rich languages. MaltOptimizer is a tool, that given a data set, searches for the optimal parameters, parsing algorithm and optimal feature set achieving the best results that it can find for parsers trained with MaltParser. In this paper, we present an extension of MaltOptimizer that explores, one by one and in combination, the features that are geared towards morphology. From our experiments in the context of the Shared Task on Parsing Morphologically Rich Languages, we extract an in-depth study that shows which features are actually useful for transition-based parsing and we provide competitive results, in a fast and simple way.

1 Introduction

Since the CoNLL Shared Tasks on Syntactic Dependency parsing (Buchholz and Marsi, 2006; Nivre et al., 2007), the number of treebanks and new parsing methods have considerably increased. Thanks to that, it has been observed that parsing morphologically rich languages (henceforth, MRLs) is a challenge because these languages include multiple levels of information that are difficult to classify and, therefore, to parse. This is why there has been recent research in this direction, with for instance a Special Issue in Computational Linguistics (Tsarfaty et al., 2012b).

MaltOptimizer (Ballesteros and Nivre, 2012b; Ballesteros and Nivre, 2012a) is a system that is capable of providing optimal settings for training models with MaltParser (Nivre et al., 2006a), a freely available transition-based parser generator. MaltOptimizer, among other things, performs an in-depth feature selection, selecting the attributes that help to achieve better parsing results. In this paper – and in this participation in the Shared Task on Parsing Morphologically Rich Languages (Seddah et al., 2013) – we present an extension of MaltOptimizer that performs a deeper search over the morphological features that are somewhat one of the keys to parsing MRLs. Instead of lumping all morphosyntactic features together, we define a different field for each individual feature (case, number, gender, etc.). Hence, we are able to extract a study that shows which features are actually useful for parsing MRLs with MaltParser.

The new *SPMRL-MaltOptimizer* implementation is available for download at *http://nil.fdi.ucm.es/maltoptimizer/spmrl.html*. It is worth noting that it can be applied to any treebank in CoNLL data format.[1]

The rest of the paper is organized as follows. Section 2 describes MaltOptimizer. Section 3 shows how we modified MaltOptimizer to make it able to perform a more complete morphological feature selection. Section 4 describes the experiments that we carried out with the data sets of the Shared Task on Parsing Morphologically Rich Languages. Section 5 reports the results of the experiments and the conclusions that we can extract. Section 6 discusses related work on MaltOptimizer and parsing morphologically rich languages. And finally, Section 7 con-

[1] http://ilk.uvt.nl/conll/#dataformat

cludes.

2 MaltOptimizer

MaltOptimizer is a system written in Java that implements a full optimization procedure for MaltParser based on the experience acquired from previous experiments (Hall et al., 2007; Nivre and Hall, 2010). MaltOptimizer attempts to find the best model that it can find, but it does not guarantee that the outcome is the best model possible because of the difficulty of exploring all the possibilities that are provided by the parameters, parsing algorithms and different feature windows. The optimization procedure is divided in 3 different phases, as follows:

1. Data analysis and initial optimization.
2. Parsing algorithm selection.
3. Feature selection and LIBLINEAR optimization.

MaltOptimizer divides the treebank into a training set and a held-out test set for evaluation. In the first phase, MaltOptimizer makes an analysis of the treebank in order to set up the rest of the optimization, and it attempts the optimization with some general parameters, such as the way of handling covered roots.[2] After that, it tests the parsing algorithms that are available in MaltParser by selecting the one that provides best results in default settings. In the third phase, it explores a wide range of features that are based on previous parsing steps and/or the information annotated in the treebanks. Finally, it also explores the single hyper-parameter (c) of the LIBLINEAR classifier.

In the next Section, we present how we updated MaltOptimizer for our participation in the Shared Task of parsing MRLs.

3 Morphological Feature Exploration

The CoNLL data format contains several columns of information that help to perform the dependency parsing of a sentence. One of the columns is the FEATS column that normally contains a set of morphological features, which is normally of the format $a{=}x|b{=}y|c{=}z$. At the time of writing, the available version of MaltOptimizer explores the features included in this column as a single feature, by lumping all morphosyntactic features in the MaltParser classifier, and by splitting the information but including all of them at the same time without making any distinctions. This is what MaltParser allows by using the standard CoNLL format, which contains the following information per column.

1. ID: Identifier.
2. FORM: Word form.
3. LEMMA: Lemma or stemmed version of the word.
4. CPOSTAG: Coarse-grained part-of-speech tag.
5. POSTAG: Fine-grained part-of-speech tag.
6. FEATS: Morphosyntactic features (e.g., case, number, tense, etc.). It is normally of the format $a{=}x|b{=}y|c{=}z$.
7. HEAD: Head node.
8. DEPREL: Dependency relation to head.
9. PHEAD: Projective head node.
10. PDEPREL: Projective dependency relation to head.

However, MaltParser also provides the option of parsing new data formats that are derived from the original CoNLL format. Therefore, there is the possibility to add new columns that may contain useful information for parsing. The new MaltOptimizer implementation automatically generates a new data format and a new data set. It creates new columns that only contain the information of a single feature which is included in the FEATS column.

Figure 1 shows two versions of a sentence annotated in the French treebank from the Shared Task. The one shown above is in the standard CoNLL format, and the one shown below is the extended format generated by MaltOptimizer in which the FEATS column has been divided in 10 different columns.

[2] A covered root is a root node covered by a dependency arc.

```
1  En      en      P      P      mwehead=ADV+|pred=y         4        mod
2  tout    tout    D      DET    g=m|n=s|s=ind|pred=y        1        dep_cpd
3  cas     cas     N      NC     g=m|s=c|pred=y  1           dep_cpd
4  est     łtre    V      V      m=ind|n=s|p=3|t=pst         0        root
5  -il     il      CL     CLS    g=m|n=s|p=3|s=suj           4        suj
6  plus    plus    ADV    ADV    _          7        mod
7  nuanc   nuanc   A      ADJ    g=m|n=s|s=qual  4        ats
8  .       .       PONCT  PONCT  s=s        4        ponct

1  En      en      P      P      _     _    _    _    _    _    ADV+  y    _    _    4   mod
2  tout    tout    D      DET    ind   m    s    _    _    _    _     y    _    _    1   dep_cpd
3  cas     cas     N      NC     c     m    _    _    _    _    _     y    _    _    1   dep_cpd
4  est     łtre    V      V      _     _    s    3    ind  pst  _     _    _    _    0   root
5  -il     il      CL     CLS    suj   m    s    3    _    _    _     _    _    _    4   suj
6  plus    plus    ADV    ADV    _     _    _    _    _    _    _     _    _    _    7   mod
7  nuanc   nuanc   A      ADJ    qual  m    s    _    _    _    _     _    _    _    4   ats
8  .       .       PONCT  PONCT  s     _    _    _    _    _    _     _    _    _    4   ponct
```

Figure 1: A sentence from the French treebank in the standard (above) and complex (below) formats. The projective columns have been removed for simplicity.

4 Experiments

With the intention of both assessing the usefulness of the new MaltOptimizer implementation and testing which features are useful for each targeted language, we carried out a series of experiments over the data sets from the Shared Task on Parsing MRLs (Seddah et al., 2013). We run the new MaltOptimizer implementation for all the data sets provided by the Shared Task organizers and we run MaltParser with the model suggested. Therefore, we had 36 different runs, 4 for each language (*gold* and *predicted* scenarios with *5k* treebanks, and *gold* and *predicted* scenarios with *full* treebanks).

In order to have a comparable set of results, we performed all the optimization processes with the smaller versions of the treebanks (*5k*) and both optimization and training steps with both the small and larger version for all languages. Each MaltOptimizer run took approximately 3-4 hours for optimization (the running time also depends on the size of the set of morphological features, or other parameters, such as the number of dependency relations) and it takes around 20 extra minutes to get the final model with MaltParser. These estimates are given with an Intel Xeon server with 8 cores, 2.8GHz and a heap space of, at least, 8GB.

5 Results and Discussion

Table 1 shows the results for *gold*-standard input while Table 2 shows the results for the provided *predicted* inputs for the best model that the new MaltOptimizer implementation can find (Dev-5k, Dev, Test-5k and Test) and a baseline, which is MaltParser in default settings (Malt-5k and Malt) on the test sets. The first conclusion to draw is that the difference between *gold* and *predicted* inputs is normally of 2 points, however for some languages such as French the drop reaches 6 points. It is also evidenced that, as shown by Ballesteros and Nivre (2012a), some languages benefit more from the feature selection phase, while others achieve higher improvements by selecting a different parsing algorithm.

In general terms, almost all languages benefit from having an accurate stemmed version of the word in the LEMMA column, providing very substantial improvements when accurately selecting this feature. Another key feature, for almost all languages, is the grammatical CASE that definitely enhances the performance; we can therefore conclude that it is essential for MRLs. Both aspects evidence the lexical challenge of parsing MRLs without using this information.

There is a positive average difference comparing with the MaltParser baseline of 4.0 points training over the full treebanks and predicted scenario and 5.6 points training over the full treebanks and gold scenario. It is therefore evident how useful MaltOptimizer is when it can perform an in-depth morphological feature exploration. In the following subsections we explain the results for each targeted language, giving special emphasis to the ones that turn out to be more meaningful.

5.1 Arabic

For Arabic, we used the shared task Arabic data set, originally provided by the LDC (Maamouri et

Language	Default	Phase 1	Phase 2	Phase 3	Diff	Dev-5k	Dev	Malt-5k	Malt	Test-5k	Test
Arabic	83.48	83.49	83.49	87.95	4.47	85.98	87.60	80.36	82.28	85.30	87.03
Basque	67.05	67.33	67.45	79.89	13.30	80.35	81.65	67.13	69.19	81.40	82.07
French	77.96	77.96	78.27	85.24	7.28	85.19	86.30	78.16	79.86	84.93	85.71
German	79.90	81.09	84.85	87.70	7.80	87.32	90.40	76.64	79.98	83.59	86.96
Hebrew	76.78	76.80	79.37	80.17	3.39	79.83	79.83	76.61	76.61	80.03	80.03
Hungarian	70.37	71.11	71.98	81.91	11.54	80.69	80.74	71.27	72.34	82.37	83.14
Korean	87.22	87.22	87.22	88.94	1.72	86.52	90.20	81.69	88.43	83.74	89.39
Polish	75.52	75.58	79.28	80.27	4.75	81.58	81.91	76.64	77.70	79.79	80.49
Swedish	76.75	76.75	78.91	79.76	3.01	74.85	74.85	75.73	75.73	77.67	77.67

Table 1: Labeled attachment score per phase compared to default settings for all training sets from the Shared Task on PMRLs in the *gold* scenario on the held-out test set for optimization. The first columns shows results per phase (the procedure of each phase is briefly described in Section 2) on the held-out sets for evaluation. The **Dev-5k** and **Dev** columns report labeled attachment score on the development sets. The columns **Malt** and **Malt-5k** report results of MaltParser in default settings on the test sets. And the columns, **Test-5k** and **Test** report results for the best model found by SPMRL-MaltOptimizer on the test sets.

Language	Default	Phase 1	Phase 2	Phase 3	Diff	Dev-5k	Dev	Malt-5k	Malt	Test-5k	Test
Arabic	83.20	83.21	83.21	85.68	2.48	80.35	82.28	78.30	80.36	79.64	81.90
Basque	68.80	69.33	69.89	77.24	8.44	78.12	79.46	68.12	70.11	77.59	78.58
French	77.43	77.43	77.63	79.42	1.99	77.65	79.33	76.54	77.98	77.56	79.00
German	78.69	79.87	82.58	83.97	5.28	83.39	86.63	74.81	77.81	79.22	82.75
Hebrew	76.29	76.31	79.01	79.67	3.38	73.40	73.40	69.97	69.97	73.01	73.01
Hungarian	68.26	69.12	69.96	78.71	10.45	76.82	77.62	69.08	70.15	79.00	79.63
Korean	80.08	80.08	80.08	81.63	1.55	77.96	83.02	74.87	82.06	75.90	82.65
Polish	74.43	74.49	76.93	78.41	3.98	80.61	80.83	75.29	75.63	79.50	80.49
Swedish	74.53	74.53	76.51	77.66	3.13	72.90	72.90	73.21	73.21	75.82	75.82

Table 2: Labeled attachment score per phase compared to default settings for all training sets from the Shared Task on PMRLs in the *predicted* scenario on the held-out test set for optimization. The columns of this table report the results in the same way as Table 1 but using predicted inputs.

al., 2004), specifically its SPMRL 2013 dependency instance, derived from the Columbia Catib Treebank (Habash and Roth, 2009; Habash et al., 2009), extended according to the SPMRL 2013 extension scheme (Seddah et al., 2013).

For the *gold* input, the most useful feature is, by far, DASHTAG[3] with an improvement of 2 points. CASE is also very useful, as it is for most of the languages, with 0.67 points. Moreover, SUBCAT (0.159) and CAT (0.129) provide improvements as well.

In the *pred* scenario, there is no DASHTAG, and this allows other features to rise, for instance, CASE (0.66), CPOSTAG (0.12), GENDER (0.08), SUBCAT (0.07) and CAT (0.06) provide improvements. Finally it is worth noting that the TED accuracy (Tsarfaty et al., 2011) for the lattices is 0.8674 with the full treebanks and 0.8563 with 5k treebanks, which overcomes the baseline in more than 0.06 points, this shows that MaltOptimizer is also useful under TED evaluation constraints.

[3]DASHTAG comes from the original constituent data, when a DASHTAG was present in a head node label, this feature was kept in the Catib corpus.

5.2 Basque

The improvement provided by the feature selection for Basque (Aduriz et al., 2003) is really high. It achieves almost 13 points improvement with the *gold* input and around 8 points with the *predicted* input. The results in the gold scenario are actually a record if we also consider the experiments performed over the treebanks of the CoNLL Shared Tasks (Ballesteros and Nivre, 2012a). One of the reasons is the treatment of covered roots that is optimized during the first phase of optimization. This corpus has multiple root labels, ROOT being the most common one and the one selected by MaltOptimizer as default.

For the *gold* input, the CPOSTAG and LEMMA columns turn out to be very useful, providing an improvement of 2.5 points and slightly less than 1 point respectively, MaltOptimizer selects them all over the more central tokens over the stack and the buffer. The Basque treebank contains a very big set of possible features in the FEATS column, however only some of them provide significant improvements, which evidences the usefulness of selecting them one by one. The most useful feature with a huge difference is *KASE* (or CASE) that provides 5.9 points by itself. MaltOptimizer fills out all the available positions of the stack and the buffer with this feature. Another useful feature is ERL [type of subordinated sentence], providing almost 0.8 points. Moreover, NUMBER (0.3), NORK2 (0.15), ASP [aspect] (0.09), NOR1 (0.08), and NMG (0.06) provide slighter, but significant, improvements as well.[4]

Surprisingly, the *predicted* input provides better results in the first 2 phases, which means that for some reason MaltParser is able to parse better by using just the predicted POS column, however, the improvement achieved by MaltOptimizer during Phase 3 are (just) a bit more than 7 points. In this case, the CPOSTAG column is less useful, providing only 0.13 points, while the LEMMA (1.2) is still very useful. CASE provides 4.5 points, while NUM (0.17), ASP (0.13) and ADM (0.11) provide improvements as well.

5.3 French

For French (Abeillé et al., 2003) there is a huge difference between the results with *gold* input and the results with *predicted* input. With *gold* input, the feature selection provides a bit less than 8 points while there is just an improvement of around 2 points with *predicted* input. In this case, the lack of quality in the predicted features is evident. It is also interesting that the lexical column, FORM, provides a quite substantial improvement when MaltOptimizer attempts to modify it, which is something that does not happen with the rest of languages.

For the *gold* input, apart from LEMMA that provides around 0.7 points, the most useful feature is MWEHEAD [head of a multi word expression, if exists] that does not exist in the *predicted* scenario. MWEHEAD provides more than 4 points; this fact invites us to think that a predicted version of this feature would be very useful for French, if possible. PRED [automatically predicted] (0.8), G [gender] (0.6), N [number] (0.2) and S [subcat] (0.14) are also useful.

In the *predicted* scenario, the CPOSTAG column provides some improvements (around 0.1) while the LEMMA is less useful than the one in the gold scenario (0.2). The morphological features that are useful are S [subcat] (0.3) and G [gender] (0.3).

5.4 German

For German (Brants et al., 2002) the results are more or less in the average. For the *gold* input, LEMMA is the best feature providing around 0.8 points; from the morphological features the most useful one is, as expected, CASE with 0.58 points. GENDER (0.16) and NUMBER (0.16) are also useful.

In the *predicted* scenario, CASE is again very useful (0.67). Other features, such as, NUMBER (0.10) and PERSON (0.10) provide improvements, but as we can observe a little bit less than the improvements provided in the *gold* scenario.

5.5 Hebrew

For the Hebrew (Sima'an et al., 2001; Tsarfaty, 2013) treebank, unfortunately we did not see a lot of improvements by adding the morphological features. For the *gold* input, only CPOSTAG (0.08) shows some improvements, while the *predicted* scenario shows improvements for NUM (0.08) and PER (0.08). It is worth noting that the TED accuracy (Tsarfaty et al., 2011) for the lattices is 0.8305 which is ranked second.

This outcome is different from the one obtained by Goldberg and Elhadad (2010), but it is also true that perhaps by selecting a different parsing algorithm it may turn out different, because two parsers may need different features, as shown by Zhang and Nivre (2012). This is why, it would be very interesting to perform new experiments with MaltOptimizer by testing different parsing algorithms included in MaltParser with the Hebrew treebank.

[4] NORK2, NOR1 and NMG are auxiliaries case markers.

5.6 Hungarian

The Hungarian (Vincze et al., 2010) results are also very consistent. During the feature selection phase, MaltOptimizer achieves an improvement of 10 points by the inclusion of morphological features. This also happens in the initial experiments performed with MaltOptimizer (Ballesteros and Nivre, 2012a), by using the Hungarian treebank of the CoNLL 2007 Shared Task. The current Hungarian treebank presents covered roots and multiple root labels and this is why we also get substantial improvements during Phase 1.

For the *gold* input, as expected the LEMMA column is very useful, providing more than 1.4 points, while MaltOptimizer selects it all over the available feature windows. The best morphological feature is again CASE providing an improvement of 5.7 points just by itself, in a similar way as in the experiments with Basque. In this case, the SUBPOS [grammatical subcategory] feature that is included in the FEATS column is also very useful, providing around 1.2 points. Other features that are useful are NUMP [number of the head] (0.2), NUM [number of the current token] (0.16), DEF [definiteness] (0.11) and DEG [degree] (0.09).

In the *predicted* scenario, we can observe a similar behavior for all features. MOOD provides 0.4 points while it does not provide improvements in the *gold* scenario. The results of the SUBPOS feature are a bit lower in this case (0.5 points), which evidences the quality lost by using *predicted* inputs.

5.7 Korean

As Korean (Choi, 2013) is the language in which our submission provided the best results comparing to other submissions, it is interesting to dedicate a section by showing its results. For the *5k* input, our model provides the best results of the Shared Task, while the results of the model trained over the *full* treebank qualified the second.

For the *gold* input, the most useful feature is CPOSTAG providing around 0.6 points. Looking into the morphological features, CASE, as usual, is the best feature with 0.24 points, AUX-Type (0.11), FNOUN-Type (0.08) are also useful.

In the *predicted* scenario, MaltOptimizer performs similarly, having CPOSTAG (0.35) and CASE (0.32) as most useful features. ADJ-Type (0.11) and PUNCT-Type (0.06) are also useful. The results of the features are a bit lower with the *predicted* input, with the exception of CASE which is better.

5.8 Polish

Polish (Świdziński and Woliński, 2010) is one of the two languages (with Swedish) in which our model performs with the worst results.

In the *gold* scenario only the LEMMA (0.76) shows some substantial improvements during the optimization process; unfortunately, the morphological features that are extracted when MaltOptimizer generates the new complex data format did not fire.

For the *predicted* input, LEMMA (0.66) is again the most useful feature, but as happened in the *gold* scenario, the rest of the features did not fire during the feature selection.

5.9 Swedish

As happened with Polish, the results for Swedish (Nivre et al., 2006b) are not as good as we could expect; however we believe that the information shown in this paper is useful because MaltOptimizer detects which features are able to outperform the best model found so far and the model trained with MaltParser in default settings by a bit less than 2 points in the predicted scenario and more than 2 points in the gold scenario.

For the *gold* scenario only two features are actually useful according to MaltOptimizer, MaltOptimizer shows improvements by adding GENDER (0.22) and PERFECTFORM (0.05).

For the *predicted* input, MaltOptimizer shows improvements by adding DEGREE (0.09), GENDER (0.08) and ABBRV (0.06). However, as we can see the improvements for Swedish are actually lower compared to the rest of languages.

6 Related Work

There has been some recent research making use of MaltOptimizer. For instance, Seraji et al. (2012) used MaltOptimizer to get optimal models for parsing Persian. Tsarfaty et al. (2012a) worked with MaltOptimizer and Hebrew by including the optimization for presenting new ways of evaluating statistical parsers. Mambrini and Passarotti (2012),

Agirre et al. (2012), Padró et al. (2013) and Ballesteros et al. (2013) applied MaltOptimizer to test different features of Ancient Greek, Basque and Spanish (the last 2) respectively; however at that time MaltOptimizer did not allow the FEATS column to be divided. Finally, Ballesteros et al. (2012) applied MaltOptimizer for different parsing algorithms that are not included in the downloadable version showing that it is also possible to optimize different parsing algorithms.

7 Conclusions

This new MaltOptimizer implementation helps the developers to adapt MaltParser models to new languages in which there is a rich set of features. It shows which features are able to make a change in the parsing results and which ones are not, in this way, it is possible to focus annotation effort for the purpose of parsing. We clearly observe that MaltOptimizer outperforms very substantially the results shown in the baseline, which is MaltParser in default settings, and it is also nice to see that the improvements provided by MaltOptimizer for the morphological features are actually very high, if we compare to the ones obtained by MaltOptimizer for the corpora of the CoNLL shared tasks (Ballesteros and Nivre, 2012a).

It is worth noting that the experiments with MaltOptimizer do not take so long. The time needed to perform the optimization is actually very short if we compare to the efforts needed to achieve results in the same range of accuracy by careful manual optimization. The MaltOptimizer process was sped up following heuristics derived from deep proven experience (Nivre and Hall, 2010), which means that there are several combinations that are untested; however, it is worth noting that these heuristics resulted in similar performance to more exhaustive search for a big set of languages (Ballesteros, 2013).

From the feature study shown in Section 5, we expect that it could be useful for people doing parsing research and interested in parsing MRLs. Finally, comparing our submission with the results of other teams, we believe that we provide a fast and effective parser optimization for parsing MRLs, having competitive results for most of the languages.

Acknowledgments

I would like to thank Koldo Gojenola who initially gave me the idea presented in this paper. I am also very thankful to Joakim Nivre for his constant help and support. Finally, special thanks to the organizers Djamé Seddah, Reut Tsarfaty and Sandra Kübler.

References

Anne Abeillé, Lionel Clément, and François Toussenel. 2003. Building a treebank for french. In Anne Abeillé, editor, *Treebanks*. Kluwer, Dordrecht.

I. Aduriz, M. J. Aranzabe, J. M. Arriola, A. Atutxa, A. Díaz de Ilarraza, A. Garmendia, and M. Oronoz. 2003. Construction of a Basque dependency treebank. In *Proceedings of the 2nd Workshop on Treebanks and Linguistic Theories (TLT)*, pages 201–204.

Eneko Agirre, Aitziber Atutxa, and Kepa Sarasola. 2012. Contribution of complex lexical information to solve syntactic ambiguity in Basque. In *Proceedings of the 24th International Conference on Computational Linguistics (COLING 2012)*, Mumbai, India, 12/2012.

Miguel Ballesteros and Joakim Nivre. 2012a. MaltOptimizer: A System for MaltParser Optimization. In *Proceedings of the Eighth International Conference on Language Resources and Evaluation (LREC 2012)*.

Miguel Ballesteros and Joakim Nivre. 2012b. MaltOptimizer: An Optimization Tool for MaltParser. In *Proceedings of the System Demonstration Session of the Thirteenth Conference of the European Chapter of the Association for Computational Linguistics (EACL 2012)*.

Miguel Ballesteros, Carlos Gómez-Rodríguez, and Joakim Nivre. 2012. Optimizing Planar and 2-Planar Parsers with MaltOptimizer. *Procesamiento del Lenguaje Natural*, 49, 09/2012.

Miguel Ballesteros, Simon Mille, and Alicia Burga. 2013. Exploring Morphosyntactic Annotation Over a Spanish Corpus for Dependency Parsing . In *Proceedings of the Second International Conference on Dependency Linguistics (DEPLING 2013)*.

Miguel Ballesteros. 2013. Exploring Automatic Feature Selection for Transition-Based Dependency Parsing. *Procesamiento del Lenguaje Natural*, 51.

Sabine Brants, Stefanie Dipper, Silvia Hansen, Wolfgang Lezius, and George Smith. 2002. The TIGER treebank. In Erhard Hinrichs and Kiril Simov, editors, *Proceedings of the First Workshop on Treebanks and Linguistic Theories (TLT 2002)*, pages 24–41, Sozopol, Bulgaria.

Sabine Buchholz and Erwin Marsi. 2006. CoNLL-X shared task on multilingual dependency parsing. In

Proceedings of the 10th Conference on Computational Natural Language Learning (CoNLL), pages 149–164.

Jinho D. Choi. 2013. Preparing Korean Data for the Shared Task on Parsing Morphologically Rich Languages. *ArXiv e-prints*, September.

Yoav Goldberg and Michael Elhadad. 2010. Easy first dependency parsing of modern hebrew. In *Proceedings of the NAACL HLT 2010 First Workshop on Statistical Parsing of Morphologically-Rich Languages*, SPMRL '10, pages 103–107, Stroudsburg, PA, USA. Association for Computational Linguistics.

Nizar Habash and Ryan Roth. 2009. Catib: The columbia arabic treebank. In *Proceedings of the ACL-IJCNLP 2009 Conference Short Papers*, pages 221–224, Suntec, Singapore, August. Association for Computational Linguistics.

Nizar Habash, Reem Faraj, and Ryan Roth. 2009. Syntactic Annotation in the Columbia Arabic Treebank. In *Proceedings of MEDAR International Conference on Arabic Language Resources and Tools*, Cairo, Egypt.

Johan Hall, Jens Nilsson, Joakim Nivre, Gülsen Eryiğit, Beáta Megyesi, Mattias Nilsson, and Markus Saers. 2007. Single malt or blended? A study in multilingual parser optimization. In *Proceedings of the CoNLL Shared Task of EMNLP-CoNLL 2007*, pages 933–939.

Mohamed Maamouri, Ann Bies, Tim Buckwalter, and Wigdan Mekki. 2004. The Penn Arabic Treebank: Building a Large-Scale Annotated Arabic Corpus. In *NEMLAR Conference on Arabic Language Resources and Tools*.

Francesco Mambrini and Marco Carlo Passarotti. 2012. Will a Parser Overtake Achilles? First experiments on parsing the Ancient Greek Dependency Treebank. In *Proceedings of the Eleventh International Workshop on Treebanks and Linguistic Theories (TLT11)*.

Joakim Nivre and Johan Hall. 2010. A quick guide to MaltParser optimization. Technical report, maltparser.org.

Joakim Nivre, Johan Hall, and Jens Nilsson. 2006a. Maltparser: A data-driven parser-generator for dependency parsing. In *Proceedings of the 5th International Conference on Language Resources and Evaluation (LREC)*, pages 2216–2219.

Joakim Nivre, Jens Nilsson, and Johan Hall. 2006b. Talbanken05: A Swedish treebank with phrase structure and dependency annotation. In *Proceedings of LREC*, pages 1392–1395, Genoa, Italy.

Joakim Nivre, Johan Hall, Sandra Kübler, Ryan McDonald, Jens Nilsson, Sebastian Riedel, and Deniz Yuret. 2007. The CoNLL 2007 shared task on dependency parsing. In *Proceedings of the CoNLL Shared Task of EMNLP-CoNLL 2007*, pages 915–932.

Muntsa Padró, Miguel Ballesteros, Hector Martínez, and Bernd Bohnet. 2013. Finding dependency parsing limits over a large spanish corpus. In *IJCNLP*, Nagoya, Japan. Association for Computational Linguistics.

Djamé Seddah, Reut Tsarfaty, Sandra Kübler, Marie Candito, Jinho Choi, Richárd Farkas, Jennifer Foster, Iakes Goenaga, Koldo Gojenola, Yoav Goldberg, Spence Green, Nizar Habash, Marco Kuhlmann, Wolfgang Maier, Joakim Nivre, Adam Przepiorkowski, Ryan Roth, Wolfgang Seeker, Yannick Versley, Veronika Vincze, Marcin Woliński, and Alina Wróblewska. 2013. Overview of the spmrl 2013 shared task: A cross-framework evaluation of parsing morphologically rich languages. In *Proceedings of the 4th Workshop on Statistical Parsing of Morphologically Rich Languages: Shared Task*, Seattle, WA.

Mojgan Seraji, Beáta Megyesi, and Joakim Nivre. 2012. Dependency parsers for persian. In *Proceedings of 10th Workshop on Asian Language Resources, at 24th International Conference on Computational Linguistics (COLING 2012)*. ACL Anthology.

Khalil Sima'an, Alon Itai, Yoad Winter, Alon Altman, and Noa Nativ. 2001. Building a Tree-Bank for Modern Hebrew Text. In *Traitement Automatique des Langues*.

Marek Świdziński and Marcin Woliński. 2010. Towards a bank of constituent parse trees for Polish. In *Text, Speech and Dialogue: 13th International Conference (TSD)*, Lecture Notes in Artificial Intelligence, pages 197—204, Brno, Czech Republic. Springer.

Reut Tsarfaty, Joakim Nivre, and Evelina Andersson. 2011. Evaluating dependency parsing: Robust and heuristics-free cross-annotation evaluation. In *EMNLP*, pages 385–396, Edinburgh, Scotland, UK., July. Association for Computational Linguistics.

Reut Tsarfaty, Joakim Nivre, and Evelina Andersson. 2012a. Cross-framework evaluation for statistical parsing. In *EACL*, pages 44–54.

Reut Tsarfaty, Djamé Seddah, Sandra Kuebler, and Joakim Nivre. 2012b. Parsing Morphologically Rich Languages: Introduction to the Special Issue. *Computational Linguistics*, November.

Reut Tsarfaty. 2013. *A Unified Morpho-Syntactic Scheme of Stanford Dependencies*. Proceedings of ACL.

Veronika Vincze, Dóra Szauter, Attila Almási, György Móra, Zoltán Alexin, and János Csirik. 2010. Hungarian dependency treebank. In *LREC*.

Yue Zhang and Joakim Nivre. 2012. Analyzing the effect of global learning and beam-search on transition-based dependency parsing. In *COLING*, pages 1391–1400.

Exploiting the Contribution of Morphological Information to Parsing: the BASQUE_TEAM system in the SPRML'2013 Shared Task

Iakes Goenaga, Nerea Ezeiza
IXA NLP Group
Faculty of Computer Science
Univ. of the Basque Country UPV/EHU
iakesg@gmail.com, n.ezeiza@ehu.es

Koldo Gojenola
IXA NLP Group
Technical School of Engineering, Bilbao
Univ. of the Basque Country UPV/EHU
koldo.gojenola@ehu.es

Abstract

This paper presents a dependency parsing system, presented as BASQUE_TEAM at the SPMRL'2013 Shared Task, based on the analysis of each morphological feature of the languages. Once the specific relevance of each morphological feature is calculated, this system uses the most significant of them to create a series of analyzers using two freely available and state of the art dependency parsers, MaltParser and Mate. Finally, the system will combine previously achieved parses using a voting approach.

1 Introduction

Morphologically rich languages present new challenges, as the use of state of the art parsers for more configurational and non-inflected languages like English does not reach similar performance levels in languages like Basque, Greek or Turkish (Nivre et al., 2007). Using morphological information as features in parsing has been a commonly used method for parsing MRLs (Tsarfaty et al., 2010). In some cases the effect of this information is positive but in others it does not help or causes a negative effect.

In most of the work on dependency parsing, the specific relevance of each morphological feature in the final result is unknown. The authors include all the morphological features[1] in their systems with the aim of taking advantage of the diversity of the used information. This approach commonly produces very good results but they are not always the best ones (see table 2).
On the other hand, some authors have made experiments to specify which is the real impact of the morphological features. Ambati et al. (2010) explore ways of integrating local morphosyntactic features into Hindi dependency parsing. They experiment with different sets of features on a graph-based and a transition-based dependency parser. They show that using some morphological features (root, case, and suffix) outperforms a baseline using POS as the only feature, with both gold and predicted settings .

Bengoetxea and Gojenola (2010) make use of MaltParser's feature configuration file to take advantage of morphological features in parsing with gold data. Their experiments show that case and subordination type considerably increase parsing accuracy.

Marton et al. (2013) also explore which morphological features could be useful in dependency parsing of Arabic. They observe the effect of features by adding them one at a time separately and comparing the outcomes. Experiments showed that when gold morphology is provided, case markers help the most, whereas when the morphology is automatically predicted the outcome is the opposite: using case harms the results the most. When features are combined in a greedy heuristic, using definiteness, person, number, and gender information improves accuracy.

Similarly, Seeker and Kuhn (2013) also determine that the use of case is specially relevant for parsing, demonstrating that morpho-syntactic constraints can delimit the search space of a statistical dependency parser to outperform state-of-the-art baselines for Czech, German and Hungarian.

Following this line of research, our first step will be to determine which is the concrete value of each feature on dependency parsing, adding one of the morphological features at a time starting with an empty *FEATS* column.

Çetinoğlu and Kuhn (2013) have shown that some parsers tend to improve the results when swapping or replacing *POS* by some of the mor-

[1] That is, they treat all the morphological features in the same way in the feature specification, and let the learning algorithms decide the weight assigned to each one.

phological features. They have made use of the METU-Sabanc Turkish Treebank (Oflazer et al., 2003) for training and the ITU validation set (Eryigit, 2007) for testing. In their work, it is observed that moving *CASE* to the *POS* field helps with a 0.3% LAS absolute increase in the gold pipeline settings and using *CASE* instead of nominal *POS* improves the labelled accuracy by 0.3% absolute for the training set.

These experiments suggest that in some way the parser is not making an optimal use of all the available morpho-syntactic information, and that the parser algorithm (or the feature specification for the learning phase) is geared towards *POS* and *CPOS*, giving a lower status to other types of information. Although this strategy is good in general, it seems that, at least for some languages, specific features (e.g. *CASE*) are crucial in obtaining a high parsing performance. Taking these ideas into consideration, we will work on three different approaches:

- We will experiment the effect of using only the best three morphological features in the FEATS column (see table 1), compared to working with the full set of morpho-syntactic features. This can have the effect of speeding the learning and parsing processes, as the number of features can be smaller. On the other hand, the elimination of non-relevant features can also help to improve the parser's results, because some features can even be detrimental for parsing.

- Following Çetinoğlu and Kuhn (2013), once our system resolves which feature is the most significant, it will be used to replace the *POS* and *CPOS* fields one by one and we will test the effect of these variants on the parsers. Finally, we will also try right-to-left versions of those 3 variants (baseline, and replacing *POS* and *CPOS*) completing a set of 6 different parsers.

- Finally, we will experiment the combination of the different or parsers with a voting approach (Hall et al., 2010) using the MaltBlender tool[2].

All of the experiments will be performed on automatically predicted *POS* and morphosyntactic data, taking the tags given in the Shared Task data, that is, we will not made use of any specifically trained morphological tagger.

In the rest of this paper we will first present the resources we have used to carry out our experiments in section 2, followed by a study of the contribution of the morphological information to parsing in section 3 and the effect of this information on the individual parsers in subsection 4.1. The final results of the best parser combinations are showed in subsection 4.2 and the main conclusions of the work in section 5.

2 Resources

This section will describe the main resources that have been used in the experiments. Subsection 2.1 will describe the languages we have used in our experiments, subsection 2.2 will explain the parsers we use, while subsection 2.3 will present briefly the *MaltBlender* tool.

2.1 Selected Languages

Although the *SPMRL'2013 Shared Task* (Seddah et al., 2013) offers the opportunity to parse nine morphologically rich languages, to carry out our experiments we have selected five of them, due in part to time constraints, but also taking into account the relevance of the morpho-syntactic information (*FEATS* column, see table 1) . The selected five languages are: Basque (Aduriz et al., 2003), French (Abeillé et al., 2003), German (Seeker and Kuhn, 2012), Hungarian (Vincze et al., 2010) and Swedish (Nivre et al., 2006).

2.2 Parsers

We have made use of MaltParser (Nivre et al., 2007b) and Mate (Bohnet and Nivre, 2012), two state of the art dependency parsers[3] representing the dominant approaches in data-driven dependency parsing, and that have been successfully applied to typologically different languages and treebanks.

MaltParser is a representative of local, greedy, transition-based dependency parsing models, where the parser obtains deterministically a dependency tree in a single pass over the input using two data structures: a stack of partially analyzed items and the remaining input sequence. To determine the best action at each step, the

[2]http://w3.msi.vxu.se/users/jni/blend/

[3]Due to time constraints, we did not have enough time to experiment with other options such as the MST parser or the EasyFirst parser.

parser uses history-based feature models and discriminative machine learning. The specification of the learning configuration can include any kind of information (such as word-form, lemma, category, subcategory or morphological features). We will use one of its latest versions (MaltParser version 1.7).

To fine-tune Maltparser we have used MaltOptimizer (Ballesteros and Nivre, 2012a; Ballesteros and Nivre, 2012b). This tool is an interactive system that first performs an analysis of the training set in order to select a suitable starting point for optimization and then guides the user through the optimization of parsing algorithm, feature model, and learning algorithm. Empirical evaluation on data from the CoNLL 2006 and 2007 shared tasks on dependency parsing shows that MaltOptimizer consistently improves over the baseline of default settings and sometimes even surpasses the result of manual optimization.

The Mate parser (Bohnet and Nivre, 2012) is a development of the algorithms described in (Carreras, 2007; Johansson and Nugues, 2008). It basically adopts the second order maximum spanning tree dependency parsing algorithm. In particular, this parser exploits a hash kernel, a new parallel parsing and feature extraction algorithm that improves accuracy as well as parsing speed (Bohnet, 2010).

2.3 Parser Combinations

The MaltBlender tool makes a two-stage optimization of the result of several parser outcomes, based on the work of Sagae and Lavie (2006), and it was used for the first time for the ten languages in the multilingual track of the CoNLL 2007 shared task on dependency parsing(Hall et al., 2010). The first stage consists in tuning several single-parser systems. The second stage consists in building an ensemble system that will combine the different parsers. When this system was evaluated on the official test sets at the CoNLL 2007 shared task, the ensemble system significantly outperformed the single-parser system and achieved the highest average labelled attachment score of all participating systems.

3 Contribution of Morphological Information to Parsing

We examined the effect of each type of morphological information, contained in the *FEATS* column, to investigate their overall contribution to parsing. This will help us to determine which are the most relevant features for parsing. To carry out this task we have used the Mate parser, due to lack of time for testing, and also taking into consideration that it gives better results than MaltParser for all the languages's baselines. Firstly, we will obtain the baseline for each language parsing the files with an empty *FEATS* column. This baseline will help us to determine the contribution of each morphological feature to parsing. Next, we trained the parsers using one feature at a time obtaining as many results as features for each language. Table 1 shows the effect of each information on the Mate parser.

In this table we can observe that Basque is one of the most sensitive languages regarding the influence of its features. Using case (KAS) as a unique feature improves the labelled attachment score over using an empty *FEATS* column by almost 5.7%. The next two better features are number (NUM) and type of subordinate sentence (ERL). They help with a 1.1% and 0.6% increase, respectively. The rest of the features do not contribute much in isolation, with a maximum of 0.2%. On the other hand, including all the features results in an improvement of 6.5%.

If we analyze the results for French we see that, in contrast to Basque, the influence of the features on the parser is minimum. The most significant feature is gender (g), which helps with a 0.1% increase. With respect to the improvement using the other features, although they do not provide big increases all of them contribute positively. In closing, including all the features we obtain a 84.6% labelled attachment score with a 0.4% improvement over not using any features.

As with French, the German morphological features provide small increases. The most two significant features are case and gender, which obtain increases of 0.2%, 0.13%, respectively. It is interesting to observe how including all the features we obtain worse results than using only the case, although the difference is not significant. That could occur due to the weak influence of its features in the final result and the negative influence of some of them.

Hungarian is the language which offers more features, 14 altogether. This language, in line with Basque, tends to vary significantly its labelled attachment score depending on the used morpholog-

Basque	French	German	Hungarian	Swedish
all feats 83.0	**all feats 84.6**	all feats 91.0	**all feats 82.8**	all feats 76.7
no feats 76.5	no feats 84.2	no feats 90.9	no feats 75.3	no feats 76.9
KAS 82.2	g 84.3	**case 91.0**	Cas 80.9	**verbform 77.0**
NUM 77.7	n 84.3	gender 91.0	PerP 76.3	definiteness 76.8
ERL 77.1	p 84.3	number 90.9	NumP 76.3	degree 76.8
DADUDIO 76.8	c 84.2	person 90.9	SubPOS 75.9	case 76.8
NORK 76.7	m 84.2	tense 90.9	Def 75.7	number 76.3
MDN 76.6	s 84.2	degree 90.8	Num 75.7	perfectform 76.3
NOR 76.6	t 84.2	mood 90.8	PerP 75.7	abbrv 76.3
ASP 76.4	_	_	Mood 75.5	mood 76.2
NORI 76.2	_	_	NumPd 75.4	pronounform 76.1
ADM 76.5	_	_	Coord 75.3	gender 76.0
_	_	_	Form 75.3	_
_	_	_	Tense 75.3	_
_	_	_	Type 75.3	_
_	_	_	Deg 75.0	_

Table 1: The effect of each feature sorted by language (MATE parser)

ical feature. If we focus on the three most significant features, the case (Cas) helps with a 5.6% increase, person of possessor (PerP) with a 1%, while number of possessor helps with a 0.9%. The grammatical subcategory within the main part of speech (SubPOS) improves the baseline in a 0.6% and the number and person in a 0.4%. The remaining features do not contribute very appreciatively even obtaining negative results. Including all the features we obtain a labelled attachment score of 82.83%. That means the real contribution of all the features is 7.5%, this improvement being the most important among all the used languages.

In common with French and German, the Swedish morphological features do not seem to help the parsers to achieve significant improvements in terms of *LAS*. However, we can observe some interesting phenomena. While in the other languages the case is one of the best features, in Swedish is does not help, achieving a negative result. In general, excluding the verb form (verbform), all the features obtain negative results with respect to not using any feature. In this scenario it is not surprising to verify that including all the features does not help the Mate parser. Having said this, the best three features are the verb form (verbform), definiteness (definiteness) and degree (degree).

4 Testing the Effect of Different Morphosyntactic features on parsers

We examined the effect of the most significant morphological features, examined in the previous step, to investigate their overall contribution to parsing. For this task, we created three variants for each parser, apart from the baseline using all the morphosyntactic features. We obtain these variants by: i) using the most 3 relevant features in the *FEATS* column (see table 1 in previous section), ii) moving the most relevant feature for each language to the *POS* column and iii) moving the most relevant feature to the *CPOS* column. Next, we have tested parser combinations including all the baselines and their variants in subsection 4.2.

4.1 Individual Parsers

Table 2 shows the effect of each information on both parsers, Maltparser and Mate parser. If we analyze the results on Basque, the difference between the two parsers is noticeable, as Mate obtains on average a 3 point improvement with respect to MaltParser. A similar difference occurs on all the used languages. The best *LAS* in Basque is acquired using the 3 best features in the *FEATS* column with the Mate parser (83.4%). On a comparison with the *LAS* obtained by the Mate baseline (All-Feats), that means a 0.4 improvement. Regarding Maltparser's results for Basque, we get the best *LAS* (81.0%) moving the best feature (case) to *POS* in its right-to-left version, increasing the *LAS* baseline (All-Feats) by 1.0. We notice that Maltparser and Mate tend to improve their baseline scores using some of the presented variants.

On the other hand, the best score for French is obtained using the baseline (All-Feats and

	Basque	French	German	Hungarian	Swedish
Baselines					
$All - Feats_{Malt}$	80.0	79.9	87.6	77.3	73.4
$All - Feats_{Mate}$	83.0	84.6	91.0	82.3	76.7
Left2right					
$3 - best_{Malt}$	79.9	**79.9**	**87.6**	75.9	73.4
$CPOS - best_{Malt}$	80.3	79.7	87.5	76.6	**72.9**
$POS - best_{Malt}$	78.7	78.7	86.6	**77.2**	72.8
$3 - best_{Mate}$	**83.4**	84.3	90.8	82.4	76.6
$CPOS - best_{Mate}$	82.7	84.3	91.0	**82.7**	76.8
$POS - best_{Mate}$	82.2	83.4	90.5	82.5	76.5
Right2left					
$3 - best_{Malt}$	80.1	78.9	86.9	75.3	69.3
$CPOS - best_{Malt}$	80.0	79.0	86.7	76.6	69.3
$POS - best_{Malt}$	**81.0**	77.8	85.4	74.9	70.2
$3 - best_{Mate}$	83.3	84.3	90.9	82.1	76.5
$CPOS - best_{Mate}$	83.1	**84.6**	**91.0**	82.6	**77.0**
$POS - best_{Mate}$	81.6	83.5	90.6	82.4	76.4

Table 2: Testing the effect of features on MaltParser and Mate

the Mate parser, 84,6%). Contrary to Basque, in French, although some of the used variants achieve similar scores with respect to their baselines (All-Feats), they do not give noticeable increases. The unique variant that equals its baseline (79,9%) is $3 - best_{Malt}$ using the left-to-right version and the three best features (gender, number and person) in the *FEATS* column using Maltparser.

With respect to German, the only variant that equals the baseline is $CPOS - best_{Mate}$ with 91.0% *LAS*. . If we focus on Maltparser's (MaltOptimizer) scores, we get the best result among the variants with $3 - best_{Malt}$ (87.6%) using the left-to-right version. The variants do not improve Maltparser's baseline.

Although some of the Hungarian variant scores are very similar to their baselines, they give some improvements over the baseline. The best two results on the Mate parser are 82.7% and 82.6%. We obtain the first score moving the best feature (case) to *CPOS* in its left-to-right version, and the second one using the same configuration in its right-to-left version. The best two scores on Maltparser without taking the baseline into account are 77.2% and 76.6%, obtained when moving the best feature to *POS* and moving the best feature to *CPOS* in its right-to-left version, respectively.

The best two results for Swedish on the Mate parser are 77.0% and 76.8%. We get the first result moving the best feature (verbform) to *CPOS* in its right-to-left version and the second one in its standard version. These two results are the only variants that improve the baseline (76.7% *LAS*) with a 0.30 and 0.17 increase, respectively. On the other hand, if we focus on Maltparser, the variants do not improve the baseline (73.4% *LAS*) where the best two results are 73.4% and 72.9% *LAS*. For the best result we use the three best features (verbform, definiteness and degree) in the *FEATS* column, while for the second one the best feature (verbform) has been moved to *CPOS*.

Despite that only the Basque and Swedish variants haven been able to significantly improve their baselines, in the next subsection we present a combination system expecting to take advantage on the variety of the parsed files (Surdeanu and Manning, 2010).

4.2 Parser Combinations

Although in several cases the use of specific morphosyntactic information does not give noticeable increases, we also tested the effect on parser combinations. Table 3 presents the result of combining the extended parsers with the baselines (using all the features) obtained in individual parsers. The table shows that the Basque language has achieved the biggest increase. Parser combination in Basque helps with an improvement of 3.2 with respect to the Mate baseline. Contrary to Basque, French is the language that has obtained the smallest increases in parser combination if we compare it with the Mate (highest) parser baseline. The combined system improves the Mate parser base-

	Basque	French	German	Hungarian	Swedish
MaltParser baseline	80.0	79.9	87.6	77.3	73.4
Mate parser baseline	83.0	84.6	91.0	82.8	76.7
Parser combination	86.2	85.1	91.8	84.1	78.1

Table 3: Results of parser combinations

line by 0.5. Parser combination in German gives a 0.8 increase with respect to the best single parser (Mate, 91.0). Our system achieves a 1.3 increase for Hungarian with respect to the Mate parser's baseline. Finally, if we focus on Swedish, the parser combination helps with a 1.4 increase with respect to the Mate parser.

After examining the parsers involved in parser combinations we noticed that there are always several variants included in the best parser combinations, although the only variant that appears in all the best parser combinations is $CPOS - best_{Mate}$ in its left-to-right version. Taking into account that the most relevant feature for Basque, German and Hungarian is the case, it would be interesting to use the $CPOS - case_{Mate}$ variant for other languages. Finally, the presented results suggest that the introduced variants contribute positively on parsing and they help to improve the scores obtained by the base parsers.

5 Conclusion and Future Work

We have presented a combined system that was designed after analyzing the relevance of the morphological features in order to take advantage on the effect of those features on some parsers. In general the improvements have been noticeable, specially for Basque. We can point out some interesting avenues for research:

- Use of new parsing algorithms for testing the effect of different morphological features. The results of this work show that the used techniques are specially useful for languages where the *FEATS* column, containing morpho-syntactic information, gives the biggest increments with respect to not using the features, like Basque and Hungarian. We expect that similar improvements could be obtained for languages like Turkish or Czech, which share many characteristics with Basque and Hungarian.

- Experimenting different models for parser combinations using new parsers. Several of the parser variants we have used give only slight modifications over the base algorithms, even though when combined they give significant increases. Widening the spectrum of parsers and adding new algorithms can imply an important boost in parser combination.

- Application to the rest of the languages of the *SPMRL 2013 Shared Task*: Korean, Hebrew, Arabic and Polish.

Acknowledgements

This research was supported by the Department of Industry of the Basque Government (IT344-10, S PE11UN114), the University of the Basque Country (GIU09/19) and the Spanish Ministry of Science and Innovation (MICINN, TIN2010-20218).

References

Anne Abeillé, Lionel Clément, and François Toussenel. 2003. Building a treebank for french. In Anne Abeillé, editor, *Treebanks*. Kluwer, Dordrecht.

I. Aduriz, M. J. Aranzabe, J. M. Arriola, A. Atutxa, A. Díaz de Ilarraza, A. Garmendia, and M. Oronoz. 2003. Construction of a Basque dependency treebank. pages 201–204.

Bharat Ram Ambati, Samar Husain, Sambhav Jain, Dipti Misra Sharma, and Rajeev Sangal. 2010. Two methods to incorporate local morphosyntactic features in hindi dependency parsing. In *Proceedings of the NAACL HLT 2010 First Workshop on Statistical Parsing of Morphologically-Rich Languages*, pages 22–30.

Miguel Ballesteros and Joakim Nivre. 2012a. Maltoptimizer: A system for maltparser optimization. In *LREC*, pages 2757–2763.

Miguel Ballesteros and Joakim Nivre. 2012b. Maltoptimizer: an optimization tool for maltparser. In *Proceedings of the Demonstrations at the 13th Conference of the European Chaptr of the Association for Computational Linguistics*, pages 58–62.

Kepa Bengoetxea and Koldo Gojenola. 2010. Application of different techniques to dependency parsing of basque. In *Proceedings of the NAACL HLT 2010 First Workshop on Statistical Parsing of Morphologically-Rich Languages*, pages 31–39.

Bernd Bohnet and Joakim Nivre. 2012. A transition-based system for joint part-of-speech tagging and labeled non-projective dependency parsing. In *Proceedings of the 2012 Joint Conference on Empirical Methods in Natural Language Processing and Computational Natural Language Learning*, pages 1455–1465.

Bernd Bohnet. 2010. Very high accuracy and fast dependency parsing is not a contradiction. In *Proceedings of the 23rd International Conference on Computational Linguistics*, pages 89–97.

Xavier Carreras. 2007. Experiments with a higher-order projective dependency parser. In *Proceedings of the CoNLL Shared Task Session of EMNLP-CoNLL 2007*, Prague, Czech Republic, June.

Özlem Çetinoğlu and Jonas Kuhn. 2013. Towards joint morphological analysis and dependency parsing of turkish. In *Proceedings of the Second International Conference on Dependency Linguistics (DepLing 2013)*, pages 23–32, Prague, Czech Republic, August. Charles University in Prague, Matfyzpress, Prague, Czech Republic.

Gülsen Eryigit. 2007. Itu validation set for metu-sabancı turkish treebank. *URL: http://www3. itu. edu. tr/ gulsenc/papers/validationset. pdf.*

Johan Hall, Jens Nilsson, and Joakim Nivre. 2010. Single malt or blended? a study in multilingual parser optimization. In *Trends in Parsing Technology*, pages 19–33. Springer.

Richard Johansson and Pierre Nugues. 2008. Dependency-based syntactic-semantic analysis with propbank and nombank. In *Proceedings of the Twelfth Conference on Computational Natural Language Learning*, pages 183–187.

Yuval Marton, Nizar Habash, and Owen Rambow. 2013. Dependency parsing of modern standard arabic with lexical and inflectional features. *Computational Linguistics*, 39(1):161–194.

Joakim Nivre, Jens Nilsson, and Johan Hall. 2006. Talbanken05: A Swedish treebank with phrase structure and dependency annotation. In *Proceedings of LREC*, pages 1392–1395, Genoa, Italy.

Joakim Nivre, Johan Hall, Sandra Kübler, Ryan McDonald, Jens Nilsson, Sebastian Riedel, and Deniz Yuret. 2007. The CoNLL 2007 shared task on dependency parsing. In *Proceedings of the CoNLL Shared Task Session of EMNLP-CoNLL 2007*, Prague, Czech Republic, June.

Joakim Nivre, Johan Hall, Jens Nilsson, Atanas Chanev, Gülsen Eryigit, Sandra Kübler, Svetoslav Marinov, and Erwin Marsi. 2007b. Maltparser: A language-independent system for data-driven dependency parsing. *Natural Language Engineering*, 13(2):95–135.

Kemal Oflazer, Bilge Say, Dilek Zeynep Hakkani-Tür, and Gökhan Tür. 2003. Building a turkish treebank. *Building and Exploiting Syntactically-annotated Corpora.*

Kenji Sagae and Alon Lavie. 2006. Parser combination by reparsing. In *Proceedings of the Human Language Technology Conference of the North American Chapter of the ACL.*

Djamé Seddah, Reut Tsarfaty, Sandra Kübler, Marie Candito, Jinho Choi, Richárd Farkas, Jennifer Foster, Iakes Goenaga, Koldo Gojenola, Yoav Goldberg, Spence Green, Nizar Habash, Marco Kuhlmann, Wolfgang Maier, Joakim Nivre, Adam Przepiorkowski, Ryan Roth, Wolfgang Seeker, Yannick Versley, Veronika Vincze, Marcin Woliński, Alina Wróblewska, and Eric Villemonte de la Clérgerie. 2013. Overview of the spmrl 2013 shared task: A cross-framework evaluation of parsing morphologically rich languages. In *Proceedings of the 4th Workshop on Statistical Parsing of Morphologically Rich Languages: Shared Task*, Seattle, WA.

Wolfgang Seeker and Jonas Kuhn. 2012. Making Ellipses Explicit in Dependency Conversion for a German Treebank. In *Proceedings of the 8th International Conference on Language Resources and Evaluation*, pages 3132–3139, Istanbul, Turkey. European Language Resources Association (ELRA).

Wolfgang Seeker and Jonas Kuhn. 2013. Morphological and syntactic case in statistical dependency parsing. *Computational Linguistics*, 39(1):23–55.

Mihai Surdeanu and Christopher D. Manning. 2010. Ensemble models for dependency parsing: Cheap and good? In *Proceedings of the North American Chapter of the Association for Computational Linguistics Conference (NAACL-2010)*, Los Angeles, CA, June.

Reut Tsarfaty, Djam Seddah, Yoav Goldberg, Sandra Kübler, Marie Candito, Jennifer Foster, Yannick Versley, Ines Rehbein, and Lamia Tounsi. 2010. Statistical parsing of morphologically rich languages (spmrl) what, how and whither. In *In Proceedings of the NAACL HLT 2010 First Workshop on Statistical Parsing of Morphologically-Rich Languages.*

Veronika Vincze, Dóra Szauter, Attila Almási, György Móra, Zoltán Alexin, and János Csirik. 2010. Hungarian dependency treebank. In *LREC.*

The AI-KU System at the SPMRL 2013 Shared Task : Unsupervised Features for Dependency Parsing

Volkan Cirik **Husnu Sensoy**
Artificial Intelligence Laboratory
Koç University, İstanbul, Turkey
{vcirik,hsensoy}@ku.edu.tr

Abstract

We propose the use of the word categories and embeddings induced from raw text as auxiliary features in dependency parsing. To induce word features, we make use of contextual, morphologic and orthographic properties of the words. To exploit the contextual information, we make use of substitute words, the most likely substitutes for target words, generated by using a statistical language model. We generate morphologic and orthographic properties of word types in an unsupervised manner. We use a co-occurrence model with these properties to embed words onto a 25-dimensional unit sphere. The AI-KU system shows improvements for some of the languages it is trained on for the first Shared Task of Statistical Parsing of Morphologically Rich Languages.

1 Introduction

For the first shared task of Workshop on Statistical Parsing of Morphologically Rich Languages (Seddah et al., 2013), we propose to use unsupervised features as auxillary features for dependency parsing.

We induce the unsupervised features using contextual, morphological and orthographic properties of the words. We use possible substitutes of the target word which are generated by a statistical language model to exploit the contextual information. We induce morphological features with a HMM-based model (Creutz and Lagus, 2005). We combine contextual, morphological and orthographic features of co-occurring words within the co-occurrence data embedding framework (Maron et al., 2010). The framework embeds word types sharing similar context, morphological and orthographic properties closely on a 25-dimensional sphere. Thus, it provides the word embeddings on a 25 dimensional sphere. We conduct experiments using these word embeddings with MaltParser (Nivre et al., 2007) and MaltOptimizer (Ballesteros and Nivre, 2012). In addition to CONLL features (Buchholz and Marsi, 2006a), they are added as additional features and the parsers are configured such that they are able to exploit these additional features. As a first step we use real valued word embeddings as they are. Secondly, we discretize the real valued word embeddings. Finally, we cluster them and find fine-grained word categories for word types.

Our experiments show that, the AI-KU system leads to better results than the baseline experiments for some languages. We claim that with the correct parameter settings, these unsupervised features could be useful for dependency parsing.

In the following sections, we introduce the related work, the algorithm, experiments, results and provide a conclusion.

2 Related Work

The features extracted from unlabeled corpora are already used for all major NLP tasks. Early studies mainly use clustering based representations (especially Brown clustering (Brown et al., 1992)) to obtain those features. Miller et al. (2004; Freitag (2004) utilized Brown Clusters to improve Named Entity Recognition (NER) performance whereas Biemann et al. (2007) used them for NER, Word Sense Disambiguation(WSD), and chunking. Ushioda (1996) extended Brown Clustering to cluster not only words but also phrases using hierarcical clustering and uses them to improve supervised part-of-speech (PoS) tagging. More recently, Brown Clusters are used for Chinese word segmentation and NER (Liang, 2005).

Just like other tasks, clustering based representations are used to improve parser performance. Koo et al. (2008; Suzuki et al. (2009) improved dependency parsing by using Brown clusters. While Candito and Seddah (2010; Candito and Crabbé (2009) improved PCFG parsing by using them and Goldberg et al. (2009) improved PCFG parser for Hebrew by using HMM generated features. More recently Socher et al. (2010) used word embeddings computed using method explained in (Collobert and Weston, 2008) for syntactic parsing.

3 Algorithm

In this section, the general flow of the algorithm will be presented. First, we explain how we generate the substitute vectors. Then, we explain the induction procedure of morphological features. In the following subsection, we explain how we use substitute vectors and morphological features and generate word embeddings. The same flow is followed for all languages we work on.

3.1 Substitute Vectors

A target word's substitute vector is represented by the vocabulary of words and their corresponding probabilities of occurring in the position of the target word.

(1) " Nobody **thought** you could just inject DNA into someone 's body and they would just suck it up."

Probability	Substitute Word
0.123	thought
0.091	knew
0.064	felt
0.062	said
0.052	believed
0.037	wish

Table 1: Substitute Vector for "thought" in above sentence.

Table 1 illustrates the substitute vector of "thought" in (1). There is a row for each word in the vocabulary. For instance, probability of "knew" occurring in the position of "thought" is 9.1% in this context.

To calculate these probabilities, as described in (Yatbaz et al., 2012), a 4-gram language model is built with SRILM (Stolcke, 2002) on the corpora of the target languages. For French, Hungarian, Polish and Swedish we used Europarl Corpus[1](Koehn, 2005). For German, CONLL-X German Corpus is used (Buchholz and Marsi, 2006b). For Hebrew, we combined HaAretz and Arutz 7 corpora of MILA[2](Itai and Wintner, 2008). For the tokens seen less than 5 times we replace them with an unknown tag to handle unseen words in training and test data. We should note that these corpora are not provided to the other participants.

To estimate probabilities of lexical substitutes, for every token in our datasets, we use three tokens each on the left and the right side of the token as a context. Using Fastsubs (Yuret, 2012) we generated top 100 most likely substitute words. Top 100 substitute probabilities are then normalized to represent a proper probability distribution.

We should emphasize that a substitute vector is a function of the context and does not depend on the target word.

3.2 Morphological Features

In order to generate unsupervised word features, the second set of features that we use are morphological and orthographic features.

The orthographic feature set used is similar to the one defined in (Berg-Kirkpatrick et al.,2010)

INITIAL-CAP	Capitalized words with the exception of sentence initial words.
NUMBER	The token starts with a digit.
CONTAINS-HYPHEN	Lowercase words with an internal hyphen.
INITIAL-APOSTROPHE	Tokens that start with an apostrophe.

The morpological features are obtained using the unlabeled corpora that are used for the generation

[1]http://www.statmt.org/europarl/

[2]http://www.mila.cs.technion.ac.il

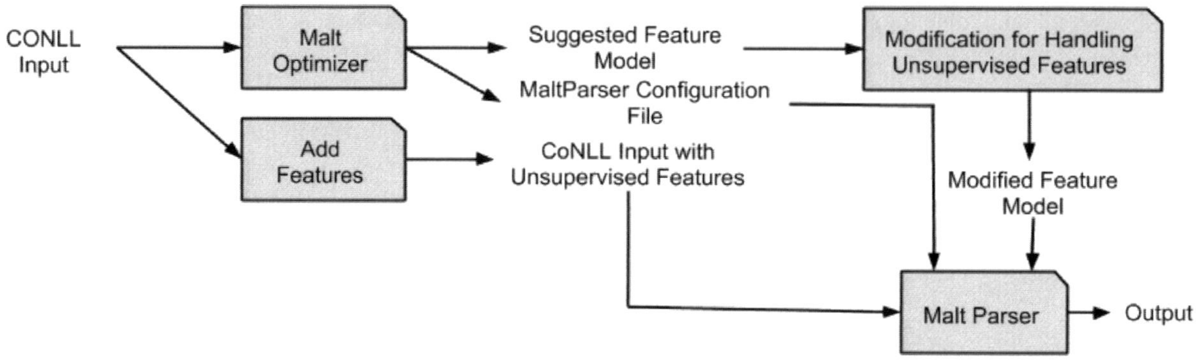

Figure 1: The Flow of The Modification for Handling New Features

of substitute vectors, using Morfessor defined in (Creutz and Lagus, 2005). We will only give a brief sketch of the model used. Morfessor splits each word into morphemes (word itself may also be a morpheme) which can be categorized under four groups, namely prefix, stem, suffix, non-morpheme. The model is defined as *a maximum a posteriori* (MAP) estimate which maximizes the lexicon (set of morphemes) over the corpus.

The maximization problem is solved by using a greedy algorithm that iteratively splits and merges morphemes, then re-segments corpus using Viterbi algorithm and reestimates probabilities until convergence. Finally, a final merge step takes place to remove all non-morphemes.

3.3 Co-occurence Embedding

For a pair of categorical variables, the Spherical Co-occurrence Data Embedding (S-CODE) framework (Maron et al., 2010) represents each of their values on a sphere such that frequently co-occurring values are positioned closely on this sphere.

The input of S-CODE are tuples of values of categorical variables. In our case, these are word tokens, their substitutes, morphological and orthograpic features. We construct the tuples by sampling substitute words using substitute vectors, their corresponding morphological and orthographic features of the tokens. On each row of the co-occurrence input, there are the target token, its substitute sampled from its substitute vector, morphological and orthographic features. Tokens having the similar substitutes, morphological and orthographic features will be closely located on the sphere at the end of this process. As in (Yatbaz et al., 2012), the dimension of the sphere is 25, in other words for each word type seen in the corpora we have a 25 dimensional vector[3].

4 Experiments

We conduct experiments using MaltParser (Nivre et al., 2007) and MaltOptimizer (Ballesteros and Nivre, 2012) with features provided in CONLL format and the additional unsupervised features that we generated with default settings of the parsers. To make use of additional features, we need to modify MaltParser accordingly. Figure 1 shows that how we use MaltOptimizer and MaltParser with new features. In order to handle auxiliary features, the feature model file is modified in two different ways. We handle new features with feature functions Input[0] and Stack[0][4]. We should note that other feature functions should also be experimented as a future work.

The following subsections explain the details of the experiments.

4.1 Experiment I

Our first approach was trying to use word embeddings as they are with the MaltParser. For each token in the training and the test set, we added the corresponding 25-dimensional word vector from the word embeddings file to the training and test sets. If the word type is not present in the word embeddings, then, we use the unknown word vector.

[3]The vectors can be downloaded here : https://github.com/wolet/sprml13-word-embeddings

[4]Thanks for Joakim Nivre for his suggestions on this

	Stack[0]			Input[0]		
	LAS	UAS	LaA	LAS	UAS	Labeled Accuracy
Real Valued Vectors	80.56	84.33	85.78	80.63	84.38	85.92
Binning, b=5	80.25	84.07	85.58	80.45	84.20	85.79
Binning, b=2	80.41	84.19	85.79	80.47	84.26	85.77
Clustering, k = 50	80.48	84.29	85.79	80.50	84.24	85.78
Clustering k = 300	80.49	84.23	85.83	80.58	84.31	85.82

	LAS	UAS	LaS
Baseline	80.36	84.11	85.72

Table 2: Results on German with MaltParser of Development Set with Default Settings

	Stack[0]			Input[0]		
	LAS	UAS	LaS	LAS	UAS	LaS
Real Valued Vectors	87.30	89.33	93.35	87.29	89.30	93.32
Binning, b =2	87.12	89.20	93.20	87.04	89.11	93.16
Clustering, k = 300	90.30	91.80	95.09	90.49	91.94	95.19

	LAS	UAS	LaS
Baseline	90.38	91.88	95.14

Table 3: Results on German with MaltOptimizer of Development Set

	Gold			Predicted		
	LAS	UAS	LaS	LAS	UAS	LaS
Best System	90.29	91.92	95.95	85.86	89.19	92.20
AI-KU 1	86.39	88.21	94.07	72.57	78.54	82.39
AI-KU 2	86.31	88.14	94.05	72.55	78.55	82.36
Baseline	85.71	87.50	93.70	79.00	83.35	87.73

	Predicted (Unofficial)		
	LAS	UAS	LaS
AI-KU 1	79.92	83.94	88.51
AI-KU 2	79.84	83.85	88.45

Table 4: Results on French

	Gold			Predicted		
	LAS	UAS	LaS	LAS	UAS	LaS
Best System	91.83	93.20	96.06	86.95	91.64	94.38
AI-KU 1	86.98	88.71	93.70	82.32	85.31	89.95
AI-KU 2	86.95	88.67	93.67	82.29	85.30	89.95
Baseline	86.96	87.67	93.67	82.75	85.38	90.15

	Predicted (Unofficial)		
	LAS	UAS	LaS
AI-KU 1	84.08	86.71	91.13
AI-KU 2	83.93	86.54	91.05

Table 5: Results on German

	Gold			Predicted		
	LAS	UAS	LaS	LAS	UAS	LaS
Best System	83.87	88.95	89.19	80.89	86.7	86.93
AI-KU 1	79.42	84.48	86.52	69.01	75.84	79.01
AI-KU 2	78.73	83.79	85.98	62.27	75.84	79.01
Baseline	80.03	84.9	86.97	73.01	79.89	81.28

Table 6: Results on Hebrew

	Gold			Predicted		
	LAS	UAS	LaS	LAS	UAS	LaS
Best System	88.06	91.14	92.58	86.13	89.81	90.92
AI-KU 1	83.67	87.08	89.64	78.92	83.77	85.98
AI-KU 2	83.63	87.06	89.58	78.76	83.60	85.95
Baseline	83.14	86.56	89.20	79.63	83.71	85.89

	Predicted (Unofficial)		
	LAS	UAS	LaS
AI-KU 1	79.98	84.42	87.12
AI-KU 2	79.74	84.12	86.93

Table 7: Results on Hungarian

	Gold			Predicted		
	LAS	UAS	LaS	LAS	UAS	LaS
Best System	89.58	93.24	93.42	87.07	91.75	91.24
AI-KU 1	85.16	88.86	90.87	81.86	86.96	88.06
AI-KU 2	85.12	88.79	90.84	78.31	84.18	85.64
Baseline	80.49	86.41	86.94	79.89	85.80	86.24

Table 8: Results on Polish

	Gold			Predicted		
	LAS	UAS	LaS	LAS	UAS	LaS
Best System	83.97	89.11	87.63	82.13	88.06	85.93
AI-KU 1	78.87	85.19	83.44	76.35	83.30	81.37
AI-KU 2	78.57	85.12	83.25	76.35	83.24	81.35
Baseline	77.67	84.6	82.36	75.82	83.20	80.88

Table 9: Results on Swedish

	Gold			Predicted		
	Precision	Recall	F1	Precision	Recal	F1
Best System	99.41	99.38	99.39	81.68	79.97	80.81
AI-KU 1	99.41	99.38	99.39	74.47	71.51	72.96
AI-KU 2	99.38	99.36	99.37	74.34	71.51	72.89
MaltOptimizer Baseline	98.77	99.18	99.26	72.64	68.09	70.29

Table 10: Results of Multi Word Expressions on French

4.2 Experiment II

The second approach is discretizing the real valued vectors. For each dimension of word embeddings, we separate b equal sized bins. Then, for each vector's dimensions, we assign their corresponding bin numbers.

4.3 Experiment III

The third approach is clustering the word embeddings. We use a modified k-means algorithm (Arthur and Vassilvitskii, 2007). We experiment with varying number of clusters k.

For each token in training and test file, we use word type's cluster id as an auxiliary feature. Again, if the token is not in the word embeddings file, we used the unknown word's cluster id.

5 Results

In Table 2, the experiments on German with MaltParser without the optimization step are demonstrated. We use the default settings of the MaltParser as our baseline. We use training data consisting of 5000 sentences with gold tags as training set and the provided development data as test set.

When we use real valued word embeddings as an auxiliary feature, we observe slight improvement compared to MaltParser baseline. The large binning size results in worse results compared to baseline due to sparsity. Clustering again leads to some improvement compared to MaltParser baseline. We also observe that increasing the number of clusters result in better scores compared to smaller k.

In Table 3, the results on German with MaltOptimizer can be seen. As a baseline, again, we use training data consisting of 5000 sentences with gold tags as training set and the provided development data as test set. We use the baseline experiment's parsing algorithm, feature model and learning algorithm to experiment with word embedding, binning and clustering on MaltParser.

Unlike in Table 2, in Table 3 we observe that only the clustering experiment outperforms the baseline but not significantly. Since clustering is leads to best results, for all other languages, we apply the same optimization and clustering pipeline. The only difference is that when the MaltOptimizer suggests Stack Projective as the best algorithm, instead of Input[0] ve use Stack[0], Stack[1], Stack[2] as feature functions. The two systems of AI-KU only differ in these feature functions.

In Table 3-7, the results of the best system, baseline MaltOptimizer result and our two submitted systems can be seen. For Polish, our system outperfoms the MaltOptimizer baseline significantly. For the rest of the languages, our systems are not significantly better or worse than the baseline. We make an assumption that we need to find the optimum settings, for instance the number of clusters, for each language separately, instead of using the fixed settings for all languages.

For French, German, Hungarian the model trained on the data with gold features is mistakenly used for testing on the data with predicted features. To correct these, for those languages, we report the unofficial results that are obtained by training on predicted features.

For French, there is also another evaluation metric. It is about capturing the Multi Word Expressions(MWE). Table 10 reports the results of MWE and it shows that our system is significantly better than MaltOptimizer baseline.

6 Conclusion

We can speculate on these results in couple of ways. First, for all languages we used the same number of clusters. The optimum number of clusters may vary with the syntactic properties of these languages. Similarly, the optimum dimension of the word embeddings may vary with the languages. In addition, for co-occurence embedding and morphological induction we use the parameter settings of (Yatbaz et al., 2012) which is optimized for Part-of-Speech induction on Penn Treebank data. We suggest to find the optimum parameter settings for co-occurrence embedding and morphological induction as a future work.

We only experimented with simple feature functions, namely Input and Stack functions. Other configuration of these functions may lead to better results. Lastly, as a future direction, we propose to use real valued word embeddings and unsupervised word categories as auxiliary features in the training phase of the MaltOptimizer.

Acknowledgments

We would like to thank Joakim Nivre and Deniz Yuret for valuable suggestions and their support.

References

D. Arthur and S. Vassilvitskii. 2007. k-means++: The advantages of careful seeding. In *Proceedings of the eighteenth annual ACM-SIAM symposium on Discrete algorithms*, pages 1027–1035. Society for Industrial and Applied Mathematics.

Miguel Ballesteros and Joakim Nivre. 2012. Maltoptimizer: A system for maltparser optimization. In *LREC*, pages 2757–2763.

Chris Biemann, Claudio Giuliano, and Alfio Gliozzo. 2007. Unsupervised part-of-speech tagging supporting supervised methods. In *Proceedings of RANLP*, volume 7.

Peter F Brown, Peter V Desouza, Robert L Mercer, Vincent J Della Pietra, and Jenifer C Lai. 1992. Class-based n-gram models of natural language. *Computational linguistics*, 18(4):467–479.

S. Buchholz and E. Marsi. 2006a. CoNLL-X shared task on multilingual dependency parsing. SIGNLL.

Sabine Buchholz and Erwin Marsi. 2006b. Conll-x shared task on multilingual dependency parsing. In *Proceedings of the Tenth Conference on Computational Natural Language Learning*, CoNLL-X '06, pages 149–164, Stroudsburg, PA, USA. Association for Computational Linguistics.

Marie Candito and Benoît Crabbé. 2009. Improving generative statistical parsing with semi-supervised word clustering. In *Proceedings of the 11th International Conference on Parsing Technologies*, pages 138–141. Association for Computational Linguistics.

Marie Candito and Djamé Seddah. 2010. Parsing word clusters. In *Proceedings of the NAACL HLT 2010 First Workshop on Statistical Parsing of Morphologically-Rich Languages*, pages 76–84. Association for Computational Linguistics.

Ronan Collobert and Jason Weston. 2008. A unified architecture for natural language processing: Deep neural networks with multitask learning. In *Proceedings of the 25th international conference on Machine learning*, pages 160–167. ACM.

Mathias Creutz and Krista Lagus. 2005. Inducing the morphological lexicon of a natural language from unannotated text. In *Proceedings of AKRR'05, International and Interdisciplinary Conference on Adaptive Knowledge Representation and Reasoning*, pages 106–113, Espoo, Finland, June.

Dayne Freitag. 2004. Trained named entity recognition using distributional clusters. *In Proceedings of EMNLP*, pages 262–269.

Yoav Goldberg, Reut Tsarfaty, Meni Adler, and Michael Elhadad. 2009. Enhancing unlexicalized parsing performance using a wide coverage lexicon, fuzzy tag-set mapping, and em-hmm-based lexical probabilities. In *Proceedings of the 12th Conference of the European Chapter of the Association for Computational Linguistics*, pages 327–335. Association for Computational Linguistics.

Alon Itai and Shuly Wintner. 2008. Language resources for Hebrew. *Language Resources and Evaluation*, 42(1):75–98, March.

Philipp Koehn. 2005. Europarl: A parallel corpus for statistical machine translation. In *MT summit*, volume 5.

Terry Koo, Xavier Carreras, and Michael Collins. 2008. Simple semi-supervised dependency parsing. Columbus, Ohio USA, June. ACL.

Percy Liang. 2005. Semi-supervised learning for natural language. Master's thesis, MIT, May.

Yariv Maron, Michael Lamar, and Elie Bienenstock. 2010. Sphere embedding: An application to part-of-speech induction. In J. Lafferty, C. K. I. Williams, J. Shawe-Taylor, R.S. Zemel, and A. Culotta, editors, *Advances in Neural Information Processing Systems 23*, pages 1567–1575.

Scott Miller, Jethran Guinness, and Alex Zamanian. 2004. Name tagging with word clusters and discriminative training. In *In Proceedings of HLT-NAACL*, pages 337–342.

Joakim Nivre, Johan Hall, Jens Nilsson, Atanas Chanev, Gülsen Eryigit, Sandra Kübler, Svetoslav Marinov, and Erwin Marsi. 2007. Maltparser: A language-independent system for data-driven dependency parsing. *Natural Language Engineering*, 13(2):95–135.

Djame Seddah, Reut Tsarfaty, Sandra Kubler, Marie Candito, Jinho Choi, Richard Farkas, Jennifer Foster, Iakes Goenaga, Koldo Gojenola, Yoav Goldberg, Spence Green, Nizar Habash, Marco Kuhlmann, Wolfgang Maier, Joakim Nivre, Adam Przepiorkowski, Ryan Roth, Wolfgang Seeker, Yannick Versley, Veronika Vincze, Marcin Wolinski, Alina Wroblewska, and Eric Villemonte de la Clergerie. 2013. Overview of the spmrl 2013 shared task: A cross-framework evaluation of parsing morphologically rich languages. In *Proceedings of the 4th Workshop on Statistical Parsing of Morphologically Rich Languages: Shared Task*, Seattle, WA.

Richard Socher, Christopher D Manning, and Andrew Y Ng. 2010. Learning continuous phrase representations and syntactic parsing with recursive neural networks. In *Proceedings of the NIPS-2010 Deep Learning and Unsupervised Feature Learning Workshop*.

Andreas Stolcke. 2002. Srilm-an extensible language modeling toolkit. In *Proceedings International Conference on Spoken Language Processing*, pages 257–286, November.

Jun Suzuki, Hideki Isozaki, Xavier Carreras, and Michael Collins. 2009. An empirical study of semi-supervised structured conditional models for dependency parsing. In *Proceedings of the 2009 Conference on Empirical Methods in Natural Language Processing: Volume 2-Volume 2*, pages 551–560. Association for Computational Linguistics.

Akira Ushioda. 1996. Hierarchical clustering of words and applications to nlp tasks. *In Proceedings of the Fourth Workshop on Very Large Corpora*, pages 28–41.

Mehmet Ali Yatbaz, Enis Sert, and Deniz Yuret. 2012. Learning syntactic categories using paradigmatic representations of word context. In *Proceedings of the 2012 Joint Conference on Empirical Methods in Natural Language Processing and Computational Natural Language Learning*, pages 940–951, Jeju Island, Korea, July. Association for Computational Linguistics.

Deniz Yuret. 2012. Fastsubs: An efficient and exact procedure for finding the most likely lexical substitutes based on an n-gram language model. *Signal Processing Letters, IEEE*, 19(11):725–728, Nov.

SPMRL'13 Shared Task System: The CADIM Arabic Dependency Parser

Yuval Marton
Microsoft Corporation
City Center Plaza
Bellevue, WA, USA

Nizar Habash, Owen Rambow
CCLS
Columbia University
New York, NY, USA

Sarah Alkuhlani
CS Department
Columbia University
New York, NY, USA

cadim@ccls.columbia.edu

Abstract

We describe the submission from the Columbia Arabic & Dialect Modeling group (CADIM) for the Shared Task at the Fourth Workshop on Statistical Parsing of Morphologically Rich Languages (SPMRL'2013). We participate in the Arabic Dependency parsing task for predicted POS tags and features. Our system is based on Marton et al. (2013).

1 Introduction

In this paper, we discuss the system that the Columbia Arabic & Dialect Modeling group (CADIM) submitted to the 2013 Shared Task on Parsing Morphologically Rich Languages (Seddah et al., 2013). We used a system for Arabic dependency parsing which we had previously developed, but retrained it on the training data splits used in this task. We only participated in the Arabic dependency parsing track, and in it, only optimized for predicted (non-gold) POS tags and features.

We first summarize our previous work (Section 2). We then discuss our submission and the results (Section 3).

2 Approach

In this section, we summarize Marton et al. (2013). We first present some background information on Arabic morphology and then discuss our methodology and main results. We present our best performing set of features, which we also use in our SPMRL'2013 submission.

2.1 Background

Morphology interacts with syntax in two ways: agreement and assignment. In *agreement*, there is coordination between the morphological features of two words in a sentence based on their syntactic configuration (e.g., subject-verb or noun-adjective agreement in GENDER and/or NUMBER). In *assignment*, specific morphological feature values are assigned in certain syntactic configurations (e.g., CASE assignment for the subject or direct object of a verb).

The choice of optimal linguistic features for a parser depends on three factors: relevance, redundancy and accuracy. A feature has **relevance** if it is useful in making an attachment (or labeling) decision. A particular feature may or may not be relevant to parsing. For example, the GENDER feature may help parse the Arabic phrase باب السيارة الجديد/الجديدة *bAb AlsyAr¯hAljdyd/Aljdyd¯h* 'door the-car the-new$_{masc.sg/fem.sg}$ [lit.]' using syntactic agreement: if *the-new* is masculine (*Aljdyd* الجديد), it should attach to the masculine *door* (*bAb* باب), resulting in the meaning 'the car's new door'; if *the-new* is feminine (*Aljdyd¯h* الجديدة), it should attach to the feminine *the-car* (*AlsyAr¯h* السيارة), resulting in 'the door of the new car'. In contrast, the ASPECT feature does

[1] Arabic orthographic transliteration is presented in the HSB scheme (Habash et al., 2007): (in alphabetical order)
ا ب ت ث ج ح خ د ذ ر ز س ش ص ض ط ظ ع غ ف ق ك ل م ن ه و ي
A b t θ j H x d ð r z s š S D T Ď ς γ f q k l m n h w y
and the additional letters: ' ء, Â أ, Ǎ إ, Ā آ, ŵ ؤ, ŷ ئ, ¯h ة, ý ى.

not constrain any syntactic decision.[2] Even if relevant, a feature may not necessarily contribute to optimal performance since it may be **redundant** with other features that surpass it in relevance. For example, the DET and STATE features alone both help parsing because they help identify the *idafa* construction (the modificiation of a nominal by a genitive noun phrase), but they are redundant with each other and the DET feature is more helpful since it also helps with adjectival modification of nouns. Finally, the **accuracy** of automatically predicting the feature values (ratio of correct predictions out of all predictions) of course affects the value of a feature on unseen text. Even if relevant and non-redundant, a feature may be hard to predict with sufficient accuracy by current technology, in which case it will be of little or no help for parsing, even if helpful when its gold values are provided. The CASE feature is very relevant and not redundant, but it cannot be predicted with high accuracy and overall it is not useful.

Different languages vary with respect to which features may be most helpful given various tradeoffs among these three factors. It has been shown previously that if the relevant morphological features in assignment configurations can be recognized well enough, then they contribute to parsing accuracy. For example, modeling CASE in Czech improves Czech parsing (Collins et al., 1999): CASE is relevant, not redundant, and can be predicted with sufficient accuracy. However, it had been more difficult showing that agreement morphology helps parsing, with negative results for dependency parsing in several languages (Nivre et al., 2008; Eryigit et al., 2008; Nivre, 2009). In contrast to these negative results, Marton et al. (2013) showed positive results for using agreement morphology for Arabic.

2.2 Methodology

In Marton et al. (2013), we investigated morphological features for dependency parsing of Modern Standard Arabic (MSA). The goal was to find a set of relevant, accurate and non-redundant features. We used both the MaltParser (Nivre, 2008) and the Easy-First Parser (Goldberg and Elhadad, 2010). Since the Easy-First Parser performed better, we use it in all experiments reported in this paper.

For MSA, the space of possible morphological features is quite large. We determined which morphological features help by performing a search through the feature space. In order to do this, we separated part-of-speech (POS) from the morphological features. We defined a core set of 12 POS features, and then explored combinations of morphological features in addition to this POS tagset. This core set of POS tags is similar to those proposed in cross-lingual work (Rambow et al., 2006; Petrov et al., 2012). We performed this search independently for Gold input features and predicted input features. We used our MADA+TOKAN system (Habash and Rambow, 2005; Habash et al., 2009; Habash et al., 2012) for the prediction. As the Easy-First Parser predicts links separately before labels, we first optimized for unlabeled attachment score, and then optimized the Easy-First Parser labeler for label score.

As had been found in previous results, assignment features, specifically CASE and STATE, are very helpful in MSA. However, in MSA this is true only under gold conditions: since CASE is rarely explicit in the typically undiacritized written MSA, it has a dismal accuracy rate, which makes it useless when used in machine-predicted (real, non-gold) condition. In contrast with previous results, we showed that agreement features are quite helpful in both gold and predicted conditions. This is likely a result of MSA having a rich agreement system, covering both verb-subject and noun-adjective relations.

Additionally, almost all work to date in MSA morphological analysis and part-of-speech (POS) tagging has concentrated on the morphemic form of the words. However, often the functional morphology (which is relevant to agreement, and relates to the meaning of the word) is at odds with the "surface" (form-based) morphology; a well-known example of this are the "broken" (irregular) plurals of nominals, which often have singular-form morphemes but are in fact plurals and show plural agreement if the referent is rational. In Marton et al. (2013), we showed that by modeling the functional morphology rather than the form-based morphology, we obtain a further increase in parsing performance

[2] For more information on Arabic morphology in the context of natural language processing see Habash (2010). For a detailed analysis of morpho-syntactic agreement, see Alkuhlani and Habash (2011).

Feature Type	Feature	Explanation
Part-of-speech	CORE12	12 tags for core parts-of-speech: verb, noun, adjective, adverb, proper noun, pronoun, preposition, conjunction, relative pronoun, particle, abbreviation, and punctuation
Inflectional features	DET	Presence of the determiner morpheme ال *Al*
	PERSON	1st, 2nd, or 3rd
	FN*N	Functional number: singular, dual, plural
	FN*G	Functional gender: masculine or feminine
Lexical features	FN*R	Rationality: rational, irrational, ambiguous, unknown or N/A
	LMM	Undiacritized lemma

Table 1: Features used in the CADIM submission with the Easy-First Parser (Goldberg and Elhadad, 2010).

Training Set	Test Set	LAS	UAS	LaS
5K (SPMRL'2013)	dev $\leq$ 70	81.7	84.7	92.7
All (SPMRL'2013)	dev $\leq$ 70	84.8	87.4	94.2
Marton et al. (2013)	test (old split) $\leq$ 70	81.7	84.6	92.8
5K (SPMRL'2013)	dev	81.1	84.2	92.7
All (SPMRL'2013)	dev	84.0	86.6	94.1
5K (SPMRL'2013)	test	80.5	83.5	92.7
All (SPMRL'2013)	test	83.2	85.8	93.9
Marton et al. (2013)	test (old split)	81.0	84.0	92.7

Table 2: Results of our system on Shared Task test data, Gold Tokenization, Predicted Morphological Tags; and for reference also on the data splits used in our previous work (Marton et al., 2013); "$\leq$ 70" refers to the test sentences with 70 or fewer words.

Training Set	Test Set	Labeled Tedeval Score	Unlabeled Tedeval Score
5K (SPMRL'2013)	test $\leq$ 70	86.4	89.9
All (SPMRL'2013)	test $\leq$ 70	87.8	90.8

Table 3: Results of our system on on Shared Task test data, Predicted Tokenization, Predicted Morphological Tags; "$\leq$ 70" refers to the test sentences with 70 or fewer words

(again, both when using gold and when using predicted POS and morphological features).

We also showed that for parsing with predicted POS and morphological features, training on a combination of gold and predicted POS and morphological feature values outperforms the alternative training scenarios.

2.3 Best Performing Feature Set

The best performing set of features on non-gold input, obtained in Marton et al. (2013), are shown in Table 1. The features are clustered into three types.

- First is part-of-speech, represented using a "core" 12-tag set.
- Second are the inflectional morphological features: determiner clitic, person and functional gender and number.
- Third are the rationality (humanness) feature, which participates in morphosyntactic agreement in Arabic (Alkuhlani and Habash, 2011), and a form of the lemma, which abstract over all inflectional morphology.

For the training corpus, we use a combination of the gold and predicted features.

3 Our Submission

3.1 Data Preparation

The data split used in the shared task is different from the data split we used in (Marton et al., 2013), so we retrained our models on the new splits (Diab et al., 2013). The data released for the Shared Task showed inconsistent availability of lemmas across gold and predicted input, so we used the ALMOR analyzer (Habash, 2007) with the SAMA databases (Graff et al., 2009) to determine a lemma given the word form and the provided (gold or predicted) POS tags. In addition to the lemmas, the ALMOR analyzer also provides morphological features in the feature-value representation our approach requires. Finally, we ran our existing converter (Alkuhlani and Habash, 2012) over this representation to obtain functional number and gender, as well as the rationality feature.[3] For simplicity reasons, we used the MLE:W2+CATiB model (Alkuhlani and Habash, 2012), which was the best performing model on seen words, as opposed to the combination system that used a syntactic component with better results on unseen words. We did not perform Alif or Ya normalization on the data.

We trained two models: one on 5,000 sentences of training data and one on the entire training data.

3.2 Results

Our performance in the Shared Task for Arabic Dependency, Gold Tokenization, Predicted Tags, is shown in Table 2. Our performance in the Shared Task for Arabic Dependency, Predicted Tokenization, Predicted Tags, is shown in Table 3. For predicted tokenization, only the IMS/Szeged system which uses system combination (Run 2) outperformed our parser on all measures; our parser performed better than all other single-parser systems. For gold tokenization, our system is the second best single-parser system after the IMS/Szeged single system (Run 1). For gold tokenization and predicted morphology (Table 2), we also give the performance reported in our previous work (Marton et al., 2013). The increase over the previously reported work may simply be due to the different split for training and test, but it may also be due to improvements to the functional feature prediction (Alkuhlani and Habash, 2012), and the predicted features provided by the Shared Task organizers.

[3]The functional feature generator of (Alkuhlani and Habash, 2012) was trained on a different training set from the parser, but the functional feature generator was not trained on any of the test corpus for the Shared Task.

References

Sarah Alkuhlani and Nizar Habash. 2011. A corpus for modeling morpho-syntactic agreement in Arabic: gender, number and rationality. In *Proceedings of the 49th Annual Meeting of the Association for Computational Linguistics (ACL)*, Portland, Oregon, USA.

Sarah Alkuhlani and Nizar Habash. 2012. Identifying broken plurals, irregular gender, and rationality in Arabic text. In *Proceedings of the 13th Conference of the European Chapter of the Association for Computational Linguistics*, pages 675–685. Association for Computational Linguistics.

Michael Collins, Jan Hajic, Lance Ramshaw, and Christoph Tillmann. 1999. A statistical parser for Czech. In *Proceedings of the 37th Annual Meeting of the Association for Computational Linguistics (ACL)*, pages 505–512, College Park, Maryland, USA, June.

Mona Diab, Nizar Habash, Owen Rambow, and Ryan Roth. 2013. LDC Arabic Treebanks and Associated Corpora: Data Divisions Manual. Technical Report CCLS-13-02, Center for Computational Learning Systems, Columbia University.

Gülsen Eryigit, Joakim Nivre, and Kemal Oflazer. 2008. Dependency parsing of Turkish. *Computational Linguistics*, 34(3):357–389.

Yoav Goldberg and Michael Elhadad. 2010. An efficient algorithm for easy-first non-directional dependency parsing. In *Proceedings of Human Language Technology (HLT): the North American Chapter of the Association for Computational Linguistics (NAACL)*, pages 742–750, Los Angeles, California.

David Graff, Mohamed Maamouri, Basma Bouziri, Sondos Krouna, Seth Kulick, and Tim Buckwalter. 2009. Standard Arabic Morphological Analyzer (SAMA) Version 3.1. Linguistic Data Consortium LDC2009E73.

Nizar Habash and Owen Rambow. 2005. Arabic Tokenization, Part-of-Speech Tagging and Morphological Disambiguation in One Fell Swoop. In *Proceedings of the 43rd Annual Meeting of the Association for Computational Linguistics (ACL)*, pages 573–580, Ann Arbor, Michigan.

Nizar Habash, Abdelhadi Soudi, and Tim Buckwalter. 2007. On Arabic Transliteration. In A. van den Bosch and A. Soudi, editors, *Arabic Computational Morphology: Knowledge-based and Empirical Methods*. Springer.

Nizar Habash, Owen Rambow, and Ryan Roth. 2009. MADA+TOKAN: A toolkit for Arabic tokenization, diacritization, morphological disambiguation, POS tagging, stemming and lemmatization. In Khalid Choukri and Bente Maegaard, editors, *Proceedings of the Second International Conference on Arabic Language Resources and Tools*. The MEDAR Consortium, April.

Nizar Habash, Owen Rambow, and Ryan Roth. 2012. MADA+TOKAN Manual. Technical report, Technical Report CCLS-12-01, Columbia University.

Nizar Habash. 2007. Arabic Morphological Representations for Machine Translation. In Antal van den Bosch and Abdelhadi Soudi, editors, *Arabic Computational Morphology: Knowledge-based and Empirical Methods*. Kluwer/Springer.

Nizar Habash. 2010. *Introduction to Arabic Natural Language Processing*. Morgan & Claypool Publishers.

Yuval Marton, Nizar Habash, and Owen Rambow. 2013. Dependency parsing of Modern Standard Arabic with lexical and inflectional features. *Computational Linguistics*, 39(1).

Joakim Nivre, Igor M. Boguslavsky, and Leonid K. Iomdin. 2008. Parsing the SynTagRus Treebank of Russian. In *Proceedings of the 22nd International Conference on Computational Linguistics (COLING)*, pages 641–648.

Joakim Nivre. 2008. Algorithms for Deterministic Incremental Dependency Parsing. *Computational Linguistics*, 34(4).

Joakim Nivre. 2009. Parsing Indian languages with MaltParser. In *Proceedings of the ICON09 NLP Tools Contest: Indian Language Dependency Parsing*, pages 12–18.

Slav Petrov, Dipanjan Das, and Ryan McDonald. 2012. A universal part-of-speech tagset. In *Proceedings of the Conference on Language Resources and Evaluation (LREC)*, May.

Owen Rambow, Bonnie Dorr, David Farwell, Rebecca Green, Nizar Habash, Stephen Helmreich, Eduard Hovy, Lori Levin, Keith J. Miller, Teruko Mitamura, Florence Reeder, and Siddharthan Advaith. 2006. Parallel syntactic annotation of multiple languages. In *Proceedings of the Fifth Conference on Language Resources and Evaluation (LREC)*, Genoa, Italy.

Djamé Seddah, Reut Tsarfaty, Sandra Kübler, Marie Candito, Jinho Choi, Richárd Farkas, Jennifer Foster, Iakes Goenaga, Koldo Gojenola, Yoav Goldberg, Spence Green, Nizar Habash, Marco Kuhlmann, Wolfgang Maier, Joakim Nivre, Adam Przepiorkowski, Ryan Roth, Wolfgang Seeker, Yannick Versley, Veronika Vincze, Marcin Woliński, Alina Wróblewska, and Eric Villemonte de la Clérgerie. 2013. Overview of the spmrl 2013 shared task: A cross-framework evaluation of parsing morphologically rich languages. In *Proceedings of the 4th Workshop on Statistical Parsing of Morphologically Rich Languages: Shared Task*, Seattle, WA.

A Statistical Approach to Prediction of Empty Categories in Hindi Dependency Treebank

Puneeth Kukkadapu, Prashanth Mannem
Language Technologies Research Center
IIIT Hyderabad, India
{puneeth.kukkadapu,prashanth}@research.iiit.ac.in

Abstract

In this paper we use statistical dependency parsing techniques to detect NULL or Empty categories in the Hindi sentences. We have currently worked on Hindi dependency treebank which is released as part of COLING-MTPIL 2012 Workshop. Earlier Rule based approaches are employed to detect Empty heads for Hindi language but statistical learning for automatic prediction is not explored. In this approach we used a technique of introducing complex labels into the data to predict Empty categories in sentences. We have also discussed about shortcomings and difficulties in this approach and evaluated the performance of this approach on different Empty categories.

1 Introduction

Hindi is a morphologically rich and a relatively free word order language (MoR-FWO). Parsing is a challenging task for such MoR-FWO languages like Turkish, Basque, Czech, Arabic, etc. because of their non-configurable nature. Previous research showed that the dependency based annotation scheme performs better than phrase based annotation scheme for such languages (Hudson, 1984; Bharati et al., 1995). Dependency annotation for Hindi is based on Paninian framework for building the treebank (Begum et al., 2008). In recent years data driven parsing on Hindi has shown good results, the availability of annotated corpora is a definite factor for this improvement (Nivre et al., 2006; McDonald et al., 2005; Martins et al., 2009; Mannem and Dara, 2011). Other approaches such as rule-based and hybrid of rule-based and data-driven (Bharati et al., 2009a) for Hindi language have also been tried out. In the shared task for Hindi Parsing organized with COLING workshop Singla et al. (2012) achieved best results for Gold-Standard data with 90.99% (Labeled Attachment Score or LAS) and 95.87% (Unlabeled Attachment Score or UAS).

Empty category is a nominal element which does not have any phonological content and is therefore unpronounced. Empty categories are annotated in sentences to ensure a linguistically plausible structure. Empty categories play a crucial role in the annotation framework of the Hindi dependency treebank (Begum et al., 2008; Bharati et al., 2009b). If dependency structure of a sentence do not form a fully connected tree then Empty category (denoted by NULL in Hindi Treebank) is inserted in the sentence. In the Hindi treebank, an Empty category has at least one child. Traditional parsing algorithms do not insert Empty categories and require the Empty categories to be part of the input. These Empty categories are manually annotated in the treebank. In real time scenarios, like translation between languages, it is not possible to add the Empty categories into the sentences manually. So we require an approach which can identify the presence of these Empty categories and insert into appropriate positions in the sentence.

Figure 1 shows an Example of a Hindi sentence annotated with a NULL category. The English translation for this sentence is, "Its not fixed what his big bank will do". The aim of this paper is to investigate the problem of automatically predicting the Empty categories in the sentences using the statistical de-

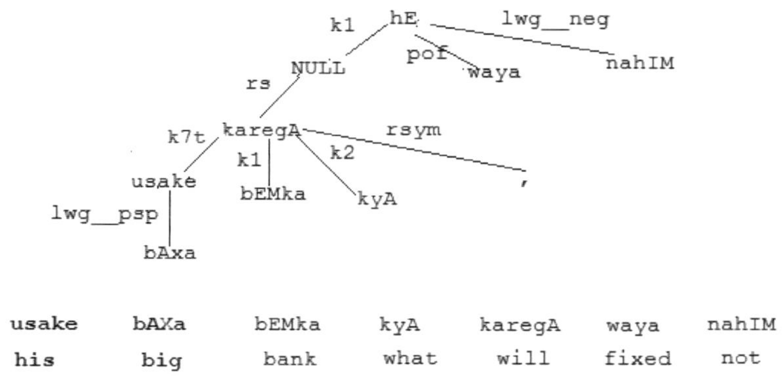

Figure 1: An Example of a Hindi sentence annotated with a NULL category.

pendency parsing technique and to shed some light on the challenges of this problem. As the data-driven parsing on Hindi language has achieved good results (Singla et al., 2012), we try to use this approach to predict Empty categories in the sentence. In this approach the information about NULL categories is encoded into the label set of the structure. In these experiments we have used only Projective sentences from the treebank. Non-projectivity makes it difficult to identify the exact position of NULLs during introduction of NULLs in the sentence.

The rest of the paper is divided into the following sections: Section 2 discusses about the related work. Section 3 gives an overview of the Hindi data we have used for our experiments. Section 4 contains the details of our approach and section 5 discusses about experiments, parser, results and discussion. We conclude the paper in section 6 with a summary and the future work.

2 Related Work

Previous work related to Empty categories prediction on Hindi data is done by Gsk et al. (2011) which is a rule based approach for detection of Empty categories and also presented detailed analysis of different types of Empty categories present in the Hindi treebank. They used hand-crafted rules in order to identify each type of Empty category. As this is a rule based approach it becomes language specific. There are many approaches for the recovery of empty categories in the treebanks like Penn treebank, both ML based (Collins, 1997; Johnson, 2002; Seeker et al., 2012), and rule based (Campbell, 2004). Some approaches such as Yang and Xue (2010) follow a post processing step of recovering empty categories after parsing the text. Gsk et al. (2011) have discussed about different types of Empty categories in Hindi Treebank in detailed manner. The main types of Empty categories are:

- Empty Subject where a clause is dependent on missing subject (NP) of the verb, denoted as NULL_NP or NULL_PRP.
- Backward Gapping where the verb (VM) is absent in the clause that occurs before a coordinating conjunct, denoted as NULL_VM
- Forward Gapping where the verb (VM) is absent in the clause that occurs after a coordinating conjunct, denoted as NULL_VM.
- Conjunction Ellipses where the Conjunction (CC) is absent in the sentence, denoted as NULL_CC.

3 Data

We have used COLING-MTPIL workshop 2012 data for our experiments. This was released by the organizers as part of the shared task in two different settings. One being the manually annotated data with POS tags, chunks and other information such as gender, number, person etc. whereas the other one contains only automatic POS tags without any other information. We have used Gold standard data with

Type of NULL	No. of Instances
NULL_VM	247
NULL_CC	184
NULL_NP	71
NULL_PRP	25

Table 1: Empty categories in Training + Development Dataset of Hindi treebank.

Type of NULL	No. of instances
NULL_VM	26
NULL_CC	36
NULL_NP	9
NULL_PRP	4

Table 2: Empty categories in Testing Dataset of Hindi treebank.

all features provided for our experiments. Training set contains 12,041 sentences, development data set consists of 1233 sentences and testing data set consists of 1828 sentences. In our experiments we have worked with only projective sentences. We have combined the training and development data sets into one data set and used as training in the final experiments.

Training and Development data together consists of 544 NULL instances (in 436 sentences) of 10,690 sentences. The major types of Empty categories present in the training data are of type NULL_CC, NULL_VM, NULL_NN and NULL_PRP categories. Table 1 and Table 2 show the number of instances of each category. Testing data consists of 80 instances (72 sentences) of 1455 sentences.

4 Approach

There are 3 main steps involved in this process.

4.1 Pre-Processing

In the first step, we encode information about presence of Empty categories in a sentence into the dependency relation label set of the sentence. If NULLs are present in a sentence, we remove the NULLs from the respective sentence in the treebank. In a sentence the dependents or children of a NULL category are attached to the parent of the NULL category and their respective labels are combined with dependency label of NULL category which indicates the presence of NULL and also says that such words or tokens are children of NULL category. Instead of just combining the labels we also add a sense of direction to the complex label which indicates whether the position of NULL is to the right or left of this token in the sentence and subsequently NULLs are also detached from its parent node. Therefore a complex label in a sentence indicates the presence of a NULL category in the sentence.

Example: **Null-label_r_dep-label** is a generic type of a complex label. In this format 'r' indicates that a NULL instance is to the right of this token. Null-label is the dependency relation label joining the Null instance and its parent and dep-label is the dependency relation label joining the current token or word to its parent which is a NULL instance. Figure 2 illustrates this step.

4.2 Data-driven parsing

In the second step a Data-driven parser is trained using the training data (with complex dependency relation labels) and when this parser model is used on the test data it predicts the complex labels in the output. In this approach we have tried out different data-driven parsers such as Malt (Nivre et al., 2006), Turbo (Martins et al., 2010) and MST (McDonald et al., 2005) for this experiment which were shown earlier to be performing better for Hindi Parsing by Kukkadapu et al. (2012) and found that Malt parser performs better than the rest on this data with complex labels.

4.3 Post-processing

In the final step, Post-processing is applied on the output predicted by the parser in the above step. In this step presence of NULLs are identified using the complex labels and their position in the sentence is identified using sense of direction in these labels (i.e., whether NULL instance is to the left 'l' or right 'r' of this token). During the insertion of NULLs into the sentence Projectivity of the sentence must be preserved. Keeping this constraint intact and using the direction information from the dependency relation labels, NULLs are introduced into the sentence. Figure 2 illustrates this step.

The advantage in using statistical approach rather than a rule based approach to predict NULLs is, it

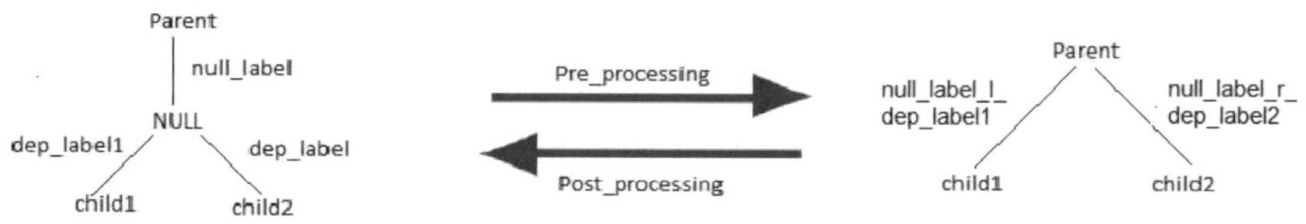

Figure 2: Process

can be easily used to predict NULLs in other MoR-FWO languages. The problem with this approach is, it can't handle Empty categories occurring as Leaf nodes (or Terminal nodes in the dependency tree) and as Root nodes. As we have mentioned earlier, the dependency annotation scheme of Hindi language does not allow for Empty categories to occur as Leaf nodes (or Terminal nodes). But if these Empty categories occur as Root nodes in the dependency tree then such cases are not disturbed in our approach.

5 Experiments and Results

5.1 Parser settings

As mentioned earlier we had used Malt parser for our experiments. Malt Parser implements the transition based approach to dependency parsing which has two components:
1) A transition system for mapping sentences into dependency trees.
2) A classifier for predicting the next transition for every possible system configuration.

Malt parser provides two learning algorithms LIBSVM and LIBLINEAR. It also provides various options for parsing algorithms and we have experimented on nivre-eager, nivre-standard and stack-proj parsing algorithms. Nivre-eager has shown good results in our experiments.

5.2 Features and Template

Feature model is the template, which governs the learning from the given training data. We observed feature model used by Kosaraju et al. (2010) performs best.

In order to get best results in the second step (Data-driven parsing) we have experimented with various features provided in the data. Kosaraju et al. (2010) and Husain et al. (2010) showed the best features that can be used in FEATS column in CoNLL-X format. These features are vibhakti (post positional marker), TAM (tense, aspect and modality), chunk features like chunk head, chunk distance and chunk boundary information have proved to be effective in parsing of Hindi language and our results on overall accuracy of data is consistent with their results.

Type of NULL Category	Recall
NULL_VM	50
NULL_CC	69.45
NULL_NN	88.89
NULL_PRP	50

Table 3: Empty categories Predicted by this approach on test data.

5.3 Results and Discussion

The Results obtained on the test dataset are shown below and Recall on each Empty category are given in Table 3:

The Results obtained by using this approach on the test set including all the Empty category types is as follows:

Precision = **84.9**

Recall = **69.23**

F-measure = **76.26**

In computation of the above results the exact position of NULLs in the sentence are not considered. These values indicate the efficiency of the system in identifying the presence of the Empty categories in the system. However, this approach inserted the

NULLs in exact positions with a Precision of more than 85%, i.e., of all the NULL instances it has inserted correctly, it has inserted 85% of them in exact positions in the sentences.

The approach was able to insert NULL_NP tokens with good accuracy but it had a tough time predicting NULL_VM tokens. This was also consistent with Gsk et al. (2011) conclusions about Empty categories in Hindi treebank.

In case of NULL_VM categories we have observed some inconsistency in the annotation of these sentences. In these sentences which have multiple clauses with main verb (VM) token missing, certain sentences are annotated with NULL_VM for each clause where main verb (VM) token is missing and certain sentences are annotated with one NULL_VM for all the clauses with main verb (VM) missing. This may be a reason for accuracy drop in predicting NULL_VM tokens. The main reason for low accuracy as we have observed is that the output predicted by the parser is low for these complex labels. The test data consists of 202 complex labels whereas the parser has been able to predict only 102 of them, which is a huge drop in accuracy for complex labels. The overall accuracy of parser on the test data (only projective sentences) has been high 91.11%(LAS), 95.86%(UAS) and 92.65%(LS). The low accuracy of the parser on complex labels may be due to less number of these instances compared to size of the corpus. Another reason may be due to the introduction of complex labels the size of label set has increased significantly and it may be difficult for the parser to learn the rare labels.

6 Conclusion and Future work

In this paper, we presented a statistical approach to Empty category prediction using Data-driven parsing. We have used state-of-the-art parser for Hindi language with an accuracy above 90% and have achieved a decent F-score of 76.26 in predicting Empty categories. We look to try out this approach for other MoR-FWO languages and compare the performances on different languages. We need to identify Features which would help in identifying NULL_CC category and also should try this approach on a big data set with a significant number of instances of NULLs and also look to extend this approach to Non-Projective sentences.

References

Rafiya Begum, Samar Husain, Arun Dhwaj, Dipti Misra Sharma, Lakshmi Bai, and Rajeev Sangal. 2008. Dependency annotation scheme for indian languages. In *Proceedings of IJCNLP*.

A. Bharati, V. Chaitanya, R. Sangal, and KV Ramakrishnamacharyulu. 1995. *Natural language processing: A Paninian perspective*. Prentice-Hall of India.

Akshar Bharati, Samar Husain, Dipti Misra, and Rajeev Sangal. 2009a. Two stage constraint based hybrid approach to free word order language dependency parsing. In *Proceedings of the 11th International Conference on Parsing Technologies*, pages 77–80. Association for Computational Linguistics.

Akshara Bharati, Dipti Misra Sharma, Samar Husain, Lakshmi Bai, Rafiya Begam, and Rajeev Sangal. 2009b. Anncorra: Treebanks for indian languages, guidelines for annotating hindi treebank.

Richard Campbell. 2004. Using linguistic principles to recover empty categories. In *Proceedings of the 42nd annual meeting on association for computational linguistics*, page 645. Association for Computational Linguistics.

Michael Collins. 1997. Three generative, lexicalised models for statistical parsing. In *Proceedings of the eighth conference on European chapter of the Association for Computational Linguistics*, pages 16–23. Association for Computational Linguistics.

Chaitanya Gsk, Samar Husain, and Prashanth Mannem. 2011. Empty categories in hindi dependency treebank: Analysis and recovery. In *Proceedings of the 5th Linguistic Annotation Workshop*, pages 134–142. Association for Computational Linguistics.

R.A. Hudson. 1984. *Word grammar*. Blackwell Oxford.

Samar Husain, Prashanth Mannem, Bharat Ram Ambati, and Phani Gadde. 2010. The icon-2010 tools contest on indian language dependency parsing. *Proceedings of ICON-2010 Tools Contest on Indian Language Dependency Parsing, ICON*, 10:1–8.

Mark Johnson. 2002. A simple pattern-matching algorithm for recovering empty nodes and their antecedents. In *Proceedings of the 40th Annual Meeting on Association for Computational Linguistics*, pages 136–143. Association for Computational Linguistics.

P. Kosaraju, S.R. Kesidi, V.B.R. Ainavolu, and P. Kukkadapu. 2010. Experiments on indian language dependency parsing. *Proceedings of the ICON10 NLP Tools Contest: Indian Language Dependency Parsing*.

Puneeth Kukkadapu, Deepak Kumar Malladi, and Aswarth Dara. 2012. Ensembling various dependency parsers: Adopting turbo parser for indian languages. In *24th International Conference on Computational Linguistics*, page 179.

P. Mannem and A. Dara. 2011. Partial parsing from bitext projections. In *Proceedings of the 49th Annual Meeting of the Association for Computational Linguistics: Human Language Technologies*, pages 1597–1606.

A.F.T. Martins, N.A. Smith, and E.P. Xing. 2009. Concise integer linear programming formulations for dependency parsing. In *Proceedings of the Joint Conference of the 47th Annual Meeting of the ACL and the 4th International Joint Conference on Natural Language Processing of the AFNLP: Volume 1-Volume 1*, pages 342–350.

A.F.T. Martins, N.A. Smith, E.P. Xing, P.M.Q. Aguiar, and M.A.T. Figueiredo. 2010. Turbo parsers: Dependency parsing by approximate variational inference. In *Proceedings of the 2010 Conference on Empirical Methods in Natural Language Processing*, pages 34–44.

R. McDonald, F. Pereira, K. Ribarov, and J. Hajič. 2005. Non-projective dependency parsing using spanning tree algorithms. In *Proceedings of the conference on Human Language Technology and Empirical Methods in Natural Language Processing (EMNLP)*, pages 523–530.

J. Nivre, J. Hall, and J. Nilsson. 2006. Maltparser: A data-driven parser-generator for dependency parsing. In *Proceedings of LREC*, volume 6, pages 2216–2219.

Wolfgang Seeker, Richárd Farkas, Bernd Bohnet, Helmut Schmid, and Jonas Kuhn. 2012. Data-driven dependency parsing with empty heads. In *Proceedings of COLING 2012: Posters*, pages 1081–1090, Mumbai, India, December. The COLING 2012 Organizing Committee.

Karan Singla, Aniruddha Tammewar, Naman Jain, and Sambhav Jain. 2012. Two-stage approach for hindi dependency parsing using maltparser. *Training*, 12041(268,093):22–27.

Yaqin Yang and Nianwen Xue. 2010. Chasing the ghost: recovering empty categories in the chinese treebank. In *Proceedings of the 23rd International Conference on Computational Linguistics: Posters*, pages 1382–1390. Association for Computational Linguistics.

An Empirical Study on the Effect of Morphological and Lexical Features in Persian Dependency Parsing

Mojtaba Khallash, **Ali Hadian** and **Behrouz Minaei-Bidgoli**
Department of Computer Engineering
Iran University of Science and Technology
{khallash,hadian}@comp.iust.ac.ir, b_minaei@iust.ac.ir

Abstract

This paper investigates the impact of different morphological and lexical information on data-driven dependency parsing of Persian, a morphologically rich language. We explore two state-of-the-art parsers, namely MSTParser and MaltParser, on the recently released Persian dependency treebank and establish some baselines for dependency parsing performance. Three sets of issues are addressed in our experiments: effects of using gold and automatically derived features, finding the best features for the parser, and a suitable way to alleviate the data sparsity problem. The final accuracy is 87.91% and 88.37% labeled attachment scores for MaltParser and MSTParser, respectively.

1 Introduction

Researchers have paid a lot of attention to data-driven dependency parsing in recent years (Bohnet and Kuhn, 2012; Bohnet and Nivre, 2012; Ballesteros and Nivre, 2013). This approach is language-independent and is solely dependent on the availability of annotated corpora. Using data-driven parsers for some languages requires careful selection of features and tuning of the parameters to reach maximum performance. Difficulty of dependency parsing in each language depends on having either free word order or morphological information. Languages with free word order have a high degree of freedom in arranging the words of a sentence. Consequently, they usually have a high percentage of non-projective structures. Morphology is determined by large inventory of word forms (Tsarfaty et al., 2010).

According to the results from CoNLL shared task 2007, languages are classified to three classes, namely *low*, *medium* and *high* accuracy languages. Among them, low-accuracy languages have high degree of free word order along with inflection (Nivre et al., 2007a). Languages which are more challenging in parsing are called morphologically rich languages (MRLs). In MRLs, multiple levels of information, concerning syntactic units and relations, are expressed at the word-level (Tsarfaty et al., 2010).

Free word order can be handled by non-projective parsing algorithms via either post-processing the output of a strictly projective parser (Nivre and Nilsson, 2005), combining adjacent (Nivre, 2009) or non-adjacent sub-structures (McDonald et al., 2005). Nevertheless, there is no general solution for resolving rich morphology issue and hence many researcher focus on features of a specific language. Most data-driven dependency parsers do not use any information that is specific to the language being parsed, but it is shown that using language specific features has a crucial role in improving the overall parsing accuracy (Ambati et al., 2010a).

Persian is an Indo-European language that is written in Perso-Arabic script (written from right to left). The canonical word order of Persian is SOV (subject-object-verb), but there are a lot of frequent exceptions in word order that turn this language into a free word order language (Shamsfard, 2011). This language has a high degree of free word order and complex inflections. As an example of rich morphology, there are more than 100 conjugates and 2800 declensions for some lemmas in Persian (Rasooli et al., 2011).

Dependency treebank for Persian (Rasooli et al., 2013) language has newly become available. Due to the lack of deep research on dependency parsing in Persian, we establish some baselines for dependency parsing performance. We also conduct a set of experiments in order to estimate the effect of errors in morphological disambiguation on the parsers. We show that with two simple changes to the input data, performance of the two parsers can be improved for both gold (manually annotated) and predicted data.

The remainder of the paper is organized as follows. Section 2 presents a brief overview of recent studies on parsing morphologically rich languages. In section 3, we introduce available morphological features annotated in our experiments. Section 4 describes the experimental setup, including corpus and parsers we use, and presents our experiments. Experimental evaluation and analysis of parsing errors are demonstrated in Section 5. Finally, we draw conclusions and suggest future work in Section 6.

2 Related work

Many studies have been done on using morphological features for parsing morphologically rich languages, (e.g. Bengoetxea and Gojenola (2010), Seeker and Kuhn (2013), etc.). Koo et al. (2008) introduce cluster-based features that incorporate word clusters derived from a large corpus of plain text, to improve statistical dependency parsing for English and Czech. Agirre et al. (2011) use lexical semantic information derived from WordNet.

Marton et al. (2011) augment the baseline model for Arabic with nine morphological features. They show that using predicted features causes a substantial drop in accuracy while it greatly improves performance in the gold settings. They show that using noisy morphological information is worse than using nothing at all. Same phenomenon is reported for Hebrew (Goldberg and Elhadad, 2010), except that using morphological-agreement feature improves the accuracy of both gold and predicted morphological information.

Another interesting research direction is to find the most beneficial features for dependency parsing for each language. Ambati et al. (2010b) explored the pool of features for Hindi through a series of experiments. In their setting, features are incrementally selected to create the best parser feature set. In Korean, Choi and Palmer (2011b) focus on feature extraction and suggest a rule-based way of selecting important morphemes to use only these as features to build dependency parsing models.

For the Persian language, Seraji et al. (2012b) investigated state-of-the-art dependency parsing algorithms on UPDT[1] (Seraji et al., 2012a). They test three feature settings, namely gold POS tags for both the training and the test sets (GG), gold POS tags for the training set and auto-generated POS tags for the test set (GA), and auto-generated POS tags for both the training and the test sets (AA). The best result is obtained in GG setting with 68.68% and 63.60% LAS, for MaltParser (Nivre et al., 2007b) and MSTParser (McDonald et al., 2005) respectively. Using AA and GA settings show worse results than GG, namely 2.29% and 3.66% drop in accuracy for MaltParser, and 1.8% and 3.23% drop for MSTParser. They only explore the effect of gold and non-gold POS tags with a small treebank with about 1,300 sentences. We apply GG and AA settings in our experiments on a larger treebank that contains richer morphological information. We define pool of 10 morphological and lexical semantic features in order to create the best feature set for the parser.

3 Features of Persian

In this section, among possible morphological and semantic features that exist in Persian, we briefly review a subset of them that is either annotated in Persian dependency treebank (Rasooli et al., 2013) or is available from other studies.

3.1 Features from Treebank

Table 1 represents the features available in the Persian dependency treebank, along with possible values for each feature.

[1]Uppsala Persian Dependency Treebank

Feature	Values
Attachment	{NXT, PRV, ISO}
Animacy	{animate, inanimate}
Number	{singular, plural}
Person	{1, 2, 3}
Comparison	{positive, comparative, superlative}
TMA	see Table 2

Table 1: Description of features in Treebank

In some special cases, we have to break a word into smaller parts in order to capture the syntactic relations between the elements of the sentence. For example, the two-word sentence صدایم کرد 'se-dAyam kard' (called me), consist of three morphemes: صدا (calling), یم (me), and کرد (to do) that have NXT (attached to the next word), PRV (attached to the previous word), and ISO (isolated word) attachment, respectively.

Person and number play a role in constraining syntactic structure. Verbs usually agree with subject in person and number (Shamsfard, 2011). This agreement is useful feature to detect subject of sentence. for example in "پسر، بچه‌ها رفتند" (hey boy, the kids are gone) sentence, both *boy* and *kids* are noun, but only kids has number agreement with verb.

Tense, mood, and aspect are not separately annotated in the treebank, but they can be induced from the TMA value. Table 2 shows the conversion table which consists of 14 valid TMA values. There is not a unique mapping from TMA to aspect, because in some conditions there is interference between the aspects. For example, in indicative imperfective perfect, the verb has perfect or continuous aspects.

3.2 Automatic Semantic Features

Word Clusters [WC] We use all the words of the treebank as inputs to the modified version of Brown clustering algorithm (Liang, 2005). In order to tune the parameters for the two parsers, we tweak the cluster count from 50 to 300 with steps of 50, and bit strings from 4 to 14. Finally, we choose 300 clusters and 6–bit strings for MaltParser and 150 clusters and 10–bit strings for MSTParser[2].

TMA	Meaning	Mood	Tense
HA	Imperative	Imp.	Pres.
AY	Indicative Future	Ind.	Fut.
GNES	Indicative Imperfective Perfect	Ind.	Past
GBES	Indicative Imperfective Pluperfect	Ind.	Past
GES	Indicative Imperfective Preterit	Ind.	Past
GN	Indicative Perfect	Ind.	Past
GB	Indicative Pluperfect	Ind.	Past
H	Indicative Present	Ind.	Pres.
GS	Indicative Preterit	Ind.	Past
GBESE	Subjunctive Imperfective Pluperfect	Sub.	Past
GESEL	Subjunctive Imperfective Preterit	Sub.	Past
GBEL	Subjunctive Pluperfect	Sub.	Past
HEL	Subjunctive Present	Sub.	Pres.
GEL	Subjunctive Preterit	Sub.	Past

Table 2: Tense/Mood/Aspect types in Persian verbs. Imp., Ind., Sub., Fut., and Pres. stand for imperative, indicative, subjunctive, future and present, respectively.

Semantic Verb Clustering [VC]: Semantic verb cluster is a generalization over verbs according to their semantic properties that capture large amounts of verb meaning without defining details for each verb. Aminian et al. (2013) clustered 1082 Persian verbs into 43 (fine-grained) semantic classes using spectral clustering. For each verb in the treebank, we included the corresponding cluster ID if the verb exists in the list of clustered verbs[3].

Synset Identifier [SID]: FarsNet (Shamsfard et al., 2010) is a lexical ontology for the Persian language that contains approximately 10000 synsets. For each word in the treebank, we look up for possible synsets in FarsNet. If any synset is found, we add the ID of the first synset to our feature set. About 59% of words in the treebank were supplied with a synset.

Semantic File [SF]: In English WordNet, each synset belongs to a unique semantic file. There is a total of 45 semantic files (1 for adverbs, 3 for adjectives, 15 for verbs, and 26 for nouns), based on syntactic and semantic categories (Agirre et al., 2011). FarsNet has a mapping to those of WordNet synsets. We use both synsetID and semantic files as instances of fine-grained and coarse-grained semantic representations, respectively. Thus, we can

[2]https://github.com/mojtaba-khallash/word-clustering

[3]https://github.com/mojtaba-khallash/verb-spectral-cluster

learn what level of granularity in semantic features can help improve performance of the parser[4].

4 Experiments

Corpus Persian dependency treebank version 1.0 (Rasooli et al., 2013) is a freely-available resource[5] with about 30,000 sentences, and half a million tokens, annotated with syntactic roles in addition to morpho-syntactic features. The annotation employs 17 coarse-grained and 30 fine-grained POS tags, 22 morphological feature values and 43 dependency labels. 21.93% of the sentences and 2.47% of the edges are non-projective.

Table 3 provides statistical properties of Persian dependency treebank, compared to UPDT[6]. In Persian dependency treebank, syntactic and/or morphological features are represented as key-value pairs separated by vertical bars ('|'), while in UPDT, they are represented as a single atomic feature.

Treebank	Persian DT	UPDT
Tok	498081	151671
Sen	29982	6000
AvgSL	16.61	25.28
Lem	yes	no
CPoS	17	15
PoS	30	30
MSF	22	30
Dep	43	48
NPT	2.47%	0.17%
NPS	21.93%	2.73%

Table 3: Comparison of UPDT (Seraji et al., 2012a) and Persian dependency treebank (Rasooli et al., 2013). Tok = number of tokens; Sen = number of sentences; AvgSL = Average sentence length; Lem = lemmatization present; CPoS = number of coarse-grained part-of-speech tags; PoS = number of (fine-grained) part-of-speech tags; MSF = number of morphosyntactic features (split into atoms); Dep = number of dependency types; NPT = proportion of non-projective dependencies/tokens (%); NPS = proportion of non-projective dependency graphs/sentences (%)

The data is split into standard train, development and test sets by the ratio of 80-10-10 percent in the CoNLL dependency format. Furthermore, the treebank is released in two representations with little changes in their annotations. A sample comparison between the two annotations is shown in Figure 1. In the first representation, which is manually annotated, the accusative case marker را /rɑ/ is supposed to be the head of the object plus rɑ. In the second representation, which is an automatic conversion of the first one obtained by reverse ordering the manual annotation, rɑ is not the head of the object word. Instead, rɑ is regarded as the accusative case marker for the direct object.

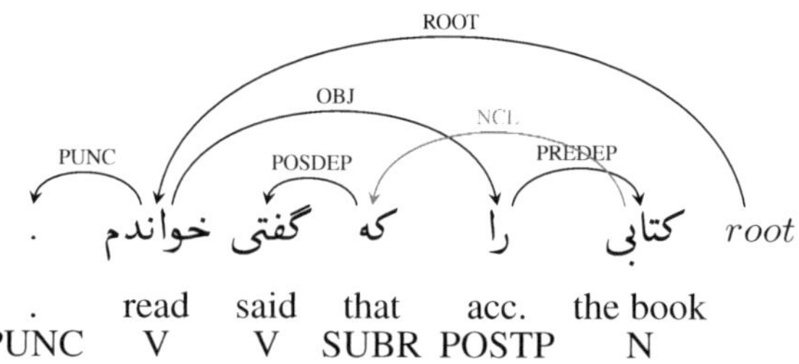

(a) First representation: Manually annotating accusative case marker را as object of the sentence

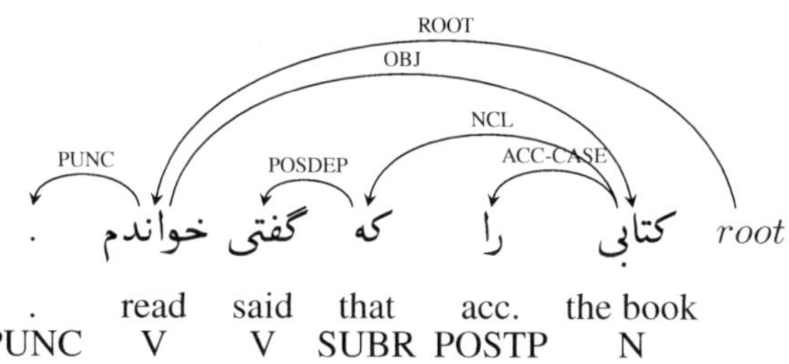

(b) Second representation: Automatic conversion of first representation. The accusative case marker را depends on original object of the sentence.

Figure 1: Two representation of object-verb relation for "I read the book that you mentioned." (Rasooli et al., 2013).

Evaluation metric The most commonly used metrics for dependency parsing are unlabeled attachment score (UAS), labeled attachment score (LAS) and label accuracy (LA). UAS is the proportion of words that are assigned the correct head, LAS is the proportion of words that are assigned the correct head and dependency type, and LA is the proportion of words that are assigned the correct dependency

[4] https://github.com/mojtaba-khallash/semantic-tagger

[5] http://www.dadegan.ir/en

[6] Freely available at http://stp.lingfil.uu.se/~mojgan/UPDT.html

type. We use LAS as our evaluation metric and take punctuation into account as for evaluating out parsing results. We use McNemars statistical significance test as implemented by (Nilsson and Nivre, 2008), and denote $p < 0.05$ and $p < 0.01$ with $^{+}$ and $^{++}$, respectively.

Parsers We use two off-the-shelf data-driven parsers, namely MaltParser (Nivre et al., 2007b) and MSTParser (McDonald et al., 2005), which are the two state-of-the-art dependency parsers that represent dominant approaches in data-driven dependency parsing.

MaltParser[7] is based on a transition-based approach to dependency parsing. Transition-based approach is based on transition systems for deriving dependency trees, that greedily searches for highest scoring transitions and uses features extracted from parse history to predict the next transition (Choi and Palmer, 2011a). We use MaltParser 1.7.1 along with nine different parsing algorithms. In order to select the best algorithm and tune the parameters of MaltParser, we use *MaltOptimizer* (Ballesteros and Nivre, 2012) on the whole of training data. MaltOptimizer analyzes data in three-phase optimization process: data analysis, parsing algorithm selection, and feature selection.

MSTParser[8] is based on a graph-based approach to dependency parsing. The algorithm searches globally in a complete graph to extract a spanning tree during derivations using dynamic programming. We use MSTParser 0.5 which has two implementations of maximum spanning tree (MST) algorithm with projective and non-projective models[9].

Baseline Experiments We run three phases of MaltOptimizer on the training set in order to find the best parsing algorithm in MaltParser. The first phase validates the data and gains 84.02% LAS with the default settings. In the second phase, using non-projective version of the Covington algorithm, which has the best accuracy, and after parameter tuning, 85.86% LAS was obtained. In the third phase, the feature model was optimized and by tuning the regularization parameter of the multiclass SVM; it led to 87.43% LAS. Finally, we trained the best algorithm with optimized settings on training set and parsed on development set, thereby we reached 87.70% LAS as the baseline of MaltParser.

We tested four parsing algorithms that exist in MSTParser and as a result, non-projective algorithm with a second-order feature decoder gave 88.04% LAS, which shows the highest improvement. Therefore, we selected that as our baseline for MSTParser.

The baselines are obtained on the first representation of the treebank. We found baselines for the second representation of the treebank on the development set. Results are compared in Table 4.

The first representation performs better than the second one. This was expected before, since rɑ is a constant word that is annotated as the object of a sentence in the first representation. This helps parsers to find the object in a sentence. Moreover, as shown in Figure 1, rɑ is closer to the verb than the direct object, hence it has more chance to select.

Representation	**Malt**	**MST**
First	87.70	88.04
Second	87.22 (-0.48)	87.03 (-1.01)

Table 4: Comparison of two representations of Persian treebank

Results In our experiments, we use the first representation of treebank with algorithms and new configurations presented in previous paragraph. For all experiments in this section, we use training and development sets of the treebank. In order to study the effects of morphology in dependency parsing of Persian, we organize experiments into three types of challenges which are presented by Tsarfaty et al. (2010): architecture and setup, representation and modeling, and estimation and smoothing.

Architecture and Setup When using dependency parsing on real-world tasks, we usually face with sentences that must be tokenized, lemmatized, and tagged with part of speech and morphological information to offer those information as input features to the parsing algorithms. Bijankhan corpus (Bijankhan, 2004) is the first manually tagged Persian

[7]`http://www.maltparser.org/`

[8]`http://www.seas.upenn.edu/~strctlrn/MSTParser/MSTParser.html`

[9]We developed an all-in-one *dependency parsing toolbox* that integrates different dependency parsing algorithms: `https://github.com/mojtaba-khallash/dependency-parsing-toolbox`

corpus that consists of morpho-syntactic and minimal semantic annotation of words. It is commonly used to train POS tagger, but its POS tagset is different from tagset of the treebank that we use. Sarabi et al. (2013) introduce PLP Toolkit which is a comprehensive Persian Language Processing (PLP) toolkit that contains fundamental NLP tools such as tokenizer, POS tagger, lemmatizer and dependency parser. They merged the POS tagset of 10 million words from bijankhan corpus with Persian dependency treebank in order to create a bigger corpus with the same tagset. They choose the tagset of Persian dependency treebank as the base setting and convert Bijankhan tagset to them. They have 11 coarse-grained and 45 fine-grained POS tags. PLP POS tagger can automatically recognize three morphological features, namely number, person, and TMA. TMA values of the PLP tool are not the same as Persian dependency treebank. Despite 14 possible TMA values in dependency treebank (Table 2), only four out of the 14 values exist in PLP (AY, GS, H, and HA), because there is no other value in Bijankhan tagset for verbs. The accuracy of PLP POS tagger on the fine grained tagset is about 98.5%. We use this tagger and apply it on our training, development, and test data. Results from these experiments are presented in Table 5.

POS tags type	Malt	MST
Gold	87.70	88.04
Predicted	86.98 (-0.72)	86.81 (-1.23)

Table 5: Effect of gold vs. predicted POS tags and morphological information in dependency parsers for Persian.

Representation and Modeling In our experiment, we use ten features of morphological and semantic information. Using a forward selection procedure, the best feature set for each parser can be found. Beside morphological features which exist in the treebank (**Attachment [A]**, **Person [P]**, **Number [N]**, **TMA**), we add **Tense [T]** and **Mood [M]** with a simple conversion table, shown in Table 2, based on the value of TMA.

Table 6 shows the effect of each feature for MaltParser and MSTParser parser. For the former, mood with slight differences achieves the best result and for the latter, TMA has the highest accuracy than other features. TMA and two derivate features, namely T and M, stands at the top of this ranking, and four semantic features are placed in the middle. This means that our newly added features can help to improve performance of each parser.

Feature	Malt	Feature	MST
Baseline	87.70	Baseline	88.04
M	**87.77**	**TMA**	**88.21**$^{+}$
TMA	87.77	M	88.17
T	87.73	P	88.09
SF	87.70	T	88.04
WC	87.69	N	88.04
VC	87.68	SID	88.03
SID	87.67	SF	88.03
A	87.67	WC	88.02
P	87.66	VC	87.98
N	87.65	A	87.93

Table 6: Effect of each feature on two parsers

In the next steps, we incrementally add one feature to the best result from previous step. As shown in Table 7, combination of M and SF obtains the best result for MaltParser (87.81%), while for MSTParser, combination of TMA and WC is the best (88.25%). In the second step, adding one semantic feature gets the best result. By trying to continue this approach, we do not see any improvement in the accuracy for both parser[10].

Feature	Malt	Feature	MST
{M,SF}	**87.81**	**{TMA,WC}**	**88.25**
{M,T}	87.79	{TMA,SID}	88.21
{M,VC}	87.78	{TMA,N}	88.16
{M,TMA}	87.77	{TMA,P}	88.14
{M,N}	87.76	{TMA,M}	88.13
{M,WC}	87.75	{TMA,A}	88.11
{M,A}	87.75	{TMA,T}	88.11
{M,P}	87.73	{TMA,VC}	88.07
{M,SID}	87.69	{TMA,SF}	88.05

Table 7: Combinations of two features

[10]https://github.com/mojtaba-khallash/treebank-transform

Estimation and Smoothing Using a few training data, especially for languages with rich morphology, lexical features may infrequently appear during training. In MRLs like Persian, due to many feature combination by the inflectional system, we face a high rate of out-of-vocabulary. There are some ways to cope with this problem:

- **Replacing word forms by lemma:** Lemma of a word has less data sparsity than word form.
- **Number Normalization** This is the default approach in MSTParser, in which each number is replaced by a constant. We apply this approach for numbers written either in English or Persian scripts.
- **Word Clustering** and **Semantic File**: The cluster ID of a word or its semantic file can be used instead of the original word form. These are two ways to categorize words into a group bigger than their lemma.

Table 8 illustrates the effect of each smoothing method on the accuracy for parsing MaltParser and MSTParser. For MaltParser, number normalization is the only technique that improves the accuracy. For MSTParser, replacing word forms by lemma and number normalization improves the accuracy. In the case of MSTParser, we apply each method separately and simultaneously on the development set, but replacing word forms by lemma gets the best improvement, and hence we use it in our final configuration.

Smoothing	Malt	MST
Baseline	87.70	88.04
Replacing word forms by lemma	87.38	**88.10**
Number Normalization	**87.71**	88.09
Word Clustering	86.98	87.47
Semantic File	87.31	85.25

Table 8: Accuracy obtained after applying different sparsity-reduction tricks.

5 Error Analysis

We use the best configurations from the previous section on the training and test data, for gold annotation and an automatically derived one. Table 9 shows the final test results of the two parsers for Persian. In addition to LAS, we also include UAS and LA to facilitate comparisons in the future. Baseline results are included in the table. In the case of MaltParser, after applying new configurations on data, we repeat the third phase of MaltOptimizer in order to find the best feature template for the new training data. It seems that the graph-based parser performs better than transitions-based parsers in general. Despite a high overall parsing accuracy, only 1017 and 922 (33.91% and 30.74%) of sentences in the test set (with 2999 sentences) are parsed without errors by MaltParser and MSTParser, respectively. MaltParser has lower overall accuracy compared to MSTParser, but the number of completely correct parsed sentences for MaltParser is more than MSTParser. In the case of predicted setting, as mentioned in section 4, there are four values for TMA. This means that we cannot create tense and mood from TMA. For this reason, we force to use TMA in the final configuration of both parsers in the predicted setting.

In order to evaluate parsing errors, we use the same approach as (McDonald and Nivre, 2011) to shows a set of linguistic and structural properties of the baseline and our best setting for each parser[11].

Length Factors Figure 2 shows the accuracy relative to the sentence length in test data. Since there are very limited long sentences in our treebank, the parser cannot predict longer sentences correctly. Consequently, the two parsers tend to have lower accuracies for longer sentences. Both parsers have the same performance, but MSTParser tends to perform better on shorter sentences, that is in contrast with results showed by McDonald and Nivre (2011). We compare each parser with its corresponding baselines. Both parsers in all lengths perform better than their baselines. For MaltParser, improvements occur for longer sentences while for MSTParser improvements occur at smaller sentences. These results are in contrast with the results reported by McDonald and Nivre (2011).

Graph Factors Figure 3 shows the accuracy for arcs relative to their distance to the artificial root node[12]. The area under the curve of final MaltParser

[11] In our analysis, we use MaltEval (Nilsson and Nivre, 2008).

[12] Number of arcs in the reverse path from the modifier of the arc to the root.

Parser	Method	LAS		UAS		LA	
Malt	Baseline	87.68	(87.04)	90.41	(89.92)	90.03	(89.49)
	Final	87.91^{++}	(87.16)$^{+}$	90.58^{+}	(90.05)$^{++}$	90.22^{+}	(89.60)$^{+}$
	Diff.	+0.23	(+0.12)	+0.17	(+0.13)	+0.19	(+0.11)
MST	Baseline	87.98	(86.82)	91.30	(90.27)	90.53	(89.90)
	Final	88.37^{++}	(86.97)	91.55^{++}	(90.36)	90.86^{++}	(90.05)
	Diff.	+0.39	(+0.15)	+0.25	(+0.09)	+0.33	(+0.15)

Table 9: Baseline and final results of gold (predicted) test data for MaltParser

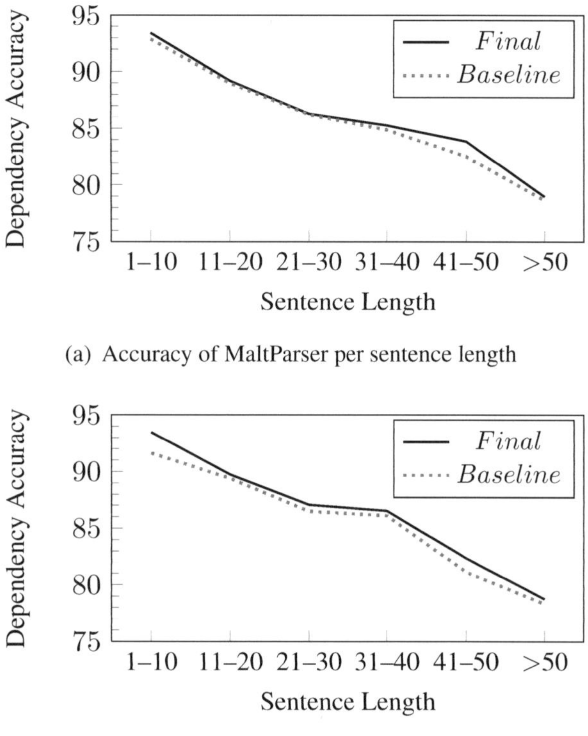

(a) Accuracy of MaltParser per sentence length

(b) Accuracy of MSTParser per sentence length

Figure 2: Accuracy relative to sentence length. Both parsers perform better than their baselines.

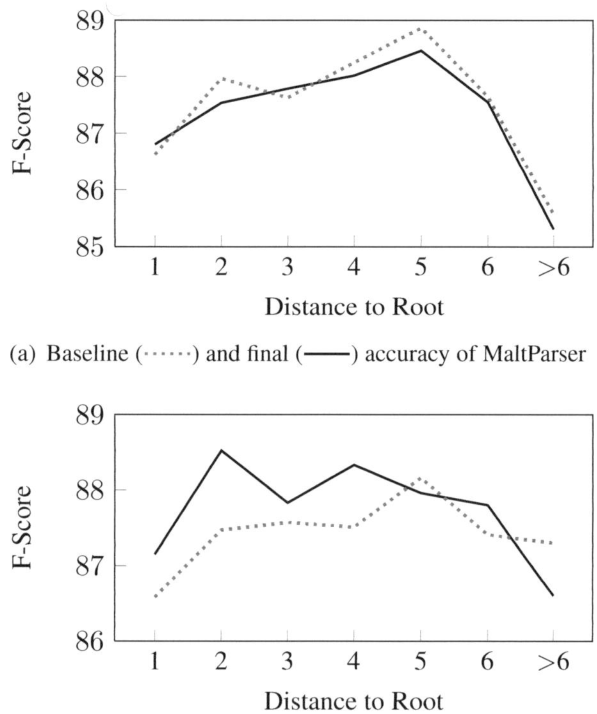

(a) Baseline (······) and final (——) accuracy of MaltParser

(b) Baseline (······) and final (——) accuracy of MSTParser

Figure 3: Dependency arc F-score relative to the distance to root

is less than baseline, but it is over baseline for MSTParser. F-score of MSTParser for shorter distance is much better than the baseline and by increasing the distance to root, F-score degrades to be less than the baseline.

Linguistic Factors MaltParser and MSTParser can find 90.22% and 90.86% of all labels correctly. Figure 4 shows the F-score of some important dependency labels in the test data. MaltParser only improves subject and object categories, while MSTParser improves object, ROOT, and adverb categories. If we only consider the final results, MaltParser performs better for predicting subject and object, while MSTParser performs better for predicting ROOT and ezafe dependent (MOZ)[13], and both have the same accuracy for adverb.

Table 10 gives the accuracy of arcs for each dependent part-of-speech. Final MSTParser performs

[13] *Ezafe construction* is referred to nouns or pronouns that imply a possessed-possessor relation (like first name-last name). The relation between the possessed and possessor is called mozaf (MOZ) that its sign is a vowel /e/ that pronounced right after the head noun (Dadegan Research Group, 2012).

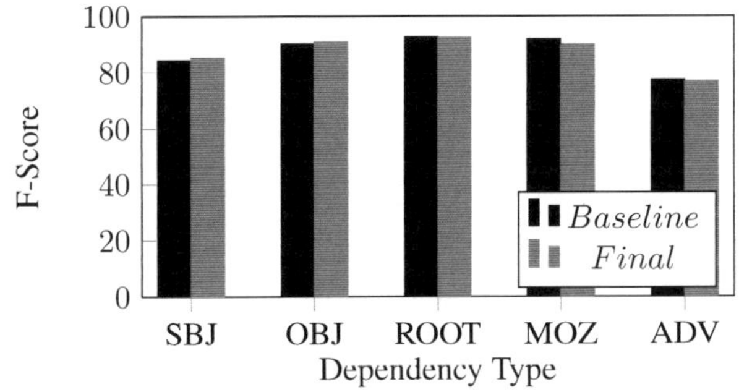

(a) Accuracy of MaltParser per dependency type

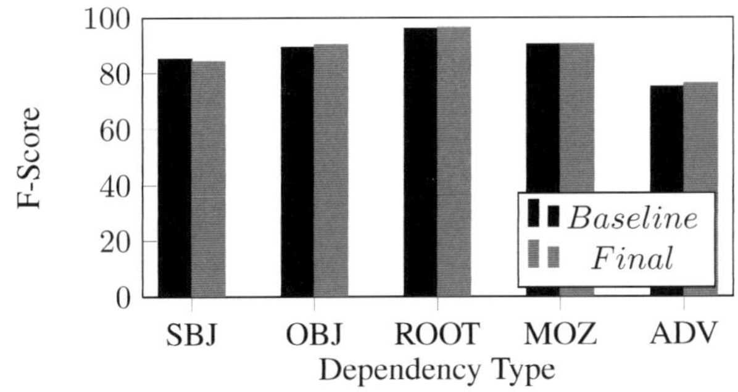

(b) Accuracy of MSTParser per dependency type

Figure 4: Dependency label F-score relative to some dependency types.

better than its baseline for all categories, except pronouns and better than MaltParser for all categories, except preposition. Final MaltParser, performs better than its baseline in all categories, except preposition.

6 Conclusion

In this paper, we have investigated a number of issues in data-driven dependency parsing of Persian. Because there is no previous study on parsing the Persian dependency treebank (Rasooli et al., 2013), we first have drawn the baseline for each parser, by selecting best performing algorithm and tuning its parameters. For MaltParser (Nivre et al., 2007b) different between best algorithm (non-projective version of Covington) with default settings and after optimizing feature template by the third phase of MaltOptimizer (Ballesteros and Nivre, 2012) is about 1.5 percent. This shows that the definition of feature template is a crucial aspect of transition-based parsing.

Our first experiment shows the effect of using automatic annotation of POS tags and morphological information. Our new configuration improves two parsers in both gold and predicted setting, but the improvement for MSTParser is higher than for MaltParser. MSTParser has higher accuracy in the gold setting, while MaltParser has better performance in predicted setting. It might mean that MaltParser is more robust against noisy information.

In the second experiment, we have explored the best combination of morphological and lexical semantic features for dependency parsing of Persian. We find that the combination of one morphological feature and one lexical semantic feature gets the best combination for each parser. Our lexical semantic features can be automatically produced for any word and thus we need to predict one morphological feature for real-world settings.

Finally we have proposed two simple methods for reducing data sparsity of each parser. After applying our solutions to three types of challenges, we reached 87.91% and 88.37% LAS on the test set (0.23% and 0.39% improvement over our baseline) for MaltParser and MSTParser, respectively.

Note that all of the experiments we reported in this paper use existing parsers as black boxes. We only changed the input data to obtain the best possible performance given our data sets. We plan to explore modifications of the underlying parsing algorithms to better make use of morphological information.

POS	**Malt**		**MST**	
	Baseline	**Final**	**Baseline**	**Final**
Verb	89.96	90.09	90.96	**91.86**
Noun	89.67	90.13	90.15	**90.23**
Pronoun	92.56	92.94	**93.53**	93.43
Adjective	87.80	88.37	87.77	**88.56**
Adverb	80.80	82.37	82.61	**83.94**
Conjunction	86.03	86.40	86.58	**87.36**
Preposition	**70.93**	70.32	69.74	70.76

Table 10: Accuracy for each dependent part of speech

Acknowledgments

We would like to thank Mohammad-Sadegh Rasooli and our anonymous reviewers for helpful feedback and suggestions. We would also thank Zahra Sarabi for providing us the data and information about the PLP toolkit.

References

Eneko Agirre, Kepa Bengoetxea, Koldo Gojenola, and Joakim Nivre. 2011. Improving Dependency Parsing with Semantic Classes. In *Proceedings of the 49th Annual Meeting of the Association for Computational Linguistics (ACL '11): shortpapers*, pages 699–703.

Baharat Ram Ambati, Samar Husain, Sambhav Jain, Dipti Misra Sharma, and Rajeev Sangal. 2010a. Two methods to incorporate local morphosyntactic features in Hindi dependency parsing. In *Proceedings of NAACL HLT 2010 First workshop on Statistical Parsing of Morphologically-Rich Languages (SPMRL 2010)*, pages 22–30.

Baharat Ram Ambati, Samar Husain, Joakim Nivre, and Rajeev Sangal. 2010b. On the Role of Morphosyntactic Features in Hindi Dependency Parsing. In *Proceedings of the NAACL HLT 2010 First Workshop on Statistical Parsing of Morphologically-Rich Languages*, pages 94–102.

Maryam Aminian, Mohammad Sadegh Rasooli, and Hossein Sameti. 2013. Unsupervised Induction of Persian Semantic Verb Classes Based on Syntactic Information. In *Language Processing and Intelligent Information Systems*, pages 112–124.

Miguel Ballesteros and Joakim Nivre. 2012. MaltOptimizer: A System for MaltParser Optimization. In *Proceedings of the Eighth International Conference on Language Resources and Evaluation (LREC 2012)*, pages 23–27.

Miguel Ballesteros and Joakim Nivre. 2013. Going to the Roots of Dependency Parsing. *Computational Linguistics*, pages 5–13.

Kepa Bengoetxea and Koldo Gojenola. 2010. Application of Different Techniques to Dependency Parsing of Basque. In *Proceedings of the NAACL HLT 2010 First Workshop on Statistical Parsing of Morphologically-Rich Languages*, pages 31–39.

Mahmood Bijankhan. 2004. The role of the corpus in writing a grammar: An introduction to a software. *Iranian Journal of Linguistics*.

Bernd Bohnet and Jonas Kuhn. 2012. The Best of Both Worlds A Graph-based Completion Model for Transition-based Parsers. In *Proceedings of the 13th Conference of the European Chapter of the Association for Computational Linguistics*, pages 77–87.

Bernd Bohnet and Joakim Nivre. 2012. A Transition-Based System for Joint Part-of-Speech Tagging and Labeled Non-Projective Dependency Parsing. In *Proceedings of the 2012 Joint Conference on Empirical Methods in Natural Language Processing and Computational Natural Language Learning (EMNLP-CoNLL 2012)*, pages 1455–1465.

Jinho D. Choi and Martha Palmer. 2011a. Getting the Most out of Transition-based Dependency Parsing. In *Proceedings of the 49th Annual Meeting of the Association for Computational Linguistics (ACL '11): shortpapers*, pages 687–692.

Jinho D. Choi and Martha Palmer. 2011b. Statistical Dependency Parsing in Korean: From Corpus Generation To Automatic Parsing. In *Proceedings of the 2nd Workshop on Statistical Parsing of Morphologically-Rich Languages (SPMRL 2011)*, pages 1–11.

Dadegan Research Group. 2012. Persian Dependency Treebank Annotation Manual and User Guide. Technical report, SCICT.

Yoav Goldberg and Michael Elhadad. 2010. Easy First Dependency Parsing of Modern Hebrew. In *Proceedings of the NAACL HLT 2010 First Workshop on Statistical Parsing of Morphologically-Rich Languages*, pages 103–107.

Terry Koo, Xavier Carreras, and Michael Collins. 2008. Simple Semi-supervised Dependency Parsing. In *Proceedings of ACL-08: HLT*, pages 595–603.

Percy Liang. 2005. *Semi-Supervised Learning for Natural Language*. Ph.D. thesis, Massachusetts Institute of Technology.

Yuval Marton, Nizar Habash, and Owen Rambow. 2011. Improving Arabic Dependency Parsing with Form-based and Functional Morphological Features. In *Proceedings of the 49th Annual Meeting of the Association for Computational Linguistics (ACL '11)*, pages 1586–1596.

Ryan McDonald and Joakim Nivre. 2011. Analyzing and Integrating Dependency Parsers. *Computational Linguistics*, pages 197–230.

Ryan McDonald, Fernando Pereira, Kiril Ribarov, and Jan Hajič. 2005. Non-projective Dependency Parsing using Spanning Tree Algorithms. In *Proceedings of the conference on Human Language Technology and Empirical Methods in Natural Language Processing*, pages 523–530.

Jens Nilsson and Joakim Nivre. 2008. MaltEval: An Evaluation and Visualization Tool for Dependency Parsing. In *Proceedings of the Sixth International Language Resources and Evaluation (LREC '08)*.

Joakim Nivre and Jens Nilsson. 2005. Pseudo-Projective Dependency Parsing. In *Proceedings of the 43rd Annual Meeting of the Association for Computational Linguistics (ACL '05)*, pages 99–106.

Joakim Nivre, Johan Hall, Sandra Kübler, Ryan McDonald, Jens Nilsson, Sebastian Riedel, and Deniz Yuret. 2007a. The CoNLL 2007 Shared Task on Dependency

Parsing. In *Proceedings of the CoNLL Shared Task Session of EMNLP-CoNLL 2007*, pages 915–932.

Joakim Nivre, Johan Hall, Jens Nilsson, Atanas Chanev, Gülsen Eryigit, Sandra Kübler, Svetoslav Marinov, and Erwin Marsi. 2007b. MaltParser: A language-independent system for data-driven dependency parsing. *Natural Language Engineering*, pages 95–135.

Joakim Nivre. 2009. Non-Projective Dependency Parsing in Expected Linear Time. In *Proceedings of the Joint Conference of the 47th Annual Meeting of the ACL and the 4th International Joint Conference on Natural Language Processing (IJCNLP) of the AFNLP*, pages 351–359.

Mohammad Sadegh Rasooli, Omid Kashefi, and Behrouz Minaei-Bidgoli. 2011. Effect of Adaptive Spell Checking in Persian. In *7th International Conference on Natural Language Processing andKnowledge Engineering (NLP-KE)*, pages 161–164.

Mohammad Sadegh Rasooli, Manouchehr Kouhestani, and Amirsaeid Moloodi. 2013. Development of a Persian Syntactic Dependency Treebank. In *Proceedings of the 2013 Conference of the North American Chapter of the Association for Computational Linguistics: Human Language Technologies*, pages 306–314.

Zahra Sarabi, Hooman Mahyar, and Mojgan Farhoodi. 2013. PLP Toolkit: Persian Language Processing Toolkit. In *3rd International eConference on Computer and Knowledge Engineering (ICCKE 2013)*.

Wolfgang Seeker and Jonas Kuhn. 2013. Morphological and Syntactic Case in Statistical Dependency Parsing. *Computational Linguistics*, pages 23–55.

Mojgan Seraji, Beáta Megyesi, and Joakim Nivre. 2012a. Bootstrapping a Persian Dependency Treebank. *Linguistic Issues in Language Technology*, pages 1–10.

Mojgan Seraji, Beáta Megyesi, and Joakim Nivre. 2012b. Dependency Parsers for Persian. In *Proceedings of 10th Workshop on Asian Language Resources, COLING 2012, 24th International Conference on Computational Linguistics.*

Mehrnoush Shamsfard, Akbar Hesabi, Hakimeh Fadaei, Niloofar Mansoory, Ali Famian, Somayeh Bagherbeigi, Elham Fekri, Maliheh Monshizadeh, and S. Mostafa Assi. 2010. Semi Automatic Development Of FarsNet: The Persian Wordnet. In *Proceedings of 5th Global WordNet Conference (GWA2010).*

Mehrnoush Shamsfard. 2011. Challenges and Open Problems in Persian Text processing. In *The 5th Language and Technology Conference (LTC 2011)*, pages 65–69.

Reut Tsarfaty, Djamé Seddah, Yoav Goldberg, Sandra Kübler, Marie Candito, Jennifer Foster, Yannick Versley, Ines Rehbein, and Lamia Tounsi. 2010. Statistical Parsing of Morphologically Rich Languages (SPMRL) What, How and Whither. In *Proceedings of the NAACL HLT 2010 First Workshop on Statistical Parsing of Morphologically-Rich Languages*, pages 1–12.

Constructing a Practical Constituent Parser from a Japanese Treebank with Function Labels

Takaaki Tanaka and **Masaaki Nagata**
NTT Communication Science Laboratories
Nippon Telegraph and Telephone Corporation

{tanaka.takaaki, nagata.masaaki}@lab.ntt.co.jp

Abstract

We present an empirical study on constructing a Japanese constituent parser, which can output function labels to deal with more detailed syntactic information. Japanese syntactic parse trees are usually represented as unlabeled dependency structure between bunsetsu chunks, however, such expression is insufficient to uncover the syntactic information about distinction between complements and adjuncts and coordination structure, which is required for practical applications such as syntactic reordering of machine translation. We describe a preliminary effort on constructing a Japanese constituent parser by a Penn Treebank style treebank semi-automatically made from a dependency-based corpus. The evaluations show the parser trained on the treebank has comparable bracketing accuracy as conventional bunsetsu-based parsers, and can output such function labels as the grammatical role of the argument and the type of adnominal phrases.

1 Introduction

In Japanese NLP, syntactic structures are usually represented as dependencies between grammatical chunks called *bunsetsus*. A bunsetsu is a grammatical and phonological unit in Japanese, which consists of an independent-word such as noun, verb or adverb followed by a sequence of zero or more dependent-words such as auxiliary verbs, postpositional particles or sentence final particles. It is one of main features of Japanese that bunsetsu order is much less constrained than phrase order in English. Since dependency between bunsetsus can treat flexible bunsetsu order, most publicly available Japanese parsers including CaboCha (Kudo et al., 2002) and KNP (Kawahara et al., 2006) return bunsetsu-based dependency as syntactic structure. Such bunsetsu-based parsers generally perform with high accuracy and have been widely used for various NLP applications.

However, bunsetsu-based representations also have serious shortcomings for dealing with Japanese sentence hierarchy. The internal structure of a bunsetsu has strong morphotactic constraints in contrast to flexible bunsetsu order. A Japanese predicate bunsetsu consists of a main verb followed by a sequence of auxiliary verbs and sentence final particles. There is an almost one-dimensional order in the verbal constituents, which reflects the basic hierarchy of the Japanese sentence structure including voice, tense, aspect and modality. Bunsetsu-based representation cannot provide the linguistic structure that reflects the basic sentence hierarchy.

Moreover, bunsetsu-based structures are unsuitable for representing such nesting structure as coordinating conjunctions. For instance, bunsetsu representation of a noun phrase "技術-の (technology-GEN) / 向上-と (improvement-CONJ) / 経済-の (economy-GEN) / 発展 (growth) " *technology improvement and economic growth* does not allow us to easily interpret it, which means *((technology improvement) and (economic growth))* or *(technology (improvement and economic growth))*, because bunsetsu-based dependencies do not convey information about left boundary of each noun phrase (Asahara, 2013). This drawback complicates operating syntactically meaningful units in such applications as statistical machine translation, which needs to recognize syntactic units in building a translation model (e.g. tree-to-string and tree-to-tree) and in preordering source language sentences.

Semantic analysis, such as predicate-argument structure analysis, is usually done as a pipeline process after syntactic analysis (Iida et al., 2011 ; Hayashibe et al., 2011); but in Japanese, the discrepancy between syntactic and semantic units cause difficulties integrating semantic analysis with syntactic analysis.

Our goal is to construct a practical constituent parser that can deal with appropriate grammatical units and output grammatical functions as semi-semantic information, e.g., grammatical or semantic roles of arguments and gapping types of relative clauses. We take an approach to deriving a grammar from manually annotated corpora by training probabilistic models like current statistical constituent parsers of de facto standards (Petrov et al., 2006; Klein et al., 2003 ; Charniak, 2000; Bikel, 2004). We used a constituent-based treebank that Uematsu et al. (2013) converted from an existing bunsetsu-based corpus as a base treebank, and retag the non-terminals and transform the tree structures in described in Section 3. We will present the results of evaluations of the parser trained with the treebank in Section 4, and show some analyses in Section 5.

2 Related work

The number of researches on Japanese constituent-based parser is quite few compared to that of bunsetsu-dependency-based parser. Most of them have been conducted under lexicalized grammatical formalism.

HPSG (Head-driven Phrase Structure Grammar) (Sag et al., 2003) is a representative one. Gunji et al. (1987) proposed JPSG (Japanese Phrase Structure Grammar) that is theoretically precise to handle the free word order problem of Japanese. Nagata et al. (1993) built a spoken-style Japanese grammar and a parser running on it. Siegel et al (2002) constructed a broad-coverage linguistically precise grammar JACY, which integrates semantics, MRS (Minimal Recursion Semantics) (Copestake, 2005). Bond et al. (2008) built a large-scale Japanese treebank Hinoki based on JACY and used it for parser training.

Masuichi et al.(2003) developed a Japanese LFG (Lexicalized-Functional Grammar) (Kaplan et al., 1982) parser whose grammar is sharing the design with six languages. Uematsu et al. (2013) constructed a CCG (Combinatory Categorial Grammar) bank based on the scheme proposed by Bekki (2010), by integrating several corpora including a constituent-based treebank converted from a dependency-base corpus.

These approaches above use a unification-based parser, which offers rich information integrating syntax, semantics and pragmatics, however, generally requires a high computational cost. We aim at constructing a more light-weighted and practical constituent parser, e.g. a PCFG parser, from Penn Treebank style treebank with function labels. Gabbard et al. (2006) introduced function tags by modifying those in Penn Treebank to their parser. Even though Noro et al. (2005) built a Japanese corpus for deriving Japanese CFG, and evaluated its grammar, they did not treat the predicate-argument structure or the distinction of adnominal phrases.

This paper is also closely related to the work of Korean treebank transformations (Choi et al., 2012). Most of the Korean corpus was built using grammatical chunks *eojeols*, which resemble Japanese bunsetsus and consist of content words and morphemes that represent grammatical functions. Choi et al. transformed the eojeol-based structure of Korean treebanks into entity-based to make them more suitable for parser training. We converted an existing bunsetsu-based corpus into a constituent-based one and integrating other information into it for training a parser.

3 Treebank for parser training

In this section, we describe the overview of our treebank for training a parser.

3.1 Construction of a base treebank

Our base treebank is built from a bunsetsu-dependency-based corpus, the Kyoto Corpus (Kurohashi et al., 2003), which is a collection of newspaper articles, that is widely used for training data for Japanese parsers and other applications. We

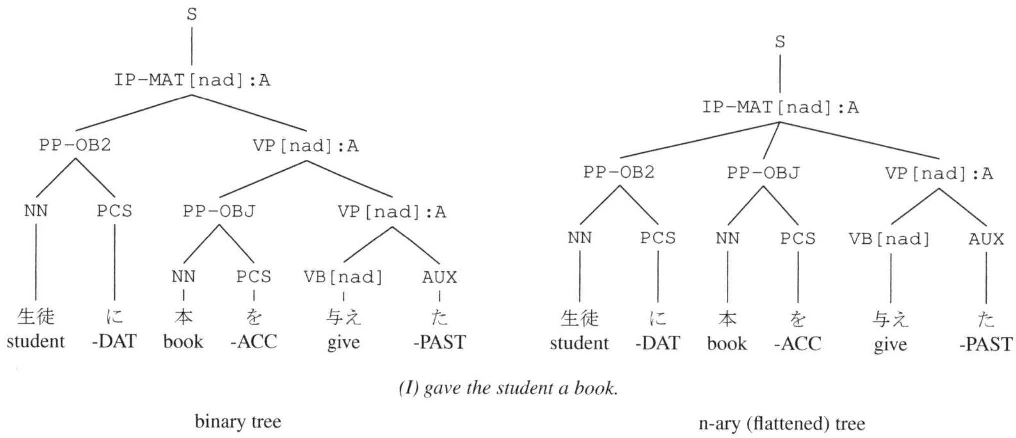

Figure 1: Verb Phrase with subcategorization and voice information

NN	General noun
NNP	Proper noun
NPR	Pronoun
NV	Verbal noun
NADJ	Adjective noun
NADV	Adverbial noun (incl. temporal noun)
NNF	Formal noun (general)
NNFV	Formal noun (adverbial)
PX	Prefix
SX	Suffix
NUM	Numeral
CL	Classifier
VB	Verb
ADJ	Adjective
ADNOM	Adnominal adjective
ADV	Adverb
PCS	Case particle
PBD	Binding particle
PADN	Adnominal particle
PCO	Parallel particle
PCJ	Conjunctive particle
PEND	Sentence-ending particle
P	Particle (others)
AUX	Auxiliary verb
CONJ	Conjunction
PNC	Punctuation
PAR	Parenthesis
SYM	Symbol
FIL	Filler

Table 1: Preterminal tags

automatically converted from dependency structure to phrase structure by the previously described method (Uematsu et al., 2013), and conversion errors of structures and tags were manually corrected.

We adopted the annotation schema used in Japanese Keyaki treebank (Butler et al., 2012) and Annotation Manual for the Penn Historical Corpora and the PCEEC (Santorini, 2010) as reference to re-tag the nonterminals and transform the tree structures.

The original Kyoto Corpus has fine-grained part-of-speech tags, which we converted into simpler preterminal tags shown in Table 1 for training by lookup tables. First the treebank's phrase tags except function tags are assigned by simple CFG rule sets, then, function tags are added by integrating the information from the other resources or manually annotated. We integrate predicate-argument information from the NAIST Text Corpus (NTC) (Iida et al., 2007) into the treebank by automatically converting and adding tag suffixes (e.g. -SBJ, -ARG0 described in section 3.3) to the original tags of the argument phrases. The structure information about coordination and apposition are manually annotated.

3.2 Complementary information

We selectively added the following information as tag suffixes and tested their effectiveness.

Inflection We introduced tag suffixes for inflection as clues to identify the attachment position of the verb and adjective phrases, because Japanese verbs and adjectives have inflections, which depends

(no label)	base form
cont	continuative form
attr	attributive form
neg	negative form
hyp	hypothetical form
imp	imperative form
stem	stem

Table 2: Inflection tag suffixes

on their modifying words and phrases (e.g. noun and verb phrases). Symbols in Table 2 are attached to tags VB, ADJ and AUX, based on their inflection form. The inflection information is propagated to the phrases governing the inflected word as a head. We adopted these symbols from the notation of Japanese CCG described in (Bekki, 2010).

Subcategorization and voice Each verb has a subcategorization frame, which is useful for building verb phrase structure. For instance, 掴む *tsukamu* "grasp" takes two arguments, nominative and accusative cases, 与える *ataeru* "give" takes three arguments: nominative, accusative and dative cases. We also added suffixes to verb tags to denote which arguments they require (n:nominative, a:accusative and d: dative). For instance, the verb 与える "give" takes three arguments (nominative, accusative and dative cases), it is tagged with VB[nad].

We retrieve this information from a Japanese case frame dictionary, Nihongo Goitaikei (Ikehara et al., 1997), which has 14,000 frames for 6,000 verbs and adjectives. As an option, we also added voice information (A:active, P:passive and C:causative) to the verb phrases, because it effectively helps to discriminate cases.

3.3 Annotation schema

We introduce phrase and function tags in Table 3 and use them selectively based on the options described below.

Tree Structure We first built a treebank with binary tree structure (except the root and terminal nodes), because it is comparably easy to convert the existing Japanese dependency-based corpus to it. We converted the dependency-based corpus by a previously described method in (Uematsu et al., 2013). The binary tree's structure has the following characteristics about verb phrase (VP) and postposition phrase (PP): VP from the same bunsetsu is a left-branching subtree and the PP-VP structure (roughly corresponding to the argument-predicate structure) is a right-branching subtree. Pure binary trees tend to be very deep and difficult to annotate and interpret by humans. We also built an n-ary tree version by flattening these structures.

NP	Noun phrase
PP	Postposition phrase
VP	Verb phrase
ADJP	Adjective phrase
ADVP	Adverbial phrase
CONJP	Conjunction phrase
S	Sentence (=root)
IP	Inflectional phrase
IP-MAT	Matrix clause
IP-ADV	Adverb clause
IP-REL	Gapping relative clause
IP-ADN	Non-gapping adnominal clause
CP	Complementizer phrase
CP-THT	Sentential complement
Function tags	
semantic role for mandatory argument (gap notation)	
-ARG0 (_arg0)	
-ARG1 (_arg1)	
-ARG2 (_arg2)	
grammatical role for mandatory argument (gap notation)	
-SBJ (_sbj)	Subjective case
-OBJ (_obj)	Objective case
-OB2 (_ob2)	Indirect object case
arbitrary argument	
-TMP	Temporal case
-LOC	Locative case
-COORD	Coordination (for n-ary)
-NCOORD	Left branch of NP coord. (for binary)
-VCOORD	Left branch of VP coord. (for binary)
-APPOS	Apposition
-QUE	Question

Table 3: Phrase tags

The predicate-argument structure, which is usually represented by PPs and a VP in the treebank, particularly tends to be deep in binary trees based on the number of arguments. To flatten the structure, we remove the internal VP nodes by intermediately re-attaching all of the argument PPs to the VP that dominates the predicate. Figure 1 shows an example of flattening the PP-VP structure.

For noun phrases, since compound nouns and numerals cause deep hierarchy, the structure that includes them is flattened under the parent NP. The coordinating structure is preserved, and each NP element of the coordination is flattened

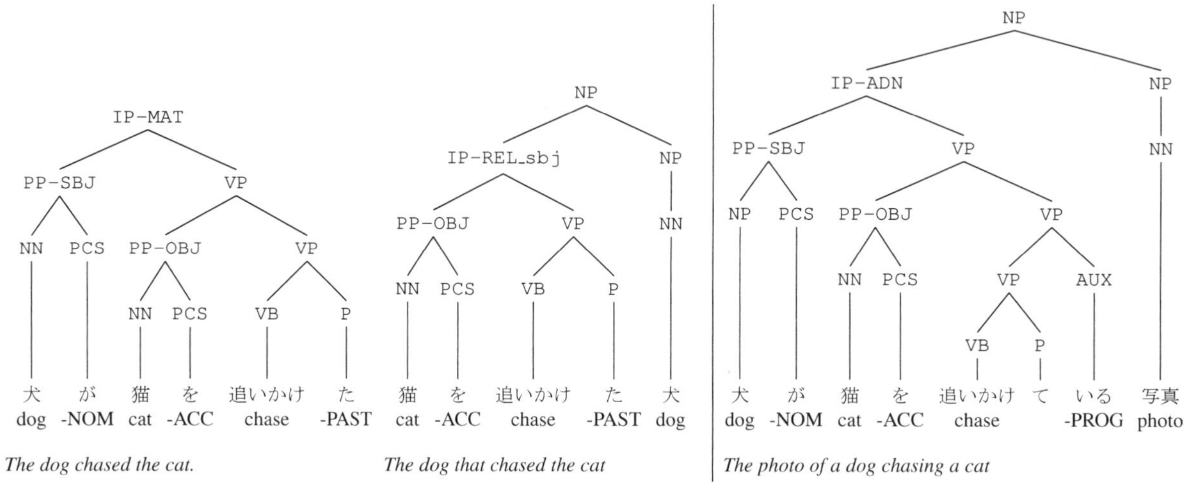

Figure 2: Leftmost tree shows annotation of grammatical roles in a basic inflectional phrase. Right two trees show examples of adnominal phrases.

Predicates and arguments The predicate's argument is basically marked with particles, which represent cases in Japanese; thus, they are represented as a postpositional phrase, which is composed of a noun phrase and particles. The leftmost tree in Figure 2 is an example of the parse result of the following sentence: 犬-が *inu-ga* "dog-NOM" 猫-を *neko-o* "cat-ACC" 追いかけた *oikaketa* "chased" (*The dog chased the cat.*)

We annotated predicate arguments by two different schemes (different tag sets) in our treebank: grammatical roles and semantic roles. In using a tag set based on grammatical roles, the arguments are assigned with the suffixes based on their syntactic roles in the sentence, like Penn Treebank: `SBJ` (subject), `OBJ` (direct object), and `OB2` (indirect object). Figure 2 is annotated by this scheme.

Alternatively, the arguments are labeled based on their semantic roles from case frame of predicates, like PropBank (Palmer et al., 2005): `ARG0`, `ARG1` and `ARG2`. These arguments are annotated by converting semantic roles defined in the case frame dictionary Goitaikei into simple labels, the labels are not influenced by case alternation.

In both annotation schemes, we also annotated two types of arbitrary arguments with semantic role labels: `LOC` (locative) and `TMP` (temporal), which can be assigned consistently and are useful for various applications.

Adnominal clauses Clauses modifying noun phrases are divided into two types: (gapping) relative and non-gapping adnominal clauses. Relative clauses are denoted by adding function tag `-REL` to phrase tag `IP`. Such a gap is directly attached to `IP-REL` tag as a suffix consisting of an underscore and small letters in our treebank, e.g., `IP-REL_sbj` for a subject-gap relative clause, so that the parser can learn the type of gap simultaneously, unlike the Penn Treebank style, where gaps are marked as trace '*T*'. For instance, note the structure of the following noun phrase, which is shown in the middle tree in Figure 2: 猫-を *neko-o* "cat-ACC" 追いかけた *oikake-ta* "to chase" 犬 *inu* "dog" "neko-o (cat-ACC) oikaketa (chase) inu" (*The dog that chased the cat.*). We also adopt another type of gap notation that resembles the predicate-argument structure: semantic role notation. In the example above, tag `IP-REL_arg0` is attached to the relative clause instead.

We attach tag `IP-ADN` to another type of adnominal clauses, which has no gap, the modified noun phrase is not an argument of the predicate in the adnominal clause. The rightmost in Figure 2 is an example of a non-gapping clause: 犬-が *inu-ga* "dog-NOM" 猫-を *neko-o* "cat-ACC" 追いかけている *oikake-teiru* "chasing" 写真 *shashin* "photo" (*A photo of a dog chasing a cat.*), where there is no predicate-argument relation between the verb 追いかける *chase* and the noun 写真 *photo*.

Coordination and apposition The notation of such parallel structure as coordination and apposition differs based on the type of tree structure. For binary trees, the coordination is represented by a left-branching tree, which is a conjunction or a conjunction particle that first joined a left hand constituent; the phrase is marked as a modifier consisting of coordination (`-NCOORD` and `-VCOORD` for NP and VP coordinations), as shown on the left side of Figure 3. On the other hand, in n-ary trees, all the coordination elements and conjunctions are aligned flatly under the parent phrase with suffix `-COORD`. The apposition is represented in the same way using tag `-APPOS` instead.

Phrase and sentential elements Since predicate arguments are often omitted in Japanese, discrimination between the fragment of larger phrases and sentential elements is not clear. In treebank, we employ `IP` and `CP` tags for inflectional and complementizer phrases, assuming that tags with function tag suffixes to the phrase correspond to the maximum projection of the predicate (verb or adjective). The matrix phrase and the adverbial phrase have `IP-MAT` and `IP-ADV` tags respectively. This annotation schema is adopted based on the Penn Historical Corpora (Santorini, 2010) and Japanese Keyaki treebank (Butler et al., 2012) as previously described, while IP in our treebank is not so flat as them.

Such sentential complements as that-clauses in English are tagged with `CP-THT`. In other words, the sentential elements, which are annotated with SBAR, S, and trace *T* in the Penn Treebank, are tagged with `CP` or `IP` in our treebank.

4 Evaluation

The original Kyoto Corpus has 38,400 sentences and they were automatically converted to constituent structures. The function tags are also added to the corpus by integrating predicate-argument information in the NAIST Text corpus. Since the conversion contains errors of structures and tags, about half of them were manually checked to avoid the effects of the conversion errors.

We evaluated our treebank's effectiveness for parser training with 18,640 sentences, which were divided into three sets: 14,895 sentences for a train-

Tag set	LF$_1$	Comp	UF$_1$	Comp
binary tree				
Base	88.4	34.0	89.6	37.9
Base_inf	88.5⋆	33.5	90.0⋆	39.3
Full$_{sr}$	80.7	13.6	88.4	35.9
Full$_{sr}$_inf	**81.1**⋆	**15.5** ⋆	**88.7**⋆	**36.9**
Full$_{sr}$_lex	79.8⋆	13.1	87.7⋆	34.3
Full$_{sr}$_vsub	80.3⋆	12.5	87.9⋆	35.1
Full$_{sr}$_vsub_alt	78.6⋆	13.3	86.7⋆	32.5⋆
Full$_{gr}$	81.0	**15.6**	88.5	**37.3**
Full$_{gr}$_inf	**81.3**⋆	15.3	**88.8**	37.2
Full$_{gr}$_lex	80.3⋆	14.2	87.9⋆	33.6⋆
Full$_{gr}$_vsub	81.2	15.5	88.5	35.2
Full$_{gr}$_vsub_alt	77.9⋆	11.7⋆	86.0⋆	29.9⋆
n-ary tree				
Full$_{sr}$	76.7	11.4	85.3	28.0
Full$_{sr}$_inf	**76.9**	**11.6**	**85.4**	**28.7**
Full$_{sr}$_lex	76.5	11.1	84.7⋆	27.9
Full$_{sr}$_vsub	76.5	10.8	84.9⋆	26.2
Full$_{sr}$_vsub_alt	76.6	11.0	84.8⋆	27.2
Full$_{gr}$	77.2	**13.2**	85.3	**29.2**
Full$_{gr}$_inf	77.4	12.0⋆	**85.5**	28.3
Full$_{gr}$_lex	**77.6**	12.2⋆	85.0	28.5
Full$_{gr}$_vsub	77.1	12.7⋆	84.8⋆	28.8
Full$_{gr}$_vsub_alt	76.9	12.2⋆	84.7⋆	26.3⋆

Table 4: Parse results displayed by labeled and unlabeled F$_1$ metrics and proportion of sentences completely matching gold standard (**Comp**). **Base** contains only basic tags, not grammatical function tags. Figures with '⋆' indicate statistically significant differences ($\alpha = 0.05$) from the results without complementary information, i.e., **Full$_{sr}$** or **Full$_{gr}$**.

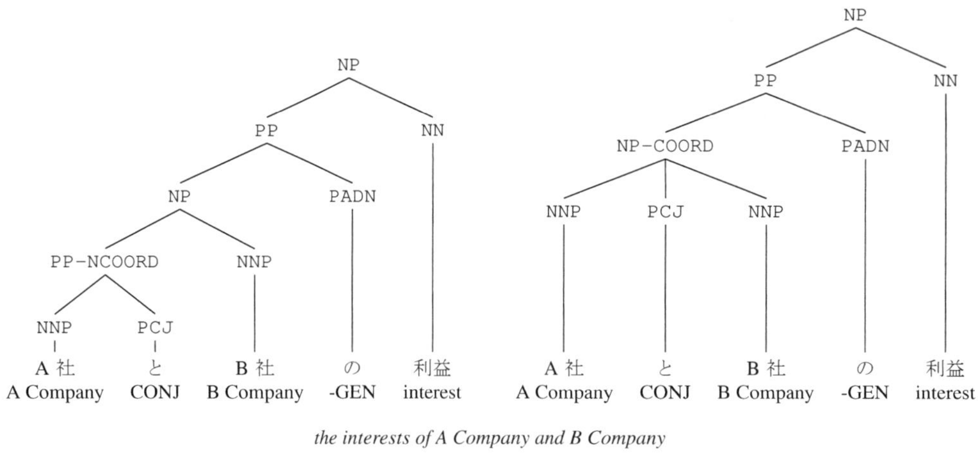

Figure 3: Noun phrase coordination

tag set	**UAS**
binary tree	
Base	89.1
Base_inf	89.4
Full$_{\mathbf{sr}}$	87.9
Full$_{\mathbf{sr}}$**_inf**	88.3
Full$_{\mathbf{gr}}$	88.0
Full$_{\mathbf{gr}}$**_inf**	88.5⋆
n-ary (flattened) tree	
Full$_{\mathbf{sr}}$	82.8
Full$_{\mathbf{sr}}$**_inf**	83.3
Full$_{\mathbf{gr}}$	82.9
Full$_{\mathbf{gr}}$**_inf**	83.0

Table 5: Dependency accuracies of the results converted into bunsetsu dependencies.

ing set, 1,860 sentences for a test set, and the remainder for a development set.

The basic evaluations were under the condition of using the original tag sets: the basic set **Base**, which contains all the preterminal tags in Table 1 and the phrase tags in Table Table 3, except the IP and CP tags, and the full set **Full**, which has **Base** + IP, CP tags, and all the function tags. The basic set **Base** is provided to evaluate the constituent parser performance in case that we need better performance at the cost of limiting the information.

We used two types of function tag sets: **Full** $_{\mathbf{sr}}$ for semantic roles and **Full** $_{\mathbf{gr}}$ for grammatical roles.

We added the following complementary information to the tags and named the new tag sets **Base** or **Full** and suffix:

_inf: add inflection information to the POS tag (verbs, adjectives, and auxiliary verbs) and the phrase tags (Table 2).

_lex: lexicalize the closed words, i.e., auxiliary verbs and particles.

_vsub: add verb subcategorization to the verb and verb phrase tags.

_vsub_alt: add verb subcategorization and case alternation to the verb and verb phrase tags.

In comparing the system output with the gold standard, we remove the complementary information to ignore different level of annotation, thus, we do not discriminate between `VB[na]` and `VB[nad]` for example.

We used the Berkeley parser (Petrov et al., 2006) for our evaluation and trained with six iterations for latent annotations. In training the n-ary trees, we used a default Markovization parameter ($h = 0, v = 1$), because the parser performed the best with the development set.

Table 4 shows the parsing results of the test sets. On the whole, the binary tree outperformed the n-ary tree. This indicates that the binary tree structure was converted from bunsetsu-based dependencies, whose characteristics are described in Section 3.3, and is better for parser training than the partially flattened structure.

As for additional information, the inflection suffixes slightly improved the F_1-metrics. This is mainly because the inflection information gives the category of the attached phrase (e.g., the attributive form for noun phrases). The others did not provide any improvement, even though we expected the subcategorization and case alternation information to help the parser detect and discriminate the grammatical roles, probably because we simply introduced the information by concatenating the suffixes to the base tags to adapt an off-the-shelf parser in our evaluation. For instance, `VB[n]` and `VB[na]` are recognized as entirely independent categories; a sophisticated model, which can treat them hierarchically, would improve the performance.

For comparison with a bunsetsu-based dependency parser, we convert the parser output into unlabeled bunsetsu dependencies by the following simple way. We first extract all bunsetsu chunks in a sentence and find a minimum phrase including each bunsetsu chunk from a constituent structure. For each pair of bunsetsus having a common parent phrase, we add a dependency from the left bunsetsu to the right one, since Japanese is a head-final language.

The unlabeled attachment scores of the converted dependencies are shown as the accuracies in Table 5, since most bunsetsu-based dependency parsers output only unlabeled structure.

The **Base_inf** results are comparable with the bunsetsu-dependency results (90.46%) over the same corpus (Kudo et al., 2002)[1], which has only the same level of information. Constituent parsing with treebank almost matched the current bunsetsu parsing.

5 Analysis

In this section, we analyze the error of parse results from the point of view of the discrimination of grammatical and semantic roles, adnominal clause and coordination.

Grammatical and semantic roles Predicate arguments usually appeared as PP, which is composed of noun phrases and particles. We focus on PPs with function labels. Table 6 shows the PP results with

[1]The division for the training and test sets is different.

tag	P	R	F_1
PP-ARG0	64.9	75.0	69.6
PP-ARG1	70.6	80.1	75.1
PP-ARG2	60.3	68.5	64.1
PP-TMP	40.1	43.6	41.8
PP-LOC	23.8	17.2	20.0

tag	P	R	F_1
PP-SBJ	69.6	81.5	75.1
PP-OBJ	72.6	83.5	77.7
PP-OB2	63.6	71.4	67.3
PP-TMP	45.0	48.0	46.5
PP-LOC	21.3	15.9	18.2

Table 6: Discrimination of semantic role and grammatical role labels (upper: semantic roles, lower: grammatical role)

system \ gold	PP-SBJ	PP-OBJ	PP-OB2
PP-SBJ	*74.9	6.5	2.3
PP-OBJ	5.8	*80.1	0.5
PP-OB2	1.7	0.3	*68.5
PP-TMP	0.2	0.0	0.5
PP-LOC	0.2	0.0	0.4
PP	6.5	2.0	16.8
other labels	0.5	0.2	0.3
no span	10.2	10.9	11.0
system \ gold	**PP-TMP**	**PP-LOC**	
PP-SBJ	4.7	4.1	
PP-OBJ	0.0	0.0	
PP-OB2	6.0	13.8	
PP-TMP	*43.6	2.8	
PP-LOC	2.0	*17.2	
PP	37.6	49.7	
other labels	1.4	5.0	
no span	4.7	7.4	

Table 7: Confusion matrix for grammatical role labels (recall). Figures with '*' indicate recall.(binary tree, $\mathbf{Full_{gr}}$)

tag	P	R	F_1
IP-REL_sbj	48.4	54.3	51.1
IP-REL_obj	27.8	22.7	24.9
IP-REL_ob2	17.2	29.4	21.7
IP-ADN	50.9	55.4	53.1
CP-THT	66.1	66.6	66.3

Table 8: Results of adnominal phrase and sentential element (binary tree, $\mathbf{Full_{gr}}$)

grammatical and semantic labels under the **Full**$_{sr}$ and **Full**$_{gr}$ conditions respectively.

The precision and the recall of mandatory arguments did not reach a high level. The results are related to predicate argument structure analysis in Japanese. But, they cannot be directly compared, because the parser in this evaluation must output a correct target phrase and select it as an argument, although most researches select a word using a gold standard parse tree. Hayashibe et al. (2011) reported the best precision of ARG0 discrimination to be 88.42 % [2], which is the selection results from the candidate nouns using the gold standard parse tree of NTC. If the cases where the correct candidates did not appear in the parser results are excluded (10.8 %), the precision is 72.7 %. The main remaining error is to label to non-argument PP with suffix `-ARG0` (17.0%), thus, we must restrain the overlabeling to improve the precision.

The discrimination of grammatical role is higher than that of semantic role, which is more directly estimated by case particles following the noun phrases. The confusion matrix for the recall in Table 7 shows main problem is parse error, where correct phrase span does not exist (no span), and marks 10-11%. The second major error is discrimination from bare PPs (PPs without suffixes), mainly because the clues to judge whether the arguments are mandatory or arbitrary lack in the treebank. Since even the mandatory arguments are often omitted in Japanese, it is not facilitate to identify arguments of predicates by using only syntactic information.

Adnominal phrases We need to discriminate between two types of adnominal phrases as described in Section 3.3: `IP-REL` and `IP-ADN`. Table 8 shows the discrimination results of the adnominal phrase types. The difference between `IP-REL` (gapped relative clauses) and `IP-ADN` is closely related to the discrimination of the grammatical role: whether the antecedent is the argument of the head predicate of the relative clause.

Table 8 shows the discrimination results of the adnominal phrases. The results indicate the difficulties of discriminating the type of gaps of relative clause `IP-REL`. The confusion matrix in Table 9 shows that the discrimination between gaps and non-gaps, i.e., `IP-REL` and `IP-ADN`, is moderate as for `IP-REL_sbj` and `IP-REL_obj`. However, `IP-REL_ob2` is hardly recognized, because it is difficult to determine whether the antecedent, which is marked with particle 'ni', is a mandatory argument (`IP-REL_ob2`) or not (`IP-ADN`). Increasing training samples would improve the discrimination, since there are only 290 `IP-REL_ob2` tags for 8,100 `IP-ADN` tags in the training set.

Naturally discrimination only by syntactic information has limitation; this baseline can be improved by incorporating semantic information.

Coordination Figure 10 shows the coordination results, which are considered the baseline for only using syntactic information. Improvement is possible by incorporating semantic information, since the disambiguation of coordination structure essentially needs semantic information.

6 Conclusion

We constructed a Japanese constituent-based parser to be released from the constraints of bunsetsu-based analysis to simplify the integration of syntactic and semantic analysis. Our evaluation results indicate that the basic performance of the parser trained with the treebank almost equals bunsetsus-based parsers and has the potential to supply detailed syntactic information by grammatical function labels for semantic analysis, such as predicate-argument structure analysis.

Future work will be to refine the annotation scheme to improve parser performance and to evaluate parser results by adapting them to such NLP applications as machine translation.

Acknowledgments

We would like to thank Associate Professor Yusuke Miyao, Associate Professor Takuya Matsuzaki of National Institute of Informatics and Sumire Uematsu of the University of Tokyo for providing us the language resources and giving us valuable suggestions.

[2]The figure is calculated only for the arguments that appear as the dependents of predicates, excluding the omitted arguments.

system \ gold	IP-REL_sbj	IP-REL_obj
IP-REL_sbj	*55.0	30.3
IP-REL_obj	8.5	*33.3
IP-REL_ob2	0.5	0.0
IP-ADN	10.0	9.0
IP-ADV	0.3	0.0
VP	8.5	7.6
other labels	1.2	6.2
no span	16.0	13.6
system \ gold	IP-REL_ob2	IP-ADN
IP-REL_sbj	29.4	7.5
IP-REL_obj	0.0	0.6
IP-REL_ob2	*11.8	0.0
IP-ADN	23.5	*57.3
IP-ADV	0.5	0.3
VP	17.6	9.3
other labels	5.4	3.0
no span	11.8	22.0

Table 9: Confusion matrix for adnominal phrases (recall). Figures with '*' indicate recall.(binary tree, $\mathbf{Full}_{\mathbf{gr}}$)

tag	P	R	F_1
NP-COORD	62.6	60.7	61.6
VP-COORD	57.6	50.0	53.5
NP-APPOS	46.0	40.0	42.8

Table 10: Results of coordination and apposition (binary tree, $\mathbf{Full}_{\mathbf{gr}}$)

References

Masayuki Asahara. 2013. Comparison of syntactic dependency annotation schemata . In *Proceedings of the 3rd Japanese Corpus Linguistics Workshop*, In Japanese.

Daisuke Bekki. 2010. Formal theory of Japanese syntax. Kuroshio Shuppan, In Japanese.

Daniel M. Bikel. 2004. A distributional analysis of a lexicalized statistical parsing model. In *Proceedings of Empirical Methods in Natural Language Processing (EMNLP 2004)*, Vol.4, pp. 182–189.

Francis Bond, Sanae Fujita and Takaaki Tanaka. 2008. The Hinoki syntactic and semantic treebank of Japanese. In *Journal of Language Resources and Evaluation*, Vol.42, No. 2, pp. 243–251

Alastair Butler, Zhu Hong, Tomoko Hotta, Ruriko Otomo, Kei Yoshimoto and Zhen Zhou. 2012. Keyaki Treebank: phrase structure with functional information for Japanese. In *Proceedings of Text Annotation Workshop*.

Eugene Charniak. 2000. A maximum-entropy-inspired parser. In *Proceedings of the 1st North American chapter of the Association for Computational Linguistics conference, (NAACL 2000)*, pp. 132–139.

DongHyun Choi, Jungyeul Park and Key-Sun Choi. 2012. Korean treebank transformation for parser training. In *Proceedings of the 50th Annual Meeting of the Association for Computational Linguistics (ACL 2012)*, pp. 78-88.

Ann Copestake, Dan Flickinger, Carl Pollard and Ivan A. Sag. 2005. Minimal recursion semantics: an introduction. *Research on Language and Computation*, Vol. 3, No. 4, pp. 281-332.

Ryan Gabbard, Mitchell Marcus and Seth Kulick. 2006. Fully parsing the Penn Treebank. In *Proceedings of the Human Language Technology Conference of the North American Chapter of the Association of Computational Linguistics (HLT-NAACL 2006)*, pp. 184–191.

Takao Gunji. 1987 Japanese phrase structure grammar: a unification-based approach. D.Reidel.

Yuta Hayashibe, Mamoru Komachi and Yujzi Matsumoto. 2011. Japanese predicate argument structure analysis exploiting argument position and type. In *Proceedings of the 5th International Joint Conference on Natural Language Processing (IJCNLP 2011)*, pp. 201-209.

Ryu Iida, Mamoru Komachi Kentaro Inui and Yuji Matsumoto. 2007. Annotating a Japanese text corpus with predicate-argument and coreference relations. In *Proceedings of Linguistic Annotation Workshop*, pp. 132–139.

Ryu Iida, Massimo Poesio. 2011. A cross-lingual ILP solution to zero anaphora resolution. In *Proceedings of the 49th Annual Meeting of the Association for Computational Linguistics: Human Language Technologies (ACL-HLT 2011)*, pp. 804-813.

Satoru Ikehara, Masahiro Miyazaki, Satoshi Shirai, Akio Yokoo, Kentaro Ogura, Yoshifumi Ooyama and Yoshihiko Hayashi. 1998. Nihongo Goitaikei. Iwanami Shoten, In Japanese.

Ronald M. Kaplan and Joan Bresnan. 1982. Lexical-Functional Grammar: a formal system for grammatical representation. In *the Mental Representation of Grammatical Relations* (Joan Bresnan ed.), pp. 173–281. The MIT Press.

Daisuke Kawahara and Sadao Kurohashi. 2006. A fully-lexicalized probabilistic model for Japanese syntactic and case structure analysis. In *Proceedings of the Human Language Technology Conference of the North American Chapter of the Association of Computational Linguistics (HLT-NAACL 2006)*, pp. 176–183.

Dan Klein and Christopher D. Manning. 2003. Fast exact inference with a factored model for natural language processing. *Advances in Neural Information Processing Systems*, 15:3–10.

Taku Kudo and Yuji Matsumoto. 2002. Japanese dependency analysis using cascaded chunking. In *Proceedings of the 6th Conference on Natural Language Learning (CoNLL-2002)*, Volume 20, pp. 1–7.

Sadao Kurohashi and Makoto Nagao. 2003. Building a Japanese parsed corpus – while improving the parsing system. In Abeille (ed.), *Treebanks: Building and using parsed corpora*, Chap. 14, pp. 249–260. Kluwer Academic Publishers.

Mitchell P. Marcus, Beatrice Santorini, Mary Ann Marcinkiewicz. 1993. Building a large annotated corpus of English: the Penn Treebank. In *Journal of Computational Linguistics*. Vol.19, No.2, pp. 313–330.

Hiroshi Masuichi, Tomoko Okuma, Hiroki Yoshimura and Yasunari Harada. 2003 Japanese parser on the basis of the Lexical-Functional Grammar formalism and its evaluation. In *Proceedings of the 17th Pacific Asia Conference on Language, Information and Computation (PACLIC 17)*, pp. 298-309.

Masaaki Nagata and Tsuyoshi Morimoto,. 1993. A unification-based Japanese parser for speech-to-speech translation. In *IEICE Transaction on Information and Systems*. Vol.E76-D, No.1, pp. 51–61.

Tomoya Noro, Taiichi Hashimoto, Takenobu Tokunaga and Hotsumi Tanaka. 2005. Building a large-scale Japanese syntactically annotated corpus for deriving a CFG. in *Proceedings of Symposium on Large-Scale Knowledge Resources (LKR2005)*, pp..159 – 162.

Matha Palmer, Daniel Gildea and Paul Kingsbury. 2005. The Proposition Bank: n annotated corpus of semantic roles. *Computational Linguistics*, Vol.31 No. 1, pp. 71–106.

Slav Petrov, Leon Barrett, Romain Thibaux and Dan Klein.. 2006. Learning accurate, compact, and interpretable tree annotation. In *Proceedings of the 21st International Conference on Computational Linguistics and the 44th Annual Meeting of the Association for Computational Linguistics (COLING-ACL 2006)*, pp. 433-440.

Ivan A. Sag, Thomas Wasow and Emily M. Bender,. 2003. Syntactic theory: a formal introduction. *2nd Edition, CSLI Publications*.

Beatrice Santorini. 2010. Annotation manual for the Penn Historical Corpora and the PCEEC (Release 2). Department of Linguistics, University of Pennsylvania.

Melanie Siegel and Emily M. Bender. 2002. Efficient deep processing of Japanese. In *Proceedings of the 3rd Workshop on Asian Language Resources and International Standardization at the 19th International Conference on Computational Linguistics*, Vol. 12, pp. 1–8.

Sumire Uematsu, Takuya Matsuzaki, Hiroaki Hanaoka, Yusuke Miyao and Hideki Mima. 2013. Integrating multiple dependency corpora for inducing wide-coverage Japanese CCG resources. In *Proceedings of the 51st Annual Meeting of the Association for Computational Linguistics (ACL 2013)*, pp. 1042–1051.

Context Based Statistical Morphological Analyzer and its Effect on Hindi Dependency Parsing

Deepak Kumar Malladi and **Prashanth Mannem**
Language Technologies Research Center
International Institute of Information Technology
Hyderabad, AP, India - 500032
{deepak.malladi, prashanth}@research.iiit.ac.in

Abstract

This paper revisits the work of (Malladi and Mannem, 2013) which focused on building a *Statistical Morphological Analyzer* (SMA) for Hindi and compares the performance of SMA with other existing statistical analyzer, *Morfette*. We shall evaluate SMA in various experiment scenarios and look at how it performs for unseen words. The later part of the paper presents the effect of the predicted morph features on dependency parsing and extends the work to other morphologically rich languages: Hindi and Telugu, without any language-specific engineering.

1 Introduction

Hindi is one of the widely spoken language in the world with more than 250 million native speakers[1]. Language technologies could play a major role in removing the digital divide that exists between speakers of various languages. Hindi, being a morphologically rich language with a relatively free word order (Mor-FOW), poses a variety of challenges for NLP that may not be encountered when working on English.

Morphological analysis is the task of analyzing the structure of morphemes in a word and is generally a prelude to further complex tasks such as parsing, machine translation, semantic analysis etc. These tasks need an analysis of the words in the sentence in terms of lemma, affixes, parts of speech (POS) etc.

NLP for Hindi has suffered due to the lack of a high coverage automatic morphological analyzer. For example, the 2012 Hindi Parsing Shared Task (Sharma et al., 2012) held with COLING-2012 workshop had a gold-standard input track and an automatic input track, where the former had gold-standard morphological analysis, POS tags and chunks of a sentence as input and the automatic track had only the sentence along with automatic POS tags as input. The morphological information which is crucial for Hindi parsing was missing in the automatic track as the existing analyzer had limited coverage. Parsing accuracies of gold-standard input track were significantly higher than that of the other track. But in the real scenario NLP applications, gold information is not provided. Even Ambati et al. (2010b) and Bharati et al. (2009a) have exploited the role of morpho-syntactic features in Hindi dependency parsing. Hence we need a high coverage and accurate morphological analyzer.

2 Related work

Previous efforts on Hindi morphological analysis concentrated on building rule based systems that give all the possible analyses for a word form irrespective of its context in the sentence. The paradigm based analyzer (PBA) by Bharati et al. (1995) is one of the most widely used applications among researchers in the Indian NLP community. In paradigm based analysis, words are grouped into a set of paradigms based on the inflections they take. Each paradigm has a set of add-delete rules to account for its inflections and words belonging to a paradigm take the same inflectional forms. Given a

[1] http://www.ethnologue.com/statistics/size

	L	G	N	P	C	T/V
	↓	↓	↓	↓	↓	↓
xeSa (*country*)	xeSa	m	sg	3	d	0
	xeSa	m	pl	3	d	0
	xeSa	m	sg	3	o	0
cAhie (*want*)	cAha	any	sg	2h	_	ie
	cAha	any	pl	2h	_	eM

L-lemma, G-gender, N-number, P-person
C-case, T/V-TAM or Vibhakti

Table 1: Multiple analyses given by the PBA for the words xeSa and cAhie

word, the PBA identifies the *lemma*, *coarse POS tag*, *gender*, *number*, *person*, *case marker*, *vibhakti*[2] and *TAM* (tense, aspect, modality). Being a rule-based system, the PBA takes a word as input and gives all the possible analyses as output. (Table 1 presents an example). It doesn't pick the correct analysis for a word in its sentential context.

Goyal and Lehal's analyser (2008), which is a re-implementation of the PBA with few extensions, has not done any comparative evaluation. Kanuparthi et al. (2012) built a derivational morphological analyzer for Hindi by introducing a layer over the PBA. It identifies 22 derivational suffixes which helps in providing derivational analysis for the word whose suffix matches with one of these 22 suffixes.

The large scale machine translation projects[3] that are currently under way in India use shallow parser built on PBA and an automatic POS tagger. The shallow parser prunes the morphological analyses from PBA to select the correct one using the POS tags from the tagger. Since it is based on PBA, it suffers from similar coverage issues for out of vocabulary (OOV) words.

The PBA, developed in 1995, has a limited vocabulary and has received only minor upgrades since then. Out of 17,666 unique words in the Hindi Treebank (HTB) released during the 2012 Hindi Parsing Shared Task (Sharma et al., 2012), the PBA does not have entries for 5,581 words (31.6%).

Apart from the traditional rule-based approaches, Morfette (Chrupała et al., 2008) is a modular, data-driven, probabilistic system which learns to perform joint morphological tagging and lemmatization from morphologically annotated corpora. The system is composed of two learning modules, one for morphological tagging and one for lemmati- zation, and one decoding module which searches for the best sequence of pairs of morphological tags and lemmas for an input sequence of wordforms.

Malladi and Mannem (2013) have build a *Statistical Morphological Analyzer* (SMA) with minimal set of features but they haven't compared their system with Morfette. In our work we shall discuss in detail about SMA with more concentration on evaluating the system in various scenarios and shall extend the approach to other morphologically rich languages. Later we evaluate the effect of the predicted morph features (by SMA) on Hindi dependency parsing.

Data	#Sentences	#Words
Training	12,041	268,096
Development	1,233	26,416
Test	1,828	39,775

Table 2: HTB statistics

3 Hindi Dependency Treebank (HTB)

A multi layered and multi representational treebank for Hindi is developed by annotating with morpho-syntactic (morphological analyses, POS tags, chunk) and syntacto-semantic (dependency relations labeled in the computational paninian framework) information. A part of the HTB (constituting of 15,102 sentences) was released for Hindi Parsing Shared Task. Table 2 shows the word counts of training, development and test sections of HTB.

With the existing morph analyzer (PBA) performing poorly on OOV words and the availability of an annotated treebank, Malladi and Mannem (2013) set out to build a high-coverage automatic Hindi morph analyzer by learning each of the seven morphological attributes separately from the Hindi Treebank. During this process, it was realized that vibhakti and TAM can be better predicted using heuristics on fine-grained POS tags than by training on the HTB.

In the rest of the section, we discuss the methods used by SMA to predict each of the seven mor-

[2] Vibhakti is a Sanskrit grammatical term that encompasses post-positionals and case endings for nouns, as well as inflection and auxiliaries for verbs (Pedersen et al., 2004).

[3] http://sampark.iiit.ac.in/

MorphFeature	Values
Gender	masculine, feminine, any, none
Number	singular, plural, any, none
Person	1, 1h, 2, 2h, 3, 3h, any, none
CaseMarker	direct, oblique, any, none

Table 3: Morph features and the values they take

source	target	gloss
k i y A	k a r a	*do*
l a d a k e	l a d a k A	*boy*
l a d a k I	l a d a k I	*girl*
l a d a k I y A M	l a d a k I	*girl*

Table 4: Sample parallel corpus for lemma prediction

phological attributes and their effect on Hindi dependency parsing. Table 3 lists the values that each of the morph attributes take in HTB.

4 Statistical Morphological Analyzer (SMA)

The output of a morphological analyzer depends on the language that it is developed for. Analyzers for English (Goldsmith, 2000) predict just the lemmas and affixes mainly because of its restricted agreement based on semantic features such as animacy and *natural* gender. But in Hindi, agreement depends on *lexical* features such as *grammatical* gender, number, person and case. Hence, it is crucial that Hindi analyzers predict these along with TAM and vibhakti which have been found to be useful for syntactic parsing (Ambati et al., 2010b; Bharati et al., 2009a).

Hindi has syntactic agreement (of GNP and case) of two kinds: modifier-head agreement and noun-verb agreement. Modifiers, including determiners, agree with their head noun in gender, number and case, and finite verbs agree with some noun in the sentence in gender, number and person (Kachru, 2006). Therefore, apart from lemma and POS tags, providing gender, number and person is also crucial for syntactic parsing.[4]

[4]While nouns, pronouns and adjectives have both GNP and case associated with them, verbs only have GNP. TAM is valid only for verbs and vibhakti (post-position) is only associated with nouns and pronouns.

4.1 Lemma prediction

The PBA uses a large vocabulary along with paradigm tables consisting of add-delete rules to find the lemma of a given word. All possible add-delete rules are applied on a given word form and the resulting lemma is checked against the vocabulary to find if it is right or not. If no such lemma exists (for OOV words), it returns the word itself as the lemma.

While the gender, number and person of a word form varies according to the context (due to syntactic agreement with head words), there are very few cases where a word form can have more than one lemma in a context. For example, vaha can either be masculine or feminine depending on the form that the verb takes. It is feminine in vaha Gara gayI (*she went home*) and masculine in vaha Gara gayA (*he went home*). The lemma for vaha can only be vaha irrespective of the context and also the lemma for gayI and gayA is jA. This makes lemma simpler to predict among the morphological features, provided there is access to a dictionary of all the word forms along with their lemmas. Unfortunately, such a large lemma dictionary doesn't exist. There are 15,752 word types in training, 4,292 word types in development and 5,536 word types in test sections of HTB respectively. Among these 18.5% of the types in development and 20.2% in test data are unseen in training data.

SMA analyzer perceives lemma prediction from a machine translation perspective, with the characters in the input word form treated as the source sentence and those in the lemma as the target. The strings on source and target side are split into sequences of characters separated by space, as shown in Table 4. The phrase based model (Koehn et al., 2007) in Moses is trained on the parallel data created from the training part of HTB. The translation model accounts for the changes in the affixes (sequence of characters) from word form to lemma whereas the language model accounts for which affixes go with which stems. In this perspective, the standard MT experiment of switching source and target to attain better accuracy would not apply since it is unreasonable to predict the word form from the lemma without taking the context into account.

Apart from the above mentioned approach, we apply a heuristic on top of SMA, wherein proper nouns

Gender	Word	Gloss
`masculine`	`cAvala, paMKA`	*rice, fan*
`feminine`	`rela, xAla`	*train, pulse*
`any`	`jA`	*go*
`none`	`karIba`	*near*

Table 5: Gender value examples

Number	Word	Gloss
`singular`	`ladZake`	*boy-Sg-Oblique*
`plural`	`ladZake`	*boy-Pl-Direct*
`any`	`banA`	*make*
`none`	`karIba`	*near*

Table 6: Number value examples

(NNP) take the word form itself as the lemma.

4.2 Gender, Number, Person and Case Prediction

Unlike lemma prediction, SMA uses SVM (support vector machine) machine learning algorithm to predict GNP and case.

Though knowing the syntactic head of a word helps in enforcing agreement (and thereby accurately predicting the correct GNP), parsing is usually a higher level task and is not performed before morphological analysis. Hence, certain cases of GNP prediction are similar in nature to the standard chicken and egg problem.

4.2.1 Gender

Gender prediction is tricky in Hindi as even native speakers tend to make errors while annotating. Gender prediction in English is easy when compared to Hindi since gender in English is inferred based on the biological characteristics the word is referring to. For example, `Train` has neuter gender in English whereas in Hindi, it exhibits feminine characteristics. A dictionary of word-gender information may usually suffice for gender prediction in English but in Hindi it isn't the case as gender could vary based on its agreement with verb/modifier. The values that gender can take for a word in a given context are *masculine*(*m*), *feminine*(*f*), *any* (either *m* or *f*) or *none* (neither *m* nor *f*). Table 5 gives example for each gender value.

Nouns inherently carry gender information. Pronouns (of genitive form), adjectives and verbs inflect according to the gender of the noun they refer to.

Case	Word	Gloss
`direct`	`ladZake`	*boy-Pl*
`oblique`	`ladZake`	*boy-sg*
`any`	`bAraha`	*twelve (cardinals)*
`none`	`kaha`	*say*

Table 7: Case value examples

4.2.2 Number

Every noun belongs to a unique number class. Noun modifiers and verbs have different forms for each number class and inflect accordingly to match the grammatical number of the nouns to which they refer.

Number takes the values *singular* (*sg*), *plural* (*pl*), *any* (either *sg* or *pl*) and *none* (neither *sg* nor *pl*). Table 6 lists examples for each of the values. In it, `ladZake` takes the grammatical number *sg* (in *direct* case) or *pl* (in *oblique* case) depending on the context in which it occurs. It may be noted that since PBA does not consider the word's context, it outputs both the values and leaves the disambiguation to the subsequent stages.

4.2.3 Person

Apart from *first*, *second* and *third* persons, Hindi also has the honorific forms, resulting in *1h*, *2h* and *3h*. Postpositions do not have person information, hence *none* is also a possible value. Apart from the above mentioned grammatical person values, *any* is also a feasible value.

4.2.4 Case Marker

Case markers in Hindi (*direct* and *oblique*) are attributed to nouns and pronouns. Table 7 lists few examples.

Words which inflect for gender, number, person and case primarily undergo affixation at the end.

Features for GNP & Case Marker

The following features were tried out in building the models for gender, number, person and case prediction:

- Word level features
  - Word

    - Last 2 characters
    - Last 3 characters
    - Last 4 characters
    - Character N-grams of the word
    - Lemma
    - Word Length

- Sentence level features
    - Lexical category[5]
    - Next word
    - Previous word

Combinations of these features have been tried out to build the SVM models for GNP and case. For each of these tasks, feature tuning was done separately. In Malladi and Mannem (2013), a linear SVM classification (Fan et al., 2008) is used to build statistical models for GNP and case but we found that with RBF kernel (non-linear SVM)[6] we achieve better accuracies. Furthermore, the parameters (C, γ) of the RBF kernel are learned using grid search technique.

4.3 Vibhakti and TAM

Vibhakti and TAM are helpful in identifying the *karaka*[7] dependency labels in HTB. While nouns and pronouns take vibhakti, verbs inflect for TAM. Both TAM and vibhakti occur immediately after the words in their respective word classes.

Instead of building statistical models for vibhakti and TAM prediction, SMA uses heuristics on POS tag sequences to predict the correct value. The POS tags of words following nouns, pronouns and verbs give an indication as to what the vibhakti/TAM are. Words with PSP (postposition) and NST (noun with spatial and temporal properties) tags are generally considered as the vibhakti for the preceding nouns and pronouns. A postposition in HTB is annotated as PSP only if it is written separately (`usane`/PRP vs `usa`/PRP `ne`/PSP). For cases where the postposition is not written separately SMA relies on the treebank data to get the suffix. Similarly, words with VAUX tag form the TAM for the immediately preceding verb.

The PBA takes individual words as input and hence does not output the entire vibhakti or TAM of the word in the sentence. It only identifies these values for those words which have the information within the word form (e.g. `usakA` *he+Oblique*, `kiyA` *do+PAST*).

In the sentence,

> `rAma`/NNP `kA`/PSP `kiwAba`/NN `cori`/NN `ho`/VM `sakawA`/VAUX `hE`/VAUX

PBA identifies `rAma`'s vibhakti as *0* and `ho`'s TAM as *0*. Whereas in HTB, vibhakti and TAM of `rAma` and `ho` are annotated as *0_kA* and *0_saka+wA_hE* respectively. SMA determines this information precisely and Morfette which can predict other morph features, is not capable of predicting TAM and Vibhakti as these features are specific to Indian languages.

5 Evaluation Systems

SMA is compared with a baseline system, Morfette and two versions of the PBA wherever relevant. The *baseline* system takes the word form itself as the lemma and selects the most frequent value for the rest of the attributes.

Since PBA is a rule based analyzer which gives more than one analysis for words, we use two versions of it for comparison. The first system is the oracle PBA (referred further as O-PBA) which uses an oracle to pick the *best* analysis from the list of all analyses given by the PBA. The second version of the PBA (F-PBA) picks the *first* analysis from the output as the correct analysis.

Morfette can perdict lemma, gender, number, person and case attributes but it cannot predict TAM and Vibhakti as they do not have a definite set of predefined values unlike other morphological attributes.

6 Experiments and Results

SMA approach to Hindi morphological analysis is based on handling each of the seven attributes (*lemma, gender, number, person, case, vibhakti* and *TAM*) separately. However, evaluation is performed

[5]POS is considered as a sentence level feature since tagging models use the word ngrams to predict the POS category

[6]LIBSVM tool is used to build non-linear SVM models for our experiments (Chang and Lin, 2011).

[7]karakas are syntactico-semantic relations which are employed in Paninian framework (Begum et al., 2008; Bharati et al., 2009b)

Analysis	Test Data - Overall(%)					Test Data - OOV of SMA(%)				
	Baseline	F-PBA	O-PBA	Morfette	SMA	Baseline	F-PBA	O-PBA	Morfette	SMA
L	71.12	83.10	86.69	94.14	95.84	78.10	82.08	82.48	90.30	89.51
G	37.43	72.98	79.59	95.05	96.19	60.22	43.07	44.06	72.03	82.65
N	52.87	72.22	80.50	94.09	95.37	69.60	44.53	47.56	84.89	90.44
P	45.59	74.33	84.13	94.88	96.38	78.30	52.51	53.89	84.76	94.85
C	29.31	58.24	81.20	93.91	95.32	43.60	31.40	47.36	80.21	88.52
V/T	65.40	53.05	59.65	NA	97.04	58.31	33.58	34.56	NA	96.04
L+C	16.46	48.84	72.06	88.56	91.39	32.52	28.50	44.66	72.89	79.09
L+V/T	54.78	44.57	51.71	NA	93.06	53.56	31.73	32.72	NA	86.41
G+N+P	23.05	61.10	73.81	88.36	91.11	47.49	35.75	39.58	62.33	76.52
G+N+P+C	9.72	45.73	70.87	84.43	87.78	21.04	20.91	35.95	55.74	69.99
L+G+N+P	20.27	53.29	66.28	83.44	87.51	44.72	34.63	38.46	57.85	69.13
L+G+N+P+C	8.57	38.25	63.41	79.73	**84.25**	19.33	19.92	34.89	51.52	**63.06**
L+G+N+P+C+V/T	1.25	32.53	42.80	NA	**82.12**	4.02	14.51	18.67	NA	**60.07**

L-lemma, G-gender, N-number, P-person, C-case, V/T-Vibhakti/TAM

Table 8: Accuracies of SMA compared with F-PBA, O-PBA and baseline systems.

on individual attributes as well as on the combined output.

SMA builds models for lemma, gender, number, person and case prediction trained on the training data of the HTB. All the models are tuned on development data and evaluated on test data of the HTB.

Table 8 presents the accuracies of five systems (baseline, F-PBA, O-PBA, Morfette and SMA) in predicting the morphological attributes of all the words in the HTB's test data and also for OOV words of SMA (i.e. words that occur in the test section but not in training section of HTB)[8]. The accuracies are the percentages of words in the data with the correct analysis. It may be noted that SMA performs significantly better than the best analyses of PBA and the baseline system in all the experiments conducted. As far as Morfette is concerned, it performs on par with SMA in terms of overall accuracy but for OOV words, except for lemma prediction, SMA outperforms Morfette by significant margin.

Table 13 lists the accuracies of lemma, gender, number, person and case for the most frequently occurring POS tags. Table 12 reports the same for OOV words. The number of OOV words in postposition and pronoun categories is quite less and hence have not been included in the table.

[8]OOV words for SMA need not be *out of vocabulary* for PBA's dictionaries. Table 8 lists accuracies for OOV words of SMA. We shall also report accuracies for OOV words of PBA in the later part of the paper (Table 11).

Metric	Exp-1[a]	Exp-2[b]	Exp-3[c]
LAS	87.75	89.41	89.82
UAS	94.41	94.50	94.81
LA	89.89	91.67	91.96

Table 9: MALT Parser's accuracies on HTB test data. Unlabeled Attachment Score (UAS) is the percentage of words with correct heads. Labeled Accuracy (LA) is the percentage of words with correct dependency labels. Labeled Attachment Score (LAS) is the percentage of words with both correct heads and labels.

[a]Exp-1: Without morph features
[b]Exp-2: With morph features predicted by SMA
[c]Exp-3: With gold morph features (as annotated in HTB)

Hindi derivational morph analyzer (Kanuparthi et al., 2012) and the morph analyzer developed by Punjab University (Goyal and Lehal, 2008) do not add much to PBA accuracy since they are developed with PBA as the base. Out of 334,287 words in HTB, the derivational morph analyzer identified only 9,580 derivational variants. For the remaining words, it gives similar analysis as PBA.

6.1 Lemma

The evaluation metric for lemma's model is *accuracy*, which is the percentage of predicted lemmas that are correct. The phrase based translation system used to predict lemmas achieved an accuracy of 95.84% compared to O-PBA's 86.69%. For OOV words, the PBA outputs the word itself as the lemma whereas the translation-based lemma model is robust enough to give the analysis.

The translation-based lemma model and O-PBA report accuracies of 89.51% and 82.48% respectively for OOV words of SMA. In terms of both overall and OOV accuracies, translation-based model outperforms PBA. Though SMA performs better than Morfette in terms of overall accuracy, but for OOV accuracy Morfette narrowly outperforms SMA.

The postposition accuracy is significantly worse than the overall accuracy. This is because the confusion is high among postpositions in HTB. For example, out of 14,818 occurrences of `ke`, it takes the lemma `kA` in 7,763 instances and `ke` in 7,022 cases. This could be the result of an inconsistency in the annotation process of HTB. The accuracies for verbs are low (when compared to Nouns, Adjectives) as well mainly because verbs in Hindi take more inflections than the rest. The accuracy for verbs is even lower for OOV words (69.23% in Table 12).

6.2 Gender, Number, Person and Case

The accuracies of gender, number, person and case hover around 95% but the combined (G+N+P) accuracy drops to 91.11%. This figure is important if one wants to enforce agreement in parsing.

The OOV accuracy for person is close to overall accuracy as most of the OOV words belong to the 3rd person category. It is not the same case for gender and number. Gender particularly suffers a significant drop of 14% for OOV words confirming the theory that gender prediction is a difficult problem without knowing the semantics of the word.

The number and person accuracies for verbs are consistently low for OOV words as well as for seen words. This could be because SMA doesn't handle long distance agreement during GNP prediction.

Until now, we reported accuracies for OOV words of SMA. Table 11 lists accuracies for OOV words of the PBA (i.e. words which are not analyzed by the PBA) in the test section of HTB. SMA clearly outperforms baseline system and also performs better than F-PBA and O-PBA as they do not give any analyses.

Analysis	Accuracy	OOV Accuracy
Gender	95.74	80.08
Number	95.29	89.71
Person	96.12	94.06
Case	95.16	88.32
G+N+P	90.92	74.14
G+N+P+C	87.72	68.47

Table 10: Joint Model for Gender, Number, Person, Case

In a nutshell, we have evaluated SMA for OOV words of the PBA as well as for OOV words of SMA. In both the cases, SMA performed better than other systems. We shall evaluate SMA in a challenging scenario wherein *training* data consists of the words from the HTB which are analyzed by the PBA and *test* data consists of the remaining unanalyzed words by the PBA. Thereby, the entire test data contains only *out of vocabulary* instances for both SMA and PBA. Table 14 presents the results of this new evaluation. The results are almost similar with that of OOV results shown in Table 8 except for *Person*. The reason behind that could be, in the training data there are only 0.1% instances of *3h* class but in test data their presence is quite significant (approximately 10%). The training instances for *3h* class were not sufficient for the model to learn and hence very few of these instances were identified correctly. This explains the drop in *Person* accuracy for this experiment scenario.

It may be noted that, we have used gold POS tags for all our experiments related to GNP and case prediction. There are numerous efforts on building POS taggers for Hindi. The ILMT pos tagger[9] is 96.5% accurate on the test data of the HTB. Table 15 reports the accuracies of gender, number, person and case using the automatic POS tags predicted by the ILMT tagger. The results are similar to that of the experiments conducted with gold POS tags.

Malladi and Mannem (2013) have build separate models for gender, number, person and case. Table 10 reports the results of *Joint Model* for these morph attributes. In terms of accuracy, Joint Model is as efficient as individual models.

[9]http://ilmt.iiit.ac.in/

Analysis	Baseline	SMA
Lemma	65.40	95.96
Gender	57.09	95.93
Number	76.79	95.17
Person	65.76	96.42
Case	46.39	95.17

Table 11: Accuracy for OOV words of PBA

Analysis	Noun	Verb	Adjective
Lemma	92.18	69.23	88.35
Gender	80.49	86.15	92.23
Number	92.35	76.92	87.38
Person	96.64	75.38	100.00
Case	88.81	98.46	70.87

Table 12: OOV accuracies for words (by POS tags)

Analysis	Baseline	SMA
Gender	57.09	73.09
Number	76.79	85.71
Person	65.76	77.93
Case	33.62	89.05

Table 14: Evaluation of SMA in a challenging scenario: training data consists only of words analyzed by PBA and test data consists of remaining unanalyzed words.

Analysis	Overall	OOV
Gender	95.68	80.41
Number	94.97	90.30
Person	96.09	96.17
Case	94.61	88.19

Table 15: Accuracy of SMA with auto POS tags

6.3 TAM and Vibhakti

The proposed heuristics for Vibhakti and TAM prediction gave accuracy of 97.04% on test data set of HTB. On the entire HTB data, SMA achieved accuracy of 98.88%. O-PBA gave accuracy of 59.65% for TAM and Vibhakti prediction on test part of HTB. The reason behind low performance of O-PBA is that it identifies the TAM and vibhakti values for each word separately and doesn't consider the neighbouring words in the sentence.

7 Effect on Parsing

The effect of morphological features on parsing is well documented (Ambati et al., 2010a). Previous works used gold morphological analysis to prove their point. In this work, we also evaluated the effect of *automatic* morph features (predicted by SMA) on dependency parsing. MALT parser was trained on gold-standard POS tagged HTB data with and with out morph features. Table 9 lists the evaluation scores for these settings. While the unlabeled attachment score (UAS) does not show significant improvement, the labeled attachment score (LAS) and label accuracy (LA) have increased significantly. Ambati et al. (2010a) also reported similar results with *gold-standard* morph features. Lemma, case, vibhakti and TAM features contribute to the increase in label accuracy because of the karaka labels in Paninian annotation scheme (Begum et al., 2008).

Table 9 also lists the performance of MALT parser with gold morph features (as annotated in HTB). It may be noted that, predicted morph features had similar effect on hindi dependency parsing as of gold features which is desirable making SMA usable for real scenario applications.

Analysis	N	V	PSP	JJ	PRP
Lemma	98.50	94.28	89.41	97.99	98.78
Gender	93.30	95.34	98.93	98.42	94.24
Number	96.26	89.67	96.45	96.26	88.98
Person	98.58	85.28	99.45	99.57	90.94
Case	94.67	98.95	93.26	83.76	95.90
N:Noun, V:Verb, PSP:postposition, JJ:adjective, PRP:pronoun					

Table 13: Overall accuracies for words (by POS tags)

8 Extending the work to Telugu and Urdu

We shall look at how SMA performs in prediciting GNP and case for other morphologically rich Indian languages: Telugu and Urdu. At this stage, we have not done any language-dependent engineering effort

Language	#Sentences	#Words
Urdu	5230	68588
Telugu	1600	6321

Table 16: Telugu and Urdu Treebank Statistics

Analysis	Telugu		Urdu	
	Overall	OOV	Overall	OOV
Gender	96.49	89.85	89.14	88.18
Number	90.65	75.13	91.62	91.35
Person	94.82	85.79	93.37	95.53
Case	96.49	89.34	85.49	79.01

Table 17: SMA for other Mor-FOW languages: Telugu and Urdu

in improving the results rather we want to see how well the system works for other languages using the minimalistic feature set employed for Hindi morphological analysis.

Telugu Treebank was released for ICON 2010 Shared Task(Husain et al., 2010) and a modified version of that data is used for our experiments. Urdu Treebank which is still under development at IIIT Hyderabad[10] is used for experiments related to Urdu morph analysis. Refer table 16 for treebank statistics.

Table 17 shows the evaluation results for Telugu and Urdu.

9 Conclusion and Future work

In conclusion, SMA is a robust state-of-the-art statistical morphological analyzer which outperforms previous analyzers for Hindi by a considerable margin. SMA achieved an accuracy of 63.06% for lemma, gender, number, person and case whereas PBA and Morfette are 34.89% and 51.52% accurate respectively. With the predicted morphological attributes by SMA, we achieve a labeled attachment score of 89.41 while without these morphological attributes the parsing accuracy drops to 87.75.

The agreement phenomenon in Hindi provides challenges in predicting gender, number and person of words in their sentential context. These can be better predicted if dependency relations are given as input. However, the standard natural language analysis pipeline forbids using parse information during morphological analysis. This provides an opportunity to explore joint modelling of morphological analysis and syntactic parsing for Hindi. We plan to experiment this as part of our future work.

Performance of Morfette is comparable to SMA and for lemma prediction in the case of OOV words, Morfette outperforms SMA. We plan to build a hybrid system whose feature set includes features from both the systems.

[10]iiit.ac.in

References

Bharat Ram Ambati, Samar Husain, Sambhav Jain, Dipti Misra Sharma, and Rajeev Sangal. 2010a. Two methods to incorporate local morphosyntactic features in hindi dependency parsing. In *Proceedings of the NAACL HLT 2010 First Workshop on Statistical Parsing of Morphologically-Rich Languages*, pages 22–30. Association for Computational Linguistics.

Bharat Ram Ambati, Samar Husain, Joakim Nivre, and Rajeev Sangal. 2010b. On the role of morphosyntactic features in hindi dependency parsing. In *Proceedings of the NAACL HLT 2010 First Workshop on Statistical Parsing of Morphologically-Rich Languages*, pages 94–102. Association for Computational Linguistics.

Rafiya Begum, Samar Husain, Arun Dhwaj, Dipti Misra Sharma, Lakshmi Bai, and Rajeev Sangal. 2008. Dependency annotation scheme for indian languages. In *Proceedings of IJCNLP*.

Akshar Bharati, Vineet Chaitanya, Rajeev Sangal, and KV Ramakrishnamacharyulu. 1995. *Natural language processing: A Paninian perspective*. Prentice-Hall of India New Delhi.

Akshar Bharati, Samar Husain, Meher Vijay, Kalyan Deepak, Dipti Misra Sharma, and Rajeev Sangal. 2009a. Constraint based hybrid approach to parsing indian languages. *Proc of PACLIC 23. Hong Kong*.

Akshara Bharati, Dipti Misra Sharma, Samar Husain, Lakshmi Bai, Rafiya Begam, and Rajeev Sangal. 2009b. Anncorra: Treebanks for indian languages, guidelines for annotating hindi treebank.

Chih-Chung Chang and Chih-Jen Lin. 2011. LIBSVM: A library for support vector machines. *ACM Transactions on Intelligent Systems and Technology*, 2:27:1–27:27.

Grzegorz Chrupała, Georgiana Dinu, and Josef Van Genabith. 2008. Learning morphology with morfette.

Rong-En Fan, Kai-Wei Chang, Cho-Jui Hsieh, Xiang-Rui Wang, and Chih-Jen Lin. 2008. LIBLINEAR: A library for large linear classification. *Journal of Machine Learning Research*, 9:1871–1874.

John Goldsmith. 2000. Linguistica: An automatic morphological analyzer. In *Proceedings of 36th meeting of the Chicago Linguistic Society*.

Vishal Goyal and G. Singh Lehal. 2008. Hindi morphological analyzer and generator. In *Emerging Trends in*

Engineering and Technology, 2008. ICETET'08. First International Conference on, pages 1156–1159. IEEE.

Samar Husain, Prashanth Mannem, Bharat Ram Ambati, and Phani Gadde. 2010. The icon-2010 tools contest on indian language dependency parsing. *Proceedings of ICON-2010 Tools Contest on Indian Language Dependency Parsing, ICON*, 10:1–8.

Yamuna Kachru. 2006. *Hindi*, volume 12. John Benjamins Publishing Company.

Nikhil Kanuparthi, Abhilash Inumella, and Dipti Misra Sharma. 2012. Hindi derivational morphological analyzer. In *Proceedings of the Twelfth Meeting of the Special Interest Group on Computational Morphology and Phonology*, pages 10–16. Association for Computational Linguistics.

Philipp Koehn, Hieu Hoang, Alexandra Birch, Chris Callison-Burch, Marcello Federico, Nicola Bertoldi, Brooke Cowan, Wade Shen, Christine Moran, Richard Zens, et al. 2007. Moses: Open source toolkit for statistical machine translation. In *Proceedings of the 45th Annual Meeting of the ACL on Interactive Poster and Demonstration Sessions*, pages 177–180. Association for Computational Linguistics.

Deepak Kumar Malladi and Prashanth Mannem. 2013. Statistical morphological analyzer for hindi. In *Proceedings of 6th International Joint Conference on Natural Language Processing*.

Mark Pedersen, Domenyk Eades, Samir K Amin, and Lakshmi Prakash. 2004. Relative clauses in hindi and arabic: A paninian dependency grammar analysis. *COLING 2004 Recent Advances in Dependency Grammar*, pages 9–16.

Dipti Misra Sharma, Prashanth Mannem, Joseph Van-Genabith, Sobha Lalitha Devi, Radhika Mamidi, and Ranjani Parthasarathi, editors. 2012. *Proceedings of the Workshop on Machine Translation and Parsing in Indian Languages*. Mumbai, India, December.

Representation of Morphosyntactic Units and Coordination Structures in the Turkish Dependency Treebank

Umut Sulubacak **Gülşen Eryiğit**
Department of Computer Engineering
Istanbul Technical University
Istanbul, 34469, Turkey
{sulubacak, gulsen.cebiroglu}@itu.edu.tr

Abstract

This paper presents our preliminary conclusions as part of an ongoing effort to construct a new dependency representation framework for Turkish. We aim for this new framework to accommodate the highly agglutinative morphology of Turkish as well as to allow the annotation of unedited web data, and shape our decisions around these considerations. In this paper, we firstly describe a novel syntactic representation for morphosyntactic sub-word units (namely inflectional groups (IGs) in Turkish) which allows inter-IG relations to be discerned with perfect accuracy without having to hide lexical information. Secondly, we investigate alternative annotation schemes for coordination structures and present a better scheme (nearly 11% increase in recall scores) than the one in Turkish Treebank (Oflazer et al., 2003) for both parsing accuracies and compatibility for colloquial language.

1 Introduction

In recent years, dependency parsing has globally seen great deal of attention, and has constituted the underlying framework for the syntactic parsing of many multilingual studies. Even though constituency parsing and grammars are still the preferred formalism for some well-researched languages, others may have certain traits that put constituency parsing in an unfavorable position against dependency parsing, such as flexible constituent ordering, which is typical of several prominent languages including Turkish. Although Turkish is decidedly more workable over the dependency formalism, it has invariably fallen short of usual parsing accuracies compared to other languages, as seen clearly in some recent works such as (McDonald and Nivre, 2011).

There are more parameters to parsing than the formalism alone, among which the correctness of the corpora used in learning procedures and the annotation schemes of syntactic relations are held in consideration as part of this work. Between the two, the emphasis is on the annotation scheme, which is proven to significantly affect the parsing performance (Bosco et al., 2010; Boyd and Meurers, 2008). Our motivation for this research is that these factors must also contribute to some extent to the performance deficiency in parsing Turkish, besides the inherent difficulty of parsing the language. Our aim is to investigate these points and suggest improvements where applicable.

2 Parsing Framework and Data Set

As our parsing framework, we use MaltParser (Nivre et al., 2007) which is a data-driven dependency parser with an underlying SVM learner based on LIBSVM (Chang and Lin, 2001). MaltParser is widely used and has shown high performances across various languages (Nivre et al., 2006a). We run MaltParser with Nivre's Arc-Standard parsing algorithm (Nivre, 2003) and use the same optimized parameters as in (Eryiğit et al., 2008). We also use the learning features from the last cited work as our baseline feature set and an updated version from (Eryiğit et al., 2011) of the same data set (Oflazer, 2003). The only difference from the configuration of (Eryiğit et al., 2011) is that our baseline parser does not exclude non-projective sentences from the corpus for training, which explains the baseline ac-

I

ID	FORM	LEMMA	CPOSTAG	POSTAG	FEATS	HEAD	DEPREL
13	_	sağlam	Adj	Adj	_	14	DERIV
14	_	_	Verb	Become	_	15	DERIV
15	_	_	Verb	Caus	_	16	DERIV
16	_	_	Verb	Pass	Pos	17	DERIV
17	sağlamlaştırılmasının	_	Noun	Inf2	A3sg|P3sg|Gen	18	POSSESSOR

II

ID	FORM	LEMMA	CPOSTAG	POSTAG	FEATS	HEAD	DEPREL	IG
13	sağlam	sağlam	Adj	Adj	_	14	DERIV	1
14	sağlamlaş	sağlam	Verb	Become	_	15	DERIV	1
15	sağlamlaştır	sağlamlaş	Verb	Caus	_	16	DERIV	1
16	sağlamlaştırıl	sağlamlaştır	Verb	Pass	Pos	17	DERIV	1
17	sağlamlaştırılmasının	sağlamlaştırıl	Noun	Inf2	A3sg|P3sg|Gen	18	POSSESSOR	0

Figure 1: The original and the novel IG representations for the word *sağlamlaştırılmasının*, which respectively comes to mean *strong*, *to become strong*, *to strengthen*, *to be strengthened* and *of the strengthening of* after each derivation. The new morphological tags introduced after each derivation pertain to the relevant IG, and common morphological features for the IGs of a single word such as the agreement are given under the final IG. Model I is the original representation, while Model II is the new representation we propose.

curacy differences (e.g. 67.4% against our 65.0% in labelled attachment score).

3 Proposed Annotation Schemes

3.1 IGs

Within the context of data-driven parsing, the most apparent problem of languages with productive derivational morphology is that words can potentially yield a very large morphological tag set, which causes severe sparsity in the morphological features of words. To alleviate this problem, words are split into morphosyntactic parts called inflectional groups (IGs), taking intermediate derivational affixes as boundaries. It is a known fact that analyzing sentences as being composed of IGs rather than surface word forms yields better results in major NLP problems such as morphological disambiguation (Hakkani-Tür et al., 2002) and syntactic parsing (Eryiğit et al., 2008).

Within the domain of dependency parsing, IGs as syntactic tokens are not as free as independent words, since the IGs of each word must be connected to each other with an exclusive dependency relation named `DERIV`. However, other tokens are free to be connected to an arbitrary IG of a word, with the added benefit of more compact morphological feature sets to help make the distinction.

Other languages with productive derivation, such as Uralic or Ugric languages, or those orthographically differing from the well-studied European languages, such as Semitic languages, can also benefit from using non-word-based morphosyntactic parsing tokens, as evidenced for instance by the recent considerations of splitting up tokens based on morphemes for Hebrew (Tsarfaty and Goldberg, 2008).

3.1.1 Current IG Representation

Since MaltParser accepts input in the standard data format of the CoNLL-X Shared Task (Buchholz and Marsi, 2006), the ways in which IGs can be represented for the parser are limited. The standard method for annotating IGs using the CoNLL-X data fields, as described in (Eryiğit et al., 2008), involves marking up the `FORM` and `LEMMA` fields with underscores rather than with lexical data as shown in Figure 1. At first, this method is convenient, as current feature vectors readily take lexical information into account, and as such, a linear transition-based parser would easily learn to connect adjacent words as IGs of the same word as long as the head word has an underscore for a stem. However, an obvious drawback is that the actual lexical information gets lost in favor of marking IGs, preventing the potential usage of that information in deciding on inter-word dependencies.

3.1.2 Proposed IG Representation

As an improvement over the original IG representation described in Section 3.1.1, we propose a slightly different annotation scheme which does not lock out the lexical data columns, by making use of a new column named IG. This new column takes a boolean value that is true for non-final IGs of multi-IG words much like the original FORM column, effectively marking the dependents that must be connected to the next token in line with the dependency relation DERIV. Once this representation gets integrated, lexical information may be assigned to the FORM and LEMMA columns, of which the former gets surface lexical forms of the current stage of derivation, and the latter gets the FORM data of the previous IG.

3.2 Coordination Structures

Among the most controversial annotation schemes are those of coordination structures (CS), which are groups of two or more tokens that are in coordination with each other, usually joined with conjunctions or punctuation, such as an *"and"* relation. The elements in coordination are the *conjuncts* of the CS, all of which are semantically linked to a single external head. A large variety of annotation methods are employed by different corpora, as thoroughly explained in (Popel et al., 2013). We chose three schemes to compare for our parser, which are illustrated in Figure 2. There does not seem to be a standard annotation rising as the best scheme, which is convenient because different schemes would have advantages and disadvantages against different formalisms and algorithms.

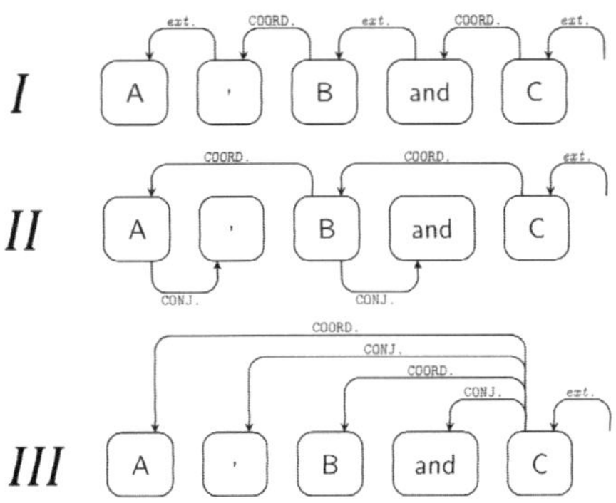

Figure 2: I) The original annotation scheme in the Turkish Treebank. II) *Swedish Style*, an alternative scheme in the manner of Talbanken (Nivre et al., 2006b). III) *Stanford Style*, another alternative scheme in the manner of the Stanford dependencies (De Marneffe and Manning, 2008), all with a head-right configuration as per (Popel et al., 2013), as would be appropriate for the predominantly head-final Turkish.

3.2.1 Current Coordination Representation

In the original Turkish Treebank, CSs are annotated as shown in scheme I in Figure 2, which appears to be problematic in several ways. This structure requires a prior conjunct to be connected to an intermediate conjunction, which in turn would be connected to a posterior conjunct, completing the coordination. The CS is then represented by the posterior conjunct, and the dependency relation between the prior conjunct and the conjunction must be identical to the dependency relation between the posterior conjunct and the external head, even if it would not semantically make sense.

Considering the tokens are processed incrementally from left to right during parsing, one difficulty with this method lies in correctly guessing the dependency relation between the prior argument and the conjunction before the posterior argument and the external head are even encountered, and unsurprisingly, directional parsers fail at this task more often than usual, resulting in added recall error for many dependency relations not necessarily related to coordinations. Another problem is that the scheme requires an intermediate conjunction or punctuation to work, which cannot be relied on even for edited texts, and would fare much worse if applied on web data. One final drawback of this method is that it is arguably more confusing for human annotators compared to a straightforward method in which the arguments in coordination are directly connected.

3.3 Proposed Coordination Representation

The drawbacks we have identified in the original CS annotation scheme encourage us to explore alternative approaches to coordinations. After investigating many annotation methods, we expect that the representation shown as the *Swedish Style* in Figure 2 will have the best performance in alleviating the issues described in Section 3.2.1.

Evaluating the *Swedish Style* representation, we observe that the CS does not depend on correctly placed conjunctions between the arguments, which increases compatibility in the absence of well-formatted sentences. Additionally, the dependency relation between the CS and the external head is not duplicated with this method, which should contribute to the reduction of recall error for many dependency types. Finally, we believe this scheme is easier for human annotators to understand and apply, and decreases the risk of annotation errors, which are very common in the Turkish Treebank.

4 Experiments

In order to practically evaluate our proposed IG and coordination representations, we first took our initial data set as our baseline, and then applied certain manual and automatic transformations to the data in order to create the experimental data sets. Since all of our data were based on a training corpus without an exclusive validation set, we decided to apply 10-fold cross-validation on all of our models to better evaluate the results.

For our tests on IG representations, we attempted to automatically transform our baseline corpus by populating the new `IG` column with boolean data derived from the IG relations in the gold-standard, and then automatically fill out the null lexical fields by an automatic morphological synthesis procedure using our morphological tool (Oflazer, 1994). The synthesis procedure, albeit a non-trivial implementation, successfully covered the majority (over 95%) of the lexical data, and we were able to manually annotate the remaining unrecognized tokens. To allow MaltParser to recognize the new fields, the CoNLL-X sentence format has been slightly adjusted and submitted as a custom input data format, and the baseline feature vector has been augmented with two extra features for the IG column information from the tokens on top of the Stack and Input pipes. The final model is named the *LexedIG* model.

On the other hand, we needed to perform a complete selective manual review of the corpus and correct numerous annotation errors in CSs before a healthy conversion could be made. Afterwards, we ran automatic conversion routines to map all CSs to the aforementioned *Swedish Style* and the commonly used *Stanford Style* in order to compare their specific performances. Since a sizeable amount of manual corrections were made before the conversions, we took the manually reviewed version as an intermediate model in order to distinguish the contribution of the automatic conversions from the manual review.

4.1 Metrics

For every model we evaluated via cross-validation, we made specific accuracy analyses and report the precision (P), recall (R) and F scores per dependency relation. Furthermore, we also calculated general accuracies as micro-averages from the cross-validation sets, for which we used two metrics, namely the labelled attachment score AS_L and the unlabelled attachment score AS_U, which are both accuracy metrics that compute the percentage of correctly parsed dependencies over all tokens, where the unlabelled metric only requires a match with the correct head, and the labelled metric additionally requires the correct dependency relation to be chosen.

	Baseline			LexedIG		
	P	R	F	P	R	F
ABLAT	61,46%	77,44%	0,69	61,50%	76,67%	0,68
APPOS	66,67%	12,87%	0,22	58,97%	11,39%	0,19
CLASS	72,98%	71,80%	0,72	72,57%	71,61%	0,72
COORD	83,95%	53,70%	0,66	83,57%	54,87%	0,66
DATIV	60,69%	71,57%	0,66	61,08%	70,68%	0,66
DERIV	**100,00%**	**100,00%**	**1,00**	**100,00%**	**100,00%**	**1,00**
DETER	91,18%	93,70%	0,92	91,23%	93,80%	0,92
INSTR	44,64%	38,38%	0,41	45,87%	40,96%	0,43
INTEN	87,99%	81,95%	0,85	87,35%	81,84%	0,85
LOCAT	73,40%	79,25%	0,76	73,90%	79,60%	0,77
MODIF	86,04%	81,58%	0,84	86,33%	81,74%	0,84
MWE	71,72%	58,72%	0,65	71,50%	59,42%	0,65
NEGAT	92,56%	70,00%	0,80	92,86%	73,13%	0,82
OBJEC	77,90%	71,36%	0,74	78,32%	71,92%	0,75
POSSE	87,44%	80,80%	0,84	86,58%	81,27%	0,84
QUEST	86,10%	77,16%	0,81	85,77%	77,16%	0,81
RELAT	70,00%	49,41%	0,58	70,49%	50,59%	0,59
ROOT	68,83%	99,77%	0,81	69,63%	99,77%	0,82
S.MOD	54,25%	50,25%	0,52	54,29%	50,92%	0,53
SENTE	93,25%	89,63%	0,91	93,20%	89,68%	0,91
SUBJE	69,54%	68,94%	0,69	69,87%	69,65%	0,70
VOCAT	69,61%	29,46%	0,41	69,23%	29,88%	0,42

Table 1: Specific accuracies per dependency relation for the IG-related models.

4.2 Results and Discussion

Our test results with the *LexedIG* model suggest that our proposed IG representation works perfectly well, as the perfect precision and recall scores of the original model for `DERIV` relations are preserved in the new model. Besides this, the reconstructed lexical information that we had populated the new model with caused only slight changes in overall accuracy that are not statistically significant, which is likely due to the sparsity of lexical data. Regardless, a model with lexical information for all tokens is essentially superior to a similarly performing model without such information. We foresee that being able to see lexical forms in the data would increase both the speed and the accuracy of human annotation. Additionally, as these experiments were done in preparation for the parsing of web data, we believe that in the near future, with the ability to unsupervisedly parse large amounts of data found on

	Baseline			Corrected			Swedish Style			Stanford Style		
	P	R	F	P	R	F	P	R	F	P	R	F
ABLAT	61,46%	77,44%	0,69	61,70%	79,46%	0,69	61,25%	79,19%	0,69	61,84%	80,20%	0,70
APPOS	66,67%	12,87%	0,22	62,86%	9,78%	0,17	65,79%	12,82%	0,21	67,57%	12,82%	0,22
CLASS	72,98%	71,80%	0,72	72,54%	71,76%	0,72	72,33%	74,52%	0,73	72,78%	74,22%	0,73
CONJU	*N/A*	*N/A*	*N/A*	*N/A*	*N/A*	*N/A*	79,78%	72,38%	0,76	76,99%	60,85%	0,68
COORD	83,95%	**53,70%**	0,66	83,88%	**54,23%**	0,66	79,15%	**64,64%**	0,71	73,82%	**58,68%**	0,65
DATIV	60,69%	71,57%	0,66	61,57%	71,77%	0,66	60,62%	72,83%	0,66	61,36%	73,81%	0,67
DERIV	100,00%	100,00%	1,00	100,00%	100,00%	1,00	100,00%	100,00%	1,00	100,00%	100,00%	1,00
DETER	91,18%	93,70%	0,92	91,08%	93,74%	0,92	91,14%	94,28%	0,93	91,15%	93,97%	0,93
INSTR	44,64%	38,38%	0,41	46,72%	39,48%	0,43	46,05%	41,08%	0,43	45,25%	41,49%	0,43
INTEN	87,99%	81,95%	0,85	87,30%	82,71%	0,85	87,46%	82,47%	0,85	87,83%	82,26%	0,85
LOCAT	73,40%	79,25%	0,76	73,92%	79,35%	0,77	72,33%	78,91%	0,75	72,42%	79,73%	0,76
MODIF	86,04%	81,58%	0,84	85,80%	81,47%	0,84	85,80%	81,84%	0,84	85,83%	81,06%	0,83
MWE	71,72%	58,72%	0,65	72,46%	59,09%	0,65	74,11%	58,87%	0,66	72,55%	60,18%	0,66
NEGAT	92,56%	70,00%	0,80	92,68%	66,28%	0,77	92,91%	73,29%	0,82	92,00%	71,43%	0,80
OBJEC	77,90%	71,36%	0,74	77,61%	71,54%	0,74	78,42%	72,12%	0,75	78,67%	72,08%	0,75
POSSE	87,44%	80,80%	0,84	87,03%	80,68%	0,84	87,69%	83,37%	0,85	87,25%	82,89%	0,85
QUEST	86,10%	77,16%	0,81	86,15%	77,78%	0,82	86,15%	78,05%	0,82	86,15%	78,05%	0,82
RELAT	70,00%	49,41%	0,58	71,67%	49,43%	0,59	72,13%	50,57%	0,59	69,35%	49,43%	0,58
ROOT	68,83%	99,77%	0,81	68,84%	99,49%	0,81	70,41%	99,79%	0,83	66,28%	99,81%	0,80
S.MOD	54,25%	50,25%	0,52	51,31%	49,28%	0,50	53,55%	50,09%	0,52	53,88%	49,91%	0,52
SENTE	93,25%	89,63%	0,91	92,74%	89,02%	0,91	93,50%	88,80%	0,91	93,36%	88,90%	0,91
SUBJE	69,54%	68,94%	0,69	69,61%	68,14%	0,69	69,89%	69,70%	0,70	69,75%	69,60%	0,70
VOCAT	69,61%	29,46%	0,41	67,86%	24,78%	0,36	61,05%	25,66%	0,36	69,62%	24,34%	0,36

Table 2: Specific accuracies per dependency relation for the coordination-related models.

the web, sparse data will no longer be a significant problem, and lexical data will gain further value.

A comparison of the alternative CS models with the baseline suggests that, while the manual correction itself did not cause a noticeable change, the automatic conversion procedures that it made possible resulted in significant improvements. The *Swedish Style* and *Stanford Style* models fared slightly better in the accuracy of some dependency types commonly joined in CSs such as `SUBJECT`, `OBJECT`, and `DATIVE`, `INSTRUMENTAL` and `ABLATIVE.ADJUNCT`s, but not always enough to warrant statistical significance. Apart from those, the largest improvement is in the `COORDINATION` relation itself, which had a slight drop in precision for both final models (likely due to the increased average dependency distances) but at the great benefit of the recall increasing from 53.70% to 58.68% for the *Stanford Style* and 64.64% for the *Swedish Style*.

	AS_U	AS_L
Baseline	$74.5\% \pm 0.2$	$65.0\% \pm 0.2$
LexedIG	$74.6\% \pm 0.1$	$65.1\% \pm 0.2$
Baseline	$74.5\% \pm 0.2$	$65.0\% \pm 0.2$
Corrected	$74.5\% \pm 0.1$	$65.0\% \pm 0.2$
Swedish Style	$74.5\% \pm 0.2$	$\mathbf{65.6}\% \pm 0.2$
Stanford Style	$73.2\% \pm 0.2$	$64.1\% \pm 0.2$

Table 3: General parsing accuracies for all models, including standard error.

5 Conclusion

In this paper, we proposed novel annotation schemes for Turkish morphosyntactic sub-word units and coordination structures that are superior to the Turkish Treebank representations in terms of ease of use, parsing performance and/or compatibility with sentences that are not well-formed. Our findings substantiate our thesis that annotation schemes have both room for improvement and a high impact potential on parsing performance. In the light of our results, we intend to sustain our research and draw better annotation schemes for other syntactic structures such as copulae and modifier sub-types to serve not only Turkish, but also other languages with rich morphology.

Acknowledgments

The authors would like to acknowledge that this work is part of a research project supported by ICT COST Action IC1207 and TÜBİTAK 1001 (Grant Number 112E276).

References

Cristina Bosco, Simonetta Montemagni, Alessandro Mazzei, Vincenzo Lombardo, Felice dell'Orletta, Alessandro Lenci, Leonardo Lesmo, Giuseppe Attardi, Maria Simi, Alberto Lavelli, et al. 2010. Comparing the influence of different treebank annotations on dependency parsing. In *LREC*.

Adriane Boyd and Detmar Meurers. 2008. Revisiting the impact of different annotation schemes on pcfg parsing: A grammatical dependency evaluation. In *Proceedings of the Workshop on Parsing German*, pages 24–32. Association for Computational Linguistics.

Sabine Buchholz and Erwin Marsi. 2006. Conll-x shared task on multilingual dependency parsing. In *Proceedings of the Tenth Conference on Computational Natural Language Learning*, pages 149–164. Association for Computational Linguistics.

Chih-Chung Chang and Chih-Jen Lin, 2001. *LIBSVM: A Library for Support Vector Machines*. Software available at http://www.csie.ntu.edu.tw/~cjlin/libsvm.

Marie-Catherine De Marneffe and Christopher D Manning. 2008. The stanford typed dependencies representation. In *Coling 2008: Proceedings of the workshop on Cross-Framework and Cross-Domain Parser Evaluation*, pages 1–8. Association for Computational Linguistics.

Gülşen Eryiğit, Tugay Ilbay, and Ozan Arkan Can. 2011. Multiword expressions in statistical dependency parsing. In *Proceedings of the Second Workshop on Statistical Parsing of Morphologically Rich Languages (IWPT)*, pages 45–55, Dublin, Ireland, October. Association for Computational Linguistics.

Gülşen Eryiğit, Joakim Nivre, and Kemal Oflazer. 2008. Dependency parsing of Turkish. *Computational Linguistics*, 34(3):357–389.

Dilek Hakkani-Tür, Kemal Oflazer, and Gökhan Tür. 2002. Statistical morphological disambiguation for agglutinative languages. *Journal of Computers and Humanities*, 36(4):381–410.

Ryan McDonald and Joakim Nivre. 2011. Analyzing and integrating dependency parsers. *Computational Linguistics*, 37(1):197–230.

Joakim Nivre, Johan Hall, Jens Nilsson, Gülşen Eryiğit, and Stetoslav Marinov. 2006a. Labeled pseudo-projective dependency parsing with support vector machines. In *Proceedings of the 10th Conference on Computational Natural Language Learning*, pages 221–225, New York, NY.

Joakim Nivre, Jens Nilsson, and Johan Hall. 2006b. Talbanken05: A swedish treebank with phrase structure and dependency annotation. In *Proceedings of the fifth International Conference on Language Resources and Evaluation (LREC)*, pages 1392–1395.

Joakim Nivre, Johan Hall, Jens Nilsson, Atanas Chanev, Gülşen Eryiğit, Sandra Kübler, Stetoslav Marinov, and Erwin Marsi. 2007. Maltparser: A language-independent system for data-driven dependency parsing. *Natural Language Engineering Journal*, 13(2):99–135.

Joakim Nivre. 2003. An efficient algorithm for projective dependency parsing. In *Proceedings of the 8th International Workshop on Parsing Technologies*, pages 149–160, Nancy.

Kemal Oflazer, Bilge Say, Dilek Z. Hakkani-Tür, and Gökhan Tür. 2003. Building a Turkish treebank. In A. Abeillé, editor, *Treebanks: Building and Using Parsed Corpora*, pages 261–277. Kluwer, London.

Kemal Oflazer. 1994. Two-level description of Turkish morphology. *Literary and Linguistic Computing*, 9(2):137–148.

Kemal Oflazer. 2003. Dependency parsing with an extended finite-state approach. *Computational Linguistics*, 29(4):515–544.

Martin Popel, David Mareček, Jan Štěpánek, Daniel Zeman, and Zdeněk Žabokrtský. 2013. Coordination structures in dependency treebanks. In *Proceedings of the 51st Annual Meeting of the Association for Computational Linguistics (Volume 1: Long Papers)*, pages 517–527, Sofia, Bulgaria, August. Association for Computational Linguistics.

Reut Tsarfaty and Yoav Goldberg. 2008. Word-based or morpheme-based? annotation strategies for modern hebrew clitics. In Nicoletta Calzolari (Conference Chair), Khalid Choukri, Bente Maegaard, Joseph Mariani, Jan Odijk, Stelios Piperidis, and Daniel Tapias, editors, *Proceedings of the Sixth International Conference on Language Resources and Evaluation (LREC'08)*, Marrakech, Morocco, may. European Language Resources Association (ELRA). http://www.lrec-conf.org/proceedings/lrec2008/.

(Re)ranking Meets Morphosyntax: State-of-the-art Results from the SPMRL 2013 Shared Task*

Anders Björkelund[§], **Özlem Çetinoğlu**[§], **Richárd Farkas**[†], **Thomas Müller**[§‡], and **Wolfgang Seeker**[§]

[§]Institute for Natural Language Processing , University of Stuttgart, Germany
[†]Department of Informatics, University of Szeged, Hungary
[‡]Center for Information and Language Processing, University of Munich, Germany
{anders,ozlem,muellets,seeker}@ims.uni-stuttgart.de
rfarkas@inf.u-szeged.hu

Abstract

This paper describes the IMS-SZEGED-CIS contribution to the SPMRL 2013 Shared Task. We participate in both the constituency and dependency tracks, and achieve state-of-the-art for all languages. For both tracks we make significant improvements through high quality preprocessing and (re)ranking on top of strong baselines. Our system came out first for both tracks.

1 Introduction

In this paper, we present our contribution to the 2013 Shared Task on Parsing Morphologically Rich Languages (MRLs). MRLs pose a number of interesting challenges to today's standard parsing algorithms, for example a free word order and, due to their rich morphology, greater lexical variation that aggravates out-of-vocabulary problems considerably (Tsarfaty et al., 2010).

Given the wide range of languages encompassed by the term MRL, there is, as of yet, no clear consensus on what approaches and features are generally important for parsing MRLs. However, developing tailored solutions for each language is time-consuming and requires a good understanding of the language in question. In our contribution to the SPMRL 2013 Shared Task (Seddah et al., 2013), we therefore chose an approach that we could apply to all languages in the Shared Task, but that would also allow us to fine-tune it for individual languages by varying certain components.

For the **dependency track**, we combined the n-best output of multiple parsers and subsequently ranked them to obtain the best parse. While this approach has been studied for constituency parsing (Zhang et al., 2009; Johnson and Ural, 2010; Wang and Zong, 2011), it is, to our knowledge, the first time this has been applied successfully within dependency parsing. We experimented with different kinds of features in the ranker and developed feature models for each language. Our system ranked first out of seven systems for all languages except French.

For the **constituency track**, we experimented with an alternative way of handling unknown words and applied a products of Context Free Grammars with Latent Annotations (PCFG-LA) (Petrov et al., 2006), whose output was reranked to select the best analysis. The additional reranking step improved results for all languages. Our system beats various baselines provided by the organizers for all languages. Unfortunately, no one else participated in this track.

For both settings, we made an effort to automatically annotate our data with the best possible preprocessing (POS, morphological information). We used a multi-layered CRF (Müller et al., 2013) to annotate each data set, stacking with the information provided by the organizers when this was beneficial. The high quality of our preprocessing considerably improved the performance of our systems.

The Shared Task involved a variety of settings as to whether gold or predicted part-of-speech tags and morphological information were available, as well as whether the full training set or a smaller (5k sen-

*Authors in alphabetical order.

	Arabic	Basque	French	German	Hebrew	Hungarian	Korean	Polish	Swedish
MarMoT	97.38/92.22	97.02/87.08	97.61/90.92	98.10/91.80	97.09/97.67	98.72/97.59	94.03/87.68	98.12/90.84	97.27/97.13
Stacked		98.23/89.05						98.56/92.63	97.83/97.62

Table 1: POS/morphological feature accuracies on the development sets.

tences) training set was used for training. Throughout this paper we focus on the settings with **predicted** preprocessing information with gold segmentation and the **full**[1] training sets. Unless stated otherwise, all given numbers are drawn from experiments in this setting. For all other settings, we refer the reader to the Shared Task overview paper (Seddah et al., 2013).

The remainder of the paper is structured as follows: We present our preprocessing in Section 2 and afterwards describe both our systems for the constituency (Section 3) and for the dependency tracks (Section 4). Section 5 discusses the results on the Shared Task test sets. We conclude with Section 6.

2 Preprocessing

We first spent some time on preparing the data sets, in particular we automatically annotated the data with high-quality POS and morphological information. We consider this kind of preprocessing to be an essential part of a parsing system, since the quality of the automatic preprocessing strongly affects the performance of the parsers.

Because our tools work on CoNLL09 format, we first converted the training data from the CoNLL06 format to CoNLL09. We thus had to decide whether to use coarse or fine part-of-speech (POS) tags. In a preliminary experiment we found that fine tags are the better option for all languages but Basque and Korean. For Korean the reason seems to be that the fine tag set is huge ($>$ 900) and that the same information is also provided in the feature column.

We predict POS tags and morphological features jointly using the Conditional Random Field (CRF) tagger MarMoT[2] (Müller et al., 2013).

MarMoT incrementally creates forward-backward lattices of increasing order to prune the sizable space of possible morphological analyses. We use MarMoT with the default parameters.

Since morphological dictionaries can improve automatic POS tagging considerably, we also created such dictionaries for each language. For this, we analyzed the word forms provided in the data sets with language-specific morphological analyzers except for Hebrew and German where we just extracted the morphological information from the lattice files provided by the organizers. For the other languages we used the following tools: Arabic: AraMorph a reimplementation of Buckwalter (2002), Basque: Apertium (Forcada et al., 2011), French: an IMS internal tool,[3] Hungarian: Magyarlanc (Zsibrita et al., 2013), Korean: HanNanum (Park et al., 2010), Polish: Morfeusz (Woliński, 2006), and Swedish: Granska (Domeij et al., 2000).

The created dictionaries were shared with the other Shared Task participants. We used these dictionaries as additional features for MarMoT.

For some languages we also integrated the predicted tags provided by the organizers into the feature model. These *stacked* models gave improvements for Swedish, Polish and Basque (cf. Table 1 for accuracies).

For the full setting the training data was annotated using 5-fold jackknifing. In the 5k setting, we additionally added all sentences not present in the parser training data to the training data sets of the tagger. This is similar to the predicted 5k files provided by the organizers, where more training data than the 5k was also used for prediction.

Table 3 presents a comparison between our graph-based baseline parser using the preprocessing explained in this section (denoted mate) and the preprocessing provided by the organizers (denoted mate'). Our preprocessing yields improvements for all languages but Swedish. The worse performance for Swedish is due to the fact that the predictions provided by the organizers were produced by models that were trained on a much larger data

[1] Although, for Hebrew and Swedish only 5k sentences were available for training, and the two settings thus coincide.

[2] `https://code.google.com/p/cistern/`

[3] The French morphology was written by Zhenxia Zhou, Max Kisselew and Helmut Schmid. It is an extension of Zhou (2007) and implemented in SFST (Schmid, 2005).

	Arabic	Basque	French	German	Hebrew	Hungarian	Korean	Polish	Swedish
Berkeley	78.24	69.17	79.74	81.74	87.83	83.90	70.97	84.11	74.50
Replaced	78.70	84.33	79.68	82.74	89.55	89.08	82.84	87.12	75.52
Product	80.30	86.21	81.42	84.56	**90.49**	89.80	84.15	88.32	79.25
Reranked	**81.24**	**87.35**	**82.49**	**85.01**	**90.49**	**91.07**	**84.63**	**88.40**	**79.53**

Table 2: PARSEVAL scores on the development sets.

set. The comparison with other parsers demonstrates that for some languages (e.g., Hebrew or Korean) the improvements due to better preprocessing can be greater than the improvements due to a better parser. For instance, for Hebrew the parser trained on the provided preprocessing is more than three points (LAS) behind the three parsers trained on our own preprocessing. However, the difference between these three parsers is less than a point.

3 Constituency Parsing

The phrase structure parsing pipeline is based on products of Context Free Grammars with Latent Annotations (PCFG-LA) (Petrov et al., 2006) and discriminative reranking. We further replace rare words by their predicted morphological analysis.

We preprocess the treebank trees by removing the morphological annotation of the POS tags and the function labels of all non-terminals. We also reduce the 177 compositional Korean POS tags to their first atomic tag, which results in a POS tag set of 9 tags.

PCFG-LAs are incrementally built by splitting non-terminals, refining parameters using EM-training and reversing splits that only cause small increases in likelihood.

Running the Berkeley Parser[4] – the reference implementation of PCFG-LAs – on the data sets results in the PARSEVAL scores given in Table 2 (Berkeley). The Berkeley parser only implements a simple signature-based unknown word model that seems to be ineffective for some of the languages, especially Basque and Korean.

We thus replace rare words (frequency < 20) by the predicted morphological tags of Section 2 (or the true morphological tag for the gold setup). The intuition is that our discriminative tagger has a more sophisticated unknown word treatment than the Berkeley parser, taking for example prefixes, suffixes and the immediate lexical context into account. Furthermore, the morphological tag contains most of the necessary syntactic information. An exception, for instance, might be the semantic information needed to disambiguate prepositional attachment. We think that replacing rare words by tags has an advantage over constraining the pre-terminal layer of the parser, because the parser can still decide to assign a different tag, for example in cases were the tagger produces errors due to long-distance dependencies. The used frequency threshold of 20 results in token replacement rates of 18% (French) to 57% (Korean and Polish), which correspond to 209 (for Polish) to 3221 (for Arabic) word types that are not replaced. The PARSEVAL scores for the described method are again given in Table 2 (Replaced). The method yields improvements for all languages except for French where we observe a drop of 0.06. The improvements range from 0.46 for Arabic to 1.02 for Swedish, 3.1 for Polish and more than 10 for Basque and Korean.

To further improve results, we employ the product-of-grammars procedure (Petrov, 2010), where different grammars are trained on the same data set but with different initialization setups. We trained 8 grammars and used tree-level inference. In Table 2 (Product) we can see that this leads to improvements from 0.72 for Hungarian to 3.73 for Swedish.

On the 50-best output of the product parser, we also carry out discriminative reranking. The reranker is trained for the maximum entropy objective function of Charniak and Johnson (2005) and use the standard feature set – without language-specific feature engineering – from Charniak and Johnson (2005) and Collins (2000). We use a slightly modified version of the Mallet toolkit (McCallum, 2002) for reranking.

Improvements range from negligible differences ($< .1$) for Hebrew and Polish to substantial differences ($> 1.$) for Basque, French, and Hungarian.

[4] `http://code.google.com/p/berkeleyparser/`

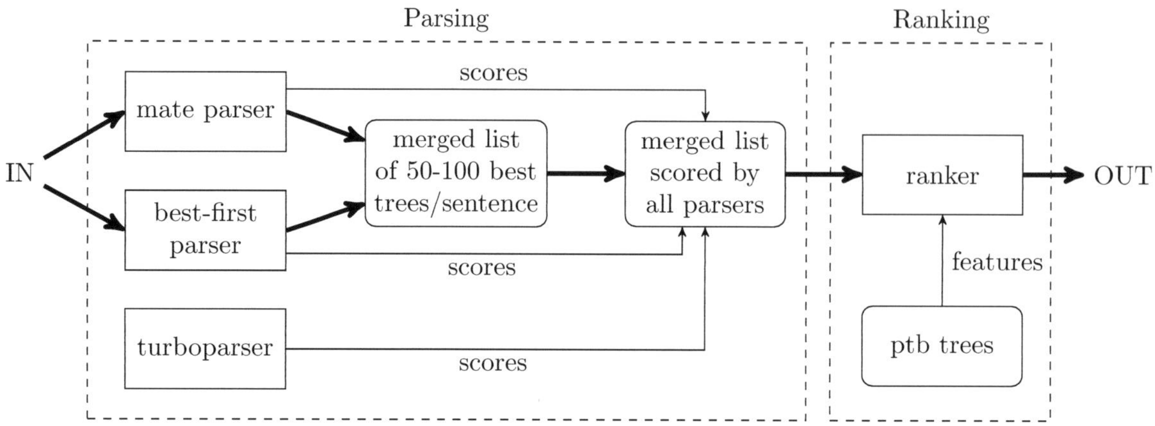

Figure 1: Architecture of the dependency ranking system.

For our final submission, we used the reranker output for all languages except French, Hebrew, Polish, and Swedish. This decision was based on an earlier version of the evaluation setting provided by the organizers. In this setup, reranking did not help or was even harmful for these four languages. The figures in Table 2 use the latest evaluation script and are thus consistent with the test set results presented in Section 5.

After the submission deadline the Shared Task organizers made us aware that we had surprisingly low exact match scores for Polish (e.g., 1.22 for the reranked setup). The reason seems to be that the Berkeley parser cannot produce unary chains of length > 2. The gold development set contains 1783 such chains while the prediction of the reranked system contains none. A particularly frequent unary chain with 908 occurences in the gold data is ff $\rightarrow$ fwe $\rightarrow$ formaczas. As this chain cannot be produced the parser leaves out the fwe phrase. Inserting new fwe nodes between ff and formacszas nodes raises the PARSEVAL scores of the reranked model from 88.40 to 90.64 and the exact match scores to 11.34. This suggests that the Polish results could be improved substantially if unary chains were properly dealt with, for example by collapsing unary chains.[5]

4 Dependency Parsing

The core idea of our dependency parsing system is the combination of the n-best output of several parsers followed by a ranking step on the combined list. Specifically, we first run two parsers that each output their 50-best analyses for each sentence. These 50-best analyses are merged together into one single n-best list of between 50 and 100 analyses (depending on the overlap between the n-best lists of the two parsers). We then use the two parsers plus an additional one to score each tree in the n-best lists according to their parsing model, thus providing us with three different scores for each tree in the n-best lists. The n-best lists are then given to a ranker, which ranks the list using the three scores and a small set of additional features in order to find the best overall analysis. Figure 1 shows a schematic of the process.

As a preprocessing step, we reduced the dependency label set for the Hungarian training data. The Hungarian dependency data set encodes ellipses through composite edge labels which leads to a proliferation of edge labels (more than 400). Since many of these labels are extremely rare and thus hard to learn for the parsers, we reduced the set of edge labels during the conversion. Specifically, we retained the 50 most frequent labels, while reducing the composite labels to their base label.

For producing the initial n-best lists, we use the mate parser[6] (Bohnet, 2010) and a variant of the EasyFirst parser (Goldberg and Elhadad, 2010), which we here call best-first parser.

The mate parser is a state-of-the-art graph-based dependency parser that uses second-order features.

[5]Thanks to Slav Petrov for pointing us to the unary chain length limit.

[6]`https://code.google.com/p/mate-tools`

The parser works in two steps. First, it uses dynamic programming to find the optimal projective tree using the Carreras (2007) decoder. It then applies the non-projective approximation algorithm proposed by McDonald and Pereira (2006) in order to produce non-projective parse trees. The non-projective approximation algorithm is a greedy hill climbing algorithm that starts from the optimal projective parse and iteratively tries to reattach all tokens, one at a time, everywhere in the sentence as long as the tree property holds. It halts when the increase in the score of the tree according to the parsing model is below a certain threshold.

n-best lists are obtained by applying the non-projective approximation algorithm in a non-greedy manner, exploring multiple possibilities. All trees are collected in a list, and when no new trees are found, or newer trees have a significantly lower score than the currently best one, search halts. The n best trees are then retrieved from the list. It should be noted that, in the standard case, the non-projective approximation algorithm may find a local optimum, and that there may be other trees that have a higher score which were not explored. Thus the best parse in the greedy case may not necessarily be the one with the highest score in the n-best list. Since the parser is trained with the greedy version of the non-projective approximation algorithm, the greedily chosen output parse tree is of special interest. We thus flag this tree as the **baseline mate parse**, in order to use that for features in the ranker. The baseline mate parse is also our overall baseline in the dependency track.

The best-first parser deviates from the EasyFirst parser in several small respects: The EasyFirst decoder creates dependency links between the roots of adjacent substructures, which gives an $O(n \log n)$ complexity, but restricts the output to projective trees. The best-first parser is allowed to choose as head any node of an adjacent substructure instead of only the root, which increases complexity to $O(n^2)$, but accounts for a big part of possible non-projective structures. We additionally implemented a swap-operation (Nivre, 2009; Tratz and Hovy, 2011) to account for the more complex structures. The best-first parser relies on a beam-search strategy[7] to pursue multiple derivations, which we also use to produce the n-best output.

In the scoring step, we additionally apply the turboparser[8] (Martins et al., 2010), which is based on linear programming relaxations.[9] We changed all three parsers such that they would return a score for a given tree. We use this to extract scores from each parser for all trees in the n-best lists. It is important to have a score from every parser for every tree, as previously observed by Zhang et al. (2009) in the context of constituency reranking.

4.1 Ranking

Table 3 shows the performance of the individual parsers measured on the development sets. It also displays the **oracle** scores over the different n-best lists, i.e., the maximal possible score over an n-best list if the best tree is always selected.

The mate parser generally performs best followed by turboparser, while the best-first parser comes last. But we can see from the oracle scores that the best-first parser often shows comparable or even higher oracle scores than mate, and that the combination of the n-best lists always adds substantial improvements to the oracle scores. These findings show that the mate and best-first parsers are providing different sets of n-best lists. Moreover, all three parsers rely on different parsing algorithms and feature sets. For these reasons, we hypothesized that the parsers contribute different views on the parse trees and that their combination would result in better overall performance.

In order to leverage the diversity between the parsers we experimented with **ranking**[10] on the n-best lists. We used the same ranking model introduced in Section 3 here as well. The model is trained to select the best parse according to the labeled attachment score (LAS). The training data for the ranker was created by 5-fold jackknifing on the training sets. The feature sets for the ranker for

[7]Due to the nature of the decoder, the parser can produce spurious ambiguities in the beam. If this occurs, only the one with the higher score is kept.

[8]`http://www.ark.cs.cmu.edu/TurboParser/`

[9]Ideally we would also extract n-best lists from the turboparser, however time prevented us from making the necessary modifications.

[10]We refrain from calling it *re*ranking in this setting, since we are using merged n-best lists and the initial ranking is not entirely clear to begin with.

	Arabic	Basque	French	German	Hebrew	Hungarian	Korean	Polish	Swedish
					Baseline results for individual parsers				
mate'		88.50/83.50	88.18/84.49	92.71/90.85	83.63/75.89	87.07/82.84	86.06/82.39	91.17/85.81	83.65/77.16
mate	87.68/85.42	89.11/84.43	88.30/84.84	93.15/91.46	86.05/79.37	88.03/84.41	87.91/85.76	91.51/86.30	83.53/77.05
bf	87.61/85.32	84.07/75.90	87.45/83.92	92.90/91.10	86.10/79.57	83.85/75.94	86.54/83.97	90.10/83.75	82.27/75.36
turbo	87.82/85.35	88.88/83.84	88.24/84.57	93.59/91.54	85.74/78.95	86.86/82.80	88.35/86.23	90.97/85.55	83.24/76.15
					Oracle scores for n-best lists				
mate	90.85/88.74	93.39/89.85	90.99/87.81	97.14/95.84	89.05/83.03	91.41/88.19	94.86/92.96	95.19/91.67	87.19/81.66
bf	91.47/89.46	91.68/86.46	91.38/88.68	97.40/96.60	91.04/85.67	87.64/81.79	94.90/92.94	96.25/93.74	87.60/82.46
merged	92.65/90.71	95.15/91.91	92.97/90.43	98.19/97.44	92.39/87.18	92.12/88.76	96.23/94.65	97.28/95.29	89.87/84.96

Table 3: Baseline performance and n-best oracle scores (UAS/LAS) on the development sets. mate' uses the preprocessing provided by the organizers, the other parsers use the preprocessing described in Section 2.

each language were optimized manually via cross-validation on the training sets. The features used for each language, as well as a default (baseline) feature set, are shown in Table 4. We now outline the features we used in the ranker:

Score from the base parsers – denoted **B**, **M**, **T**, for the best-first, mate, and turbo parsers, respectively. We also have indicator features whether a certain parse was the best according to a given parser, denoted **GB**, **GM**, **GT**, respectively. Since the mate parser does not necessarily assign the highest score to the baseline mate parse, the GM feature is a ternary feature which indicates whether a parse is the same as the baseline mate parse, or better, or worse. We also experimented with transformations and combinations of the scores from the parsers. Specifically, **BMProd** denotes the product of B and M; **BMeProd** denotes the sum of B and M in e-space, i.e., e^{B+M}; **reBMT**, **reBT**, **reMT** denote the normalized product of the corresponding scores, where scores are normalized in a softmax fashion such that all features take on values in the interval $(0, 1)$.

Projectivity features (Hall et al., 2007) – the number of non-projective edges in a tree, denoted **np**. Whether a tree is ill-nested, denoted **I**. Since ill-nested trees are extremely rare in the treebanks, this helps the ranker filter out unlikely candidates from the n-best lists. For a definition and further discussion of ill-nestedness, we refer to (Havelka, 2007).

Constituent features – from the constituent track we also have constituent trees of all sentences which can be used for feature extraction. Specifically, for every head-dependent pair, we extract the path in the constituent tree between the nodes, denoted **ptbp**.

Case agreement – on head-dependent pairs that both have a case value assigned among their morphological features, we mark whether it is the same case or not, denoted **case**.

Function label uniqueness – on each training set we extracted a list of function labels that generally occur at most once as the dependent of a node, e.g., subjects or objects. Features are then extracted from all nodes that have one or more dependents of each label aimed at capturing mistakes such as double subjects on a verb. This template is denoted **FL**.

In addition to the features mentioned above, we experimented with a variety of feature templates, including features drawn from previous work on dependency reranking (Hall, 2007), e.g., lexical and POS-based features over edges, "subcategorization" frames (i.e., the concatenation of POS-tags that are headed by a certain node in the tree), etc, although these features did not seem to help. For German we created feature templates based on the constraints used in the constraint-based parser by Seeker and Kuhn (2013). This includes, e.g., violations in case or number agreement between heads and dependents, as well as more complex features that consider labels on entire verb complexes. None of these features yielded any clear improvements though. We also experimented with features that target some specific constructions (and specifics of annotation schemes) which the parsers typically cannot fully see, such as coordination, however, also here we saw no clear improvements.

4.2 Effects of Ranking

In Table 5, we show the improvements from using the ranker, both with the baseline and optimized features sets for the ranker. For the sake of comparison,

	Arabic	Basque	French	German	Hebrew	Hungarian	Korean	Polish	Swedish
Baseline	87.68/85.42	89.11/84.43	88.30/84.84	93.15/91.46	86.05/79.37	88.03/84.41	87.91/85.76	91.51/86.30	83.53/77.05
Ranked-dflt	88.54/86.32	**89.99**/85.43	88.85/85.39	94.06/92.36	87.28/80.44	88.16/84.54	88.71/86.65	92.26/87.12	84.51/77.83
Ranked	**88.93/86.74**	89.95/**85.61**	**89.37/85.96**	**94.20/92.68**	**87.63/81.02**	**88.38/84.77**	**89.20/87.12**	**93.02/87.69**	**85.04/78.57**
Oracle	92.65/90.71	95.15/91.91	92.97/90.43	98.19/97.44	92.39/87.18	92.12/88.76	96.23/94.65	97.28/95.29	89.87/84.96

Table 5: Performance (UAS/LAS) of the reranker on the development sets. Baseline denotes our baseline. Ranked-dflt and Ranked denote the default and optimized ranker feature sets, respectively. Oracle denotes the oracle scores.

default	B, M, T, GB, GM, GT, I
Arabic	B, M, T, GB, GM, I, ptbp, reBMT
Basque	B, M, T, GB, GM, GT, I, ptbp, I, reMT, case
French	B, M, T, GB, GM, GT, I, ptbp
German	B, M, T, GM, I, BMProd, FL
Hebrew	B, M, T, GB, GM, GT, I, ptbp, FL, BMeProd
Hungarian	B, M, T, GB, GM, GT, I, ptbp, reBM, FL
Korean	B, M, T, GB, GM, GT, I, ptbp, reMT, FL
Polish	B, M, T, GB, GM, GT, I, ptbp, np
Swedish	B, M, T, GB, GM, GT, I, ptbp, reBM, FL

Table 4: Feature sets for the dependency ranker for each language. default denotes the default ranker feature set.

the baseline mate parses as well as the oracle parses on the merged n-best lists are repeated from Table 3. We see that ranking clearly helps, both with a tailored feature set, as well as the default feature set. The improvement in LAS between the baseline and the tailored ranking feature sets ranges from 1.1% (French) to 1.6% (Hebrew) absolute, with the exception of Hungarian, where improvements on the dev set are more modest (contrary to the test set results, cf. Section 5). Even with the default feature set, the improvements range from 0.5% (French) to 1.1% (Hebrew) absolute, again setting Hungarian aside. We believe that this is an interesting result considering the simplicity of the default feature set.

5 Test Set Results

In this section we outline our final results on the test sets. As previously, we focus on the setting with predicted tags in gold segmentation and the largest training set. We also present results on Arabic and Hebrew for the predicted segmentation setting. For the gold preprocessing and all 5k settings, we refer the reader to the Shared Task overview paper (Seddah et al., 2013).[11]

In Table 7, we present our results in the constituency track. Since we were the only participating team in the constituency track, we compare ourselves with the best baseline[12] provided by the organizers. Our system outperforms the baseline for all languages in terms of PARSEVAL F_1. Following the trend on the development sets, reranking is consistently helping across languages.[13] Despite the lack of other submissions in the shared task, we believe our numbers are generally strong and hope that they can serve as a reference for future work on constituency parsing on these data sets.

Table 8 displays our results in the dependency track. We submitted two runs: a baseline, which is the baseline mate parse, and the reranked trees. The table also compares our results to the best performing other participant in the shared task (denoted Other) as well as the MaltParser (Nivre et al., 2007) baseline provided by the shared task organizers (denoted ST Baseline). We obtain the highest scores for all languages, with the exception of French. It is also clear that we make considerable gains over our baseline, confirming our results on the development sets reported in Section 4. It is also noteworthy that our baseline (i.e., the mate parser with our own preprocessing) outperforms the best other system for 5 languages.

	Arabic	Hebrew
Other	90.75/8.48	88.33/12.20
Dep. Baseline	91.13/9.10	89.27/15.01
Dep. Ranked	91.74/9.83	89.47/16.97
Constituency	92.06/9.49	89.30/13.60

Table 6: Unlabeled TedEval scores (accuracy/exact match) for the test sets in the predicted segmentation setting. Only sentences of length $\leq$ 70 are evaluated.

[11] Or the results page online: http://www.spmrl.org/spmrl2013-sharedtask-results.html

[12] It should be noted that the Shared Task organizers computed 2 different baselines on the test sets. The best baseline results for each language thus come from different parsers.

[13] We remind the reader that our submission decisions are not based on figures in Table 2, cf. Section 3.

	Arabic	Basque	French	German	Hebrew	Hungarian	Korean	Polish	Swedish
ST Baseline	79.19	74.74	80.38	78.30	86.96	85.22	78.56	86.75	80.64
Product	80.81	87.18	81.83	80.70	89.46	90.58	83.49	87.55	83.99
Reranked	**81.32**	**87.86**	**82.86**	**81.27**	**89.49**	**91.85**	**84.27**	**87.76**	**84.88**

Table 7: Final PARSEVAL F_1 scores for constituents on the test set for the predicted setting. ST Baseline denotes the best baseline (out of 2) provided by the Shared Task organizers. Our submission is underlined.

	Arabic	Basque	French	German	Hebrew	Hungarian	Korean	Polish	Swedish
ST Baseline	83.18/80.36	79.77/70.11	82.49/77.98	81.51/77.81	76.49/69.97	80.72/70.15	85.72/82.06	82.19/75.63	80.29/73.21
Other	85.78/83.20	89.19/84.25	**89.19/85.86**	90.80/88.66	81.05/73.63	88.93/84.97	85.84/82.65	88.12/82.56	87.28/80.88
Baseline	86.96/84.81	89.32/84.25	87.87/84.37	90.54/88.37	85.88/79.67	89.09/85.31	87.41/85.51	90.30/85.51	86.85/80.67
Ranked	**88.32/86.21**	**89.88/85.14**	88.68/85.24	**91.64/89.65**	**86.70/80.89**	**89.81/86.13**	**88.47/86.62**	**91.75/87.07**	**88.06/82.13**

Table 8: Final UAS/LAS scores for dependencies on the test sets for the predicted setting. Other denotes the highest scoring other participant in the Shared Task. ST Baseline denotes the MaltParser baseline provided by the Shared Task organizers.

Table 6 shows the unlabeled TedEval (Tsarfaty et al., 2012) scores (accuracy/exact match) on the test sets for the predicted segmentation setting for Arabic and Hebrew. Note that these figures only include sentences of length less than or equal to 70. Since TedEval enables cross-framework comparison, we compare our submissions from the dependency track to our submission from the constituency track. In these runs we used the same systems that were used for the gold segmentation with predicted tags track. The predicted segmentation was provided by the Shared Task organizers. We also compare our results to the best other system from the Shared Task (denoted Other).

Also here we obtain the highest results for both languages. However, it is unclear what syntactic paradigm (dependencies or constituents) is better suited for the task. All in all it is difficult to assess whether the differences between the best and second best systems for each language are meaningful.

6 Conclusion

We have presented our contribution to the 2013 SPMRL Shared Task. We participated in both the constituency and dependency tracks. In both tracks we make use of a state-of-the-art tagger for POS and morphological features. In the constituency track, we use the tagger to handle unknown words and employ a product-of-grammars-based PCFG-LA parser and parse tree reranking. In the dependency track, we combine multiple parsers output as input for a ranker.

Since there were no other participants in the constituency track, it is difficult to draw any conclusions from our results. We do however show that the application of product grammars, our handling of rare words, and a subsequent reranking step outperforms a baseline PCFG-LA parser.

In the dependency track we obtain the best results for all languages except French among 7 participants. Our reranking approach clearly outperforms a baseline graph-based parser. This is the first time multiple parsers have been used in a dependency reranking setup.

Aside from minor decisions made on the basis of each language, our approach is language agnostic and does not target morphology in any particular way as part of the parsing process. We show that with a strong baseline and with no language specific treatment it is possible to achieve state-of-the-art results across all languages. Our architecture for the dependency parsing track enables the use of language-specific features in the ranker, although we only had minor success with features that target morphology. However, it may be the case that approaches from previous work on parsing MRLs, or the approaches taken by other teams in the Shared Task, can be successfully combined with ours and improve parsing accuracy even more.

Acknowledgments

Richárd Farkas is funded by the European Union and the European Social Fund through the project FuturICT.hu (grant no.: TÁMOP-4.2.2.C-11/1/KONV-

2012-0013). Thomas Müller is supported by a Google Europe Fellowship in Natural Language Processing. The remaining authors are funded by the Deutsche Forschungsgemeinschaft (DFG) via the SFB 732, projects D2 and D8 (PI: Jonas Kuhn).

We also express our gratitude to the treebank providers for each language: Arabic (Maamouri et al., 2004; Habash and Roth, 2009; Habash et al., 2009; Green and Manning, 2010), Basque (Aduriz et al., 2003), French (Abeillé et al., 2003), Hebrew (Sima'an et al., 2001; Tsarfaty, 2010; Goldberg, 2011; Tsarfaty, 2013), German (Brants et al., 2002; Seeker and Kuhn, 2012), Hungarian (Csendes et al., 2005; Vincze et al., 2010), Korean (Choi et al., 1994; Choi, 2013), Polish (Świdziński and Woliński, 2010), and Swedish (Nivre et al., 2006).

References

Anne Abeillé, Lionel Clément, and François Toussenel. 2003. Building a treebank for french. In Anne Abeillé, editor, *Treebanks*. Kluwer, Dordrecht.

I. Aduriz, M. J. Aranzabe, J. M. Arriola, A. Atutxa, A. Díaz de Ilarraza, A. Garmendia, and M. Oronoz. 2003. Construction of a Basque dependency treebank. In *TLT-03*, pages 201–204.

Bernd Bohnet. 2010. Top Accuracy and Fast Dependency Parsing is not a Contradiction. In *Proceedings of the 23rd International Conference on Computational Linguistics (Coling 2010)*, pages 89–97, Beijing, China, August. Coling 2010 Organizing Committee.

Sabine Brants, Stefanie Dipper, Silvia Hansen, Wolfgang Lezius, and George Smith. 2002. The TIGER treebank. In Erhard Hinrichs and Kiril Simov, editors, *Proceedings of the First Workshop on Treebanks and Linguistic Theories (TLT 2002)*, pages 24–41, Sozopol, Bulgaria.

Tim Buckwalter. 2002. Buckwalter Arabic Morphological Analyzer Version 1.0. *Linguistic Data Consortium, University of Pennsylvania, 2002. LDC Catalog No.: LDC2002L49.*

Xavier Carreras. 2007. Experiments with a Higher-Order Projective Dependency Parser. In *Proceedings of the CoNLL Shared Task Session of EMNLP-CoNLL 2007*, pages 957–961, Prague, Czech Republic, June. Association for Computational Linguistics.

Eugene Charniak and Mark Johnson. 2005. Coarse-to-fine n-best parsing and MaxEnt discriminative reranking. In *Proceedings of the 43rd Annual Meeting on Association for Computational Linguistics*, ACL '05, pages 173–180.

Key-Sun Choi, Young S Han, Young G Han, and Oh W Kwon. 1994. Kaist tree bank project for korean: Present and future development. In *Proceedings of the International Workshop on Sharable Natural Language Resources*, pages 7–14. Citeseer.

Jinho D. Choi. 2013. Preparing korean data for the shared task on parsing morphologically rich languages. *ArXiv e-prints*.

Michael Collins. 2000. Discriminative Reranking for Natural Language Parsing. In *Proceedings of the Seventeenth International Conference on Machine Learning*, ICML '00, pages 175–182.

Dóra Csendes, Janós Csirik, Tibor Gyimóthy, and András Kocsor. 2005. The Szeged treebank. In Václav Matoušek, Pavel Mautner, and Tomáš Pavelka, editors, *Text, Speech and Dialogue: Proceedings of TSD 2005*. Springer.

Rickard Domeij, Ola Knutsson, Johan Carlberger, and Viggo Kann. 2000. Granska-an efficient hybrid system for Swedish grammar checking. In *In Proceedings of the 12th Nordic Conference in Computational Linguistics*.

Mikel L Forcada, Mireia Ginestí-Rosell, Jacob Nordfalk, Jim O'Regan, Sergio Ortiz-Rojas, Juan Antonio Pérez-Ortiz, Felipe Sánchez-Martínez, Gema Ramírez-Sánchez, and Francis M Tyers. 2011. Apertium: A free/open-source platform for rule-based machine translation. *Machine Translation*.

Yoav Goldberg and Michael Elhadad. 2010. An Efficient Algorithm for Easy-First Non-Directional Dependency Parsing. In *Human Language Technologies: The 2010 Annual Conference of the North American Chapter of the Association for Computational Linguistics*, pages 742–750, Los Angeles, California, June. Association for Computational Linguistics.

Yoav Goldberg. 2011. *Automatic syntactic processing of Modern Hebrew*. Ph.D. thesis, Ben Gurion University of the Negev.

Spence Green and Christopher D. Manning. 2010. Better arabic parsing: Baselines, evaluations, and analysis. In *Proceedings of the 23rd International Conference on Computational Linguistics (Coling 2010)*, pages 394–402, Beijing, China, August. Coling 2010 Organizing Committee.

Nizar Habash and Ryan Roth. 2009. Catib: The columbia arabic treebank. In *Proceedings of the ACL-IJCNLP 2009 Conference Short Papers*, pages 221–224, Suntec, Singapore, August. Association for Computational Linguistics.

Nizar Habash, Reem Faraj, and Ryan Roth. 2009. Syntactic Annotation in the Columbia Arabic Treebank. In *Proceedings of MEDAR International Conference on Arabic Language Resources and Tools*, Cairo, Egypt.

Keith Hall, Jiri Havelka, and David A. Smith. 2007. Log-Linear Models of Non-Projective Trees, k-best MST Parsing and Tree-Ranking. In *Proceedings of the CoNLL Shared Task Session of EMNLP-CoNLL 2007*, pages 962–966, Prague, Czech Republic, June. Association for Computational Linguistics.

Keith Hall. 2007. K-best Spanning Tree Parsing. In *Proceedings of the 45th Annual Meeting of the Association of Computational Linguistics*, pages 392–399, Prague, Czech Republic, June. Association for Computational Linguistics.

Jiri Havelka. 2007. Beyond Projectivity: Multilingual Evaluation of Constraints and Measures on Non-Projective Structures. In *Proceedings of the 45th Annual Meeting of the Association of Computational Linguistics*, pages 608–615, Prague, Czech Republic, June. Association for Computational Linguistics.

Mark Johnson and Ahmet Engin Ural. 2010. Reranking the Berkeley and Brown Parsers. In *Human Language Technologies: The 2010 Annual Conference of the North American Chapter of the Association for Computational Linguistics*, pages 665–668, Los Angeles, California, June. Association for Computational Linguistics.

Mohamed Maamouri, Ann Bies, Tim Buckwalter, and Wigdan Mekki. 2004. The Penn Arabic Treebank: Building a Large-Scale Annotated Arabic Corpus. In *NEMLAR Conference on Arabic Language Resources and Tools*.

Andre Martins, Noah Smith, Eric Xing, Pedro Aguiar, and Mario Figueiredo. 2010. Turbo Parsers: Dependency Parsing by Approximate Variational Inference. In *Proceedings of the 2010 Conference on Empirical Methods in Natural Language Processing*, pages 34–44, Cambridge, MA, October. Association for Computational Linguistics.

Andrew Kachites McCallum. 2002. "mallet: A machine learning for language toolkit". http://mallet.cs.umass.edu.

Ryan McDonald and Fernando Pereira. 2006. Online learning of approximate dependency parsing algorithms. In *Proceedings of the 11th Conference of the European Chapter of the Association for Computational Linguistics*, pages 81–88, Trento, Italy. Association for Computational Linguistics.

Thomas Müller, Helmut Schmid, and Hinrich Schütze. 2013. Efficient Higher-Order CRFs for Morphological Tagging. In *In Proceedings of EMNLP*.

Joakim Nivre, Jens Nilsson, and Johan Hall. 2006. Talbanken05: A Swedish treebank with phrase structure and dependency annotation. In *Proceedings of LREC*, pages 1392–1395, Genoa, Italy.

Joakim Nivre, Johan Hall, Jens Nilsson, Atanas Chanev, Gülşen Eryiğit, Sandra Kübler, Svetoslav Marinov, and Erwin Marsi. 2007. MaltParser: A language-independent system for data-driven dependency parsing. *Natural Language Engineering*, 13:95–135, 6.

Joakim Nivre. 2009. Non-Projective Dependency Parsing in Expected Linear Time. In *Proceedings of the Joint Conference of the 47th Annual Meeting of the ACL and the 4th International Joint Conference on Natural Language Processing of the AFNLP*, pages 351–359, Suntec, Singapore, August. Association for Computational Linguistics.

S Park, D Choi, E-k Kim, and KS Choi. 2010. A plug-in component-based Korean morphological analyzer. In *Proceedings of HCLT2010*.

Slav Petrov, Leon Barrett, Romain Thibaux, and Dan Klein. 2006. Learning accurate, compact, and interpretable tree annotation. In *Proceedings of the 21st International Conference on Computational Linguistics and the 44th annual meeting of the Association for Computational Linguistics*, pages 433–440. Association for Computational Linguistics.

Slav Petrov. 2010. Products of Random Latent Variable Grammars. In *Human Language Technologies: The 2010 Annual Conference of the North American Chapter of the Association for Computational Linguistics*, pages 19–27, Los Angeles, California, June. Association for Computational Linguistics.

Helmut Schmid. 2005. A programming language for finite state transducers. In *FSMNLP*.

Djamé Seddah, Reut Tsarfaty, Sandra Kübler, Marie Candito, Jinho Choi, Richárd Farkas, Jennifer Foster, Iakes Goenaga, Koldo Gojenola, Yoav Goldberg, Spence Green, Nizar Habash, Marco Kuhlmann, Wolfgang Maier, Joakim Nivre, Adam Przepiorkowski, Ryan Roth, Wolfgang Seeker, Yannick Versley, Veronika Vincze, Marcin Woliński, and Alina Wróblewska. 2013. Overview of the SPMRL 2013 Shared Task: A Cross-Framework Evaluation of Parsing Morphologically Rich Languages. In *Proceedings of the 4th Workshop on Statistical Parsing of Morphologically Rich Languages: Shared Task*, Seattle, WA.

Wolfgang Seeker and Jonas Kuhn. 2012. Making Ellipses Explicit in Dependency Conversion for a German Treebank. In *Proceedings of the 8th International Conference on Language Resources and Evaluation*, pages 3132–3139, Istanbul, Turkey. European Language Resources Association (ELRA).

Wolfgang Seeker and Jonas Kuhn. 2013. Morphological and Syntactic Case in Statistical Dependency Parsing. *Computational Linguistics*, 39(1):23–55.

Khalil Sima'an, Alon Itai, Yoad Winter, Alon Altman, and Noa Nativ. 2001. Building a Tree-Bank for Modern Hebrew Text. In *Traitement Automatique des Langues*.

Marek Świdziński and Marcin Woliński. 2010. Towards a bank of constituent parse trees for Polish. In *Text, Speech and Dialogue: 13th International Conference (TSD)*, Lecture Notes in Artificial Intelligence, pages 197—204, Brno, Czech Republic. Springer.

Stephen Tratz and Eduard Hovy. 2011. A Fast, Accurate, Non-Projective, Semantically-Enriched Parser. In *Proceedings of the 2011 Conference on Empirical Methods in Natural Language Processing*, pages 1257–1268, Edinburgh, Scotland, UK., July. Association for Computational Linguistics.

Reut Tsarfaty, Djamé Seddah, Yoav Goldberg, Sandra Kuebler, Yannick Versley, Marie Candito, Jennifer Foster, Ines Rehbein, and Lamia Tounsi. 2010. Statistical Parsing of Morphologically Rich Languages (SPMRL) What, How and Whither. In *Proc. of the SPMRL Workshop of NAACL-HLT*, pages 1–12, Los Angeles, CA, USA.

Reut Tsarfaty, Joakim Nivre, and Evelina Andersson. 2012. Joint Evaluation of Morphological Segmentation and Syntactic Parsing. In *Proceedings of the 50th Annual Meeting of the Association for Computational Linguistics (Volume 2: Short Papers)*, pages 6–10, Jeju Island, Korea, July. Association for Computational Linguistics.

Reut Tsarfaty. 2010. *Relational-Realizational Parsing*. Ph.D. thesis, University of Amsterdam.

Reut Tsarfaty. 2013. *A Unified Morpho-Syntactic Scheme of Stanford Dependencies*. Proceedings of ACL.

Veronika Vincze, Dóra Szauter, Attila Almási, György Móra, Zoltán Alexin, and János Csirik. 2010. Hungarian dependency treebank. In *LREC*.

Zhiguo Wang and Chengqing Zong. 2011. Parse Reranking Based on Higher-Order Lexical Dependencies. In *Proceedings of 5th International Joint Conference on Natural Language Processing*, pages 1251–1259, Chiang Mai, Thailand, November. Asian Federation of Natural Language Processing.

Marcin Woliński. 2006. Morfeusz - A practical tool for the morphological analysis of Polish. In *Intelligent information processing and web mining*, pages 511–520. Springer.

Hui Zhang, Min Zhang, Chew Lim Tan, and Haizhou Li. 2009. K-Best Combination of Syntactic Parsers. In *Proceedings of the 2009 Conference on Empirical Methods in Natural Language Processing*, pages 1552–1560, Singapore, August. Association for Computational Linguistics.

Zhenxia Zhou. 2007. Entwicklung einer französischen Finite-State-Morphologie. Diplomarbeit, Institute for Natural Language Processing, University of Stuttgart.

János Zsibrita, Veronika Vincze, and Richárd Farkas. 2013. Magyarlanc 2.0: Szintaktikai elemzés és felgyorsított szófaji egyértelműsítés. In *IX. Magyar Számítógépes Nyelvészeti Konferencia*.

Overview of the SPMRL 2013 Shared Task: Cross-Framework Evaluation of Parsing Morphologically Rich Languages*

**Djamé Seddah[a], Reut Tsarfaty[b], Sandra Kübler[c],
Marie Candito[d], Jinho D. Choi[e], Richárd Farkas[f], Jennifer Foster[g], Iakes Goenaga[h],
Koldo Gojenola[i], Yoav Goldberg[j], Spence Green[k], Nizar Habash[l], Marco Kuhlmann[m],
Wolfgang Maier[n], Joakim Nivre[o], Adam Przepiórkowski[p], Ryan Roth[q], Wolfgang Seeker[r],
Yannick Versley[s], Veronika Vincze[t], Marcin Woliński[u],
Alina Wróblewska[v], Eric Villemonte de la Clérgerie[w]**

[a]U. Paris-Sorbonne/INRIA, [b]Weizman Institute, [c]Indiana U., [d]U. Paris-Diderot/INRIA, [e]IPsoft Inc., [f,t]U. of Szeged, [g]Dublin City U., [h,i]U. of the Basque Country, [j]Bar Ilan U., [k]Stanford U., [l,q]Columbia U., [m,o]Uppsala U., [n]Düsseldorf U., [p,u,v]Polish Academy of Sciences, [r]Stuttgart U., [s]Heidelberg U., [w]INRIA

Abstract

This paper reports on the first shared task on statistical parsing of morphologically rich languages (MRLs). The task features data sets from nine languages, each available both in constituency and dependency annotation. We report on the preparation of the data sets, on the proposed parsing scenarios, and on the evaluation metrics for parsing MRLs given different representation types. We present and analyze parsing results obtained by the task participants, and then provide an analysis and comparison of the parsers across languages and frameworks, reported for gold input as well as more realistic parsing scenarios.

1 Introduction

Syntactic parsing consists of automatically assigning to a natural language sentence a representation of its grammatical structure. Data-driven approaches to this problem, both for constituency-based and dependency-based parsing, have seen a surge of interest in the last two decades. These data-driven parsing approaches obtain state-of-the-art results on the *de facto* standard Wall Street Journal data set (Marcus et al., 1993) of English (Charniak, 2000; Collins, 2003; Charniak and Johnson, 2005; McDonald et al., 2005; McClosky et al., 2006; Petrov et al., 2006; Nivre et al., 2007b; Carreras et al., 2008; Finkel et al., 2008; Huang, 2008; Huang et al., 2010; Zhang and Nivre, 2011; Bohnet and Nivre, 2012; Shindo et al., 2012), and provide a foundation on which many tasks operating on semantic structure (e.g., recognizing textual entailments) or even discourse structure (coreference, summarization) crucially depend.

While progress on parsing English — the main language of focus for the ACL community — has inspired some advances on other languages, it has not, by itself, yielded high-quality parsing for other languages and domains. This holds in particular for morphologically rich languages (MRLs), where important information concerning the predicate-argument structure of sentences is expressed through word formation, rather than constituent-order patterns as is the case in English and other configurational languages. MRLs express information concerning the grammatical function of a word and its grammatical relation to other words at the word level, via phenomena such as inflectional affixes, pronominal clitics, and so on (Tsarfaty et al., 2012c).

The non-rigid tree structures and morphological ambiguity of input words contribute to the challenges of parsing MRLs. In addition, insufficient language resources were shown to also contribute to parsing difficulty (Tsarfaty et al., 2010; Tsarfaty et al., 2012c, and references therein). These challenges have initially been addressed by native-speaking experts using strong in-domain knowledge of the linguistic phenomena and annotation idiosyncrasies to improve the accuracy and efficiency of parsing models. More

*Contact authors: djame.seddah@paris-sorbonne.fr, reut.tsarfaty@weizmann.ac.il, skuebler@indiana.edu

recently, advances in PCFG-LA parsing (Petrov et al., 2006) and language-agnostic data-driven dependency parsing (McDonald et al., 2005; Nivre et al., 2007b) have made it possible to reach high accuracy with classical feature engineering techniques in addition to, or instead of, language-specific knowledge. With these recent advances, the time has come for establishing the state of the art, and assessing strengths and weaknesses of parsers across different MRLs.

This paper reports on the first shared task on statistical parsing of morphologically rich languages (the SPMRL Shared Task), organized in collaboration with the 4th SPMRL meeting and co-located with the conference on Empirical Methods in Natural Language Processing (EMNLP). In defining and executing this shared task, we pursue several goals. First, we wish to provide standard training and test sets for MRLs in different representation types and parsing scenarios, so that researchers can exploit them for testing existing parsers across different MRLs. Second, we wish to standardize the evaluation protocol and metrics on morphologically ambiguous input, an under-studied challenge, which is also present in English when parsing speech data or web-based non-standard texts. Finally, we aim to raise the awareness of the community to the challenges of parsing MRLs and to provide a set of strong baseline results for further improvement.

The task features data from nine, typologically diverse, languages. Unlike previous shared tasks on parsing, we include data in both dependency-based and constituency-based formats, and in addition to the *full data* setup (complete training data), we provide a *small* setup (a training subset of 5,000 sentences). We provide three parsing scenarios: one in which gold segmentation, POS tags, and morphological features are provided, one in which segmentation, POS tags, and features are automatically predicted by an external resource, and one in which we provide a lattice of multiple possible morphological analyses and allow for joint disambiguation of the morphological analysis and syntactic structure. These scenarios allow us to obtain the performance upper bound of the systems in lab settings using gold input, as well as the expected level of performance in realistic parsing scenarios — where the parser follows a morphological analyzer and is a part of a full-fledged NLP pipeline.

The remainder of this paper is organized as follows. We first survey previous work on parsing MRLs (§2) and provide a detailed description of the present task, parsing scenarios, and evaluation metrics (§3). We then describe the data sets for the nine languages (§4), present the different systems (§5), and empirical results (§6). Then, we compare the systems along different axes (§7) in order to analyze their strengths and weaknesses. Finally, we summarize and conclude with challenges to address in future shared tasks (§8).

2 Background

2.1 A Brief History of the SPMRL Field

Statistical parsing saw initial success upon the availability of the Penn Treebank (PTB, Marcus et al., 1994). With that large set of syntactically annotated sentences at their disposal, researchers could apply advanced statistical modeling and machine learning techniques in order to obtain high quality structure prediction. The first statistical parsing models were generative and based on treebank grammars (Charniak, 1997; Johnson, 1998; Klein and Manning, 2003; Collins, 2003; Petrov et al., 2006; McClosky et al., 2006), leading to high phrase-structure accuracy.

Encouraged by the success of phrase-structure parsers for English, treebank grammars for additional languages have been developed, starting with Czech (Hajič et al., 2000) then with treebanks of Chinese (Levy and Manning, 2003), Arabic (Maamouri et al., 2004b), German (Kübler et al., 2006), French (Abeillé et al., 2003), Hebrew (Sima'an et al., 2001), Italian (Corazza et al., 2004), Spanish (Moreno et al., 2000), and more. It quickly became apparent that applying the phrase-based treebank grammar techniques is sensitive to language and annotation properties, and that these models are not easily portable across languages and schemes. An exception to that is the approach by Petrov (2009), who trained latent-annotation treebank grammars and reported good accuracy on a range of languages.

The CoNLL shared tasks on dependency parsing (Buchholz and Marsi, 2006; Nivre et al., 2007a) highlighted the usefulness of an alternative linguistic formalism for the development of competitive parsing models. Dependency relations are marked between input tokens directly, and allow the annotation of non-projective dependencies that are parseable efficiently. Dependency syntax was applied to the description of different types of languages (Tesnière, 1959; Mel'čuk, 2001), which raised the hope that in these settings, parsing MRLs will further improve.

However, the 2007 shared task organizers (Nivre et al., 2007a) concluded that: *"[Performance] classes are more easily definable via language characteristics than via characteristics of the data sets. The split goes across training set size, original data format [...], sentence length, percentage of unknown words, number of dependency labels, and ratio of (C)POSTAGS and dependency labels. The class with the highest top scores contains languages with a rather impoverished morphology."* The problems with parsing MRLs have thus not been solved by dependency parsing, but rather, the challenge has been magnified.

The first event to focus on the particular challenges of parsing MRLs was a dedicated panel discussion co-located with IWPT 2009.[1] Work presented on Hebrew, Arabic, French, and German made it clear that researchers working on non-English parsing face the same overarching challenges: poor lexical coverage (due to high level of inflection), poor syntactic coverage (due to more flexible word ordering), and, more generally, issues of data sparseness (due to the lack of large-scale resources). Additionally, new questions emerged as to the evaluation of parsers in such languages – are the word-based metrics used for English well-equipped to capture performance across frameworks, or performance in the face of morphological complexity? This event provoked active discussions and led to the establishment of a series of SPMRL events for the discussion of shared challenges and cross-fertilization among researchers working on parsing MRLs.

The body of work on MRLs that was accumulated through the SPMRL workshops[2] and hosting ACL venues contains new results for Arabic (Attia et al., 2010; Marton et al., 2013a), Basque (Bengoetxea and Gojenola, 2010), Croatian (Agic et al., 2013), French (Seddah et al., 2010; Candito and Seddah, 2010; Sigogne et al., 2011), German (Rehbein, 2011), Hebrew (Tsarfaty and Sima'an, 2010; Goldberg and Elhadad, 2010a), Hindi (Ambati et al., 2010), Korean (Chung et al., 2010; Choi and Palmer, 2011) and Spanish (Le Roux et al., 2012), Tamil (Green et al., 2012), amongst others. The awareness of the modeling challenges gave rise to new lines of work on topics such as joint morpho-syntactic processing (Goldberg and Tsarfaty, 2008), Relational-Realizational Parsing (Tsarfaty, 2010), EasyFirst Parsing (Goldberg, 2011), PLCFRS parsing (Kallmeyer and Maier, 2013), the use of factored lexica (Green et al., 2013), the use of bilingual data (Fraser et al., 2013), and more developments that are currently under way.

With new models and data, and with lingering interest in parsing non-standard English data, questions begin to emerge, such as: *What is the realistic performance of parsing MRLs using today's methods? How do the different models compare with one another? How do different representation types deal with parsing one particular language? Does the success of a parsing model on a language correlate with its representation type and learning method? How to parse effectively in the face of resource scarcity?* The first step to answering all of these questions is providing standard sets of comparable size, streamlined parsing scenarios, and evaluation metrics, which are our main goals in this SPMRL shared task.

2.2 Where We Are At: The Need for Cross-Framework, Realistic, Evaluation Procedures

The present task serves as the first attempt to standardize the data sets, parsing scenarios, and evaluation metrics for MRL parsing, for the purpose of gaining insights into parsers' performance across languages. Ours is not the first cross-linguistic task on statistical parsing. As mentioned earlier, two previous CoNLL shared tasks focused on cross-linguistic dependency parsing and covered thirteen different languages (Buchholz and Marsi, 2006; Nivre et al., 2007a). However, the settings of these tasks, e.g., in terms of data set sizes or parsing scenarios, made it difficult to draw conclusions about strengths and weaknesses of different systems on parsing MRLs.

A key aspect to consider is the relation between input tokens and tree terminals. In the standard statistical parsing setup, every input token is assumed to be a terminal node in the syntactic parse tree (after deterministic tokenization of punctuation). In MRLs,

[1] `http://alpage.inria.fr/iwpt09/panel.en.html`

[2] See `http://www.spmrl.org/` and related workshops.

morphological processes may have conjoined several words into a single token. Such tokens need to be segmented and their analyses need to be disambiguated in order to identify the nodes in the parse tree. In previous shared tasks on statistical parsing, morphological information was assumed to be known in advance in order to make the setup comparable to that of parsing English. In realistic scenarios, however, morphological analyses are initially unknown and are potentially highly ambiguous, so external resources are used to predict them. Incorrect morphological disambiguation sets a strict ceiling on the expected performance of parsers in real-world scenarios. Results reported for MRLs using gold morphological information are then, at best, optimistic.

One reason for adopting this less-than-realistic evaluation scenario in previous tasks has been the lack of sound metrics for the more realistic scenario. Standard evaluation metrics assume that the number of terminals in the parse hypothesis equals the number of terminals in the gold tree. When the predicted morphological segmentation leads to a different number of terminals in the gold and parse trees, standard metrics such as ParsEval (Black et al., 1991) or Attachment Scores (Buchholz and Marsi, 2006) fail to produce a score. In this task, we use TedEval (Tsarfaty et al., 2012b), a metric recently suggested for joint morpho-syntactic evaluation, in which normalized tree-edit distance (Bille, 2005) on morpho-syntactic trees allows us to quantify the success on the joint task in realistic parsing scenarios.

Finally, the previous tasks focused on dependency parsing. When providing both constituency-based and dependency-based tracks, it is interesting to compare results across these frameworks so as to better understand the differences in performance between parsers of different types. We are now faced with an additional question: how can we compare parsing results across different frameworks? Adopting standard metrics will not suffice as we would be comparing apples and oranges. In contrast, TedEval is defined for both phrase structures and dependency structures through the use of an intermediate representation called function trees (Tsarfaty et al., 2011; Tsarfaty et al., 2012a). Using TedEval thus allows us to explore both dependency and constituency parsing frameworks and meaningfully compare the performance of parsers of different types.

3 Defining the Shared-Task

3.1 Input and Output

We define a parser as a structure prediction function that maps sequences of space-delimited *input tokens* (henceforth, *tokens*) in a language to a set of parse trees that capture valid morpho-syntactic structures in that language. In the case of *constituency parsing*, the output structures are phrase-structure trees. In *dependency parsing*, the output consists of dependency trees. We use the term *tree terminals* to refer to the leaves of a phrase-structure tree in the former case and to the nodes of a dependency tree in the latter.

We assume that input sentences are represented as sequences of tokens. In general, there may be a many-to-many relation between input tokens and tree terminals. Tokens may be identical to the terminals, as is often the case in English. A token may be mapped to multiple terminals assigned their own POS tags (consider, e.g., the token "isn't"), as is the case in some MRLs. Several tokens may be grouped into a single (virtual) node, as is the case with multiword expressions (MWEs) (consider "pomme de terre" for "potatoe"). This task covers all these cases.

In the *standard* setup, all tokens are tree terminals. Here, the task of a parser is to predict a syntactic analysis in which the tree terminals coincide with the tokens. Disambiguating the morphological analyses that are required for parsing corresponds to selecting the correct POS tag and possibly a set of morphological features for each terminal. For the languages Basque, French, German, Hungarian, Korean, Polish, and Swedish, we assume this standard setup.

In the *morphologically complex* setup, every token may be composed of multiple terminals. In this case, the task of the parser is to predict the sequence of tree terminals, their POS tags, and a correct tree associated with this sequence of terminals. Disambiguating the morphological analysis therefore requires splitting the tokens into segments that define the terminals. For the Semitic languages Arabic and Hebrew, we assume this morphologically complex setup.

In the *multiword expression* (MWEs) setup, provided here for French only, groupings of terminals are identified as MWEs (non-terminal nodes in constituency trees, marked heads in dependency trees). Here, the parser is required to predict how terminals are grouped into MWEs on top of predicting the tree.

3.2 Data Sets

The task features nine languages from six language families, from Germanic languages (Swedish and German) and Romance (French) to Slavic (Polish), Koreanic (Korean), Semitic (Arabic, Hebrew), Uralic (Hungarian), and the language isolate Basque.

These languages cover a wide range of morphological richness, with Arabic, Basque, and Hebrew exhibiting a high degree of inflectional and derivational morphology. The Germanic languages, German and Swedish, have greater degrees of phrasal ordering freedom than English. While French is not standardly classified as an MRL, it shares MRLs characteristics which pose challenges for parsing, such as a richer inflectional system than English.

For each contributing language, we provide two sets of annotated sentences: one annotated with labeled phrase-structure trees, and one annotated with labeled dependency trees. The sentences in the two representations are aligned at token and POS levels. Both representations reflect the predicate-argument structure of the same sentence, but this information is expressed using different formal terms and thus results in different tree structures.

Since some of our native data sets are larger than others, we provide the training set in two sizes: *Full* containing all sentences in the standard training set of the language, and *5k* containing the number of sentences that is equivalent in size to our smallest training set (5k sentences). For all languages, the data has been split into sentences, and the sentences are parsed and evaluated independently of one another.

3.3 Parsing Scenarios

In the shared task, we consider three parsing scenarios, depending on how much of the morphological information is provided. The scenarios are listed below, in increasing order of difficulty.

- **Gold:** In this scenario, the parser is provided with unambiguous gold morphological segmentation, POS tags, and morphological features for each input token.
- **Predicted:** In this scenario, the parser is provided with disambiguated morphological segmentation. However, the POS tags and morphological features for each input segment are unknown.
- **Raw:** In this scenario, the parser is provided with morphologically ambiguous input. The morphological segmentation, POS tags, and morphological features for each input token are unknown.

Scenario	Segmentation	PoS+Feat.	Tree
Gold	✓	✓	–
Predicted	✓	1-best	–
Raw (1-best)	1-best	1-best	–
Raw (all)	–	–	–

Table 1: A summary of the parsing and evaluation scenarios. ✓ depicts gold information, – depicts unknown information, to be predicted by the system.

The **Predicted** and **Raw** scenarios require predicting morphological analyses. This may be done using a language-specific morphological analyzer, or it may be done jointly with parsing. We provide inputs that support these different scenarios:

- **Predicted**: Gold treebank segmentation is given to the parser. The POS tags assignment and morphological features are automatically predicted by the parser or by an external resource.
- **Raw (1-best)**: The 1st-best segmentation and POS tags assignment is predicted by an external resource and given to the parser.
- **Raw (all)**: All possible segmentations and POS tags are specified by an external resource. The parser selects jointly a segmentation and a tree.

An overview of all shown in table 1. For languages in which terminals equal tokens, only **Gold** and **Predicted** scenarios are considered. For Semitic languages we further provide input for both **Raw (1-best)** and **Raw (all)** scenarios. [3]

3.4 Evaluation Metrics

This task features nine languages, two different representation types and three different evaluation scenarios. In order to evaluate the quality of the predicted structures in the different tracks, we use a combination of evaluation metrics that allow us to compare the systems along different axes.

[3]The raw Arabic lattices were made available later than the other data. They are now included in the shared task release.

In this section, we formally define the different evaluation metrics and discuss how they support system comparison. Throughout this paper, we will be referring to different evaluation dimensions:

- **Cross-Parser Evaluation in Gold/Predicted Scenarios.** Here, we evaluate the results of different parsers on a single data set in the Gold or Predicted setting. We use standard evaluation metrics for the different types of analyses, that is, **ParsEval** (Black et al., 1991) on phrase-structure trees, and **Labeled Attachment Scores** (LAS) (Buchholz and Marsi, 2006) for dependency trees. Since ParsEval is known to be sensitive to the size and depth of trees (Rehbein and van Genabith, 2007b), we also provide the **Leaf-Ancestor** metric (Sampson and Babarczy, 2003), which is less sensitive to the depth of the phrase-structure hierarchy. In both scenarios we also provide metrics to evaluate the prediction of **MultiWord Expressions**.

- **Cross-Parser Evaluation in Raw Scenarios.** Here, we evaluate the results of different parsers on a single data set in scenarios where morphological segmentation is not known in advance. When a hypothesized segmentation is not identical to the gold segmentation, standard evaluation metrics such as ParsEval and Attachment Scores break down. Therefore, we use **TedEval** (Tsarfaty et al., 2012b), which jointly assesses the quality of the morphological and syntactic analysis in morphologically-complex scenarios.

- **Cross-Framework Evaluation.** Here, we compare the results obtained by a dependency parser and a constituency parser on the same set of sentences. In order to avoid comparing apples and oranges, we use the unlabeled **TedEval** metric, which converts all representation types internally into the same kind of structures, called function trees. Here we use TedEval's cross-framework protocol (Tsarfaty et al., 2012a), which accomodates annotation idiosyncrasies.

- **Cross-Language Evaluation.** Here, we compare parsers for the same representation type across different languages. Conducting a complete and faithful evaluation across languages would require a harmonized universal annotation scheme (possibly along the lines of (de Marneffe and Manning, 2008; McDonald et al., 2013; Tsarfaty, 2013)) or task based evaluation. As an approximation we use unlabeled **TedEval**. Since it is unlabeled, it is not sensitive to label set size. Since it internally uses function-trees, it is less sensitive to annotation idiosyncrasies (e.g., head choice) (Tsarfaty et al., 2011).

The former two dimensions are evaluated on the full sets. The latter two are evaluated on smaller, comparable, test sets. For completeness, we provide below the formal definitions and essential modifications of the evaluation software that we used.

3.4.1 Evaluation Metrics for Phrase Structures

ParsEval The ParsEval metrics (Black et al., 1991) are evaluation metrics for phrase-structure trees. Despite various shortcomings, they are the de-facto standard for system comparison on phrase-structure parsing, used in many campaigns and shared tasks (e.g., (Kübler, 2008; Petrov and McDonald, 2012)). Assume that G and H are phrase-structure gold and hypothesized trees respectively, each of which is represented by a set of tuples (i, A, j) where A is a labeled constituent spanning from i to j. Assume that g is the same as G except that it discards the root, preterminal, and terminal nodes, likewise for h and H. The ParsEval scores define the accuracy of the hypothesis in terms of the normalized size of the intersection of the constituent sets.

$$\begin{aligned} Precision(g,h) &= \frac{|g \cap h|}{|h|} \\ Recall(g,h) &= \frac{|g \cap h|}{|g|} \\ F_1(g,h) &= \frac{2 \times P \times R}{P+R} \end{aligned}$$

We evaluate accuracy on phrase-labels ignoring any further decoration, as it is in standard practices. Evalb, the standard software that implements ParsEval,[4] takes a parameter file and ignores the labels specified therein. As usual, we ignore root and POS labels. Contrary to the standard practice, we do take punctuation into account. Note that, as opposed to the *official version*, we used the SANCL'2012 version[5] modified to actually penalize non-parsed trees.

[4] `http://www.spmrl.org/spmrl2013-sharedtask-metrics.html/#Evalb`

[5] Modified by Petrov and McDonald (2012) to be less sensitive to punctuation errors.

Leaf-Ancestor The Leaf-Ancestor metric (Sampson and Babarczy, 2003) measures the similarity between the path from each terminal node to the root node in the output tree and the corresponding path in the gold tree. The path consists of a sequence of node labels between the terminal node and the root node, and the similarity of two paths is calculated by using the Levenshtein distance. This distance is normalized by path length, and the score of the tree is an aggregated score of the values for all terminals in the tree (x_t is the leaf-ancestor path of t in tree x).

$$LA(h, g) \quad = \quad \frac{\sum_{t \in yield(g)} Lv(h_t, g_t)/(len(h_t) + len(g_t))}{|yield(g)|}$$

This metric was shown to be less sensitive to differences between annotation schemes in (Kübler et al., 2008), and was shown by Rehbein and van Genabith (2007a) to evaluate trees more faithfully than ParsEval in the face of certain annotation decisions. We used the implementation of Wagner (2012).[6]

3.4.2 Evaluation Metrics for Dependency Structures

Attachment Scores Labeled and Unlabeled Attachment scores have been proposed as evaluation metrics for dependency parsing in the CoNLL shared tasks (Buchholz and Marsi, 2006; Nivre et al., 2007a) and have since assumed the role of standard metrics in multiple shared tasks and independent studies. Assume that g, h are gold and hypothesized dependency trees respectively, each of which is represented by a set of arcs (i, A, j) where A is a labeled arc from terminal i to terminal j. Recall that in the gold and predicted settings, $|g| = |h|$ (because the number of terminals determines the number of arcs and hence it is fixed). So Labeled Attachment Score equals precision and recall, and it is calculated as a normalized size of the intersection between the sets of gold and parsed arcs.[7]

$$\begin{aligned} Precision(g, h) &= \frac{|g \cap h|}{|g|} \\ Recall(g, h) &= \frac{|g \cap h|}{|h|} \\ LAS(g, h) &= \frac{|g \cap h|}{|g|} = \frac{|g \cap h|}{|h|} \end{aligned}$$

[6]The original version is available at http://www.grsampson.net/Resources.html, ours at http://www.spmrl.org/spmrl2013-sharedtask-metrics.html/#Leaf.

[7]http://ilk.uvt.nl/conll/software.html.

3.4.3 Evaluation Metrics for Morpho-Syntactic Structures

TedEval The TedEval metrics and protocols have been developed by Tsarfaty et al. (2011), Tsarfaty et al. (2012a) and Tsarfaty et al. (2012b) for coping with non-trivial evaluation scenarios, e.g., comparing parsing results across different frameworks, across representation theories, and across different morphological segmentation hypotheses.[8] Contrary to the previous metrics, which view accuracy as a normalized intersection over sets, TedEval computes the accuracy of a parse tree based on the tree-edit distance between complete trees. Assume a finite set of (possibly parameterized) edit operations $\mathcal{A} = \{a_1....a_n\}$, and a cost function $c : \mathcal{A} \rightarrow 1$. An edit script is the cost of a sequence of edit operations, and the edit distance of g, h is the minimal cost edit script that turns g into h (and vice versa). The normalized distance subtracted from 1 provides the level of accuracy on the task. Formally, the TedEval score on g, h is defined as follows, where ted is the tree-edit distance, and the $|x|$ (size in nodes) discards terminals and root nodes.

$$TedEval(g, h) = 1 - \frac{ted(g, h)}{|g| + |h|}$$

In the gold scenario, we are not allowed to manipulate terminal nodes, only non-terminals. In the raw scenarios, we can add and delete both terminals and non-terminals so as to match both the morphological and syntactic hypotheses.

3.4.4 Evaluation Metrics for Multiword-Expression Identification

As pointed out in section 3.1, the French data set is provided with tree structures encoding both syntactic information and groupings of terminals into MWEs. A given MWE is defined as a continuous sequence of terminals, plus a POS tag. In the constituency trees, the POS tag of the MWE is an internal node of the tree, dominating the sequence of pre-terminals, each dominating a terminal. In the dependency trees, there is no specific node for the MWE as such (the nodes are the terminals). So, the first token of a MWE is taken as the head of the other tokens of the same MWE, with the same label (see section 4.4).

[8]http://www.tsarfaty.com/unipar/download.html.

To evaluate performance on MWEs, we use the following metrics.

- R_MWE, P_MWE, and F_MWE are recall, precision, and F-score over full MWEs, in which a predicted MWE counts as correct if it has the correct span (same group as in the gold data).
- R_MWE +POS, R_MWE +POS, and F_MWE +POS are defined in the same fashion, except that a predicted MWE counts as correct if it has both correct span and correct POS tag.
- R_COMP, R_COMP, and F_COMP are recall, precision and F-score over non-head components of MWEs: a non-head component of MWE counts as correct if it is attached to the head of the MWE, with the specific label that indicates that it is part of an MWE.

4 The SPMRL 2013 Data Sets

4.1 The Treebanks

We provide data from nine different languages annotated with two representation types: phrase-structure trees and dependency trees.[9] Statistics about size, average length, label set size, and other characteristics of the treebanks and schemes are provided in Table 2. Phrase structures are provided in an extended bracketed style, that is, Penn Treebank bracketed style where every labeled node may be extended with morphological features expressed. Dependency structures are provided in the CoNLL-X format.[10]

For any given language, the dependency and constituency treebanks are aligned at the token and terminal levels and share the same POS tagset and morphological features. That is, any form in the CoNLL format is a terminal of the respective bracketed tree. Any CPOS label in the CoNLL format is the pre-terminal dominating the terminal in the bracketed tree. The FEATS in the CoNLL format are represented as dash-features decorated on the respective pre-terminal node in the bracketed tree. See Figure 1(a)–1(b) for an illustration of this alignment.

For ambiguous morphological analyses, we provide the mapping of tokens to different segmentation possibilities through lattice files. See Figure 1(c) for an illustration, where lattice indices mark the start and end positions of terminals.

For each of the treebanks, we provide a three-way *dev/train/set* split and another train set containing the first 5k sentences of *train (5k)*. This section provides the details of the original treebanks and their annotations, our data-set preparation, including preprocessing and data splits, cross-framework alignment, and the prediction of morphological information in non-gold scenarios.

4.2 The Arabic Treebanks

Arabic is a morphologically complex language which has rich inflectional and derivational morphology. It exhibits a high degree of morphological ambiguity due to the absence of the diacritics and inconsistent spelling of letters, such as Alif and Ya. As a consequence, the Buckwalter Standard Arabic Morphological Analyzer (Buckwalter, 2004; Graff et al., 2009) produces an average of 12 analyses per word.

Data Sets The Arabic data set contains two treebanks derived from the LDC Penn Arabic Treebanks (PATB) (Maamouri et al., 2004b):[11] the Columbia Arabic Treebank (CATiB) (Habash and Roth, 2009), a dependency treebank, and the Stanford version of the PATB (Green and Manning, 2010), a phrase-structure treebank. We preprocessed the treebanks to obtain strict token matching between the treebanks and the morphological analyses. This required non-trivial synchronization at the tree token level between the PATB treebank, the CATiB treebank and the morphologically predicted data, using the PATB source tokens and CATiB feature word form as a dual synchronized pivot.

The Columbia Arabic Treebank The Columbia Arabic Treebank (CATiB) uses a dependency representation that is based on traditional Arabic grammar and that emphasizes syntactic case relations (Habash and Roth, 2009; Habash et al., 2007). The CATiB treebank uses the word tokenization of the PATB

[9] Additionally, we provided the data in TigerXML format (Brants et al., 2002) for phrase structure trees containing crossing branches. This allows the use of more powerful parsing formalisms. Unfortunately, we received no submissions for this data, hence we discard them in the rest of this overview.

[10] See `http://ilk.uvt.nl/conll/`.

[11] The LDC kindly provided their latest version of the Arabic Treebanks. In particular, we used PATB 1 v4.1 (Maamouri et al., 2005), PATB 2 v3.1 (Maamouri et al., 2004a) and PATB 3 v3.3. (Maamouri et al., 2009)

	Arabic	Basque	French	German	Hebrew	Hungarian	Korean	Polish	Swedish
train:									
#Sents	15,762	7,577	14,759	40,472		8,146	23,010	6,578	
#Tokens	589,220	96,368	443,113	719,532		170,141	351,184	68,424	
Lex. Size	36,906	25,136	27,470	77,222		40,782	11,1540	22,911	
Avg. Length	37.38	12.71	30.02	17.77		20.88	15.26	10.40	
Ratio #NT/#Tokens	0.19	0.82	0.34	0.60		0.59	0.60	0.94	
Ratio #NT/#Sents	7.40	10.50	10.33	10.70		12.38	9.27	9.84	
#Non Terminals	22	12	32	25		16	8	34	
#POS tags	35	25	29	54		16	1,975	29	
#total NTs	116,769	79,588	152,463	433,215		100,885	213,370	64,792	
Dep. Label Set Size	9	31	25	43		417	22	27	
train5k:									
#Sents	5,000	5,000	5,000	5,000	5,000	5,000	5,000	5,000	5,000
#Tokens	224,907	61,905	150,984	87,841	128,046	109,987	68,336	52,123	76,357
Lex. Size	19,433	18,405	15,480	17,421	15,975	29,009	29,715	18,632	14,110
Avg. Length	44.98	12.38	30.19	17.56	25.60	21.99	13.66	10.42	15.27
Ratio #NT/#Tokens	0.15	0.83	0.34	0.60	0.42	0.57	0.68	0.94	0.58
Ratio #NT/#Sents	7.18	10.33	10.32	10.58	10.97	12.57	9.29	9.87	8.96
#Non Terminals	22	12	29	23	60	16	8	34	8
#POS Tags	35	25	29	51	50	16	972	29	25
#total NTs	35,909	5,1691	51,627	52,945	54,856	62,889	46,484	49,381	44,845
Dep. Label Set Size	9	31	25	42	43	349	20	27	61
dev:									
#Sents	1,985	948	1,235	5,000	500	1,051	2,066	821	494
#Tokens	73,932	13,851	38,820	76,704	11,301	29,989	30,480	8,600	9,341
Lex. Size	12,342	5,551	6,695	15,852	3,175	10,673	15,826	4,467	2,690
Avg. Length	37.24	14.61	31.43	15.34	22.60	28.53	14.75	10.47	18.90
Ratio #NT/#Tokens	0.19	0.74	0.33	0.63	0.47	047	0.63	0.94	0.48
Ratio #NT/#Sents	7.28	10.92	10.48	9.71	10.67	13.66	9.33	9.90	9.10
#Non Terminals	21	11	27	24	55	16	8	31	8
#POS Tags	32	23	29	50	47	16	760	29	24
#total NTs	14,452	10,356	12,951	48,560	5,338	14,366	19,283	8,132	4,496
Dep. Label Set Size	9	31	25	41	42	210	22	26	59
test:									
#Sents	1959	946	2541	5000	716	1009	2287	822	666
#Tokens	73878	11457	75216	92004	16998	19908	33766	8545	10690
Lex. Size	12254	4685	10048	20149	4305	7856	16475	4336	3112
Avg. Length	37.71	12.11	29.60	18.40	23.74	19.73	14.76	10.39	16.05
Ratio #NT/#Tokens	0.19	0.83	0.34	0.60	0.47	0.62	0.61	0.95	0.57
Ratio #NT/#Sents	7.45	10.08	10.09	11.07	11.17	12.26	9.02	9.94	9.18
#Non Terminals	22	12	30	23	54	15	8	31	8
#POS Tags	33	22	30	52	46	16	809	27	25
#total NTs	14,610	9,537	25,657	55,398	8,001	12,377	20,640	8,175	6,118
Dep. Label Set Size	9	31	26	42	41	183	22	27	56

Table 2: Overview of participating languages and treebank properties. 'Sents' = number of sentences, 'Tokens' = number of raw surface forms. 'Lex. size' and 'Avg. Length' are computed in terms of tagged terminals. 'NT' = non-terminals in constituency treebanks, 'Dep Labels' = dependency labels on the arcs of dependency treebanks. – A more comprehensive table is available at `http://www.spmrl.org/spmrl2013-sharedtask.html/#Prop`.

(a) Constituency Tree

```
% % every line is a single tree in a bracketed Penn Treebank format

(ROOT (S (NP ( NNP-#pers=3|num=sing# John))(VP ( VB-#pers=3|num=sing# likes)(NP ( NNP-#pers=3|num=sing# Mary)))))
```

(b) Dependency Tree

```
%% every line describes a terminal: terminal-id form lemma CPOS FPOS FEATS Head Rel PHead PRel

1  John   John  NNP  NNP  pers=3|num=sing  2  sbj   _  _
2  likes  like  VB   VB   pers=3|num=sing  0  root  _  _
3  Mary   Mary  NNP  NNP  pers=3|num=sing  2  obj   _  _
```

Input Lattice

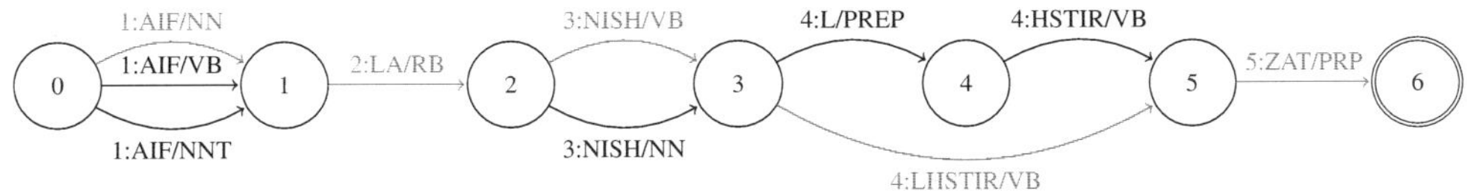


```
%% every line describes a terminal: start-id end-id form lemma CPOS FPOS FEATS token-id

0  1  AIF     AIF    NN    NN    _  1
0  1  AIF     AIF    NNT   NNT   _  1
0  1  AIF     AIF    VB    VB    _  1
1  2  LA      LA     RB    RB    _  2
2  3  NISH    NISH   VB    VB    _  3
2  3  NISH    NISH   NN    NN    _  3
3  5  LHSTIR  HSTIR  VB    VB    _  4
3  4  L       L      PREP  PREP  _  4
4  5  HSTIR   HSTIR  VB    VB    _  4
5  6  ZAT     ZAT    PRP   PRP   _  5
```

Figure 1: **File formats.** Trees (a) and (b) are aligned constituency and dependency trees for a mockup English example. Boxed labels are shared across the treebanks. Figure (c) shows an ambiguous lattice. The red part represents the yield of the gold tree. For brevity, we use empty feature columns, but of course lattice arcs may carry any morphological features, in the FEATS CoNLL format.

and employs a reduced POS tagset consisting of six tags only: NOM (non-proper nominals including nouns, pronouns, adjectives and adverbs), PROP (proper nouns), VRB (active-voice verbs), VRB-PASS (passive-voice verbs), PRT (particles such as prepositions or conjunctions) and PNX (punctuation). (This stands in extreme contrast with the Buckwalter Arabic tagset (PATB official tagset) which is almost 500 tags.) To obtain these dependency trees, we used the constituent-to-dependency tool (Habash and Roth, 2009). Additional CATiB trees were annotated directly, but we only use the portions that are converted from phrase-structure representation, to ensure that the constituent and dependency yields can be aligned.

The Stanford Arabic Phrase Structure Treebank In order to stay compatible with the state of the art, we provide the constituency data set with most of the pre-processing steps of Green and Manning (2010), as they were shown to improve baseline performance on the PATB parsing considerably.[12]

To convert the original PATB to preprocessed phrase-structure trees á la Stanford, we first discard all trees dominated by X, which indicates errors and non-linguistic text. At the phrasal level, we collapse unary chains with identical categories like NP → NP. We finally remove all traces, but, unlike Green and Manning (2010), we keep all function tags.

In the original Stanford instance, the pre-terminal morphological analyses were mapped to the shortened *Bies* tag set provided with the treebank (where Determiner markers, "DT", were added to definite noun and adjectives, resulting in 32 POS tags). Here we use the *Kulick* tagset (Kulick et al., 2006) for

[12]Both the corpus split and pre-processing code are available with the Stanford parser at `http://nlp.stanford.edu/projects/arabic.shtml`.

pre-terminal categories in the phrase-structure trees, where the *Bies* tag set is included as a morphological feature (*stanpos*) in our PATB instance.

Adapting the Data to the Shared Task We converted the CATiB representation to the CoNLL representation and added a 'split-from-previous' and 'split-from-next' markers as in LDC's tree-terminal fields.

A major difference between the CATiB treebank and the Stanford treebank lies in the way they handle paragraph annotations. The original PATB contains sequences of annotated trees that belong to a same discourse unit (e.g., paragraph). While the CATiB conversion tool considers each sequence a single parsing unit, the Stanford pre-processor treats each such tree structure rooted at S, NP or Frag as a tree spanning a single sentence. To be compatible with the predicted morphology data which was bootstrapped and trained on the CATiB interpretation, we deterministically modified the original PATB by adding pseudo XP root nodes, so that the Stanford pre-proprecessor will generate the same tree yields as the CATiB treebank.

Another important aspect of preprocessing (often-delegated as a technicality in the Arabic parsing literature) is the normalization of token forms. Most Arabic parsing work used transliterated text based on the schemes proposed by Buckwalter (2002). The transliteration schemes exhibit some small differences, but enough to increase the out-of-vocabulary rate by a significant margin (on top of strictly unknown morphemes). This phenomenon is evident in the morphological analysis lattices (in the predicted dev set there is a 6% OOV rate without normalization, and half a point reduction after normalization is applied, see (Habash et al., 2009b; Green and Manning, 2010)). This rate is much lower for gold tokenized predicted data (with an OOV rate of only 3.66%, similar to French for example). In our data set, all tokens are minimally normalized: no diacritics, no normalization.[13]

Data Splits For the Arabic treebanks, we use the data split recommended by the Columbia Arabic and Dialect Modeling (CADiM) group (Diab et al., 2013). The data of the LDC first three annotated Arabic Treebanks (ATB1, ATB2 and ATB3) were divided into roughly a 10/80/10% dev/train/test split by word volume. When dividing the corpora, document boundaries were maintained. The train5k files are simply the first 5,000 sentences of the training files.

POS Tagsets Given the richness of Arabic morphology, there are multiple POS tag sets and tokenization schemes that have been used by researchers, (see, e.g., Marton et al. (2013a)). In the shared task, we follow the standard PATB tokenization which splits off several categories of orthographic clitics, but not the definite article *Al+*. On top of that, we consider three different POS tag sets with different degrees of granularity: the *Buckwalter* tag set (Buckwalter, 2004), the *Kulick* Reduced Tag set (Kulick et al., 2006), and the *CATiB* tag set (Habash et al., 2009a), considering that granularity of the morphological analyses may affect syntactic processing. For more information see Habash (2010).

Predicted Morphology To prepare input for the Raw scenarios (§3.3), we used the MADA+TOKAN system (Habash et al., 2009b). MADA is a system for *morphological analysis and disambiguation of Arabic*. It can predict the 1-best tokenization, POS tags, lemmas and diacritization in one fell swoop. The MADA output was also used to generate the lattice files for the Raw-all scenario.

To generate input for the gold token / predicted tag input scenario, we used Morfette (Chrupała et al., 2008), a joint lemmatization and POS tagging model based on an averaged perceptron. We generated two tagging models, one trained with the *Buckwalter* tag set, and the other with the *Kulick* tag set. Both were mapped back to the CATiB POS tag set such that all predicted tags are contained in the feature field.[14]

4.3 The Basque Treebank

Basque is an agglutinative language with a high capacity to generate inflected wordforms, with free constituent order of sentence elements with respect to the main verb. Contrary to many other treebanks, the Basque treebank was originally annotated with dependency trees, which were later on converted to constituency trees.

[13]Except for the minimal normalization present in MADA's back-end tools. This script was provided to the participants.

[14]A conversion script from the rich *Buckwalter* tagset to CoNLL-like features was provided to the participants.

The Basque Dependency Treebank (BDT) is a dependency treebank in its original design, due to syntactic characteristics of Basque such as its free word order. Before the syntactic annotation, morphological analysis was performed, using the Basque morphological analyzer of Aduriz et al. (2000). In Basque each lemma can generate thousands of wordforms — differing in morphological properties such as case, number, tense, or different types of subordination for verbs. If only POS category ambiguity is resolved, the analyses remain highly ambiguous.

For the main POS category, there is an average of 1.55 interpretations per wordform, which rises to 2.65 for the full morpho-syntactic information, resulting in an overall 64% of ambiguous wordforms. The correct analysis was then manually chosen.

The syntactic trees were manually assigned. Each word contains its lemma, main POS category, POS subcategory, morphological features, and the labeled dependency relation. Each form indicates morphosyntactic features such as case, number and type of subordination, which are relevant for parsing.

The first version of the Basque Dependency Treebank, consisting of 3,700 sentences (Aduriz et al., 2003), was used in the CoNLL 2007 Shared Task on Dependency Parsing (Nivre et al., 2007a). The current shared task uses the second version of the BDT, which is the result of an extension and redesign of the original requirements, containing 11,225 sentences (150,000 tokens).

The Basque Constituency Treebank (BCT) was created as part of the CESS-ECE project, where the main aim was to obtain syntactically annotated constituency treebanks for Catalan, Spanish and Basque using a common set of syntactic categories. BCT was semi-automatically derived from the dependency version (Aldezabal et al., 2008). The conversion produced complete constituency trees for 80% of the sentences. The main bottlenecks have been sentence connectors and non-projective dependencies which could not be straightforwardly converted into projective tree structures, requiring a mechanism similar to traces in the Penn English Treebank.

Adapting the Data to the Shared Task As the BCT did not contain all of the original non-projective dependency trees, we selected the set of 8,000 matching sentences in both treebanks for the shared task.[15] This implies that around 2k trees could not be generated and therefore were discarded. Furthermore, the BCT annotation scheme does not contain attachment for most of the punctuation marks, so those were inserted into the BCT using a simple lower-left attachment heuristic. The same goes for some connectors that could not be aligned in the first phase.

Predicted Morphology In order to obtain predicted tags for the non-gold scenarios, we used the following pipeline. First, morphological analysis as described above was performed, followed by a disambiguation step. At that point, it is hard to obtain a single interpretation for each wordform, as determining the correct interpretation for each wordform may require knowledge of long-distance elements on top of the free constituency order of the main phrasal elements in Basque. The disambiguation is performed by the module by Ezeiza et al. (1998), which uses a combination of knowledge-based disambiguation, by means of Constraint Grammar (Karlsson et al., 1995; Aduriz et al., 1997), and a posterior statistical disambiguation module, using an HMM.[16]

For the shared task data, we chose a setting that disambiguates most word forms, and retains $\geq 97\%$ of the correct interpretations, leaving an ambiguity level of 1.3 interpretations. For the remaining cases of ambiguity, we chose the first interpretation, which corresponds to the most frequent option. This leaves open the investigation of more complex approaches for selecting the most appropriate reading.[17]

4.4 The French Treebank

French is not a morphologically rich language per se, though its inflectional system is richer than that of English, and it also exhibits a limited amount of word order variation occurring at different syntactic levels including the word level (e.g. pre- or post-nominal

[15] We generated a 80/10/10 split, – train/dev/test – The first 5k sentences of the train set were used as a basis for the train5k.

[16] Note that the statistical module can be parametrized according to the level of disambiguation to trade off precision and recall. For example, disambiguation based on the main categories (abstracting over morpho-syntactic features) maintains most of the correct interpretations but still gives an output with several interpretations per wordform.

[17] This is not an easy task. The ambiguity left is the hardest to solve given that the knowledge-based and statistical disambiguation processes have not been able to pick out a single reading.

adjective, pre- or post-verbal adverbs) and the phrase level (e.g. possible alternations between post verbal NPs and PPs). It also has a high degree of multi-word expressions, that are often ambiguous with a literal reading as a sequence of simple words. The syntactic and MWE analysis shows the same kind of interaction (though to a lesser extent) as morphological and syntactic interaction in Semitic languages — MWEs help parsing, and syntactic information may be required to disambiguate MWE identification.

The Data Set The French data sets were generated from the French Treebank (Abeillé et al., 2003), which consists of sentences from the newspaper Le Monde, manually annotated with phrase structures and morphological information. Part of the treebank trees are also annotated with grammatical function tags for dependents of verbs. In the SPMRL shared task release, we used only this part, consisting of 18,535 sentences,[18] split into 14,759 sentences for training, 1,235 sentences for development, and 2,541 sentences for the final evaluation.[19]

Adapting the Data to the Shared Task The constituency trees are provided in an extended PTB bracketed format, with morphological features at the pre-terminal level only. They contain slight, automatically performed, modifications with respect to the original trees of the French treebank. The syntagmatic projection of prepositions and complementizers was normalized, in order to have prepositions and complementizers as heads in the dependency trees (Candito et al., 2010).

The dependency representations are projective dependency trees, obtained through automatic conversion from the constituency trees. The conversion procedure is an enhanced version of the one described by Candito et al. (2010).

Both the constituency and the dependency representations make use of coarse- and fine-grained POS tags (CPOS and FPOS respectively). The CPOS are the categories from the original treebank. The FPOS are merged using the CPOS and specific morphological information such as verbal mood, proper/common noun distinction (Crabbé and Candito, 2008).

Multi-Word Expressions The main difference with respect to previous releases of the bracketed or dependency versions of the French treebank lies in the representation of multi-word expressions (MWEs). The MWEs appear in an extended format: each MWE bears an FPOS[20] and consists of a sequence of terminals (hereafter the "components" of the MWE), each having their proper CPOS, FPOS, lemma and morphological features. Note though that in the original treebank the only gold information provided for a MWE component is its CPOS. Since leaving this information blank for MWE components would have provided a strong cue for MWE recognition, we made sure to provide the same kind of information for every terminal, whether MWE component or not, by providing predicted morphological features, lemma, and FPOS for MWE components (even in the "gold" section of the data set). This information was predicted by the Morfette tool (Chrupała et al., 2008), adapted to French (Seddah et al., 2010).

In the constituency trees, each MWE corresponds to an internal node whose label is the MWE's FPOS suffixed by a +, and which dominates the component pre-terminal nodes.

In the dependency trees, there is no "node" for a MWE as a whole, but one node (a terminal in the CoNLL format) per MWE component. The first component of a MWE is taken as the head of the MWE. All subsequent components of the MWE depend on the first one, with the special label *dep_cpd*. Furthermore, the first MWE component bears a feature *mwe-head* equal to the FPOS of the MWE. For instance, the MWE *la veille* (*the day before*) is an adverb, containing a determiner component and a common noun component. Its bracketed representation is (ADV+ (DET la) (NC veille)), and in the dependency representation, the noun *veille* depends on the determiner *la*, which bears the feature `mwehead=ADV+`.

Predicted Morphology For the predicted morphology scenario, we provide data in which the `mwehead` has been removed and with predicted

[18]The process of functional annotation is still ongoing, the objective of the FTB providers being to have all the 20000 sentences annotated with functional tags.

[19]The first 9,981 training sentences correspond to the canonical 2007 training set. The development set is the same and the last 1235 sentences of the test set are those of the canonical test set.

[20]In the current data, we did not carry along the lemma and morphological features pertaining to the MWE itself, though this information is present in the original trees.

FPOS, CPOS, lemma, and morphological features, obtained by training Morfette on the whole train set.

4.5 The German Treebank

German is a fusional language with moderately free word order, in which verbal elements are fixed in place and non-verbal elements can be ordered freely as long as they fulfill the ordering requirements of the clause (Höhle, 1986).

The Data Set The German constituency data set is based on the TiGer treebank release 2.2.[21] The original annotation scheme represents discontinuous constituents such that all arguments of a predicate are always grouped under a single node regardless of whether there is intervening material between them or not (Brants et al., 2002). Furthermore, punctuation and several other elements, such as parentheses, are not attached to the tree. In order to make the constituency treebank usable for PCFG parsing, we adapted this treebank as described shortly.

The conversion of TiGer into dependencies is a variant of the one by Seeker and Kuhn (2012), which does not contain empty nodes. It is based on the same TiGer release as the one used for the constituency data. Punctuation was attached as high as possible, without creating any new non-projective edges.

Adapting the Data to the Shared Task For the constituency version, punctuation and other unattached elements were first attached to the tree. As attachment target, we used roughly the respective least common ancestor node of the right and left terminal neighbor of the unattached element (see Maier et al. (2012) for details), and subsequently, the crossing branches were resolved.

This was done in three steps. In the first step, the head daughters of all nodes were marked using a simple heuristic. In case there was a daughter with the edge label `HD`, this daughter was marked, i.e., existing head markings were honored. Otherwise, if existing, the rightmost daughter with edge label `NK` (noun kernel) was marked. Otherwise, as default, the leftmost daughter was marked. In a second step, for each continuous part of a discontinuous constituent, a separate node was introduced. This corresponds to the "raising" algorithm described by Boyd (2007). In a third steps, all those newly introduced nodes that did not cover the head daughter of the original discontinuous node were deleted. For the second and the third step, we used the same script as for the Swedish constituency data.

[21] This version is available from `http://www.ims.uni-stuttgart.de/forschung/ressourcen/korpora/tiger.html`

Predicted Morphology For the predicted scenario, a single sequence of POS tags and morphological features has been assigned using the MATE toolchain via a model trained on the train set via cross-validation on the training set. The MATE toolchain was used to provide predicted annotation for lemmas, POS tags, morphology, and syntax. In order to achieve the best results for each annotation level, a 10-fold jackknifing was performed to provide realistic features for the higher annotation levels. The predicted annotation of the 5k training set were copied from the full data set.[22]

4.6 The Hebrew Treebank

Modern Hebrew is a Semitic language, characterized by inflectional and derivational (templatic) morphology and relatively free word order. The function words for *from/to/like/and/when/that/the* are prefixed to the next token, causing severe segmentation ambiguity for many tokens. In addition, Hebrew orthography does not indicate vowels in modern texts, leading to a very high level of word-form ambiguity.

The Data Set Both the constituency and the dependency data sets are derived from the Hebrew Treebank V2 (Sima'an et al., 2001; Guthmann et al., 2009). The treebank is based on just over 6000 sentences from the daily newspaper 'Ha'aretz', manually annotated with morphological information and phrase-structure trees and extended with head information as described in Tsarfaty (2010, ch. 5). The unlabeled dependency version was produced by conversion from the constituency treebank as described in Goldberg (2011). Both the constituency and dependency trees were annotated with a set grammatical function labels conforming to Unified Stanford Dependencies by Tsarfaty (2013).

[22] We also provided a predicted-all scenario, in which we provided morphological analysis lattices with POS and morphological information derived from the analyses of the SMOR derivational morphology (Schmid et al., 2004). These lattices were not used by any of the participants.

Adapting the Data to the Shared Task While based on the same trees, the dependency and constituency treebanks differ in their POS tag sets, as well as in some of the morphological segmentation decisions. The main effort towards the shared task was unifying the two resources such that the two treebanks share the same lexical yields, and the same pre-terminal labels. To this end, we took the layering approach of Goldberg et al. (2009), and included two levels of POS tags in the constituency trees. The lower level is lexical, conforming to the lexical resource used to build the lattices, and is shared by the two treebanks. The higher level is syntactic, and follows the tag set and annotation decisions of the original constituency treebank.[23] In addition, we unified the representation of morphological features, and fixed inconsistencies and mistakes in the treebanks.

Data Split The Hebrew treebank is one of the smallest in our language set, and hence it is provided in only the small (5k) setting. For the sake of comparability with the 5k set of the other treebanks, we created a comparable size of dev/test sets containing the first and last 500 sentences respectively, where the rest serve as the 5k training.[24]

Predicted Morphology The lattices encoding the morphological ambiguity for the Raw (all) scenario were produced by looking up the possible analyses of each input token in the wide-coverage morphological analyzer (lexicon) of the Knowledge Center for Processing Hebrew (Itai and Wintner, 2008; MILA, 2008), with a simple heuristic for dealing with unknown tokens. A small lattice encoding the possible analyses of each token was produced separately, and these token-lattices were concatenated to produce the sentence lattice. The lattice for a given sentence may not include the gold analysis in cases of incomplete lexicon coverage.

The morphologically disambiguated input files for the Raw (1-best) scenario were produced by running the raw text through the morphological disambiguator (tagger) described in Adler and Elhadad (2006; Goldberg et al. (2008),Adler (2007). The disambiguator is based on the same lexicon that is used to produce the lattice files, but utilizes an extra module for dealing with unknown tokens Adler et al. (2008). The core of the disambiguator is an HMM tagger trained on about 70M unannotated tokens using EM, and being supervised by the lexicon.

As in the case of Arabic, we also provided data for the Predicted (gold token / predicted morphology) scenario. We used the same sequence labeler, Morfette (Chrupała et al., 2008), trained on the concatenation of POS and morphological gold features, leading to a model with respectable accuracy.[25]

4.7 The Hungarian Treebank

Hungarian is an agglutinative language, thus a lemma can have hundreds of word forms due to derivational or inflectional affixation (nominal declination and verbal conjugation). Grammatical information is typically indicated by suffixes: case suffixes mark the syntactic relationship between the head and its arguments (subject, object, dative, etc.) whereas verbs are inflected for tense, mood, person, number, and the definiteness of the object. Hungarian is also characterized by vowel harmony.[26] In addition, there are several other linguistic phenomena such as causation and modality that are syntactically expressed in English but encoded morphologically in Hungarian.

The Data Set The Hungarian data set used in the shared task is based on the Szeged Treebank, the largest morpho-syntactic and syntactic corpus manually annotated for Hungarian. This treebank is based on newspaper texts and is available in both constituent-based (Csendes et al., 2005) and dependency-based (Vincze et al., 2010) versions.

Around 10k sentences of news domain texts were made available to the shared task.[27] Each word is manually assigned all its possible morpho-syntactic

[23]Note that this additional layer in the constituency treebank adds a relatively easy set of nodes to the trees, thus "inflating" the evaluation scores compared to previously reported results. To compensate, a stricter protocol than is used in this task would strip one of the two POS layers prior to evaluation.

[24]This split is slightly different than the split in previous studies.

[25]POS+morphology prediction accuracy is 91.95% overall (59.54% for unseen tokens). POS only prediction accuracy is 93.20% overall (71.38% for unseen tokens).

[26]When vowel harmony applies, most suffixes exist in two versions – one with a front vowel and another one with a back vowel – and it is the vowels within the stem that determine which form of the suffix is selected.

[27]The original treebank contains 82,000 sentences, 1.2 million words and 250,000 punctuation marks from six domains.

tags and lemmas and the appropriate one is selected according to the context. Sentences were manually assigned a constituency-based syntactic structure, which includes information on phrase structure, grammatical functions (such as subject, object, etc.), and subcategorization information (i.e., a given NP is subcategorized by a verb or an infinitive). The constituency trees were later automatically converted into dependency structures, and all sentences were then manually corrected. Note that there exist some differences in the grammatical functions applied to the constituency and dependency versions of the treebank, since some morpho-syntactic information was coded both as a morphological feature and as decoration on top of the grammatical function in the constituency trees.

Adapting the Data to the Shared Task Originally, the Szeged Dependency Treebank contained virtual nodes for elided material *(ELL)* and phonologically covert copulas *(VAN)*. In the current version, they have been deleted, their daughters have been attached to the parent of the virtual node, and have been given complex labels, e.g. *COORD-VAN-SUBJ*, where *VAN* is the type of the virtual node deleted, *COORD* is the label of the virtual node and *SUBJ* is the label of the daughter itself. When the virtual node was originally the root of the sentence, its daughter with a predicative *(PRED)* label has been selected as the new root of the sentence (with the label *ROOT-VAN-PRED*) and all the other daughters of the deleted virtual node have been attached to it.

Predicted Morphology In order to provide the same POS tag set for the constituent and dependency treebanks, we used the dependency POS tagset for both treebank instances. Both versions of the treebank are available with gold standard and automatic morphological annotation. The automatic POS tagging was carried out by a 10-fold cross-validation on the shared task data set by `magyarlanc`, a natural language toolkit for processing Hungarian texts (segmentation, morphological analysis, POS tagging, and dependency parsing). The annotation provides POS tags and deep morphological features for each input token (Zsibrita et al., 2013).[28]

[28]The full data sets of both the constituency and dependency versions of the Szeged Treebank are available at the following website: `www.inf.u-szeged.hu/rgai/SzegedTreebank`, and `magyarlanc` is downloadable from: `www.inf.u-szeged.hu/rgai/magyarlanc`.

4.8 The Korean Treebank

The Treebank The Korean corpus is generated by collecting constituent trees from the KAIST Treebank (Choi et al., 1994), then converting the constituent trees to dependency trees using head-finding rules and heuristics. The KAIST Treebank consists of about 31K manually annotated constituent trees from 97 different sources (e.g., newspapers, novels, textbooks). After filtering out trees containing annotation errors, a total of 27,363 trees with 350,090 tokens are collected.

The constituent trees in the KAIST Treebank[29] also come with manually inspected morphological analysis based on 'eojeol'. An eojeol contains root-forms of word tokens agglutinated with grammatical affixes (e.g., case particles, ending markers). An eojeol can consist of more than one word token; for instance, a compound noun "*bus stop*" is often represented as one eojeol in Korean, 버스정류장, which can be broken into two word tokens, 버스 (bus) and 정류장 (stop). Each eojeol in the KAIST Treebank is separated by white spaces regardless of punctuation. Following the Penn Korean Treebank guidelines (Han et al., 2002), punctuation is separated as individual tokens, and parenthetical notations surrounded by round brackets are grouped into individual phrases with a function tag (`PRN` in our corpus).

All dependency trees are automatically converted from the constituent trees. Unlike English, which requires complicated head-finding rules to find the head of each phrase (Choi and Palmer, 2012), Korean is a head final language such that the rightmost constituent in each phrase becomes the head of that phrase. Moreover, the rightmost conjunct becomes the head of all other conjuncts and conjunctions in a coordination phrase, which aligns well with our head-final strategy.

The constituent trees in the KAIST Treebank do not consist of function tags indicating syntactic or semantic roles, which makes it difficult to generate dependency labels. However, it is possible to generate meaningful labels by using the rich morphology in Korean. For instance, case particles give good

[29]See Lee et al. (1997) for more details about the bracketing guidelines of the KAIST Treebank.

indications of what syntactic roles eojeols with such particles should take. Given this information, 21 dependency labels were generated according to the annotation scheme proposed by Choi (2013).

Adapting the Data to the Shared Task All details concerning the adaptation of the KAIST treebank to the shared task specifications are found in Choi (2013). Importantly, the rich KAIST treebank tag set of 1975 POS tag types has been converted to a list of CoNLL-like feature-attribute values refining coarse grained POS categories.

Predicted Morphology Two sets of automatic morphological analyses are provided for this task. One is generated by the HanNanum morphological analyzer.[30] The HanNanum morphological analyzer gives the same morphemes and POS tags as the KAIST Treebank. The other is generated by the Sejong morphological analyzer.[31] The Sejong morphological analyzer gives a different set of morphemes and POS tags as described in Choi and Palmer (2011).

4.9 The Polish Treebank

The Data Set *Składnica* is a constituency treebank of Polish (Woliński et al., 2011; Świdziński and Woliński, 2010). The trees were generated with a non-probabilistic DCG parser *Świgra* and then disambiguated and validated manually. The analyzed texts come from the one-million-token subcorpus of the National Corpus of Polish (NKJP, (Przepiórkowski et al., 2012)) manually annotated with morpho-syntactic tags.

The dependency version of *Składnica* is a result of an automatic conversion of manually disambiguated constituent trees into dependency structures (Wróblewska, 2012). The conversion was an entirely automatic process. Conversion rules were based on morpho-syntactic information, phrasal categories, and types of phrase-structure rules encoded within constituent trees. It was possible to extract dependencies because the constituent trees contain information about the head of the majority of constituents. For other constituents, heuristics were defined in order to select their heads.

The version of *Składnica* used in the shared task comprises parse trees for 8,227 sentences.[32]

Predicted Morphology For the shared task Predicted scenario, an automatic morphological annotation was generated by the *PANTERA* tagger (Acedański, 2010).

4.10 The Swedish Treebank

Swedish is moderately rich in inflections, including a case system. Word order obeys the verb second constraint in main clauses but is SVO in subordinate clauses. Main clause order is freer than in English but not as free as in some other Germanic languages, such as German. Also, subject agreement with respect to person and number has been dropped in modern Swedish.

The Data Set The Swedish data sets are taken from the Talbanken section of the Swedish Treebank (Nivre and Megyesi, 2007). Talbanken is a syntactically annotated corpus developed in the 1970s, originally annotated according to the MAMBA scheme (Teleman, 1974) with a syntactic layer consisting of flat phrase structure and grammatical functions. The syntactic annotation was later automatically converted to full phrase structure with grammatical functions and from that to dependency structure, as described by Nivre et al. (2006).

Both the phrase structure and the dependency version use the functional labels from the original MAMBA scheme, which provides a fine-grained classification of syntactic functions with 65 different labels, while the phrase structure annotation (which had to be inferred automatically) uses a coarse set of only 8 labels. For the release of the Swedish treebank, the POS level was re-annotated to conform to the current de facto standard for Swedish, which is the Stockholm-Umeå tagset (Ejerhed et al., 1992) with 25 base tags and 25 morpho-syntactic features, which together produce over 150 complex tags.

For the shared task, we used version 1.2 of the treebank, where a number of conversion errors in the dependency version have been corrected. The phrase structure version was enriched by propagating morpho-syntactic features from preterminals (POS

[30] `http://kldp.net/projects/hannanum`

[31] `http://www.sejong.or.kr`

[32] *Składnica* is available from `http://zil.ipipan.waw.pl/Sklicense`.

tags) to higher non-terminal nodes using a standard head percolation table, and a version without crossing branches was derived using the lifting strategy (Boyd, 2007).

Adapting the Data to the Shared Task Explicit attribute names were added to the feature field and the split was changed to match the shared task minimal training set size.

Predicted Morphology POS tags and morphosyntactic features were produced using the HunPoS tagger (Halácsy et al., 2007) trained on the Stockholm-Umeå Corpus (Ejerhed and Källgren, 1997).

5 Overview of the Participating Systems

With 7 teams participating, more than 14 systems for French and 10 for Arabic and German, this shared task is on par with the latest large-scale parsing evaluation campaign SANCL 2012 (Petrov and McDonald, 2012). The present shared task was extremely demanding on our participants. From 30 individuals or teams who registered and obtained the data sets, we present results for the seven teams that accomplished successful executions on these data in the relevant scenarios in the given the time frame.

5.1 Dependency Track

Seven teams participated in the dependency track. Two participating systems are based on MaltParser: MALTOPTIMIZER (Ballesteros, 2013) and AI:KU (Cirik and Şensoy, 2013). MALTOPTIMIZER uses a variant of MaltOptimizer (Ballesteros and Nivre, 2012) to explore features relevant for the processing of morphological information. AI:KU uses a combination of MaltParser and the original MaltOptimizer. Their system development has focused on the integration of an unsupervised word clustering method using contextual and morphological properties of the words, to help combat sparseness.

Similarly to MaltParser ALPAGE:DYALOG (De La Clergerie, 2013) also uses a shift-reduce transition-based parser but its training and decoding algorithms are based on beam search. This parser is implemented on top of the tabular logic programming system DyALog. To the best of our knowledge, this is the first dependency parser capable of handling word lattice input.

Three participating teams use the MATE parser (Bohnet, 2010) in their systems: the BASQUETEAM (Goenaga et al., 2013), IGM:ALPAGE (Constant et al., 2013) and IMS:SZEGED:CIS (Björkelund et al., 2013). The BASQUETEAM uses the MATE parser in combination with MaltParser (Nivre et al., 2007b). The system combines the parser outputs via MaltBlender (Hall et al., 2007). IGM:ALPAGE also uses MATE and MaltParser, once in a pipeline architecture and once in a joint model. The models are combined via a re-parsing strategy based on (Sagae and Lavie, 2006). This system mainly focuses on MWEs in French and uses a CRF tagger in combination with several large-scale dictionaries to handle MWEs, which then serve as input for the two parsers.

The IMS:SZEGED:CIS team participated in both tracks, with an ensemble system. For the dependency track, the ensemble includes the MATE parser (Bohnet, 2010), a best-first variant of the easy-first parser by Goldberg and Elhadad (2010b), and turbo parser (Martins et al., 2010), in combination with a ranker that has the particularity of using features from the constituent parsed trees. CADIM (Marton et al., 2013b) uses their variant of the easy-first parser combined with a feature-rich ensemble of lexical and syntactic resources.

Four of the participating teams use external resources in addition to the parser. The IMS:SZEGED:CIS team uses external morphological analyzers. CADIM uses SAMA (Graff et al., 2009) for Arabic morphology. ALPAGE:DYALOG and IGM:ALPAGE use external lexicons for French. IGM:ALPAGE additionally uses Morfette (Chrupała et al., 2008) for morphological analysis and POS tagging. Finally, as already mentioned, AI:KU clusters words and POS tags in an unsupervised fashion exploiting additional, un-annotated data.

5.2 Constituency Track

A single team participated in the constituency parsing task, the IMS:SZEGED:CIS team (Björkelund et al., 2013). Their phrase-structure parsing system uses a combination of 8 PCFG-LA parsers, trained using a product-of-grammars procedure (Petrov, 2010). The 50-best parses of this combination are then reranked by a model based on the reranker by Charniak and

Johnson (2005).[33]

5.3 Baselines

We additionally provide the results of two baseline systems for the nine languages, one for constituency parsing and one for dependency parsing.

For the dependency track, our baseline system is MaltParser in its default configuration (the arc-eager algorithm and liblinear for training). Results marked as BASE:MALT in the next two sections report the results of this baseline system in different scenarios.

The constituency parsing baseline is based on the most recent version of the PCFG-LA model of Petrov et al. (2006), used with its default settings and five split/merge cycles, for all languages.[34] We use this parser in two configurations: a '1-best' configuration where all POS tags are provided to the parser (predicted or gold, depending on the scenario), and another configuration in which the parser performs its own POS tagging. These baselines are referred to as BASE:BKY+POS and BASE:BKY+RAW respectively in the following results sections. Note that even when BASE:BKY+POS is given gold POS tags, the Berkeley parser sometimes fails to reach a perfect POS accuracy. In cases when the parser cannot find a parse with the provided POS, it falls back on its own POS tagging for all tokens.

6 Results

The high number of submitted system variants and evaluation scenarios in the task resulted in a large number of evaluation scores. In the following evaluation, we focus on the best run for each participant, and we aim to provide key points on the different dimensions of analysis resulting from our evaluation protocol. We invite our interested readers to browse the comprehensive representation of our results on the official shared-task results webpages.[35]

[33]Note that a slight but necessary change in the configuration of one of our metrics, which occurred after the system submission deadline, resulted in the IMS:SZEGED:CIS team to submit suboptimal systems for 4 languages. Their final scores are actually slightly higher and can be found in (Björkelund et al., 2013).

[34]For Semitic languages, we used the lattice based PCFG-LA extension by Goldberg (2011).

[35]`http://www.spmrl.org/spmrl2013-sharedtask-results.html`.

6.1 Gold Scenarios

This section presents the parsing results in gold scenarios, where the systems are evaluated on gold segmented and tagged input. This means that the sequence of terminals, POS tags, and morphological features are provided based on the treebank annotations. This scenario was used in most previous shared tasks on data-driven parsing (Buchholz and Marsi, 2006; Nivre et al., 2007a; Kübler, 2008). Note that this scenario was not mandatory. We thank our participants for providing their results nonetheless.

We start by reviewing dependency-based parsing results, both on the trees and on multi-word expression, and continue with the different metrics for constituency-based parsing.

6.1.1 Dependency Parsing

Full Training Set The results for the gold parsing scenario of dependency parsing are shown in the top block of table 3.

Among the six systems, IMS:SZEGED:CIS reaches the highest LAS scores, not only on average, but for every single language. This shows that their approach of combining parsers with (re)ranking provides robust parsing results across languages with different morphological characteristics. The second best system is ALPAGE:DYALOG, the third best system is MALTOPTIMIZER. The fact that AI:KU is ranked below the Malt baseline is due to their submission of results for 6 out of the 9 languages. Similarly, CADIM only submitted results for Arabic and ranked in the third place for this language, after the two IMS:SZEGED:CIS runs. IGM:ALPAGE and BASQUETEAM did not submit results for this setting.

Comparing LAS results across languages is problematic due to the differences between languages, treebank size and annotation schemes (see section 3), so the following discussion is necessarily tentative. If we consider results across languages, we see that the lowest results (around 83% for the best performing system) are reached for Hebrew and Swedish, the languages with the smallest data sets. The next lowest result, around 86%, is reached for Basque. Other languages reach similar LAS scores, around 88-92%. German, with the largest training set, reaches the highest LAS, 91.83%.

Interstingly, all systems have high LAS scores on the Korean Treebank given a training set size

team	Arabic	Basque	French	German	Hebrew	Hungarian	Korean	Polish	Swedish	avg.
					1) gold setting / full training set					
IMS:SZEGED:CIS	**89.83**	**86.68**	**90.29**	**91.83**	**83.87**	**88.06**	**89.59**	**89.58**	**83.97**	**88.19**
ALPAGE:DYALOG	85.87	80.39	87.69	88.25	80.70	79.60	88.23	86.00	79.80	84.06
MALTOPTIMIZER	87.03	82.07	85.71	86.96	80.03	83.14	89.39	80.49	77.67	83.61
BASE:MALT	82.28	69.19	79.86	79.98	76.61	72.34	88.43	77.70	75.73	78.01
AI:KU			86.39	86.98	79.42	83.67		85.16	78.87	55.61
CADIM	85.56									9.51
					2) gold setting / 5k training set					
IMS:SZEGED:CIS	**87.35**	**85.69**	**88.73**	**87.70**	**83.87**	**87.21**	83.38	**89.16**	**83.97**	**86.34**
ALPAGE:DYALOG	83.25	79.11	85.66	83.88	80.70	78.42	81.91	85.67	79.80	82.04
MALTOPTIMIZER	85.30	81.40	84.93	83.59	80.03	82.37	**83.74**	79.79	77.67	82.09
BASE:MALT	80.36	67.13	78.16	76.64	76.61	71.27	81.93	76.64	75.73	76.05
AI:KU			84.98	83.47	79.42	82.84		84.37	78.87	54.88
CADIM	82.67									9.19
					3) predicted setting / full training set					
IMS:SZEGED:CIS	**86.21**	**85.14**	85.24	**89.65**	**80.89**	**86.13**	**86.62**	**87.07**	**82.13**	**85.45**
ALPAGE:DYALOG	81.20	77.55	82.06	84.80	73.63	75.58	81.02	82.56	77.54	79.55
MALTOPTIMIZER	81.90	78.58	79.00	82.75	73.01	79.63	82.65	79.89	75.82	79.25
BASE:MALT	80.36	70.11	77.98	77.81	69.97	70.15	82.06	75.63	73.21	75.25
AI:KU			72.57	82.32	69.01	78.92		81.86	76.35	51.23
BASQUETEAM		84.25	84.51	88.66		84.97			80.88	47.03
IGM:ALPAGE			**85.86**							9.54
CADIM	83.20									9.24
					4) predicted setting / 5k training set					
IMS:SZEGED:CIS	**83.66**	**83.84**	83.45	**85.08**	**80.89**	**85.24**	**80.80**	**86.69**	**82.13**	**83.53**
MALTOPTIMIZER	79.64	77.59	77.56	79.22	73.01	79.00	75.90	79.50	75.82	77.47
ALPAGE:DYALOG	78.65	76.06	80.11	73.07	73.63	74.48	73.79	82.04	77.54	76.60
BASE:MALT	78.48	68.12	76.54	74.81	69.97	69.08	74.87	75.29	73.21	73.37
AI:KU			71.23	79.16	69.01	78.04		81.30	76.35	50.57
BASQUETEAM		83.19	82.65	84.70		84.01			80.88	46.16
IGM:ALPAGE			**83.60**							9.29
CADIM	80.51									8.95

Table 3: Dependency parsing: LAS scores for full and 5k training sets and for gold and predicted input. Results in bold show the best results per language and setting.

of approximately 23,000 sentences, which is a little over half of the German treebank. For German, on the other hand, only the IMS:SZEGED:CIS system reaches higher LAS scores than for Korean. This final observation indicates that more than treebank size is important for comparing system performance across treebanks. This is the reason for introducing the reduced set scenario, in which we can see how the participating system perform on a common ground, albeit small.

5k Training Set The results for the gold setting on the 5k train set are shown in the second block of Table 3. Compared with the full training, we see that there is a drop of around 2 points in this setting. Some parser/language pairs are more sensitive to data sparseness than others. CADIM, for instance, exhibit a larger drop than MALTOPTIMIZER on Arabic, and MALTOPTIMIZER shows a smaller drop than IMS:SZEGED:CIS on French. On average, among all systems that covered all languages, MALTOPTIMIZER has the smallest drop when moving to 5k training, possibly since the automatic feature optimization may differ for different data set sizes.

Since all languages have the same number of sentences in the train set, these results can give us limited insight into the parsing complexity of the different treebanks. Here, French, Arabic, Polish, and Korean reach the highest LAS scores while Swedish reaches

Team	F_MWE	F_COMP	F_MWE+POS
1) gold setting / full training set			
AI:KU	99.39	99.53	99.34
IMS:SZEGED:CIS	99.26	99.39	99.21
MALTOPTIMIZER	98.95	98.99	0
ALPAGE:DYALOG	98.32	98.81	0
BASE:MALT	68.7	72.55	68.7
2) predicted setting / full training set			
IGM:ALPAGE	80.81	81.18	77.37
IMS:SZEGED:CIS	79.45	80.79	70.48
ALPAGE:DYALOG	77.91	79.25	0
BASQUE-TEAM	77.19	79.81	0
MALTOPTIMIZER	70.29	74.25	0
BASE:MALT	67.49	71.01	0
AI:KU	0	0	0
3) predicted setting / 5k training set			
IGM:ALPAGE	77.66	78.68	74.04
IMS:SZEGED:CIS	77.28	78.92	70.42
ALPAGE:DYALOG	75.17	76.82	0
BASQUETEAM	73.07	76.58	0
MALTOPTIMIZER	65.76	70.42	0
BASE:MALT	62.05	66.8	0
AI:KU	0	0	0

Table 4: Dependency Parsing: MWE results

the lowest one. Treebank variance depends not only on the language but also on annotation decisions, such as label set (Swedish, interestingly, has a relatively rich one). A more careful comparison would then take into account the correlation of data size, label set size and parsing accuracy. We investigate these correlations further in section 7.1.

6.1.2 Multiword Expressions

MWE results on the gold setting are found at the top of Table 4. All systems, with the exception of BASE:MALT, perform exceedingly well in identifying the spans and non-head components of MWEs given gold morphology.[36] These almost perfect scores are the consequence of the presence of two gold MWE features, namely MWEHEAD and PRED=Y, which respectively indicate the node span of the whole MWE and its dependents, which do not have a gold feature field. The interesting scenario is, of course, the predicted one, where these features are not provided to the parser, as in any realistic application.

6.1.3 Constituency Parsing

In this part, we provide accuracy results for phrase-structure trees in terms of ParsEval F-scores. Since ParsEval is sensitive to the non-terminals-per-word ratio in the data set (Rehbein and van Genabith, 2007a; Rehbein and van Genabith, 2007b), and given the fact that this ratio varies greatly within our data set (as shown in Table 2), it must be kept in mind that ParsEval should only be used for comparing parsing performance over treebank instances sharing the exact same properties in term of annotation schemes, sentence length and so on. When comparing F-Scores across different treebanks and languages, it can only provide a rough estimate of the relative difficulty or ease of parsing these kinds of data.

Full Training Set The F-score results for the gold scenario are provided in the first block of Table 5. Among the two baselines, BASE:BKY+POS fares better than BASE:BKY+RAW since the latter selects its own POS tags and thus cannot benefit from the gold information. The IMS:SZEGED:CIS system clearly outperforms both baselines, with Hebrew as an outlier.[37]

As in the dependency case, the results are not strictly comparable across languages, yet we can draw some insights from them. We see considerable differences between the languages, with Basque, Hebrew, and Hungarian reaching F-scores in the low 90s for the IMS:SZEGED:CIS system, Korean and Polish reaching above-average F-scores, and Arabic, French, German, and Swedish reaching F-scores below the average, but still in the low 80s. The performance is, again, not correlated with data set sizes. Parsing Hebrew, with one of the smallest training sets, obtains higher accuracy many other languages, including Swedish, which has the same training set size as Hebrew. It may well be that gold morphological information is more useful for combatting sparseness in languages with richer morphology (though Arabic here would be an outlier for this conjecture), or it may be that certain treebanks and schemes are inherently harder to parser than others, as we investigate in section 7.

For German, the language with the largest training

[36] Note that for the labeled measure F_MWE+POS, both MALTOPTIMIZER and ALPAGE:DYALOG have an F-score of zero, since they do not attempt to predict the MWE label at all.

[37] It might be that the easy layer of syntactic tags benefits from the gold POS tags provided. See section 4 for further discussion of this layer.

team	Arabic	Basque	French	German	Hebrew	Hungarian	Korean	Polish	Swedish	avg.
1) gold setting / full training set										
IMS:SZEGED:CIS	**82.20**	**90.04**	**83.98**	**82.07**	91.64	**92.60**	**86.50**	**88.57**	**85.09**	**86.97**
BASE:BKY+POS	80.76	76.24	81.76	80.34	**92.20**	87.64	82.95	88.13	82.89	83.66
BASE:BKY+RAW	79.14	69.78	80.38	78.99	87.32	81.44	73.28	79.51	78.94	78.75
2) gold setting / 5k training set										
IMS:SZEGED:CIS	**79.47**	**88.45**	**82.25**	**74.78**	91.64	**91.87**	**80.10**	**88.18**	**85.09**	**84.65**
BASE:BKY+POS	77.54	74.06	78.07	71.37	**92.20**	86.74	72.85	87.91	82.89	80.40
BASE:BKY+RAW	75.22	67.16	75.91	68.94	87.32	79.34	60.40	78.30	78.94	74.61
3) predicted setting / full training set										
IMS:SZEGED:CIS	**81.32**	**87.86**	**81.83**	**81.27**	**89.46**	**91.85**	**84.27**	**87.55**	**83.99**	**85.49**
BASE:BKY+POS	78.66	74.74	79.76	78.28	85.42	85.22	78.56	86.75	80.64	80.89
BASE:BKY+RAW	79.19	70.50	80.38	78.30	86.96	81.62	71.42	79.23	79.18	78.53
4) predicted setting / 5k training set										
IMS:SZEGED:CIS	**78.85**	**86.65**	**79.83**	**73.61**	**89.46**	**90.53**	**78.47**	**87.46**	**83.99**	**83.21**
BASE:BKY+POS	74.84	72.35	76.19	69.40	85.42	83.82	67.97	87.17	80.64	77.53
BASE:BKY+RAW	74.57	66.75	75.76	68.68	86.96	79.35	58.49	78.38	79.18	74.24

Table 5: Constituent Parsing: ParsEval F-scores for full and 5k training sets and for gold and predicted input. Results in bold show the best results per language and setting.

set and the highest scores in dependency parsing, the F-scores are at the lower end. These low scores, which are obtained despite the larger treebank and only moderately free word-order, are surprising. This may be due to case syncretism; gold morphological information exhibits its own ambiguity and thus may not be fully utilized.

5k Training Set Parsing results on smaller comparable test sets are presented in the second block of Table 5. On average, IMS:SZEGED:CIS is less sensitive than BASE:BKY+POS to the reduced size. Systems are not equally sensitive to reduced training sets, and the gaps range from 0.4% to 3%, with German and Korean as outliers (Korean suffering a 6.4% drop in F-score and German 7.3%). These languages have the largest treebanks in the full setting, so it is not surprising that they suffer the most. But this in itself does not fully explain the cross-treebank trends. Since ParsEval scores are known to be sensitive to the label set sizes and the depth of trees, we provide LeafAncestor scores in the following section.

6.1.4 Leaf-Ancestor Results

The variation across results in the previous subsection may have been due to differences across annotation schemes. One way to neutralize this difference (to some extent) is to use a different metric. We evaluated the constituency parsing results using the Leaf-Ancestor (LA) metric, which is less sensitive to the number of nodes in a tree (Rehbein and van Genabith, 2007b; Kübler et al., 2008). As shown in Table 6, these results are on a different (higher) scale than ParsEval, and the average gap between the full and 5k setting is lower.

Full Training Set The LA results in gold setting for full training sets are shown in the first block of Table 6. The trends are similar to the ParsEval F-scores. German and Arabic present the lowest LA scores (in contrast to the corresponding F-scores, Arabic is a full point below German for IMS:SZEGED:CIS). Basque and Hungarian have the highest LA scores. Hebrew, which had a higher F-score than Basque, has a lower LA than Basque and is closer to French. Korean also ranks worse in the LA analysis. The choice of evaluation metrics thus clearly impacts system rankings – F-scores rank some languages suspiciously high (e.g., Hebrew) due to deeper trees, and another metric may alleviate that.

5k Training Set The results for the leaf-ancestor (LA) scores in the gold setting for the 5k training set are shown in the second block of Table 6. Across

team	Arabic	Basque	French	German	Hebrew	Hungarian	Korean	Polish	Swedish	avg.
				1) gold setting / full training set						
IMS:SZEGED:CIS	**88.61**	**94.90**	**92.51**	**89.63**	**92.84**	**95.01**	**91.30**	**94.52**	**91.46**	**92.31**
BASE:BKY+POS	87.85	91.55	91.74	88.47	92.69	92.52	90.82	92.81	90.76	91.02
BASE:BKY+RAW	87.05	89.71	91.22	87.77	91.29	90.62	87.11	90.58	88.97	89.37
				2) gold setting / 5k training set						
IMS:SZEGED:CIS	**86.68**	**94.21**	**91.56**	**85.74**	**92.84**	**94.79**	**88.87**	**94.17**	**91.46**	**91.15**
BASE:BKY+POS	86.26	90.72	89.71	84.11	92.69	92.11	86.75	92.91	90.76	89.56
BASE:BKY+RAW	84.97	88.68	88.74	83.08	91.29	89.94	81.82	90.31	88.97	87.53
				3) predicted setting / full training set						
IMS:SZEGED:CIS	**88.45**	**94.50**	**91.79**	**89.32**	**91.95**	**94.90**	**90.13**	**94.11**	**91.05**	**91.80**
BASE:BKY+POS	86.60	90.90	90.96	87.46	89.66	91.72	89.10	92.56	89.51	89.83
BASE:BKY+RAW	86.97	89.91	91.11	87.46	90.77	90.50	86.68	90.48	89.16	89.23
				4) predicted setting / 5k training set						
IMS:SZEGED:CIS	**86.69**	**93.85**	**90.76**	**85.20**	**91.95**	**94.05**	**87.99**	**93.99**	**91.05**	**90.61**
BASE:BKY+POS	84.76	89.83	89.18	83.05	89.66	91.24	84.87	92.74	89.51	88.32
BASE:BKY+RAW	84.63	88.50	89.00	82.69	90.77	89.93	81.50	90.08	89.16	87.36

Table 6: Constituent Parsing: Leaf-Ancestor scores for full and 5k training sets and for gold and predicted input.

parsers, IMS:SZEGED:CIS again has a smaller drop than BASE:BKY+POS on the reduced size. German suffers the most from the reduction of the training set, with a loss of approximately 4 points. Korean, however, which was also severely affected in terms of F-scores, only loses 1.17 points in the LA score. On average, the LA seem to reflect a smaller drop when reducing the training set — this underscores again the impact of the choice of metrics on system evaluation.

6.2 Predicted Scenarios

Gold scenarios are relatively easy since syntactically relevant morphological information is disambiguated in advance and is provided as input. Predicted scenarios are more difficult: POS tags and morphological features have to be automatically predicted, by the parser or by external resources.

6.2.1 Dependency Parsing

Eight participating teams submitted dependency results for this scenario. Two teams submitted for a single language. Four teams covered all languages.

Full Training Set The results for the predicted scenario in full settings are shown in the third block of Table 3. Across the board, the results are considerably lower than the gold scenario. Again, IMS:SZEGED:CIS is the best performing system, followed by ALPAGE:DYALOG and MALTOPTIMIZER. The only language for which IMS:SZEGED:CIS is outperformed is French, for which IGM:ALPAGE reaches higher results (85.86% vs. 85.24%). This is due to the specialized treatment of French MWEs in the IGM:ALPAGE system, which is thereby shown to be beneficial for parsing in the predicted setting.

If we compare the results for the predicted setting and the gold one, given the full training set, the IMS:SZEGED:CIS system shows small differences between 1.5 and 2 percent. The only exception is French, for which the LAS drops from 90.29% to 85.24% in the predicted setting. The other systems show somewhat larger differences than IMS:SZEGED:CIS, with the highest drops for Arabic and Korean. The AI:KU system shows a similar problem as IMS:SZEGED:CIS for French.

5k Training Set When we consider the predicted setting for the 5k training set, in the last block of Table 3, we see the same trends as comparing with the full training set or when comparing to the gold setting. Systems suffer from not having gold standard data, and they suffer from the small training set. Interestingly, the loss between the different training set sizes in the predicted setting is larger than in the gold setting, but only marginally so, with a difference < 0.5. In other words, the predicted setting adds a challenge to parsing, but it only minimally compounds data sparsity.

6.2.2 Multiword Expressions Evaluation

In the predicted setting, shown in the second block of table 4 for the full training set and in the third block of the same table for the 5k training set, we see that only two systems, IGM:ALPAGE and IMS:SZEGED:CIS can predict the MWE label when it is not present in the training set. IGM:ALPAGE's approach of using a separate classifier in combination with external dictionaries is very successful, reaching an F_MWE+POS score of 77.37. This is compared to the score of 70.48 by IMS:SZEGED:CIS, which predicts this node label as a side effect of their constituent feature enriched dependency model (Björkelund et al., 2013). AI:KU has a zero score for all predicted settings, which results from an erroneous training on the gold data rather than the predicted data.[38]

6.2.3 Constituency Parsing

Full Training Set The results for the predicted setting with the full training set are shown in the third block of table 5. A comparison with the gold setting shows that all systems have a lower performance in the predicted scenario, and the differences are in the range of 0.88 for Arabic and 2.54 for Basque. It is interesting to see that the losses are generally smaller than in the dependency framework: on average, the loss across languages is 2.74 for dependencies and 1.48 for constituents. A possible explanation can be found in the two-dimensional structure of the constituent trees, where only a subset of all nodes is affected by the quality of morphology and POS tags. The exception to this trend is Basque, for which the loss in constituents is a full point higher than for dependencies. Another possible explanation is that all of our constituent parsers select their own POS tags in one way or another. Most dependency parsers accept predicted tags from an external resource, which puts an upper-bound on their potential performance.

5k Training Set The results for the predicted setting given the 5k training set are shown in the bottom block of table 5. They show the same trends as the dependency ones: The results are slightly lower than the results obtained in gold setting and the ones utilizing the full training set.

6.2.4 Leaf Ancestor Metrics

Full Training Set The results for the predicted scenario with a full training set are shown in the third block of table 6. In the LA evaluation, the loss in moving from gold morphology are considerably smaller than in F-scores. For most languages, the loss is less than 0.5 points. Exceptions are French with a loss of 0.72, Hebrew with 0.89, and Korean with 1.17. Basque, which had the highest loss in F-scores, only shows a minor loss of 0.4 points. Also, the average loss of 0.41 points is much smaller than the one in the ParsEval score, 1.48.

5k Training Set The results for the predicted setting given the 5k training set are shown in the last block of table 6. These results, though considerably lower (around 3 points), exhibit the exact same trends as observed in the gold setting.

6.3 Realistic Raw Scenarios

The previous scenarios assume that input surface tokens are identical to tree terminals. For languages such as Arabic and Hebrew, this is not always the case. In this scenario, we evaluate the capacity of a system to predict both morphological segmentation and syntactic parse trees given raw, unsegmented input tokens. This may be done via a pipeline assuming a 1-st best morphological analysis, or jointly with parsing, assuming an ambiguous morphological analysis lattice as input. In this task, both of these scenarios are possible (see section 3). Thus, this section presents a realistic evaluation of the participating systems, using TedEval, which takes into account complete morpho-syntactic parses.

Tables 7 and 8 present labeled and unlabeled TedEval results for both constituency and dependency parsers, calculated only for sentence of length $<= 70$.[39] We firstly observe that labeled TedEval scores are considerably lower than unlabeled TedEval scores, as expected, since unlabeled scores evaluate only structural differences. In the labeled setup,

[38] Unofficial updated results are to to be found in (Cirik and Şensoy, 2013)

[39] TedEval builds on algorithms for calculating edit distance on complete trees (Bille, 2005). In these algorithms, longer sentences take considerably longer to evaluate.

	Arabic full training set		Arabic 5k training set		Hebrew		All	
	Acc (x100)	Ex (%)	Acc (x100)	Ex (%)	Acc (x100)	Ex (%)	Avg.	Soft Avg.
IMS:SZEGED:CIS (Bky)	83.34	1.63	82.54	0.67	56.47	0.67	69.51	69.51
IMS:SZEGED:CIS	**89.12**	**8.37**	**87.82**	**5.56**	**86.08**	**8.27**	**86.95**	**86.95**
CADIM	87.81	6.63	86.43	4.21	-	-	43.22	86.43
MALTOPTIMIZER	86.74	5.39	85.63	3.03	83.05	5.33	84.34	84.34
ALPAGE:DYALOG	86.60	5.34	85.71	3.54	82.96	6.17	41.48	82.96
ALPAGE:DYALOG (RAW)	-	-	-	-	82.82	4.35	41.41	82.82
AI:KU	-	-	-	-	78.57	3.37	39.29	78.57

Table 7: Realistic Scenario: Tedeval Labeled Accuracy and Exact Match for the Raw scenario.
The upper part refers to constituency results, the lower part refers to dependency results

	Arabic full training set		Arabic 5k training set		Hebrew		All	
	Acc (x100)	Ex (%)	Acc (x100)	Ex (%)	Acc (x100)	Ex (%)	Avg.	Soft Avg.
IMS:SZEGED:CIS (Bky)	**92.06**	9.49	**91.29**	7.13	89.30	13.60	90.30	90.30
IMS:SZEGED:CIS	91.74	**9.83**	90.85	**7.30**	**89.47**	**16.97**	90.16	90.16
ALPAGE:DYALOG	89.99	7.98	89.46	5.67	88.33	12.20	88.90	88.90
MALTOPTIMIZER	90.09	7.08	89.47	5.56	87.99	11.64	88.73	88.73
CADIM	90.75	8.48	89.89	5.67	-	-	44.95	89.89
ALPAGE:DYALOG (RAW)	-	-	-	-	87.61	10.24	43.81	87.61
AI:KU	-	-	-	-	86.70	8.98	43.35	86.70

Table 8: Realistic Scenario: Tedeval Unlabeled Accuracy and Exact Match for the Raw scenario.
Top upper part refers to constituency results, the lower part refers to dependency results.

the IMS:SZEGED:CIS dependency parser are the best for both languages and data set sizes. Table 8 shows that their unlabeled constituency results reach a higher accuracy than the next best system, their own dependency results. However, a quick look at the exact match metric reveals lower scores than for its dependency counterparts.

For the dependency-based joint scenarios, there is obviously an upper bound on parser performance given inaccurate segmentation. The transition-based systems, ALPAGE:DYALOG & MALTOPTIMIZER, perform comparably on Arabic and Hebrew, with ALPAGE:DYALOG being slightly better on both languages. Note that ALPAGE:DYALOG reaches close results on the 1-best and the lattice-based input settings, with a slight advantage for the former. This is partly due to the insufficient coverage of the lexical resource we use: many lattices do not contain the gold path, so the joint prediction can only as be high as the lattice predicted path allows.

7 Towards In-Depth Cross-Treebank Evaluation

Section 6 reported evaluation scores across systems for different scenarios. However, as noted, these results are not comparable across languages, representation types and parsing scenarios due to differences in the data size, label set size, length of sentences and also differences in evaluation metrics.

Our following discussion in the first part of this section highlights the kind of impact that data set properties have on the standard metrics (label set size on LAS, non-terminal nodes per sentence on F-score). Then, in the second part of this section we use the TedEval cross-experiment protocols for comparative evaluation that is less sensitive to representation types and annotation idiosyncrasies.

7.1 Parsing Across Languages and Treebanks

To quantify the impact of treebank characteristics on parsing parsing accuracy we looked at correlations of treebank properties with parsing results. The most highly correlated combinations we have found are shown in Figures 2, 3, and 4 for the dependency track and the constituency track (F-score and LeafAnces-

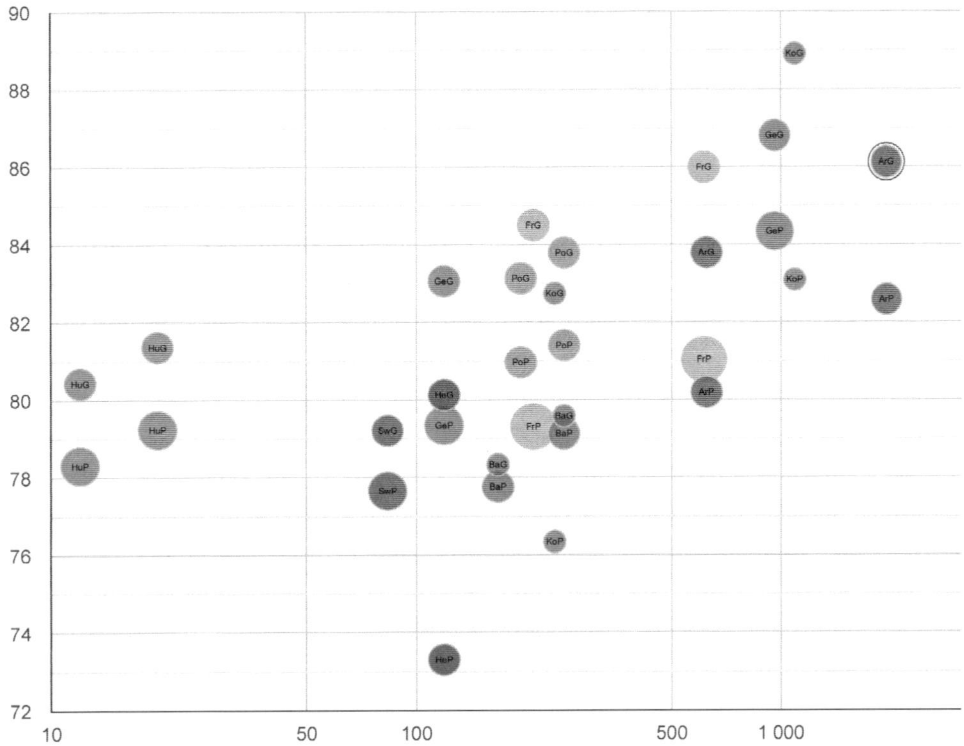

Figure 2: The correlation between treebank size, label set size, and LAS scores. *x: treebank size / #labels ; y: LAS (%)*

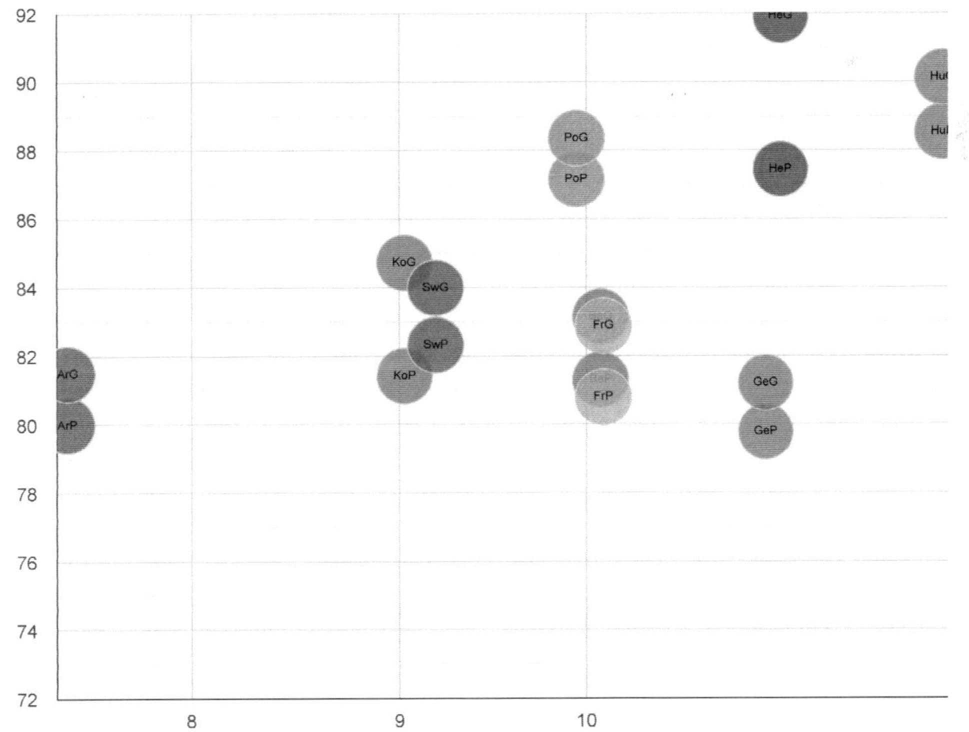

Figure 3: The correlation between the non terminals per sentence ratio and F-scores. *x: #non terminal/ #sentence ; y: F1 (%)*

tor) respectively.

Figure 2 presents the LAS against the average number of tokens relative to the number of labels. The numbers are averaged per language over all participating systems, and the size of the “bubbles” is proportional to the number of participants for a given language setting. We provide “bubbles” for all languages in the predicted (-P) and gold (-G) setting, for both training set sizes. The lower dot in terms of parsing scores always corresponds to the reduced training set size.

Figure 2 shows a clear correlation between data-set complexity and parsing accuracy. The simpler the data set is (where “simple" here translates into large data size with a small set of labels), the higher the results of the participating systems. The bubbles reflects a diagonal that indicates correlation between these dimensions. Beyond that, we see two interesting points off of the diagonal. The Korean treebank (pink) in the gold setting and full training set can be parsed with a high LAS relative to its size and label set. It is also clear that the Hebrew treebank (purple) in the predicted version is the most difficult one to parse, relative to our expectation about its complexity. Since the Hebrew gold scenario is a lot closer to the diagonal again, it may be that this outlier is due to the coverage and quality of the predicted morphology.

Figure 3[40] shows the correlation of data complexity in terms of the average number of non-terminals per sentence, and parsing accuracy (ParsEval F-score). Parsing accuracy is again averaged over all participating systems for a given language. In this figure, we see a diagonal similar to the one in figure 2, where Arabic (dark blue) has high complexity of the data (here interpreted as flat trees, low number of non terminals per sentence) and low F-scores accordingly. Korean (pink), Swedish (burgundy), Polish (light green), and Hungarian (light blue) follow, and then Hebrew (purple) is a positive outlier, possibly due to an additional layer of “easy" syntactic POS nodes which increases tree size and inflates F-scores. French (orange), Basque (red), and German (dark green) are negative outliers, falling off the diagonal. German has the lowest F-score with respect to what would be expected for the non-terminals per sentence ratio, which is in contrast to the LAS figure where German occurs among the less complex data set to parse. A possible explanation may be the crossing branches in the original treebank which were re-attached. This creates flat and variable edges which might be hard predict accurately.

Figure 4[41] presents the correlation between parsing accuracy in terms the LeafAncestor metrics (macro averaged) and treebank complexity in terms of the average number of non-terminals per sentence. As in the correlation figures, the parsing accuracy is averaged over the participanting systems for any language. The LeafAncestor accuracy is calculated over phrase structure trees, and we see a similar diagonal to the one in Figure 3 showing that flatter treebanks are harder (that is, are correlated with lower averaged scores) But, its slope is less steep than for the F-score, which confirms the observation that the LeafAncestor metric is less sensitive than F-score to the non-terminals-per-sentence ratio.

Similarly to Figure 3, German is a negative outlier, which means that this treebank is harder to parse – it obtains lower scores on average than we would expect. As for Hebrew, it is much closer to the diagonal. As it turns out, the "easy" POS layer that inflates the scores does not affect the LA ratings as much.

7.2 Evaluation Across Scenarios, Languages and Treebanks

In this section we analyze the results in cross-scenario, cross-annotation, and cross-framework settings using the evaluation protocols discussed in (Tsarfaty et al., 2012b; Tsarfaty et al., 2011; Tsarfaty et al., 2012a).

As a starting point, we select comparable sections of the parsed data, based on system runs trained on the small train set (train5k). For those, we selected subsets containing the first 5,000 tree terminals (respecting sentence boundaries) of the test set. We only used TedEval on sentences up to 70 terminals long, and projectivized non-projective sentences in all sets. We use the TedEval metrics to calculate scores on both constituency and dependency structures in all languages and all scenarios. Since the metric defines one scale for all of these different cases, we can

[40]This figure was created from the IMS:SZEGED:CIS (Const.) and our own PCFG-LA baseline in POS Tagged mode (BASE:BKY+POS) so as to avoid the noise introduced by the parser's own tagging step (BASE:BKY+RAW).

[41]This figure was created under the same condition as the F-score correlation in figure (Figure 3).

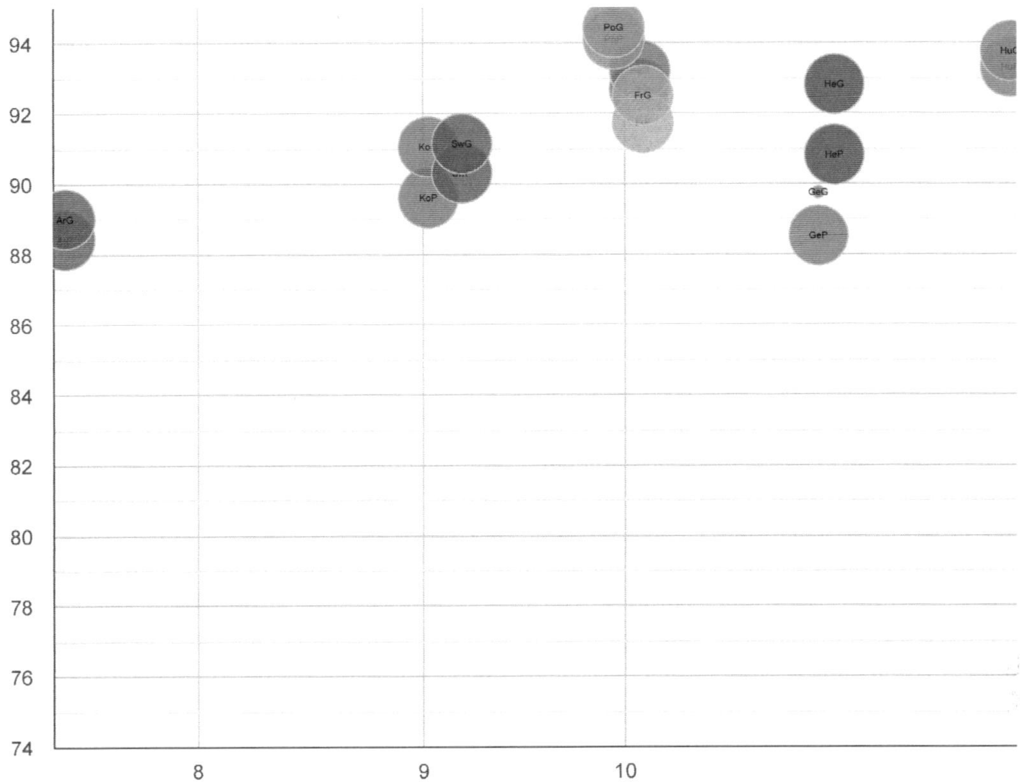

Figure 4: The correlation between the non terminals per sentence ratio and Leaf Accuracy (macro) scores. *x: #non terminal/ #sentence ; y: Acc.(%)*

compare the performance across annotation schemes, assuming that those subsets are representative of their original source.[42]

Ideally, we would be using labeled TedEval scores, as the labeled parsing task is more difficult, and labeled parses are far more informative than unlabeled ones. However, most constituency-based parsers do not provide function labels as part of the output, to be compared with the dependency arcs. Furthermore, as mentioned earlier, we observed a huge difference between label set sizes for the dependency runs. Consequently, labeled scores will not be as informative across treebanks and representation types. We will therefore only use labels across scenarios for the same language and representation type.

[42]We choose this sample scheme for replicability. We first tried sampling sentences, aiming at the same average sentence length (20), but that seemed to create artificially difficult test sets for languages as Polish and overly simplistic ones for French or Arabic.

7.2.1 Cross-Scenario Evaluation: raw vs. gold

One novel aspect of this shared task is the evaluation on non-gold segmentation in addition to gold morphology. One drawback is that the scenarios are currently not using the same metrics — the metrics generally applied for gold and predicted scenrios cannot apply for raw. To assess how well state of the art parsers perform in raw scenarios compared to gold scenarios, we present here TedEval results comparing raw and gold systems using the evaluation protocol of Tsarfaty et al. (2012b).

Table 9 presents the labeled and unlabeled results for Arabic and Hebrew (in Full and 5k training settings), and Table 10 presents unlabeled TedEval results (for all languages) in the gold settings. The unlabeled TedEval results for the raw settings are substantially lower then TedEval results on the gold settings for both languages.

When comparing the unlabeled TedEval results for Arabic and Hebrew on the participating systems, we see a loss of 3-4 points between Table 9 (raw) and Table 10 (gold). In particular we see that for the best performing systems on Arabic (IMS:SZEGED:CIS for both constituency and dependency), the gap between gold and realistic scenarios is 3.4 and 4.3 points, for the constituency and the dependency parser respectively. These results are on a par with results by Tsarfaty et al. (2012b), who showed for different settings, constituency and dependency based, that raw scenarios are considerably more difficult to parse than gold ones on the standard split of the Modern Hebrew treebank.

For Hebrew, the performance gap between unlabeled TedEval in raw (Table 9) and gold (Table 10) is even more salient, with around 7 and 8 points of difference between the scenarios. We can only speculate that such a difference may be due to the difficulty of resolving Hebrew morpho-syntactic ambiguities without sufficient syntactic information. Since Hebrew and Arabic now have standardized morphologically and syntactically analyzed data sets available through this task, it will be possible to investigate further how cross-linguistic differences in morphological ambiguity affect full-parsing accuracy in raw scenarios.

This section compared the raw and gold parsing results only on unlabeled TedEval metrics. According to what we have seen so far is expected that for labeled TedEval metrics using the same protocol, the gap between gold and raw scenario will be even greater.

7.2.2 Cross-Framework Evaluation: Dependency vs. Constituency

In this section, our focus is on comparing parsing results across constituency and dependency parsers based on the protocol of Tsarfaty et al. (2012a) We have only one submission from IMS:SZEGED:CIS in the constituency track, and. from the same group, a submission on the dependency track. We only compare the IMS:SZEGED:CIS results on constituency and dependency parsing with the two baselines we provided. The results of the cross-framework evaluation protocol are shown in Table 11.

The results comparing the two variants of the IMS:SZEGED:CIS systems show that they are very close for all languages, with differences ranging from 0.03 for German to 0.8 for Polish in the gold setting.

It has often been argued that dependency parsers perform better than a constituency parser, but we notice that when using a cross framework protocol, such as TedEval, and assuming that our test set sample is representative, the difference between the interpretation of both representation's performance is alleviated. Of course, here the metric is unlabeled, so it simply tells us that both kind of parsing models are equally able to provide similar tree structures. Said differently, the gaps in the quality of predicting the same underlying structure across representations for MRLs is not as large as is sometimes assumed.

For most languages, the baseline constituency parser performs better than the dependency baseline one, with Basque and Korean as an exception, and at the same time, the dependency version of IMS:SZEGED:CIS performs slightly better than their constituent parser for most languages, with the exception of Hebrew and Hungarian. It goes to show that, as far as these present MRL results go, there is no clear preference for a dependency over a constituency parsing representation, just preferences among particular models.

More generally, we can say that even if the linguistic coverage of one theory is shown to be better than another one, it does not necessarily mean that the statistical version of the formal theory will perform better for structure prediction. System performance is more tightly related to the efficacy of the learning and search algorithms, and feature engineering on top of the selected formalism.

7.2.3 Cross-Language Evaluation: All Languages

We conclude with an overall outlook of the TedEval scores across all languages. The results on the gold scenario, for the small training set and the 5k test set are presented in Table 10. We concentrate on gold scenarios (to avoid the variation in coverage of external morphological analyzers) and choose unlabeled metrics as they are not sensitive to label set sizes. We emphasize in bold, for each parsing system (row in the table), the top two languages that most accurately parsed by it (boldface) and the two languages it performed the worse on (italics).

We see that the European languages German and Hungarian are parsed most accurately in the constituency-based setup, with Polish and Swedish having an advantage in dependency parsing. Across all systems, Korean is the hardest to parse, with Ara-

	Arabic	Hebrew	AVG1	SOFT AVG	Arabic	Hebrew	AVG2	SOFT AVG2
				1) Constituency Evaluation				
		Labeled TedEval				*Unabeled TedEval*		
IMS:SZEGED:CIS (Bky)	83.59	56.43	70.01	70.01	**92.18**	88.02	**90.1**	90.1
				2) Dependency Evaluation				
		Labeled TedEval				*Unabeled TedEval*		
IMS:SZEGED:CIS	**88.61**	**84.74**	**86.68**	86.68	91.41	**88.58**	90	90
ALPAGE:DYALOG	87.20	81.65	40.83	81.65	90.74	87.44	89.09	89.09
CADIM	87.99	-	44	**87.99**	91.22	-	45.61	**91.22**
MALTOPTIMIZER	86.62	81.74	43.31	86.62	90.26	87.00	45.13	90.26
ALPAGE:DYALOG (RAW)	-	82.82	41.41	82.82	-	87.43	43.72	87.43
AI:KU	-	77.8	38.9	77.8	-	85.87	42.94	85.87

Table 9: Labeled and Unlabeled TedEval Results for raw Scenarios, Trained on 5k sentences and tested on 5k terminals. *The upper part refers to constituency parsing and the lower part refers to dependency parsing.*

	Arabic	Basque	French	German	Hebrew	Hungarian	Korean	Polish	Swedish
				1) Constituency Evaluation					
IMS:SZEGED:CIS (Bky)	*95.35*	96.91	95.98	**97.12**	96.22	**97.92**	*92.91*	97.19	96.65
BASE:BKY+POS	*95.11*	94.69	95.08	**97.01**	95.85	**97.08**	*90.55*	96.99	96.38
BASE:BKY+RAW	94.58	*94.32*	94.72	**96.74**	95.64	**96.15**	*87.08*	95.93	95.90
				2) Dependency Evaluation					
IMS:SZEGED:CIS	*95.76*	**97.63**	96.59	96.88	96.29	97.56	*94.62*	**98.01**	97.22
ALPAGE:DYALOG	*93.76*	95.72	95.75	96.4	95.34	95.63	*94.56*	**96.80**	**96.55**
BASE:MALT	*94.16*	95.08	*94.21*	94.55	94.98	95.25	94.27	**95.83**	**95.33**
AI:KU	-	-	95.46	96.34	*95.07*	96.53	-	**96.88**	**95.87**
MALTOPTIMIZER	*94.91*	**96.82**	95.23	**96.32**	95.46	96.30	*94.69*	96.06	95.90
CADIM	94.66	-	-	-	-	-	-	-	-

Table 10: Cross-Language Evaluation: Unlabeled TedEval Results in gold input scenario, On a 5k-sentences set set and a 5k-terminals test set. *The upper part refers to constituency parsing and the lower part refers to dependency parsing. For each system we mark the two top scoring languages in* **bold** *and the two lowest scoring languages in* italics.

team	Arabic	Basque	French	German	Hebrew	Hungarian	Korean	Polish	Swedish
				1) gold setting					
IMS:SZEGED:CIS (Bky)	95.82	97.30	96.15	97.43	**96.37**	**98.25**	94.07	97.22	96.89
IMS:SZEGED:CIS	**95.87**	**98.06**	**96.61**	**97.46**	96.31	97.93	**94.62**	**98.04**	**97.24**
BASE:BKY+POS	95.61	95.25	95.48	97.31	96.03	97.53	92.15	96.97	96.66
BASE:MALT	94.26	95.76	94.23	95.53	95.00	96.09	94.27	95.90	95.35
				2) predicted setting					
IMS:SZEGED:CIS (Bky)	**95.74**	97.07	**96.21**	**97.31**	96.10	**98.03**	94.05	96.92	96.90
IMS:SZEGED:CIS	95.18	**97.67**	96.15	97.09	**96.22**	97.63	**94.43**	**97.50**	**97.02**
BASE:BKY+POS		95.03	95.35	97.12	95.36	97.20	91.34	96.92	96.25
BASE:MALT		95.49	93.84	95.39	94.41	95.72	93.74	96.04	95.09

Table 11: Cross Framework Evaluation: Unlabeled TedEval on generalized gold trees in gold scenario, trained on 5k sentences and tested on 5k terminals.

bic, Hebrew and to some extent French following. It appears that on a typological scale, Semitic and Asian languages are still harder to parse than a range of European languages in terms of structural difficulty and complex morpho-syntactic interaction. That said, note that we cannot tell why certain treebanks appear more challenging to parse then others, and it is still unclear whether the difficulty is inherent on the language, in the currently available models, or because of the annotation scheme and treebank consistency.[43]

[43]The latter was shown to be an important factor orthogonal to the morphologically-rich nature of the treebank's language

8 Conclusion

This paper presents an overview of the first shared task on parsing morphologically rich languages. The task features nine languages, exhibiting different linguistic phenomena and varied morphological complexity. The shared task saw submissions from seven teams, and results produced by more than 14 different systems. The parsing results were obtained in different input scenarios (gold, predicted, and raw) and evaluated using different protocols (cross-framework, cross-scenario, and cross-language). In particular, this is the first time an evaluation campaign reports on the execution of parsers in realistic, morphologically ambiguous, setting.

The best performing systems were mostly ensemble systems combining multiple parser outputs from different frameworks or training runs, or integrating a state-of-the-art morphological analyzer on top of a carefully designed feature set. This is consistent with previous shared tasks such as ConLL 2007 or SANCL'2012. However, dealing with ambiguous morphology is still difficult for all systems, and a promising approach, as demonstrated by ALPAGE:DYALOG, is to deal with parsing and morphology jointly by allowing lattice input to the parser. A promising generalization of this approach would be the full integration of all levels of analysis that are mutually informative into a joint model.

The information to be gathered from the results of this shared task is vast, and we only scratched the surface with our preliminary analyses. We uncovered and documented insights of strategies that make parsing systems successful: parser combination is empirically proven to reach a robust performance across languages, though language-specific strategies are still a sound avenue for obtaining high quality parsers for that individual language. The integration of morphological analysis into the parsing needs to be investigated thoroughly, and new approaches that are morphologically aware need to be developed.

Our cross-parser, cross-scenario, and cross-framework evaluation protocols have shown that, as expected, more data is better, and that performance on gold morphological input is significantly higher than that in more realistic scenarios. We have shown that gold morphological information is more helpful to some languages and parsers than others, and that it may also interact with successful identification of multiword expressions. We have shown that differences between dependency and constituency are smaller than previously assumed and that properties of the learning model and granularity of the output labels are more influential. Finally, we observed that languages which are typologically farthest from English, such as Semitic and Asian languages, are still amongst the hardest to parse, regardless of the parsing method used.

Our cross-treebank, in-depth analysis is still preliminary, owing to the limited time between the end of the shared task and the deadline for publication of this overview. but we nonetheless feel that our findings may benefit researchers who aim to develop parsers for diverse treebanks.[44]

A shared task is an inspection of the state of the art, but it may also accelerate research in an area by providing a stable data basis as well as a set of strong baselines. The results produced in this task give a rich picture of the issues associated with parsing MRLs and initial cues towards their resolution. This set of results needs to be further analyzed to be fully understood, which will in turn contribute to new insights. We hope that this shared task will provide inspiration for the design and evaluation of future parsing systems for these languages.

Acknowledgments

We heartily thank Miguel Ballesteros and Corentin Ribeire for running the dependency and constituency baselines. We warmly thank the Linguistic Data Consortium: Ilya Ahtaridis, Ann Bies, Denise DiPersio, Seth Kulick and Mohamed Maamouri for releasing the Arabic Penn Treebank for this shared task and for their support all along the process. We thank Alon Itai and MILA, the knowledge center for processing Hebrew, for kindly making the Hebrew treebank and morphological analyzer available for us, Anne Abeillé for allowing us to use the French treebank, and Key-Sun Choi for the Kaist Korean Treebank. We thank Grzegorz Chrupała for providing the morphological analyzer *Morfette*, and Joachim

(Schluter and van Genabith, 2007)

[44]The data set will be made available as soon as possible under the license distribution of the shared-task, with the exception of the Arabic data, which will continue to be distributed by the LDC.

Wagner for his *LeafAncestor* implementation. We finally thank Özlem Çetinoğlu, Yuval Marton, Benoit Crabbé and Benoit Sagot who have been nothing but supportive during all that time.

At the end of this shared task (though watch out for further updates and analyses), what remains to be mentioned is our deep gratitude to all people involved, either data providers or participants. Without all of you, this shared task would not have been possible.

References

Anne Abeillé, Lionel Clément, and François Toussenel. 2003. Building a treebank for French. In Anne Abeillé, editor, *Treebanks*. Kluwer, Dordrecht.

Szymon Acedański. 2010. A Morphosyntactic Brill Tagger for Inflectional Languages. In *Advances in Natural Language Processing*, volume 6233 of *Lecture Notes in Computer Science*, pages 3–14. Springer-Verlag.

Meni Adler and Michael Elhadad. 2006. An unsupervised morpheme-based HMM for Hebrew morphological disambiguation. In *Proceedings COLING-ACL*, pages 665–672, Sydney, Australia.

Meni Adler, Yoav Goldberg, David Gabay, and Michael Elhadad. 2008. Unsupervised lexicon-based resolution of unknown words for full morphological analysis. In *Proceedings of ACL-08: HLT*, pages 728–736, Columbus, OH.

Meni Adler. 2007. *Hebrew Morphological Disambiguation: An Unsupervised Stochastic Word-based Approach*. Ph.D. thesis, Ben-Gurion University of the Negev.

Itziar Aduriz, José María Arriola, Xabier Artola, A Díaz de Ilarraza, et al. 1997. Morphosyntactic disambiguation for Basque based on the constraint grammar formalism. In *Proceedings of RANLP*, Tzigov Chark, Bulgaria.

Itziar Aduriz, Eneko Agirre, Izaskun Aldezabal, Iñaki Alegria, Xabier Arregi, Jose Maria Arriola, Xabier Artola, Koldo Gojenola, Aitor Maritxalar, Kepa Sarasola, et al. 2000. A word-grammar based morphological analyzer for agglutinative languages. In *Proceedings of COLING*, pages 1–7, Saarbrücken, Germany.

Itziar Aduriz, Maria Jesus Aranzabe, Jose Maria Arriola, Aitziber Atutxa, A Diaz de Ilarraza, Aitzpea Garmendia, and Maite Oronoz. 2003. Construction of a Basque dependency treebank. In *Proceedings of the 2nd Workshop on Treebanks and Linguistic Theories (TLT)*, pages 201–204, Växjö, Sweden.

Zeljko Agic, Danijela Merkler, and Dasa Berovic. 2013. Parsing Croatian and Serbian by using Croatian dependency treebanks. In *Proceedings of the Fourth Workshop on Statistical Parsing of Morphologically Rich Languages (SPMRL)*, Seattle, WA.

I. Aldezabal, M.J. Aranzabe, A. Diaz de Ilarraza, and K. Fernández. 2008. From dependencies to constituents in the reference corpus for the processing of Basque. In *Procesamiento del Lenguaje Natural, n° 41 (2008)*, pages 147–154. XXIV edición del Congreso Anual de la Sociedad Española para el Procesamiento del Lenguaje Natural (SEPLN).

Bharat Ram Ambati, Samar Husain, Joakim Nivre, and Rajeev Sangal. 2010. On the role of morphosyntactic features in Hindi dependency parsing. In *Proceedings of the NAACL/HLT Workshop on Statistical Parsing of Morphologically Rich Languages (SPMRL 2010)*, Los Angeles, CA.

Mohammed Attia, Jennifer Foster, Deirdre Hogan, Joseph Le Roux, Lamia Tounsi, and Josef van Genabith. 2010. Handling unknown words in statistical latent-variable parsing models for Arabic, English and French. In *Proceedings of the NAACL/HLT Workshop on Statistical Parsing of Morphologically Rich Languages (SPMRL)*, Los Angeles, CA.

Miguel Ballesteros and Joakim Nivre. 2012. MaltOptimizer: An optimization tool for MaltParser. In *Proceedings of EACL*, pages 58–62, Avignon, France.

Miguel Ballesteros. 2013. Effective morphological feature selection with MaltOptimizer at the SPMRL 2013 shared task. In *Proceedings of the Fourth Workshop on Statistical Parsing of Morphologically-Rich Languages*, pages 53–60, Seattle, WA.

Kepa Bengoetxea and Koldo Gojenola. 2010. Application of different techniques to dependency parsing of Basque. In *Proceedings of the NAACL/HLT Workshop on Statistical Parsing of Morphologically Rich Languages (SPMRL 2010)*, Los Angeles, CA.

Philip Bille. 2005. A survey on tree edit distance and related problems. *Theoretical Computer Science*, 337(1–3):217–239, 6.

Anders Björkelund, Ozlem Cetinoglu, Richárd Farkas, Thomas Mueller, and Wolfgang Seeker. 2013. (Re)ranking meets morphosyntax: State-of-the-art results from the SPMRL 2013 shared task. In *Proceedings of the Fourth Workshop on Statistical Parsing of Morphologically-Rich Languages*, pages 134–144, Seattle, WA.

Ezra Black, Steven Abney, Dan Flickinger, Claudia Gdaniec, Ralph Grishman, Philip Harrison, Donald Hindle, Robert Ingria, Frederick Jelinek, Judith Klavans, Mark Liberman, Mitchell Marcus, Salim Roukos, Beatrice Santorini, and Tomek Strzalkowski. 1991. A procedure for quantitatively comparing the syntactic coverage of English grammars. In *Proceedings of the DARPA Speech and Natural Language Workshop 1991*, pages 306–311, Pacific Grove, CA.

Bernd Bohnet and Joakim Nivre. 2012. A transition-based system for joint part-of-speech tagging and labeled non-projective dependency parsing. In *Proceedings of the EMNLP-CoNLL*, pages 1455–1465, Jeju, Korea.

Bernd Bohnet. 2010. Top accuracy and fast dependency parsing is not a contradiction. In *Proceedings of COLING*, pages 89–97, Beijing, China.

Adriane Boyd. 2007. Discontinuity revisited: An improved conversion to context-free representations. In *Proceedings of the Linguistic Annotation Workshop*, Prague, Czech Republic.

Sabine Brants, Stefanie Dipper, Silvia Hansen, Wolfgang Lezius, and George Smith. 2002. The TIGER treebank. In *Proceedings of the First Workshop on Treebanks and Linguistic Theories (TLT)*, pages 24–41, Sozopol, Bulgaria.

Sabine Buchholz and Erwin Marsi. 2006. CoNLL-X shared task on multilingual dependency parsing. In *Proceedings of CoNLL*, pages 149–164, New York, NY.

Tim Buckwalter. 2002. Arabic morphological analyzer version 1.0. Linguistic Data Consortium.

Tim Buckwalter. 2004. Arabic morphological analyzer version 2.0. Linguistic Data Consortium.

Marie Candito and Djamé Seddah. 2010. Parsing word clusters. In *Proceedings of the NAACL/HLT Workshop on Statistical Parsing of Morphologically Rich Languages (SPMRL 2010)*, Los Angeles, CA.

Marie Candito, Benoit Crabbé, and Pascal Denis. 2010. Statistical French dependency parsing: Treebank conversion and first results. In *Proceedings of LREC*, Valletta, Malta.

Xavier Carreras, Michael Collins, and Terry Koo. 2008. TAG, dynamic programming, and the perceptron for efficient, feature-rich parsing. In *Proceedings of CoNLL*, pages 9–16, Manchester, UK.

Eugene Charniak and Mark Johnson. 2005. Course-to-fine n-best-parsing and maxent discriminative reranking. In *Proceedings of ACL*, pages 173–180, Barcelona, Spain.

Eugene Charniak. 1997. Statistical parsing with a context-free grammar and word statistics. In *AAAI/IAAI*, pages 598–603.

Eugene Charniak. 2000. A maximum entropy inspired parser. In *Proceedings of NAACL*, pages 132–139, Seattle, WA.

Jinho D. Choi and Martha Palmer. 2011. Statistical dependency parsing in Korean: From corpus generation to automatic parsing. In *Proceedings of Second Workshop on Statistical Parsing of Morphologically Rich Languages*, pages 1–11, Dublin, Ireland.

Jinho D. Choi and Martha Palmer. 2012. Guidelines for the Clear Style Constituent to Dependency Conversion. Technical Report 01-12, University of Colorado at Boulder.

Key-sun Choi, Young S. Han, Young G. Han, and Oh W. Kwon. 1994. KAIST Tree Bank Project for Korean: Present and Future Development. In *In Proceedings of the International Workshop on Sharable Natural Language Resources*, pages 7–14, Nara, Japan.

Jinho D. Choi. 2013. Preparing Korean data for the shared task on parsing morphologically rich languages. arXiv:1309.1649.

Grzegorz Chrupała, Georgiana Dinu, and Josef van Genabith. 2008. Learning morphology with Morfette. In *Proceedings of LREC*, Marrakech, Morocco.

Tagyoung Chung, Matt Post, and Daniel Gildea. 2010. Factors affecting the accuracy of Korean parsing. In *Proceedings of the NAACL/HLT Workshop on Statistical Parsing of Morphologically Rich Languages (SPMRL 2010)*, Los Angeles, CA.

Volkan Cirik and Hüsnü Şensoy. 2013. The AI-KU system at the SPMRL 2013 shared task: Unsupervised features for dependency parsing. In *Proceedings of the Fourth Workshop on Statistical Parsing of Morphologically-Rich Languages*, pages 68–75, Seattle, WA.

Michael Collins. 2003. Head-driven statistical models for natural language parsing. *Computational Linguistics*, 29(4):589–637.

Matthieu Constant, Marie Candito, and Djamé Seddah. 2013. The LIGM-Alpage architecture for the SPMRL 2013 shared task: Multiword expression analysis and dependency parsing. In *Proceedings of the Fourth Workshop on Statistical Parsing of Morphologically-Rich Languages*, pages 46–52, Seattle, WA.

Anna Corazza, Alberto Lavelli, Giogio Satta, and Roberto Zanoli. 2004. Analyzing an Italian treebank with state-of-the-art statistical parsers. In *Proceedings of the Third Workshop on Treebanks and Linguistic Theories (TLT)*, Tübingen, Germany.

Benoit Crabbé and Marie Candito. 2008. Expériences d'analyse syntaxique statistique du français. In *Actes de la 15ème Conférence sur le Traitement Automatique des Langues Naturelles (TALN'08)*, pages 45–54, Avignon, France.

Dóra Csendes, János Csirik, Tibor Gyimóthy, and András Kocsor. 2005. The Szeged treebank. In *Proceedings of the 8th International Conference on Text, Speech and Dialogue (TSD)*, Lecture Notes in Computer Science, pages 123–132, Berlin / Heidelberg. Springer.

Eric De La Clergerie. 2013. Exploring beam-based shift-reduce dependency parsing with DyALog: Results from the SPMRL 2013 shared task. In *Proceedings of the Fourth Workshop on Statistical Parsing of*

Morphologically-Rich Languages, pages 81–89, Seattle, WA.

Marie-Catherine de Marneffe and Christopher D. Manning. 2008. The stanford typed dependencies representation. In *Proceedings of the workshop on Cross-Framework and Cross-Domain Parser Evaluation*.

Mona Diab, Nizar Habash, Owen Rambow, and Ryan Roth. 2013. LDC Arabic treebanks and associated corpora: Data divisions manual. Technical Report CCLS-13-02, Center for Computational Learning Systems, Columbia University.

Eva Ejerhed and Gunnel Källgren. 1997. Stockholm Umeå Corpus. Version 1.0. Department of Linguistics, Umeå University and Department of Linguistics, Stockholm University.

Eva Ejerhed, Gunnel Källgren, Ola Wennstedt, and Magnus Åström. 1992. The linguistic annotation system of the Stockholm–Umeå Corpus project. Technical Report 33, University of Umeå: Department of Linguistics.

Nerea Ezeiza, Iñaki Alegria, José María Arriola, Rubén Urizar, and Itziar Aduriz. 1998. Combining stochastic and rule-based methods for disambiguation in agglutinative languages. In *Proceedings of COLING*, pages 380–384, Montréal, Canada.

Jenny Rose Finkel, Alex Kleeman, and Christopher D. Manning. 2008. Efficient, feature-based, conditional random field parsing. In *Proceedings of ACL*, pages 959–967, Columbus, OH.

Alexander Fraser, Helmut Schmid, Richárd Farkas, Renjing Wang, and Hinrich Schütze. 2013. Knowledge sources for constituent parsing of German, a morphologically rich and less-configurational language. *Computational Linguistics*, 39(1):57–85.

Iakes Goenaga, Koldo Gojenola, and Nerea Ezeiza. 2013. Exploiting the contribution of morphological information to parsing: the BASQUE TEAM system in the SPRML'2013 shared task. In *Proceedings of the Fourth Workshop on Statistical Parsing of Morphologically-Rich Languages*, pages 61–67, Seattle, WA.

Yoav Goldberg and Michael Elhadad. 2010a. Easy-first dependency parsing of Modern Hebrew. In *Proceedings of the NAACL/HLT Workshop on Statistical Parsing of Morphologically Rich Languages (SPMRL 2010)*, Los Angeles, CA.

Yoav Goldberg and Michael Elhadad. 2010b. An efficient algorithm for easy-first non-directional dependency parsing. In *Proceedings of HLT: NAACL*, pages 742–750, Los Angeles, CA.

Yoav Goldberg and Reut Tsarfaty. 2008. A single framework for joint morphological segmentation and syntactic parsing. In *Proceedings of ACL*, Columbus, OH.

Yoav Goldberg, Meni Adler, and Michael Elhadad. 2008. EM can find pretty good HMM POS-taggers (when given a good start). In *Proc. of ACL*, Columbus, OH.

Yoav Goldberg, Reut Tsarfaty, Meni Adler, and Michael Elhadad. 2009. Enhancing unlexicalized parsing performance using a wide coverage lexicon, fuzzy tag-set mapping, and EM-HMM-based lexical probabilities. In *Proceedings of EALC*, pages 327–335, Athens, Greece.

Yoav Goldberg. 2011. *Automatic syntactic processing of Modern Hebrew*. Ph.D. thesis, Ben Gurion University of the Negev.

David Graff, Mohamed Maamouri, Basma Bouziri, Sondos Krouna, Seth Kulick, and Tim Buckwalter. 2009. Standard Arabic Morphological Analyzer (SAMA) version 3.1. Linguistic Data Consortium LDC2009E73.

Spence Green and Christopher D. Manning. 2010. Better Arabic parsing: Baselines, evaluations, and analysis. In *Proceedings of COLING*, pages 394–402, Beijing, China.

Nathan Green, Loganathan Ramasamy, and Zdenék Žabokrtský. 2012. Using an SVM ensemble system for improved Tamil dependency parsing. In *Proceedings of the ACL 2012 Joint Workshop on Statistical Parsing and Semantic Processing of Morphologically Rich Languages*, pages 72–77, Jeju, Korea.

Spence Green, Marie-Catherine de Marneffe, and Christopher D. Manning. 2013. Parsing models for identifying multiword expressions. *Computational Linguistics*, 39(1):195–227.

Noemie Guthmann, Yuval Krymolowski, Adi Milea, and Yoad Winter. 2009. Automatic annotation of morpho-syntactic dependencies in a Modern Hebrew Treebank. In *Proceedings of the Eighth International Workshop on Treebanks and Linguistic Theories (TLT)*, Groningen, The Netherlands.

Nizar Habash and Ryan Roth. 2009. CATiB: The Columbia Arabic Treebank. In *Proceedings of ACL-IJCNLP*, pages 221–224, Suntec, Singapore.

Nizar Habash, Ryan Gabbard, Owen Rambow, Seth Kulick, and Mitch Marcus. 2007. Determining case in Arabic: Learning complex linguistic behavior requires complex linguistic features. In *Proceedings of EMNLP-CoNLL*, pages 1084–1092, Prague, Czech Republic.

Nizar Habash, Reem Faraj, and Ryan Roth. 2009a. Syntactic Annotation in the Columbia Arabic Treebank. In *Proceedings of MEDAR International Conference on Arabic Language Resources and Tools*, Cairo, Egypt.

Nizar Habash, Owen Rambow, and Ryan Roth. 2009b. MADA+TOKAN: A toolkit for Arabic tokenization, diacritization, morphological disambiguation, POS tagging, stemming and lemmatization. In *Proceedings of the Second International Conference on Arabic Language Resources and Tools*. Cairo, Egypt.

Nizar Habash. 2010. *Introduction to Arabic Natural Language Processing*. Morgan & Claypool Publishers.

Jan Hajič, Alena Böhmová, Eva Hajičová, and Barbora Vidová-Hladká. 2000. The Prague Dependency Treebank: A three-level annotation scenario. In Anne Abeillé, editor, *Treebanks: Building and Using Parsed Corpora*. Kluwer Academic Publishers.

Péter Halácsy, András Kornai, and Csaba Oravecz. 2007. HunPos – an open source trigram tagger. In *Proceedings of ACL*, pages 209–212, Prague, Czech Republic.

Johan Hall, Jens Nilsson, Joakim Nivre, Gülşen Eryiğit, Beáta Megyesi, Mattias Nilsson, and Markus Saers. 2007. Single malt or blended? A study in multilingual parser optimization. In *Proceedings of the CoNLL Shared Task Session of EMNLP-CoNLL 2007*, pages 933–939, Prague, Czech Republic.

Chung-hye Han, Na-Rae Han, Eon-Suk Ko, Martha Palmer, and Heejong Yi. 2002. Penn Korean Treebank: Development and evaluation. In *Proceedings of the 16th Pacific Asia Conference on Language, Information and Computation*, Jeju, Korea.

Tilman Höhle. 1986. Der Begriff "Mittelfeld", Anmerkungen über die Theorie der topologischen Felder. In *Akten des Siebten Internationalen Germanistenkongresses 1985*, pages 329–340, Göttingen, Germany.

Zhongqiang Huang, Mary Harper, and Slav Petrov. 2010. Self-training with products of latent variable grammars. In *Proceedings of EMNLP*, pages 12–22, Cambridge, MA.

Liang Huang. 2008. Forest reranking: Discriminative parsing with non-local features. In *Proceedings of ACL*, pages 586–594, Columbus, OH.

Alon Itai and Shuly Wintner. 2008. Language resources for Hebrew. *Language Resources and Evaluation*, 42(1):75–98, March.

Mark Johnson. 1998. PCFG models of linguistic tree representations. *Computational Linguistics*, 24(4):613–632.

Laura Kallmeyer and Wolfgang Maier. 2013. Data-driven parsing using probabilistic linear context-free rewriting systems. *Computational Linguistics*, 39(1).

Fred Karlsson, Atro Voutilainen, Juha Heikkilae, and Arto Anttila. 1995. *Constraint Grammar: a language-independent system for parsing unrestricted text*. Walter de Gruyter.

Dan Klein and Christopher D. Manning. 2003. Accurate unlexicalized parsing. In *Proceedings of ACL*, pages 423–430, Sapporo, Japan.

Sandra Kübler, Erhard W. Hinrichs, and Wolfgang Maier. 2006. Is it really that difficult to parse German? In *Proceedings of EMNLP*, pages 111–119, Sydney, Australia, July.

Sandra Kübler, Wolfgang Maier, Ines Rehbein, and Yannick Versley. 2008. How to compare treebanks. In *Proceedings of LREC*, pages 2322–2329, Marrakech, Morocco.

Sandra Kübler. 2008. The PaGe 2008 shared task on parsing German. In *Proceedings of the Workshop on Parsing German*, pages 55–63, Columbus, OH.

Seth Kulick, Ryan Gabbard, and Mitch Marcus. 2006. Parsing the Arabic Treebank: Analysis and Improvements. In *Proceedings of the Treebanks and Linguistic Theories Conference*, pages 31–42, Prague, Czech Republic.

Joseph Le Roux, Benoit Sagot, and Djamé Seddah. 2012. Statistical parsing of Spanish and data driven lemmatization. In *Proceedings of the Joint Workshop on Statistical Parsing and Semantic Processing of Morphologically Rich Languages*, pages 55–61, Jeju, Korea.

Kong Joo Lee, Byung-Gyu Chang, and Gil Chang Kim. 1997. Bracketing Guidelines for Korean Syntactic Tree Tagged Corpus. Technical Report CS/TR-97-112, Department of Computer Science, KAIST.

Roger Levy and Christopher D. Manning. 2003. Is it harder to parse Chinese, or the Chinese treebank? In *Proceedings of ACL*, Sapporo, Japan.

Mohamed Maamouri, Ann Bies, Tim Buckwalter, and Hubert Jin. 2004a. Arabic Treebank: Part 2 v 2.0. LDC catalog number LDC2004T02.

Mohamed Maamouri, Ann Bies, Tim Buckwalter, and Wigdan Mekki. 2004b. The Penn Arabic Treebank: Building a large-scale annotated Arabic corpus. In *NEMLAR Conference on Arabic Language Resources and Tools*, pages 102–109, Cairo, Egypt.

Mohamed Maamouri, Ann Bies, Tim Buckwalter, and Hubert Jin. 2005. Arabic Treebank: Part 1 v 3.0. LDC catalog number LDC2005T02.

Mohamed Maamouri, Ann Bies, Seth Kulick, Fatma Gaddeche, Wigdan Mekki, Sondos Krouna, and Basma Bouziri. 2009. The Penn Arabic Treebank part 3 version 3.1. Linguistic Data Consortium LDC2008E22.

Wolfgang Maier, Miriam Kaeshammer, and Laura Kallmeyer. 2012. Data-driven PLCFRS parsing revisited: Restricting the fan-out to two. In *Proceedings of the Eleventh International Conference on Tree Adjoining Grammars and Related Formalisms (TAG+11)*, Paris, France.

Mitchell P. Marcus, Beatrice Santorini, and Mary Ann Marcinkiewicz. 1993. Building a large annotated corpus of English: The Penn TreeBank. *Computational Linguistics*, 19(2):313–330.

Andre Martins, Noah Smith, Eric Xing, Pedro Aguiar, and Mario Figueiredo. 2010. Turbo parsers: Dependency parsing by approximate variational inference. In *Proceedings of EMNLP*, pages 34–44, Cambridge, MA.

Yuval Marton, Nizar Habash, and Owen Rambow. 2013a. Dependency parsing of Modern Standard Arabic with lexical and inflectional features. *Computational Linguistics*, 39(1):161–194.

Yuval Marton, Nizar Habash, Owen Rambow, and Sarah Alkhulani. 2013b. SPMRL'13 shared task system: The CADIM Arabic dependency parser. In *Proceedings of the Fourth Workshop on Statistical Parsing of Morphologically-Rich Languages*, pages 76–80, Seattle, WA.

David McClosky, Eugene Charniak, and Mark Johnson. 2006. Effective self-training for parsing. In *Proceedings of HLT:NAACL*, pages 152–159, New York, NY.

Ryan T. McDonald, Koby Crammer, and Fernando C. N. Pereira. 2005. Online large-margin training of dependency parsers. In *Proceedings of ACL*, pages 91–98, Ann Arbor, MI.

Ryan McDonald, Joakim Nivre, Yvonne Quirmbach-Brundage, Yoav Goldberg, Dipanjan Das, Kuzman Ganchev, Keith Hall, Slav Petrov, Hao Zhang, Oscar Tackstrom, Claudia Bedini, Nuria Bertomeu Castello, and Jungmee Lee. 2013. Universal dependency annotation for multilingual parsing. In *Proceedings of ACL*, Sofia, Bulgaria.

Igor Mel'čuk. 2001. *Communicative Organization in Natural Language: The Semantic-Communicative Structure of Sentences*. J. Benjamins.

Knowledge Center for Processing Hebrew MILA. 2008. Hebrew morphological analyzer. http://mila.cs.technion.ac.il.

Antonio Moreno, Ralph Grishman, Susana Lopez, Fernando Sanchez, and Satoshi Sekine. 2000. A treebank of Spanish and its application to parsing. In *Proceedings of LREC*, Athens, Greece.

Joakim Nivre and Beáta Megyesi. 2007. Bootstrapping a Swedish treeebank using cross-corpus harmonization and annotation projection. In *Proceedings of the 6th International Workshop on Treebanks and Linguistic Theories*, pages 97–102, Bergen, Norway.

Joakim Nivre, Jens Nilsson, and Johan Hall. 2006. Talbanken05: A Swedish treebank with phrase structure and dependency annotation. In *Proceedings of LREC*, pages 1392–1395, Genoa, Italy.

Joakim Nivre, Johan Hall, Sandra Kübler, Ryan McDonald, Jens Nilsson, Sebastian Riedel, and Deniz Yuret. 2007a. The CoNLL 2007 shared task on dependency parsing. In *Proceedings of the CoNLL Shared Task Session of EMNLP-CoNLL 2007*, pages 915–932, Prague, Czech Republic.

Joakim Nivre, Johan Hall, Jens Nilsson, Atanas Chanev, Gülşen Eryiğit, Sandra Kübler, Svetoslav Marinov, and Erwin Marsi. 2007b. MaltParser: A language-independent system for data-driven dependency parsing. *Natural Language Engineering*, 13(2):95–135.

Slav Petrov and Ryan McDonald. 2012. Overview of the 2012 Shared Task on Parsing the Web. In *Proceedings of the First Workshop on Syntactic Analysis of Non-Canonical Language (SANCL), a NAACL-HLT 2012 workshop*, Montreal, Canada.

Slav Petrov, Leon Barrett, Romain Thibaux, and Dan Klein. 2006. Learning accurate, compact, and interpretable tree annotation. In *Proceedings of COLING-ACL*, Sydney, Australia.

Slav Petrov. 2009. *Coarse-to-Fine Natural Language Processing*. Ph.D. thesis, University of California at Bekeley, Berkeley, CA.

Slav Petrov. 2010. Products of random latent variable grammars. In *Proceedings of HLT: NAACL*, pages 19–27, Los Angeles, CA.

Adam Przepiórkowski, Mirosław Bańko, Rafał L. Górski, and Barbara Lewandowska-Tomaszczyk, editors. 2012. *Narodowy Korpus Jkezyka Polskiego*. Wydawnictwo Naukowe PWN, Warsaw.

Ines Rehbein and Josef van Genabith. 2007a. Evaluating Evaluation Measures. In *Proceedings of the 16th Nordic Conference of Computational Linguistics NODALIDA-2007*, Tartu, Estonia.

Ines Rehbein and Josef van Genabith. 2007b. Treebank annotation schemes and parser evaluation for German. In *Proceedings of EMNLP-CoNLL*, Prague, Czech Republic.

Ines Rehbein. 2011. Data point selection for self-training. In *Proceedings of the Second Workshop on Statistical Parsing of Morphologically Rich Languages*, pages 62–67, Dublin, Ireland.

Kenji Sagae and Alon Lavie. 2006. Parser combination by reparsing. In *Proceedings of HLT-NAACL*, pages 129–132, New York, NY.

Geoffrey Sampson and Anna Babarczy. 2003. A test of the leaf-ancestor metric for parse accuracy. *Natural Language Engineering*, 9(04):365–380.

Natalie Schluter and Josef van Genabith. 2007. Preparing, restructuring, and augmenting a French Treebank: Lexicalised parsers or coherent treebanks? In *Proc. of PACLING 07*, Melbourne, Australia.

Helmut Schmid, Arne Fitschen, and Ulrich Heid. 2004. SMOR: A German computational morphology covering derivation, composition and inflection. In *Proceedings of LREC*, Lisbon, Portugal.

Djamé Seddah, Grzegorz Chrupała, Ozlem Cetinoglu, Josef van Genabith, and Marie Candito. 2010. Lemmatization and statistical lexicalized parsing of morphologically-rich languages. In *Proceedings of the First Workshop on Statistical Parsing of Morphologically Rich Languages (SPMRL)*, Los Angeles, CA.

Wolfgang Seeker and Jonas Kuhn. 2012. Making ellipses explicit in dependency conversion for a German treebank. In *Proceedings of LREC*, pages 3132–3139, Istanbul, Turkey.

Hiroyuki Shindo, Yusuke Miyao, Akinori Fujino, and Masaaki Nagata. 2012. Bayesian symbol-refined tree substitution grammars for syntactic parsing. In *Proceedings of ACL*, pages 440–448, Jeju, Korea.

Anthony Sigogne, Matthieu Constant, and Eric Laporte. 2011. French parsing enhanced with a word clustering method based on a syntactic lexicon. In *Proceedings of the Second Workshop on Statistical Parsing of Morphologically Rich Languages*, pages 22–27, Dublin, Ireland.

Khalil Sima'an, Alon Itai, Yoad Winter, Alon Altmann, and Noa Nativ. 2001. Building a tree-bank of Modern Hebrew text. *Traitement Automatique des Langues*, 42:347–380.

Marek Świdziński and Marcin Woliński. 2010. Towards a bank of constituent parse trees for Polish. In *Proceedings of Text, Speech and Dialogue*, pages 197–204, Brno, Czech Republic.

Ulf Teleman. 1974. *Manual för grammatisk beskrivning av talad och skriven svenska*. Studentlitteratur.

Lucien Tesnière. 1959. *Éléments De Syntaxe Structurale*. Klincksieck, Paris.

Reut Tsarfaty and Khalil Sima'an. 2010. Modeling morphosyntactic agreement in constituency-based parsing of Modern Hebrew. In *Proceedings of the First Workshop on Statistical Parsing of Morphologically Rich Languages (SPMRL)*, Los Angeles, CA.

Reut Tsarfaty, Djame Seddah, Yoav Goldberg, Sandra Kübler, Marie Candito, Jennifer Foster, Yannick Versley, Ines Rehbein, and Lamia Tounsi. 2010. Statistical parsing for morphologically rich language (SPMRL): What, how and whither. In *Proceedings of the First workshop on Statistical Parsing of Morphologically Rich Languages (SPMRL)*, Los Angeles, CA.

Reut Tsarfaty, Joakim Nivre, and Evelina Andersson. 2011. Evaluating dependency parsing: Robust and heuristics-free cross-framework evaluation. In *Proceedings of EMNLP*, Edinburgh, UK.

Reut Tsarfaty, Joakim Nivre, and Evelina Andersson. 2012a. Cross-framework evaluation for statistical parsing. In *Proceeding of EACL*, Avignon, France.

Reut Tsarfaty, Joakim Nivre, and Evelina Andersson. 2012b. Joint evaluation for segmentation and parsing. In *Proceedings of ACL*, Jeju, Korea.

Reut Tsarfaty, Djamé Seddah, Sandra Kübler, and Joakim Nivre. 2012c. Parsing morphologically rich languages: Introduction to the special issue. *Computational Linguistics*, 39(1):15–22.

Reut Tsarfaty. 2010. *Relational-Realizational Parsing*. Ph.D. thesis, University of Amsterdam.

Reut Tsarfaty. 2013. A unified morpho-syntactic scheme of Stanford dependencies. In *Proceedings of ACL*, Sofia, Bulgaria.

Veronika Vincze, Dóra Szauter, Attila Almási, György Móra, Zoltán Alexin, and János Csirik. 2010. Hungarian Dependency Treebank. In *Proceedings of LREC*, Valletta, Malta.

Joachim Wagner. 2012. *Detecting Grammatical Errors with Treebank-Induced Probabilistic Parsers*. Ph.D. thesis, Dublin City University.

Marcin Woliński, Katarzyna Głowińska, and Marek Świdziński. 2011. A preliminary version of Składnica—a treebank of Polish. In *Proceedings of the 5th Language & Technology Conference*, pages 299–303, Poznań, Poland.

Alina Wróblewska. 2012. Polish Dependency Bank. *Linguistic Issues in Language Technology*, 7(1):1–15.

Yue Zhang and Joakim Nivre. 2011. Transition-based dependency parsing with rich non-local features. In *Proceedings of ACL:HLT*, pages 188–193, Portland, OR.

János Zsibrita, Veronika Vincze, and Richárd Farkas. 2013. magyarlanc: A toolkit for morphological and dependency parsing of Hungarian. In *Proceedings of RANLP*, pages 763–771, Hissar, Bulgaria.

Author Index

Association for Computational Linguistics
209 N. Eighth Street
Stroudsburg, Pennsylvania 18360

proceedings.com